D1570367

Two versions of George Eliot, both very influential, have emerged from the study of her life and work. One is the radical Victorian thinker, formidably learned in a whole range of intellectual disciplines, to which she made major contributions during her early years in London. The other is the reclusive novelist, enigmatic, sybilline, celebrating through her fiction the communal values which were being eroded in the modern world. This study brings the two together, and by placing her within the crisis of belief and value acted out in the mid-nineteenth century, it reveals the unity of her whole career.

George Eliot saw this crisis as one of interpretation, and the intensity of her writing comes from the vivid, almost apocalyptic, awareness that traditional modes of interpreting the world were breaking down irrevocably. This study shows how, in response to this, she redefined the nature of Victorian fiction – its presentation of character, the role of the narrator, the structure of narrative, the depiction of social and historical change. Each of her novels becomes an experiment which tests to the point of destruction a variety of Victorian myths, orthodoxies, and ideologies, as it moves towards its climax – the inevitable contradiction which disconfirms all theories of life.

George Eliot and the conflict of interpretations articulates the tension, novel by novel, between the writer's suspicion of orthodox creeds and her urgent need to restore values in a sceptical age. Each attempt to break through the conflict of interpretations acknowledges the urgency of the need and the provisional nature of any resolution.

GEORGE ELIOT AND THE CONFLICT OF INTERPRETATIONS

GEORGE ELIOT AND THE CONFLICT OF INTERPRETATIONS

A Reading of the Novels

DAVID CARROLL

Professor of English
Lancaster University

CAMBRIDGE
UNIVERSITY PRESS

Published by the Press Syndicate of the University of Cambridge
The Pitt Building, Trumpington Street, Cambridge CB2 1RP
40 West 20th Street, New York, NY 10011–4211, USA
10 Stamford Road, Oakleigh, Victoria 3166, Australia

First published 1992

Printed in Great Britain at the University Press, Cambridge

A catalogue record of this book is available from the British Library

Library of Congress cataloguing in publication data

Carroll, David.
George Eliot and the conflict of interpretations: a reading of
the novels / by David Carroll.
p.   cm.
Includes bibliographical references and index.
ISBN 0 521 40366 9
1. Eliot, George, 1819–1880 – Criticism and interpretation.
I. Title.
PR4688.C28   1992
823'.8 – dc20   91-36677 CIP

ISBN 0 521 40366 9 hardback

SE

For Dorothy, Sara, and Helen

Contents

Preface

The idea for this study of George Eliot's fiction came initially from the scene at the end of *Romola* in which the heroine seeks to interpret Savonarola's confession. With great care she examines the unreliable documents, listens to the reactions of the Florentines, and re-lives her own experience of the priest as she carries out her agonised exegesis. It is a many-layered episode in which Romola not only identifies herself with Savonarola but also comes to represent the author, the narrator, and the reader. Everyone is engaged in the difficult act of interpretation. The scene seemed to epitomise vividly a crucial and characteristic aspect of the novels and, at the same time, to place George Eliot firmly within the context of mid-nineteenth-century hermeneutics, where a crisis of interpretation was being acted out in a variety of intellectual disciplines.

This was not, of course, a new discovery. In recent years, several critics have studied the influence of many of these branches of knowledge on the form and language of George Eliot's fiction. I am thinking of such revealing studies as E. S. Shaffer's examination of the effects of biblical criticism on secular literature which culminates in a detailed analysis of *Daniel Deronda*; or Gillian Beer's tracing of the interactions between Darwin's evolutionary theories and narrative process in the last two novels. Others have examined, for example, the influence of psychology, mythology, and sociology on the fiction. All of these works demonstrate the novelist's intimate and formidable engagement with those disciplines which were at the forefront of Victorian radical thought. But my aim, which is both more general and more specific, is not to try to emulate such studies, but to show that George Eliot was fundamentally concerned with all these branches of learning because each was grappling in its different way with hermeneutics, the theory of interpretation. Consequently, I maintain that any reading of the novels should pay special attention to the various and complex ways in which the characters, communities, the narrator, and, of course, the reader, seek different and conflicting forms of coherence through the act of interpretation.

This study attempts such a reading. Though I have found some contemporary writing on interpretation theory helpful, my aim has been to assimilate this without technical language to an account of George Eliot's own hermeneutic and then to a reading of the separate novels. My main indebtedness is to the scholars and critics through whom George Eliot studies have been so well served during the last thirty or so years. I acknowledge, amongst many others, my particular debts to Gillian Beer, Felicia Bonaparte, the late Gordon Haight, Barbara Hardy, U. C. Knoepflmacher, George Levine, E. S. Shaffer, and Alexander Welsh. I am indebted to Andrew Brown for his sustained interest, to the Humanities Research Committee of Lancaster University for research funds at an opportune time, and to the staff of the libraries at St Deiniol's and Lancaster University for their assistance. My special thanks are to Michael Wheeler for his encouragement and support over many years.

Introduction: a working hypothesis

At the climax of *The Mill on the Floss*, Maggie Tulliver sits alone in an agony of complete uncertainty. Her life has reached an impasse in which the opposing claims on her are so finely balanced that decision is impossible. In the silence she listens to two voices, two texts which she knows by heart and which speak through her, offering conflicting interpretations of her dilemma. Stephen Guest's letter calls her out of her penance 'back to life and goodness', to which in counterpoint she murmurs the words of the *Imitation of Christ* like a prayer: 'I have received the Cross'. There is no possible resolution of the conflict between passion and duty, for the terms themselves have by now become interchangeable. 'Am I to struggle and fall and repent again?' asks Maggie, as she listens to each voice in turn through the rising storm. Oscillation has taken the place of narrative progression and any kind of closure seems impossible. At this moment the flood-waters rise around her and the novel proper ends as the heroine breaks through into a different fictional reality: 'She was not bewildered for an instant – she knew it was the flood'.[1]

This is the kind of culminating episode we are familiar with in novels by George Eliot. The central character, usually the heroine, experiences a moment of extreme oscillation, contradiction, or vertigo. It is a privileged moment towards which the whole narrative has been moving and it announces that the search for a coherent view of the world has finally broken down. Every possible scheme of meaning within the novel has been found partial and inadequate. Such episodes indicate the limits of intelligibility. Like Maggie, Romola is unable to make sense of her conflicting loyalties and so abandons Florence in despair, drifting away in her boat; in *Felix Holt*, Esther Lyon, appropriated in turn by the male protagonists, awaits in uncertainty for the appearance of the ghost of Transome Court; while Gwendolen Harleth, with all her escape routes finally blocked, sees herself sailing eternally on, under Grandcourt's surveillance, like the Flying Dutchman. Such highly charged moments not only question conventional morality, they also dissolve the normal co-ordinates of space and time and so challenge the verisimilitude of the fictions to which they belong. They demand a breakthrough into another kind of fictional reality.

The main purpose of this study is to examine the crisis of interpretation which these moments epitomise and upon which George Eliot's career as a novelist was based. She saw her fictions as 'experiments in life'[2] and, as such, each experiment proceeds by the testing, juxtaposing, comparing, and contrasting of different ways of making sense of the world until coherence reaches its limit and breaks down into incoherence. This process is, in fact, what life is and it is never-ending. 'None of our theories,' says the narrator in *Felix Holt* laconically, 'are quite large enough for all the disclosures of time.'[3] And in a well-known letter of 1848, before she began writing fiction, George Eliot states clearly how this lack of symmetry both energises our lives and accounts for their pathos:

Alas for the fate of poor mortals which condemns them to wake up some fine morning and find all the poetry in which their world was bathed only the evening before utterly gone – the hard angular world of chairs and tables and looking-glasses staring at them in all its naked prose. It is so in all the stages of life – the poetry of girlhood goes – the poetry of love and marriage – the poetry of maternity – and at last the very poetry of duty forsakes us for a season and we see ourselves and all about us as nothing more than miserable agglomerations of atoms – poor tentative efforts of the Natur Princip to mould a personality. This is the state of prostration – the self-abnegation through which the soul must go, and to which perhaps it must again and again return, that its poetry or religion, which is the same thing, may be a real ever-flowing river fresh from the windows of heaven and the fountains of the great deep – not an artificial basin with grotto work and gold fish.[4]

This vivid account defines some of the crucial characteristics of the moment I am seeking to isolate and also generalises it into a description of the disruptive rhythm of life itself. This rhythm consists, first, of the creation of a theory of life, a philosophy, a world-view, 'poetry or religion', whatever one calls it, which reconciles the self and the world. Inevitably and essentially, each paradigm proves to be inadequate when subjected to the 'disclosures of time' and collapses. Then, both the self and the world simultaneously become fragmentary and meaningless: the former becomes simply a heap of atoms and the latter a collection of objects. But the process must continue unless the self is to contract and rigidify, and so each phase of wholeness and coherence is succeeded by the prostration of meaninglessness. This basic pattern informs George Eliot's thinking about life at its most prosaic level and at its most apocalyptic. It is a model which accommodates both a gradualist and a catastrophist view of the world.

Such an account of the individual life is a commonplace of romantic thought: life is a vale of soul-making, periods of holistic joy alternate with the aridities of dejection as the evolving self continues its search for, and creation of, more and more comprehensive meanings. The model was most memorably redefined for the Victorians by Carlyle in *Sartor Resartus* (1833–4). My aim is to show that in George Eliot's novels this view of life is assimilated, refined, and extended to a whole new range of experiences by means of her special awareness of the crisis of interpretation which the Victorians were experiencing. She was uniquely fitted to express the implications of this crisis since her own life was a sustained response to the orthodox creeds she had rejected. As one of her contemporaries commented: 'The sleepless sense that a new code of duty and motive needed to be restored in the midst of the void left by lost sanctions and banished hopes never ceased to stimulate her faculties and to oppress her spirits'.[5] As an intellectual of formidable learning she was fully aware of the latest developments in a whole range of intellectual disciplines undergoing radical change: biblical studies, philosophy, biology, psychology, historiography, mythology, philology, sociology, and anthropology. As a novelist she could deploy her fictions to domesticate these revolutionary ideas in the lives of ordinary people. In acknowledgement of this, critics have studied the effects of many of these branches of knowledge upon the form and language of her fiction.[6] My aim is to suggest that George Eliot was fundamentally concerned with all these branches of learning because each was grappling in its own way with the problem of interpretation.

Another way of expressing the same idea is to say that George Eliot's career and fiction can best be understood in the context of nineteenth-century hermeneutics. It was during her lifetime that hermeneutics developed from a body of rules for the translation and understanding of ancient texts, biblical and classical, to the recognition that interpretation was a foundational activity in which everyone was inescapably involved. The history of this philosophical tradition, originating in Schleiermacher and Coleridge at the beginning of the century, developing through Dilthey and Heidegger, and culminating in the work of Gadamer and Ricoeur in our own time has been described on several occasions.[7] George Eliot was not only familiar with the works of the German nineteenth-century philosophers working within the tradition, but she and Lewes also knew many of them personally. And it is significant that her first two major works were examples of that central hermeneutic activity, translation, and – more significantly – translations of German works exploring radically new ways of interpreting the life of Jesus and the essence of Christianity. It was, of course, in the field of theology that some of the most innovative and radical Victorian thinking was being carried out. But my concern is not with the history of ideas. It is rather to explore the larger implications of what I see as this central concern of George Eliot, namely, that it was because of her awareness of the fundamental role of interpretation in all areas of life that she was able to redefine the nature of Victorian fiction: its presentation of character, the role of the narrator, the structure of its narrative, the depiction of social and historical change. The intensity of her career as a novelist comes from her vivid, almost apocalyptic, sense that traditional modes of interpretation – making sense of the world – were breaking down irrevocably. Each of her fictional experiments as it moves towards the inevitable episode, the contradiction, the gap which disconfirms its hypothesis, is enacting that crisis with increasing urgency.

What evidence is there in George Eliot's novels that she was aware of what I am calling the Victorian crisis of interpretation? I have already suggested that her protagonists invariably experience a series of crises which arise essentially from the difficulty of interpreting their situation in the world. This, of course, is integral to much nineteenth-century literature. But one can point to elements in her fiction which are more specifically concerned with the traditional problems of hermeneutics.[8] *Scenes of Clerical Life* parodies and then re-deploys biblical exegesis in the lives of her chosen clergymen, with particular emphasis on typology, a means of linking past, present, and future which is developed in new directions through Mordecai and the Cabbala in *Daniel Deronda*. Typology is also used as a structuring device in *Adam Bede* and *The Mill on the Floss*, as Dinah's sermon and the legend of St Ogg's are fulfilled in their antitypes at the climax of those novels. Then there is legal hermeneutics. The law-court scenes in *Adam Bede* and *Felix Holt*, and the trial scenes in *Silas Marner*, explore the difficulties of applying legal principles to the details of human circumstance and motivation. Even where there are no formal trial scenes, one senses repeatedly in George Eliot the need to confront received truths, assumptions, and conventions, with the insoluble dilemmas of her major figures in a kind of surrogate trial. The most sustained case of this occurs in the final chapters of *The Mill on the Floss* when everyone in St Ogg's 'passes judgment' on Maggie, according to their own premises. Closely related to these are those crucial confessional scenes where the mentors – such as Mr Gilfil, the Rev. Tryan, or Daniel Deronda – seek to assess the heroines' guilt or innocence by interpreting their garbled narratives. Then, there is the evidence in the novels of George Eliot's fascination with the hermeneutics of literary and historical research: in *Romola*, for example, Bardo and Baldassarre seek to recover the classical roots of the Renaissance, one through editorial reconstruction, the other through epigraphy. But perhaps the novelist's most overt acknowledgement of the centrality – and the pitfalls – of the interpretative enterprise can be found in *Middlemarch*, in the juxtaposition of Casaubon and Lydgate: one searching for the founding religious myth, the other for the original organic tissue. And finally, one could point to the end of *Romola* where, after Savonarola's trial by fire and subsequent interrogation under torture, the heroine scrutinises his printed confessions to separate, with lengthy and tortuous exegesis, the genuine from the corrupt text in order to assess his claim to martyrdom. The model here is the biblical criticism of the Gospel narratives.

These, however, are simply particular episodes and devices in the novels where interpretative activity is crystallised. My argument is that they are symptomatic of profound tendencies which affected George Eliot's fiction in more pervasive and fundamental ways. One of these is to be found in her development of that crucial convention of Victorian fiction, the omniscient narrator, into a more and more subtle means of interpretative commentary within the novels themselves. As J. Hillis Miller has pointed out, 'omniscient' is a misnomer since the narrators in this tradition, far from being divinely transcendent, 'identify themselves with a human awareness which is everywhere at all times within the world of the novel'.[9] This is certainly true of George Eliot where the sympathetic identification of commentator and the characters is stressed. And this is directly related to the increasing difficulties the narrator experiences in seeking to judge or interpret the narrative. At the end of *The Mill on the Floss*, for example, the narrator acknowledges that there is no simple interpretation of Maggie's dilemma, 'no master-key that will fit all cases', and that in the absence of 'general rules [which] . . . will lead them to justice by a ready-made patent method', the casuist is to be preferred to the man of maxims.[10] And, as a casuist, the narrator is more intent on unravelling a few human lives and 'seeing how they were woven and interwoven'[11] than in grand theory or general principles. It is true that in the later novels she appeals increasingly to science, philosophy, and historiography for illumination, but such analogies have a disturbing habit of undermining themselves. In *Middlemarch*, for example, the pier-glass analogy at the beginning of chapter twenty-seven both philosophically asserts and solipsistically questions any attempt to understand other people; while the analogy of the micro-scope directed on a water-drop in chapter six prompts 'interpreta-tions which turn out to be rather coarse' when a stronger lens is used.[12] By the time of *Daniel Deronda*, George Eliot is using her commentary to express these uncertainties even more emphatically. The paradoxical problem is, how do you assert undogmatically the unquestioned truth that things appear different in different perspectives? The narrator finds it more and more difficult to link general observations about the world and human nature to the details of the narrative; when they occur, they appear as ambiguous commonplaces protected by a kind of ironic self-deprecation. There is a growing sense that the convention of authorial omniscience is at risk if the act of interpre-tation itself needs continual explanation and justification.

Another area where George Eliot's hermeneutic awareness finds expression is in the representation of character. One of the most vivid acknowledgements of this was made by the historian Lord Acton on the news of her death in 1880. His own life has been spent, he wrote, 'in endless striving to make out the inner point of view, the *raison d'être*, the secret of fascination for powerful minds, of systems of religion and philosophy, and of politics'. But the problem – which neither the historians nor the poets have solved – is in knowing 'how to think or feel as men do who live in the grasp of the various systems'. The novelist, he maintains, had this ability.

George Eliot seemed to me capable not only of reading the diverse hearts of men, but of creeping into their skin, watching the world through their eyes, feeling their latent background of conviction, discerning theory and habit, influences of thought and knowledge, of life and descent, and having obtained this experience, recovering her independence, stripping off the borrowed shell, and exposing scientifically and indifferently the soul of a Vestal, a Crusader . . . without attraction, preference, or caricature.[13]

The terms of praise are significant. The novelist has confronted the problems of the historian and solved them in her fiction. How do people make sense of the world? What is their point of view, their *raison d'être*, their system of thought, by means of which they interpret reality? In other words, Acton implies, George Eliot depicts character as an act of interpretation.

This aspect of her writing is most apparent in those sketches of minor characters which consist essentially of an interpretative scheme or rationale. Unlike the major figures, they are the embodiment of one rather than a sequence of paradigms. Mrs Cadwallader, an aristocrat living in provincial Middlemarch, 'believed as unquestioningly in birth and no-birth a she did in game and vermin'. As a result, 'her feeling towards the vulgar rich was a sort of religious hatred . . . such people were no part of God's design in making the world; and their accent was an affliction to the ears. A town where such monsters abounded was hardly more than a sort of low comedy, which could not be taken account of in a well-bred scheme of the universe.'[14] The ironic over-statement makes the point clearly. By means of her well-bred scheme, based on blood, birth, and genealogy, Mrs Cadwallader cuts reality into her approved shape. These are the co-ordinates of her world-view, her scheme of the universe, her religion. The novels are, of course, full of such sketches, ranging from the assorted clergymen of *Scenes of Clerical Life* through the Renaissance types in *Romola* to the aristocrats of *Daniel Deronda*. George Eliot has helped to transform the Theophrastan character sketch and its later developments into a scheme by which the world is interpreted. It is worth noticing that even with such relatively minor figures the reader is provided with a double perspective; free indirect speech both enters the character's world-view and stands back from it. This fulfils, in Carlyle's words at the beginning of the Victorian period, the true methods of character depiction: 'to see into him, understand his goings-forth, decipher the whole heart of his mystery: nay, not only to see into him, but even to see out of him, to view the world altogether as he views it; so that we can theoretically construe him'.[15] The sentiments anticipate Acton's fifty years later and point to a particular obsession in this great age of biography and fiction.

The presentation of character as world-view is essentially dialectical, as these comments indicate. The self and the world are constituted simultaneously. In describing how a character shapes his world, the novelist is showing at the same time how his self takes shape; and even with minor figures this is made possible by the flexibility of omniscient narration as it enters and then disengages from the worlds being created. Explanation and understanding work together in the act of interpretation. With the major characters, the narrator's interpretative turn from explanation to understanding is announced publicly in a manner which becomes a hall-mark of George Eliot's fiction. Such a moment occurs in *Middlemarch* in the depiction of Mr Casaubon: 'Suppose we turn from outside estimates of a man, to wonder, with keener interest, what is the report of his own consciousness about his doings or capacity.'[16] There is a medical quality to this kind of shift: after the diagnosis of symptoms the doctor asks the patient how he feels. The two, of course, never coincide fully. The discrepancy, the tension between the outside and inside estimate, is what character consists of and makes the future possible.

George Eliot's vivid awareness of this both vitalises and constrains her fiction. Interpretation by its nature is never definitive; illumination and concealment are inseparable and always in tension. If life consists of a never-ending series of crises of intelligibility, if character is 'a process and an unfolding', as she says in *Middlemarch*,[17] then any attempted encapsulation – even in the terms praised by Lord Acton – is bound to falsify. There are always discrepancies between the characters' rationale of life, their feelings, and their actions; Mrs Cadwallader has, after all, married a provincial clergyman. This is also the reason why the reader-as-interpreter is warned against premature judgment. George Eliot concludes her sketch of her minor character's world-view in this way: 'Let any lady who is inclined to be hard on Mrs Cadwallader inquire into the comprehensiveness of her own beautiful views, and be quite sure that they afford accommodation for all the lives which have the honour to co-exist with hers.'[18] For as well as the narrator and the characters, the reader too is involved in the hermeneutical enterprise and should be aware of the limited horizon of her own world-view. Inevitably, such problems of analysis, explanation, and depiction are multiplied when it comes to the major characters. The problems become such an integral part of the narrator's difficulty in fulfilling his role as commentator in any conventional sense, that by the time of *Daniel Deronda* they are being additionally foregrounded in George Eliot's own chapter mottoes. 'How trace the why and wherefore in a mind reduced to the barrenness of a fastidious egoism?', she asks, before attempting to dramatise another cryptic episode in Grandcourt's life.[19] But the impossibility of the task has already been expressed in a previous motto. Since people have, like the planets, both a visible and invisible history, then 'the narrator of human actions, if he did his work with the same completeness, would have to thread the hidden pathways of feeling and thought which lead up to every moment of action'.[20] Such strict deduction is not possible in human affairs, and it is in the inevitable discrepancy between the desire for a comprehensive explanatory scheme and particular, recalcitrant circumstances that the energy and challenge of George Eliot's fiction are to be found.

The novelist's direct involvement in the changes transforming nineteenth-century hermeneutics in many areas of intellectual life and belief can be seen most vividly in her work as editor and reviewer at the beginning of her writing career, when she was most closely involved in the intellectual and literary life of London. An examination of her writings at this time will help us to understand her response to some of the major changes in nineteenth-century thought. Her persistent aim, it will be seen, was to define a state of mind appropriate to a crisis of interpretation.

In her essays and reviews, George Eliot shares with other Victorian thinkers the sense that the modern mind's predicament is a consciousness of its own belatedness. The past and its traditions had become remote and alien in a new way, to which the growth of hermeneutics in the nineteenth-century was a response. Carlyle in *Sartor Resartus* expresses a vision of the individual and society through Professor Teufelsdröckh's old-clothes philosophy as a continual discarding of old, unfashionable beliefs and systems; while Matthew Arnold, in his essay on Heine, sees 'the sense of want of correspondence between the forms of modern Europe and its spirit' as an inescapable fact of life. This is no less than 'the awakening of the modern spirit'.[21] And one of the most familiar expressions of this awareness in Victorian literature is that of lovers amidst the ruins of a past civilisation, a *topos* which reaches a kind of hermeneutical epitome in the Roman honeymoon scenes in *Middlemarch*. There, the idealistic bride and the scholar groom, both seeking 'a binding theory', are overwhelmed by the 'stupendous fragmentariness' of a Rome which had once been 'the spiritual centre and interpreter of the world.'[22] It is, however, in her non-fiction writings that George Eliot begins to explore the various responses of modern thought to this dilemma. What theories of interpretation are available to understand both the past and, by implication, the present which is its consequence?

Though the essays and reviews cover a wide range of subjects – philosophy, sociology, biblical criticism, mythology, and art as well as literary criticism – their persistent concern is to define a method of thought, a balanced, critical mental stance appropriate to the middle decades of the century. In all these areas of knowledge, George Eliot is seeking to alert her readers, principally of the *Westminster Review* and the *Leader*, to recent intellectual developments. Significantly, the major proponents of these ideas are German scholars whose thoroughness and sophistication are used to criticise the naivety and parochialism of English culture. Her most direct advocacy occurs in her essay, 'A Word for the Germans' (1865), where she seeks to revise John Bull's caricature of these continentals as 'cloudy metaphysicians'. In contrast to the 'sound British thinker [who] kicks a stone to prove that matter exists', George Eliot characterises 'the German mind [which] possesses in a high degree two tendencies which are often represented as opposed to each other: namely, largeness of theoretic conception, and thoroughness in the investigation of facts'. She is fully aware that either tendency can lapse into eccentricity – cloudy metaphysics or mind-numbing pedantry – but this again is simply the vice of that German virtue, thoroughness. George Eliot refuses to be sidetracked from the quality she admires, that ability to combine painstaking research with theoretical self-consciousness. 'Without them, historical criticism would have been simply nowhere; take away the Germans, with their patience, their thoroughness, their need for a doctrine which refers all transient and material manifestations to subtler and more permanent causes, and all that we value most in our appreciation of early history would have been wanting to us.'[23]

On these grounds she praises the work of the philosopher Gruppe ('The Future of German Philosophy'), the sociologist Riehl ('The Natural History of German Life'), the biblical scholar Von Bohlen ('Introduction to Genesis'), the classical scholar Böckh ('The

Antigone and its Moral'), and the art historian Stahr ('The Art of the Ancients').[24] Even when the work praised is British, as in the case of Robert William Mackay's *The Progress of the Intellect* (1850), the terms of praise are Germanic: 'Now and then, however, we meet with a nature which combines the faculty for amassing minute erudition with the largeness of view necessary to give it a practical bearing; a high appreciation of the genius of antiquity, with a profound belief in the progressive character of human development.' The combination of these 'antithetically mixt' qualities is, for George Eliot, essentially Germanic, and in a scholar like Mackay British culture is beginning at last 'to emulate the immense labours of Germany in the departments of mythology and biblical criticism'. Interestingly, she goes further and adds that 'when once [England] does so, the greater solidity and directness of the English mind ensure a superiority of treatment'.[25] Here, one feels, we have the ulterior motive for a majority of George Eliot's reviews: the mediation of advanced German thought – begun by Carlyle a generation earlier – so that it will be assimilated in its own way by native British empiricism. The techniques of the essays – their explication, reassurance, exhortation, and irony – are all directed to this end.

What the modern critical mind rejects is the unexamined premise, those absolutes of every kind which have been simply handed down, like old clothes, and with them the belief in watertight systems of thought. This is why George Eliot praises the philosophical work of Gruppe. He is not proposing a new system but a new method of philosophical investigation. 'The age of systems is passed . . .' he writes. 'System is the childhood of philosophy; the manhood of philosophy is investigation.' In his task of bringing together ideas and things, abstract and concrete, analytical and synthetic, he is in her opinion undertaking the true task of philosophy in the future: 'It must renounce metaphysics: it must renounce the ambitious attempt to form a theory of the universe, to know things in their causes and first principles.' Its route, she asserts, is not 'the high *priori* road' but the humble '*a posteriori* path'.[26]

The way in which the critical mind carries out this genuine investigation is by means of the hypothesis, that vital combination of those apparently antithetical qualities – the large theoretic conception and the thorough investigation of facts.[27] 'A correct generalization gives significance to the smallest detail,' she comments in her review of Mackay, 'just as the great inductions of geology demonstrate in every pebble the working of laws by which the earth has become adapted for the habitation of man.'[28] And the selection of passages from *The Progress of the Intellect* which follows, develops the central significance of the hypothesis as a method of thought. First of all, the working hypothesis takes for granted the gaps and uncertainties in our thinking: 'All human knowledge must partake of the imperfection of the faculties through which it is derived; and the limited and unsatisfactory character of what we know leaves a wide and most important void to be filled up by our belief.' Secondly, the hypothesis fills this void honestly, says Mackay, by acknowledging that it is dependent upon an act of faith 'to supply the imperfections of our knowledge': 'True faith is a belief in things probable; it is the assigning to certain inferences a hypothetical objectivity, and upon the conscious acknowledgement of this hypothetical character alone depends its advantage over fanaticism; its moral value and dignity.' This is not simply a matter of scientific method.

Thirdly, it is this kind of faith, integral to the hypothesis, that makes religion and science inseparable. If, in both areas of knowledge, the correct balance between credulity and scepticism is maintained, then the dialectic is that of necessary development. 'Faith and knowledge tend mutually to the confirmation and enlargement of each other; faith by verification being often transformed into knowledge, and every increase of knowledge supplying a wider and firmer basis of belief.' True religion and science, therefore, writes Mackay, inevitably represent 'an infinite search or approximation' in which 'finality is but another name for bewilderment or defeat'. This is another way of describing the hermeneutic circle, that basic mode of understanding which had been defined earlier by Schleiermacher in his interpretation of literary texts: knowledge is achieved not only by the gradual progression from one detail to another, but also by the anticipation of the whole, for the detail can only be understood within the whole and the whole through its constituent parts. The circle is not a vicious one, since a valid interpretation always consists of a sustained and mutually qualifying interplay between the whole and its parts.[29] It is this dialectical openness George Eliot commends in *The Progress of the Intellect*, and this is the message of her final quotation: 'A remnant of the mythical lurks in the very sanctuary of science. Forms or theories ever fall short of nature . . . To a certain extent they are reliable and complete; as a system of knowledge they are but intermediary and preparatory.' Systems and creeds must be rejected in all areas of knowledge. It is not certainty but ignorance which is 'the eyelid through which [the soul] gradually opens itself to the truth, admitting no more than it can for the time support, and, as through a veil, learning to support its lustre'.[30]

It would be difficult to exaggerate the significance of this early review in George Eliot's thinking, for in it we can find ideas which recur from the earliest fiction to *Daniel Deronda*. Mackay, in tracing the progress of the intellect 'as exemplified in the religious development of the Greeks and Hebrews', is spelling out what he considers to be the true forms of faith and revelation. He had been profoundly influenced by Strauss who, in his *Das Leben Jesu* (1835) which George Eliot translated in 1846, declared that biblical interpretation had tried for centuries to be both rationalist and supernaturalist in its assumptions, believing that the gospels were both historical and supernatural. In Strauss's view, the only way of resolving the inevitable contradictions arising from this was by means of the mythical method, the hermeneutical key which he was defining and applying to the gospels. Mackay is developing and extending this idea, as we have seen, by suggesting that myth is a form of 'hypothetical objectivity' which arises naturally in all kinds of mental activity as a means of connecting the known with the unknown, and which will be progressively superseded in the course of human development. In contrast to the vitality of this hermeneutic are the traditional biblical theories of accommodation, which George Eliot criticises in her review for failing to deliver 'the understanding from a heavy burthen of contradiction and absurdity'.[31]

Her most detailed examination of biblical hermeneutics – apart from her translations – occurs in 1856 in her review of a new translation of Von Bohlen's *Introduction to Genesis* (1835).[32] There she defines four stages of interpretation: first, there is 'extreme orthodoxy', essentially 'a deductive process, which has for its axiom the belief that the Hebrew writings are from beginning to end revealed truth'; second, there is the 'accommodation theory' which acknowledges that divine revelation had to be adapted to the culture in which it took place; this in turn leads to 'mild heterodoxy, which allows the presence of mythical and legendary elements in the Hebrew records'; and finally, there is 'extreme heterodoxy' which interprets the scriptures as any other national records using all the tools of historical criticism. Thus, the development of hermeneutics, here as in other branches of knowledge, is the gradual transition from deduction to hypothesis, from the dogmatic application of rules to the vital balancing of credulity and scepticism. George Eliot's translations were documents crucial to this transition in England and they provide further evidence of her engagement with German hermeneutics. Feuerbach, in particular, was to prove influential in the transmission of these radical ideas to England. *The Essence of Christianity* goes beyond even extreme heterodoxy, to what Paul Ricoeur has called the 'hermeneutics of suspicion', there joining the writings of Marx, Nietzsche, and Freud, which maintain that the religious like other forms of language is a coded version of hidden truths which need demystifying.[33] Feuerbach's particular aim was 'to show that the antithesis of divine and human is altogether illusory, that it is nothing else than the antithesis between the human nature in general and the human individual'.[34] Once this has been recognised, then humanity will end the process of self-alienation through which it empties its substance into an illusory absolute, God the great *a priori*. The false opposition between God and the world is nothing else than 'the opposition between the nature of abstraction and the nature of perception', and that which connects the two is the imagination. 'All religious cosmogonies are products of the imagination'.[35] Here again one sees the dialectical force of the hypothesis in Feuerbach's radical deconstructions: the second Person of the Trinity is in reality the mediation between the abstract and the concrete. In this form of German idealism the Incarnation becomes the symbol of the hypothetical method.

George Eliot acknowledged her indebtedness to Feuerbach, but one should be cautious in attributing his views to her. She was only too aware that the dismantling of orthodoxies could lead to new forms of hubris. In what seems to be an implicit reference to Feuerbach's religious anthropology, she wrote to her friend, the phrenologist Charles Bray, in 1857 objecting to elements of his *The Philosophy of Necessity* on the grounds of 'our total inability to find in our own natures a key to the Divine Mystery': 'I could more readily turn Christian and worship Jesus again than embrace a Theism which professes to explain the proceedings of God.'[36] But once the true philosophical method of enquiry has been established by means of the working hypothesis then, George Eliot believed, scholars like Mackay will be able to write a satisfactory natural history of religion. Moreover, by deploying this instrument generally, it will be realised that 'every phase of human development is part of that education of the race in which we are sharing; every mistake, every absurdity into which poor human nature has fallen, may be looked on as an experiment of which we may reap the benefit'. Interestingly, the language used here to describe the progress of the intellect is the same George Eliot employed in her letter of 1848 to articulate 'the fate of poor mortals' as they stumble through a series of inadequate world-views, each of which ends in disenchantment and prostration. But here, instead of the pathos, she stresses the beneficial effects of these 'experiments' in life. It all depends on one's position and perspective. Now she writes with historical hindsight in a confidently positivist mood that the failed experiments of the past have revealed the way forward into the future. Such revelation 'is perpetually unfolding itself to our widened experience and investigation, as firmament upon firmament becomes visible to us in proportion to the power and range of our exploring instruments'. And the act of positivist faith upon which this confidence is based is enunciated: 'The master key to this revelation, is the recognition of the presence of undeviating law in the material and moral world.' This must now be seen as the new 'divine yea and nay, the seal of prohibition and sanction'.[37]

In these writings, George Eliot clearly identifies herself with a group of closely-linked Victorian thinkers, all of whom were seeking to create synthetic philosophies based on the methods of the physical sciences. She was to make the point again fourteen years later in her review of Lecky's *History of the Rise and Influence of the Spirit of Rationalism in Europe* (1865): 'The great conception of universal regular sequence, without partiality and without caprice – the conception which is the most potent force at work in the modification of our faith, and of the practical form given to our sentiments – could only grow out of that patient watching of external fact, and that silencing of preconceived notions, which are urged upon the mind by the problems of physical science.'[38] This group of thinkers and their relationships have recently been perceptively re-examined by Diana Postlethwaite. She shows how the monistic theories and ambitions of Spinoza and Coleridge are redefined under the influence of Victorian scientific method; and in particular how the influence of John Stuart Mill's *System of Logic* (1843) in its search for a science of human nature, based upon the theory of universal causation, is eventually superseded by Comte's *Cours de Philosophie Positive* (1830–42) which seeks to carry the implications of the scientific method even further, into the realms of psychology, ethics, and social science, culminating in the fundamen-

tal reconciliation of the intellect and the emotions. This in turn –
especially what was considered to be Comte's metaphysical mysticism
– was questioned and redefined by Spencer and Lewes by means of
'the development hypothesis' which culminated in the former's
Principles of Psychology (1855). Here, the principles of evolutionary
biology are applied to the mental developments of both the individual
and the race. Spencer was to apply his key, in Postlethwaite's words,
'through the solar system, the formation of the earth, plants and
animals, man, society, language, religion, and art'.[39] Lewes's *Problems
of Life and Mind* (1873–9) became the major expression of his own
attempt, building on the same foundations, to integrate materialism
and idealism, Locke with Kant, in the search for that Victorian holy
grail, a comprehensive synthetic philosophy.

This then is the context in which George Eliot was promoting a
certain mental stance, a method of thought based on the working
hypothesis which would progressively uncover the laws of the
universe. Not only was she fascinated by these ambitious unitary
philosophies, but also through Spencer and Lewes she was directly
involved in working them out. Two aspects in particular of these
quests for unity in plurality must have influenced George Eliot's own
thinking. First, there was their basic assumption that belief and
intellect progressed through a sequence of historical phases, corresponding to the crises of the individual life. In the *Ethics*, for example,
which George Eliot also translated, Spinoza presents a three-tiered
theory of knowledge in which man starts with fragmentary, particular
perceptions, moves to a level of adequate ideas and generalisations,
and finally achieves a mystical, intuitive knowledge of particular
things in their general relation to the cosmos. For Comte, too, the
single design of history is conceived as the progress of the human mind
through its three stages: the theological, the metaphysical, the
positivist. The key mechanism of the movement in this historical plan
is the incoherence at each stage of certain ways of making sense of the
world.[40] History, as we have seen, can be viewed as a series of failed
experiments: a hypothesis seems to explain the facts, turns into a
theory, but is eventually disconfirmed by an anomaly or
contradiction.

A second feature of the work of these philosophers to which she
responded was their recognition to a greater or lesser degree of the
limitations of the experimental method. As Postlethwaite shows, their
search led invariably to the brink of the unknowable, the first cause
underpinning the laws of invariable sequence. In his seminal article,

'Progress: Its Law and Cause' (1857), for example, Spencer concludes that it was, in fact, the sincere man of science who 'alone *knows* that under all things, there lies an impenetrable mystery'.[41] It is a common refrain to which George Eliot responds. In a letter of 1857 to Sara Hennell, in which she speaks enthusiastically about Spencer's article, she comments: 'I feel every day a greater disinclination for theories and arguments about the origin of things in the presence of all this mystery and beauty and pain and ugliness, that floods one with conflicting emotions.'[42] And her well-known, low-key comment on the appearance of Darwin's *Origin of Species* underlines the point: 'To me the Development Theory and all other explanations of processes by which things come to be, produce a feeble impression compared with the mystery that lies under the process.'[43] But we have already seen, in her review of 1851, how this was fully expressed through her treatment of Mackay. The recognition of 'undeviating law' and of 'invariability of sequence' goes hand-in-hand with a vivid awareness of the unknown continually pressing in on the known, of the need for faith and knowledge, credulity and scepticism, to work together.

The scepticism about the claims of the intellect had been part of George Eliot's thinking many years before she began writing for the *Westminster Review*. In a letter to Sara Hennell in 1843, for example, shortly after losing her Christian faith, she recapitulates the stages her own beliefs have passed through: first the liberation 'from the wretched giant's bed of dogmas', then the enjoyment of 'the full use of our limbs and the bracing air of independence', but soon the sense of 'our own miserable weakness' introduces a new awareness: 'Speculative truth begins to appear but a shadow of individual minds, agreement between intellects seems unattainable, and we turn to the *truth of feeling* as the only universal bond of union.' Again, credulity and scepticism work together in any hypothesis. The individual life is seen as a process of disconfirmation as well as discovery, and part of the process is the recognition of feeling as an essential element of knowledge. But the outmoded speculative truths cannot simply be discarded as in scientific discovery: 'We find that the intellectual errors which we once fancied were a mere incrustation have grown into the living body and that we cannot in the majority of cases, wrench them away without destroying vitality.'[44] This is the complex paradigm, both organic and dialectical, which was integral to George Eliot's thinking from an early age and which was refined, enlarged, and consolidated by her later intellectual labours.

The ambiguity of this view of life persistently works against excessive positivist confidence in the findings of social science. The extension of natural science to the study of man might be a liberation from dogma of various kinds, but the knowledge acquired may encourage the view that human beings are the product of forces quite beyond their control. The dangers of this attitude are evident even in the review of 1851, when she declares that the social sciences should be employed to separate the vital from the moribund: 'Our civilization, and, yet more, our religion, are an anomalous blending of lifeless barbarisms, which have descended to us like so many petrifactions from distant ages, with living ideas, the offspring of a true process of development.'[45] But if they are 'blended' in this way, how do you distinguish the old clothes from the new? The difficulties are more explicitly acknowledged five years later in her sympathetic review of the sociologist Riehl, who 'sees in European society *incarnate history*, and any attempt to disengage it from its historical elements must, he believes, be simply destructive of social vitality'. Social science may develop 'those grand simple generalizations which trace out the inevitable march of the human race as a whole', but it also needs 'what may be called its Biology, carrying us on to innumerable special phenomena which outlie the sphere of science, and belong to Natural History'. The classification is still Comte's, but the emphasis now falls on the careful, detailed investigation for which Riehl is praised: 'the most complete equipment of theory will not enable a statesman or a political and social reformer to adjust his measures wisely, in the absence of a special acquaintance with the section of society for which he legislates'.[46] It is a note heard frequently in her literary criticism. When the discrepancy between theory and evidence is great, the effects are dangerous and vicious, especially in art and literature with their opera peasants and idyllic ploughmen. We need a true conception of 'the peasant in all his coarse apathy, and the artisan in all his suspicious selfishness', in order to check the 'tendency created by the splendid conquests of modern generalization, to believe that all relations of men to their neighbours may be settled by algebraic equations'.[47]

George Eliot was, in other words, involved in a careful balancing act with the claims of grand theory, especially with Positivism that 'one-sided system',[48] as she called it, which was to continue to the end of her career. This may be considered natural in a novelist. It is certainly part of her belief in the provisional nature of any system, her awareness of the hermeneutical problems in any comprehensive theory. This often found expression in irony at the expense of singleminded system-making, as in this comment on one of the Victorian synthesisers in a letter to her friend Sara Hennell in 1852: 'I went to Kew yesterday on a scientific expedition with Herbert Spencer, who has all sorts of theories about plants – I should have said *proof*-hunting expedition. Of course, if the flowers didn't correspond to the theories, we said, "*tant pis pour les fleurs!*"'.[49] This scepticism is expressed more solemnly in some of her non-fiction writings at the end of her life, which have only recently been published.[50] These are items written between 1872 and 1879 but omitted by Charles Lee Lewes from 'Leaves from a Notebook' (1884), probably because of their turgid style. Much of their scepticism is directed at the findings of social science – by then an orthodoxy – and its belief that the future is predetermined by the operation of discernible universal laws in the direction of social progress. These late jottings question the hubristic claims of theory in a variety of fields – social, scientific, mythological.

The two basic criteria by which grand theory is questioned are those of human limitations and of increasing complexity. 'To everything human there are limits' is the opening refrain of the first essay in the Princeton notebook, which is then applied to the imagination, to language, to clothes, and most sombrely to discovery: 'That too must end somewhere and under the name of knowledge has long been recognized as a mere parenthesis in a context of irremovable darkness.' This is not unlike the gist of some of her earliest remarks, but the tone is different: then in the triumphant progress of the intellect the glass was seen as half-full, now it is half-empty. But her commitment to the proper use of the hypothetical method remains. It is only when the 'irrational exclusiveness of theory' insists on reducing everything to its own key terms – as here in its search for the origins of myth – and ignoring the common constraints of the human that she objects.[51] Likeness is what we should expect even among remote tribes because they all share the limitations of the human. This need to check the claims of theory against the facts of human experience, explanation against understanding, is emphasised by the inclusion of two quotations which stress the need for appropriate knowledge. The first is Locke's description of the man with microscopical eyes so subtle that he can discern 'the configuration of the minute particles of the spring of a clock', but is unable to tell the time; the second is Aristotle's remark in the *Ethics* that 'we must not look for equal exactness in all departments of study, but only such as belongs to the subject matter of each, and in such a degree as is appropriate to the particular line of enquiry'. But the most vehement criticism is reserved, in a note entitled 'Moral Freedom', for the debilitating deterministic thinking which in maintaining that human action is 'a chain of necessary sequences' neutralizes practice and 'locks up [human] nature in a dark closet away from the impressions without which character must become a shrivelled unripe fruit'. Like the spurious, one-dimensional search for origins, this kind of tracking down of the cause of each impression through 'an illimitable series of antecedents' ignores the facts of the human situation: 'Life & action are prior to theorizing, & have a prior logic in the conditions necessary to maintain them. To regard any theory which supplants that logic as having supreme intellectual authority is a contradiction, unless it could be ruled that the human race should commit a slow suicide by the gradual extinction of motive – the poisoning of feeling by inference.'[52]

The second prong of her attack on grand theorising is what she calls the principle of increasing complexity: 'in whatever concerns the life of man there is a constantly increasing complexity or interaction of various conditions, so that similar phenomena may often be produced by a different concurrence of facts and events and that you can hardly find any phenomenon which is not a highly mixed product'.[53] This, too, makes the explanation of origins and derivations according to a single agency improbable, whether applied by Lyell to geology or by the sociologists to society. Consequently, the difficulties of discriminating true from false development are exacerbated. In the note, 'Historic Guidance', she examines Comte's concepts of continuity and solidarity – the cornerstones of social sympathy – in order to point out their unreliability as a simple guide to conduct. Social solidarity 'may be said to exist *avengingly* as well as beneficently', and continuity also implies that 'evil results [descend] from generation to generation'. We simply don't have the means to interpret and predict the products of social development with confidence. 'How much is tendency destined to grow?' she asks,[54] echoing a question in *Daniel Deronda*.

What this particular discussion leads to in these late jottings is a significantly 'critical estimate', as she calls it, of Comte; in particular, of his endorsement of the separation of spiritual and temporal authority to be found in medieval Catholicism. He saw this as anticipating and validating the creation of a positivist spiritual authority, unhindered by the temporal and practical, and in sole charge of the development of positive law. Comte expressed his view

in these terms: 'The wisdom of such a course is obvious ... as soon as it
becomes generally recognized that social phenomena are subject to
invariable laws; laws of so complicated a character and so dependent
upon other sciences as to make it doubly necessary that minds of the
highest order should be specially devoted to their interpretation.'[55]
She saw it as the thin end of the wedge, and it became the danger
signal for many of Comte's English followers. For George Eliot, it was
dramatic and disturbing proof of the tendency of the hypothetical
method to divide fatally into 'the natural fundamental distinction
between theory & practice'. Unless resisted, the effects will be dire:

Doctrine, no matter of what sort, is liable to putrefy when kept in close
chambers to be dispensed according to the will of men authorized to hold the
keys. It throws up 'infallibility' & damnatory edicts against heresy, & sends
fumes into the brains of the keyholders breeding strange interpretations &
inferences so that canonical doctrine itself passes into corrupt heresy.[56]

It is a dark hermeneutic vision characteristic of George Eliot. Once
doctrine or theory is seen as a key rather than a working hypothesis,
the priestly keyholders are free to concoct what interpretations they
wish without challenge.

Such a failure constantly to test theory and practice against each
other springs, in both George Eliot's and George Henry Lewes's view,
from a Comtean misunderstanding of 'invariable laws'. By her
criteria of human limitations and of increasing complexity, she
questioned the basis of such laws, while Lewes repeatedly stressed in
his *Problems of Life and Mind* that 'the laws of Nature are not objective
existences, but subjective abstractions, – formulae in which the
multifarious phenomena are stripped of their variety and reduced to
unity'. Laws are fictions that direct research; no general statement is
real, but only true 'within the limits of the formulated terms'.[57] A
crucial expression of this controversy in the 1840s and '50s was the
dispute between John Stuart Mill and William Whewell over the
nature of scientific explanation. Was a scientific law, as the former
maintained, a copy of the observable facts? Or was it, as the latter
argued, a concept not in the facts but 'superinduced' on the facts?
Lewes, significantly, changed sides in the public debate in the late
1850s from being a supporter of Mill to taking up what Michael
Mason has called a 'distinctly Whewellian position', in which the
hypothesis is accepted as essential to the very nature of scientific
discovery.[58] Again and again, in whatever area of knowledge, the true

nature of the hypothesis – in particular, an understanding of its 'hypothetical objectivity' – is returned to as a corrective against the overweening demand for certainty. Such a position for any thinker or writer to take up is both precarious and demanding, allowing no resting place in any orthodoxy. The rigours of such a life can be guessed from an episode in 1878 which has been reconstructed by K. K. Collins.

In that year Lewes died, leaving unfinished the final two volumes of his *magnum opus*, the *Problems of Life and Mind*, which he had several times referred to jokingly as his 'Key to all Psychologies'. In her intense grief, George Eliot spent six months of careful labour preparing the rough manuscript drafts for the press. Collins shows how in this process she thoroughly re-examined and to some extent revised Lewes's central conclusions about the moral sense. In doing so, it seems, she was seeking to re-assert the centrality of the true hypothetical method in the moral life. In the nineteenth-century controversy between the utilitarians and the intuitionists, George Eliot clearly felt that Lewes had misrepresented the situation by coming down too firmly on the side of the former, underestimating the 'a priori principles that make moral experience intelligible in the first place'. In her editing and revisions she performs a subtle balancing act of the *a priori* and the *a posteriori* at work in the moral sense, without reducing the significance of either. Collins summarises the revisions in these terms: 'Stated in practical terms, as an altruistic calculation of consequences, the abstract principle of duty takes a generally utilitarian colour. But the unselfish nature of the calculation . . . conserves the idea that the principle of duty is impersonal in the sense that it does not accommodate one's special advantage.'[59] It is a revealing episode. Here, while mourning her beloved companion, she sets about re-establishing the fine balance she felt had been lost in his last painful writings about the nature of the moral sense. It is a poignant reminder of where George Eliot's true priorities lay.

What emerges from this examination of George Eliot's non-fiction writing is her acute awareness of both the loss of traditional forms of belief, and the urgent need to re-create meaning and coherence. This is not simply an intellectual task. As we have seen, she is constantly seeking to widen the terms of reference to accommodate the full range of human faculties – mind, emotions, faith, and moral awareness. In response to this need, she creates her own model of the way we make sense of the world, based on certain assumptions. It is the same model which informs her comments on the role of the writer and, most significantly, on her own career as a novelist. These comments confirm the sense of uncertainty and crisis associated with the interpretative act. They reveal the role of the Victorian woman writer to be one of acute anxiety.

The first thing to notice is that, as with 'the fate of poor mortals', George Eliot saw her career as a novelist both as a unity and as a series of distinct stages. As she wrote to John Blackwood in 1861 over the publication of *Silas Marner*: 'My chief reason for wishing to publish the story now, is, that I like my writings to appear in the order in which they are written, because they belong to successive mental phases, and when they are a year behind me, I can no longer feel that thorough identification with them which gives zest to the sense of authorship.' The writer moves on having satisfactorily solved the particular problem which is now no longer relevant. She adds with characteristic ambivalence: 'I generally like them better at that distance, but then, I feel as if they might just as well have been written by somebody else.'[60] In other words, the struggle of writing identifies her fictions as her own; the pleasure of completion disengages them. Certainly, the agony of writing is intense and her letters form a litany of despondency, self-deprecation, illness, and despair, which Lewes has to use all his wiles to dispel.

The anxiety begins as soon as an idea for a novel, a hypothesis, surfaces. Writing to Blackwood in 1860, for example, she uncharacteristically describes her future plans then immediately regrets doing so: 'But just now I am quite without confidence in my future doings, and almost repent of having formed conceptions which will go on lashing me now until I have at least tried to fulfil them.'[61] And when the writing begins, it is the pain of authorship which is dwelt on, and the pain consists of giving the 'conceptions' a satisfactory embodiment, as in childbirth. 'When a subject has begun to grow in me', she writes on the completion of *Middlemarch*, 'I suffer terribly until it has wrought itself out – become a complete organism; and then it seems to take wing and go away from me.'[62] Suffering is inseparable from the act of writing: 'I am in that state of utter distrust and anxiety about my work which is usually the painful accompaniment of authorship with me until the last word of the last page has been written.'[63] But even then, future anxieties prevent her 'from tasting the quiet joy I might have in the *work done*'.[64] 'Exultation is a dream before achievement, and rarely comes after.' The reason is that the writer who is both male and female has, as it were, been used by her own conception and then discarded: 'What comes after, is rather the sense that the work has been produced within one, like offspring, developing and growing by some force of which one's own life has only served as a vehicle, and that what is left of oneself is only a poor husk.'[65] So that even the organic image contains within it the sense of sharp disruption and disengagement: 'Everything I do seems poor and trivial in the doing, and when it is quite gone from me and seems no longer my own – then I rejoice and think it fine. That is the history of my life.'[66] And then the process begins once more for 'the same demon [of despair] tries to get hold of me again whenever an old work is dismissed and a new one is being meditated'.[67] Edward Said has suggested that for the modern writer there is something dangerously illicit in the writing career, arising from the 'peculiar transgression' of confusing textuality and sexuality.[68]

These comments certainly provide us with a harrowing picture of the writer's life as one of risk, uncertainty, and incompleteness, of an almost Conradian intensity. When the disruptions of the writing career are stressed, it is as if each completed work becomes not only the end of a phase but an obituary; and yet, because writing nourishes as well as depletes the author's identity, as Said suggests, it must continue. My contention is that it shares these qualities in an accentuated form with 'the fate of poor mortals' who are all seeking in their own ways to make sense of their lives. The model which George Eliot uses to articulate both forms of life in crisis is that of the experimental method: the tentative hypothesis, the careful testing, the reformulation, the provisional theory. The peculiar difficulty of the novelist is that she invents both the hypothesis and the facts by which it is tested. It is worth looking now at her most explicit description of her writing career in these terms, which occurs in a letter of 1876 to the positivist Frederic Harrison who was seeking religious consolation on the death of his mother, which the novelist finds herself unable to provide:

But my writing is simply a set of experiments in life – an endeavour to see what our thought and emotion may be capable of – what stores of motive, actual or hinted as possible, give promise of a better after which we may strive – what gains from past revelations and discipline we must strive to keep hold of as something more than shifting theory. I become more and more timid –

with less daring to adopt any formula which does not get itself clothed for me in some human figure and individual experience, and perhaps that is a sign that if I help others to see at all it must be through that medium of art.[69]

It is a complex statement which contains both an account of the individual life and an account of the role of the novelist, and both are based on the same model. Life is seen as a striving after 'a better' based upon successive 'revelations and discipline' which no 'shifting theory' can provide. The experimental novelist, eschewing formula, articulates life in the form of a fictional hypothesis ('an endeavour to see what our thought and emotion may be capable of') which is tested against the evidence by being embodied in 'some human figure and individual experience'. The fictional experiment, unlike the scientific, results not in a new theory but in the aesthetic object which embodies a vision of life.

It is here, in such an account of the mind in action, that we can locate the basis for George Eliot's own unitary view of life. The art of the novelist, the experiment of the scientist, the struggles of the individual, all share certain crucial features. To understand this helps, in particular, to dispel certain false conceptions about art and the imagination as something quite opposed to the workings of the scientific or philosophic mind. A revealing statement to this effect occurs in Lewes's *The Principles of Success in Literature* (1865) which challenges this simplistic separation in terms similar to George Eliot's. 'Everyone', he writes, 'who has really interrogated Nature with a view to a distinct answer, will bear me out in saying that it requires intense and sustained effort of imagination.' Such scientific effort goes into the rigorous demands of the experimental method: 'The relations of sequence among the phenomena must be seen; they are hidden; they can only be seen mentally; . . . the experiments by which the problems may be solved have to be imagined; and to imagine a good experiment is as difficult as to invent a good fable, for we must have distinctly *present* – in clear mental vision – the known qualities and relations of all the objects, and must *see* what will be the effect of introducing some new qualifying agent.'[70]

In short, Lewes maintains, both 'the discoverer and the poet are inventors' and, whatever the differences in their forms of selection and abstraction from experience, 'imagination is active in both'.

From known facts the philosopher infers the facts that are unapparent. He does so by an effort of imagination (hypothesis) which has to be subjected to verification: he makes a mental picture of the unapparent fact, and then sets about to prove that his picture does in some way correspond with the reality. The correctness of his hypothesis and verification must depend on the clearness of his vision.[71]

The awareness of this essential similarity, based as it is on the facts of cognition, demystifies conventional ideas of the imagination, and also challenges simplistic empiricism as the basis of science. In both disciplines, 'the imagination is most tasked when it has to paint pictures which shall withstand the silent criticism of general experience, and to frame hypotheses which shall withstand the confrontation with facts'.[72] The statement anticipates in its turns of phrase the account of Lydgate's scientific research in *Middlemarch*.

The great danger then, in art, science or life, is that the subtle but crucial interaction of hypothesis and evidence will be jeopardised. This is why George Eliot responds so cautiously to Frederic Harrison's proposal in 1866 that she write a Positivist novel. She has 'gone through', she explains, 'again and again the severe effort of trying to make certain ideas thoroughly incarnate, as if they had revealed themselves to me first in the flesh and not in the spirit'. The two realms – flesh and spirit – are seen as separate, but the imaginative act, experiment based on hypothesis, brings them briefly together in that true 'aesthetic teaching', which becomes offensive 'if it lapses anywhere from the picture to the diagram'.[73] It is the imagination, working through the hypothesis, which brings about the aesthetic incarnation. George Eliot, it should be added, is far more aware and anxious than Lewes about the liability of the hypothesis, in all areas of life, to lapse into the formulae, dogmas, and theories, which seek to offer keys to the meaning of existence. But it is the difficulties of the writer in particular which understandably concern her, and it is her depiction of these I now wish to examine.

There are three occasions on which George Eliot represents writers, all male, grappling with the problems of writing. Two of these – 'Poetry and Prose, From the Notebook of an Eccentric' (1846–7) and *Impressions of Theophrastus Such* (1879) – bracket her writing career. Each is a collection of essays which introduces the writer, Macarthy and Such respectively, as a preliminary explanation of what follows. In both cases, the attempt to establish a point of view turns into a diagnosis of extreme instability. The eccentric Macarthy is a composite of heterogeneous qualities which, his editor tells us, are reflected in his writings. Too exquisitely constructed for this world, he belongs to the line of romantic essayists, impressionable, depressive, and androgynous. There is 'a morbid sensitiveness in his feeling of the beautiful, which I can compare to nothing but those alleged states of mesmeric lucidity, in which the patient obtains an unenviable cognizance of irregularities, happily imperceptible to us in the ordinary state of our consciousness'. The morbidity arises from the discrepancy between the shadowy ideal and the world of normal experience before which it floats, 'importunately presenting itself as a twin object with all realities, whether external or internal, and turning all their charms into mockery'.[74] The Eccentric is, in effect, the embodiment of that 'antithetical mixture' of the general idea and particular fact, out of which the experimental method is constructed but which, in this case, does not develop towards resolution and discovery, except in the form of the fragments of his notebook now published by his editor as his memorial. His death is the only possible resolution of his writing, just as it is the occasion of their publication.

Two of the subsequent essays from his notebook repeat and dramatise the discrepancy in the Eccentric's character by juxtaposing definitions of the ideal and the worldly, first, in terms of a contrast between the philosopher and the sceptic ('The Wisdom of the Child'), and secondly, in the contrast between the two hamadryads, one loving and one egoistic ('A Little Fable with a Great Moral'). But the most significant piece is one in which the Eccentric briefly locates, not simply an expression, but a resolution of his divided nature. This is a description of a painter at work in his studio ('How to Avoid Disappointment'). Here, idea and fact, general and particular, work together: 'the perfect whole exists in the imagination of the artist before his pencil has marked the canvass', and then every brushstroke, 'every dismal-looking layer of colour, conduces to the ultimate effect'. Or, to begin with the particular, the artist's eye is 'scrupulously attentive to the details of his actual labour, yet keeping ever in view the idea which that labour is to fulfil'. Whole and part vitalise each other, and the hermeneutic circle becomes a creative mode with large implications: 'I say to myself, – this is an image of what our life should be, – a series of efforts directed to the production of a contemplated whole, just as every stroke of the artist's pencil has a purpose bearing on the conception which he retains in his mind's eye.'[75]

This is a satisfactory image of life because it focuses on the process of artistic creation, the intimate and developing reciprocity of whole and parts, in which nothing is fixed or *a priori*. Through this we can see how the creative act is linked to the interpretative in George Eliot's thinking, as they were in Lewes's account of the imagination. Both kinds of activity reveal the hermeneutic circle to be a form of dynamic activity which leads to complex visions of wholeness. Her fullest and most abstract definition of this activity occurs in 'Notes on Form in Art', written halfway through her career in 1868. Form of all kinds originates in difference, 'but with this fundamental discrimination is born in necessary antithesis the sense of wholeness'. The cognitive process, its systole and diastole, proceeds from this dialectic and leads to the awareness of organic form:

And as knowledge continues to grow by its alternating processes of distinction & combination, seeing smaller & smaller unlikenesses & grouping or associating these under a common likeness, it arrives at the conception of wholes composed of parts more & more multiplied & highly differenced, yet more and more absolutely bound together by various conditions of common likeness or mutual dependence. And the fullest example of such a whole is the highest example of Form: in other words, the relation of multiplex interdependent parts to the whole which is itself in the most varied & therefore the fullest relation to other wholes.[76]

This is how the mind works in creation, comprehension, and interpretation.

The Eccentric, however, with a mind fatally divided, only occasionally glimpses a true image of perfection. When the process is disrupted, then the darker side of this organic narrative of cognition becomes apparent. The hermeneutic circle becomes a vertiginous revelation of worlds beyond worlds, of worlds within worlds, in never-ending succession. There is always present in George Eliot's thinking a Pascalian awareness of human disproportion, on the narrow isthmus between the two abysses of infinity and nothingness. And not only in her thinking, for as she writes in the 'fate of poor mortals' letter of 1848, 'I feel a sort of madness growing upon me – just the opposite of the delirium which makes people fancy that their bodies are filling the room. It seems to me as if I were shrinking into that mathematical abstraction, a point – so entirely am I destitute of contact that I am unconscious of length or breadth'.[77] In this context, her characteristic images of telescope and microscope open up alarming possibilities which it is the writer's task somehow to contain in the tension of aesthetic incarnation. In the odd literary form of the posthumous notebook, where the obituary of the neurotic Eccentric and his fragmentary essays explain and complete each other, George Eliot found an early expression of both the painful difficulty of interpreting the world and the true form of creative activity.

Many of the same elements are arranged in a similar fashion over thirty years later in George Eliot's final publication, *Impressions of Theophrastus Such*. Again, there is the random collection of essays written after the style of Theophrastus crossed with La Bruyère which seek to depict and diagnose some contemporaneous types with their fads and failings. Anxiety quickly sets in when the essayist Such feels called upon in the first piece ('Looking Inward') to present himself to the reader. The attempt to establish the point of view from which the impressions are to be delivered proves to be both precarious and convoluted, the style ironical and arch. The essayist turns out to be a bachelor with a nervous disposition, unprepossessing appearance, modest means, and a desire for authorship. But how can the significance of these details be communicated to the reader? How can the interpreter of society interpret himself? Every possible strategy of self-presentation is proposed, qualified, and deconstructed. 'Is there no remedy or corrective for that inward squint which consists in a dissatisfied egoism or other want of mental balance?'[78] The attempt to be objective leads to a denial of the self; the opposite, a theory of neurotic self-justification, sees the world in purely egocentric terms. The self is all or nothing – egotistical sublime or negative capability – but neither position makes for a balanced view of life. The dialectic of explanation and understanding keeps falling apart.

The effect, however, of making this confession confirms Such's belief that only the act of writing itself can free him from embarrassment and awkwardness. On paper, reticence becomes garrulousness, 'as the sea-lion plunges and swims the more energetically because his limbs are of a sort to make him shambling on land'. Writing creates the 'delightful illusion' of a sympathetic audience instantly approving of what he enjoys writing. And the audience can remain hazy for, like the Eccentric, he doesn't intend to publish in his own lifetime. By this manoeuvre, he fashions a medium for the self and others to interact freely without anxiety. 'Thus I make myself a charter to write, and keep the pleasing, inspiring illusions of being listened to, though I may sometimes write about myself.'[79] It is a strange charter which fabricates an imaginary readership and kills off the author, leaving simply the act of writing as the self-sustaining process of mediation. Writing originates in and, at the same time, overcomes a kind of malaise, the division between ideal and experience, the self and the world. It may result in the ironically sharpened vision of the Eccentric who observed the 'knots and blemishes' of the world with 'mesmeric lucidity', or in Such's satirical scrutiny of Victorian peccadilloes. But like his predecessor, Such is also seeking a vision of wholeness, and in the *Impressions* there are at least two expressions of this. The first is to be found again in genuine artistic activity and supremely in a poet like Dante, 'at once the most precise and homely in his reproduction of actual objects, and the most soaringly at large in his imaginative combinations'. 'Powerful imagination', we are reminded, 'is not false outward vision, but intense inward representation, and a creative energy constantly fed by susceptibility to the veriest minutiae of experience, which it reproduces and constructs in fresh and fresh wholes.'[80] The second expression is found in the final essay ('The Modern Hep! Hep! Hep!') which is essentially a defence of Jewish separateness, of 'a people taught by many concurrent influences to identify faithfulness to its national traditions with the highest social and religious blessings'. After *Daniel Deronda* this comes as no surprise, for there the spiritual unity expressed in the *Shemah* was hailed as a supreme and exemplary image of wholeness. Here, George Eliot offers another formulation: 'The Jews were steadfast in their separateness, and through that separateness Christianity was born.'[81]

If making practical sense of the world consists of the interaction of idea and experience in the form of the working hypothesis, then these two essayists fail dismally. Their writing originates in this failure, out of which come their insecurity, anxiety, their convoluted self-reflectiveness and inability to achieve a stable identity. Since the two essayists initiate and conclude George Eliot's writing career, one is tempted to see the Eccentric embodying the anxieties of trying to create a stable narrative persona, while Such announces through his neurotic self-deconstructions the demise of this Victorian narrative convention. But out of their malaise, it must be added, these essayists are occasionally granted a glimpse of possibilities, a vital synthesis in which part and whole, self and other, work together, transcending their own self-division. The wound and the bow explain each other. It is this breaking through the constraints of normal vision which is examined in detail in the third example of a writer's confessions in Eliot's work. This is the novella, 'The Lifted Veil' (1859), which comprises a failed writer's only work, presented once again as a lengthy obituary.

If the other two writers were neurotics, this piece of Gothic horror reads more like a case history narrated by the patient. In this posthumous publication, the narrator prepares for the moment of his death, of which he has had a prevision a month earlier and which is described on the first page of the story. Now is the time for recantation: 'I long for life, and there is no help. I thirsted for the unknown; the thirst is gone. O God, let me stay with the known, and be weary of it!'[82] In the remaining interval he will write the story of his life to try and win a little sympathy. Here we have the most extreme version of the writing predicament: its origin is despair, its closure death, its motive self-exoneration. At least, while the writing continues Latimer knows he is still alive.

The story is that of a mind denied the normal experiential understanding of the world and cursed instead with the gift of various kinds of insight. It begins with an uncongenial childhood, a morbid sensitivity, a 'half-womanish' beauty (295), a Gradgrind-like education, and a sense of isolation, all adding up to the frustrations of the writer *manqué*, 'the poet's sensibility without his voice' (284). After a severe illness, this sensibility is diverted into other, paranormal channels and the veils of reality begin to lift. He experiences first of all a prevision of a future visit to Prague, a city of death-in-life which confirms that his gift is a disease, 'a sort of intermittent delirium' (292). Like Tithonus, Latimer begins 'to taste something of the horror that belongs to the lot of a human being whose nature is not adjusted to simple human conditions' (293). This is compounded by a second gift, telepathic insight into other people, through which 'the web of their characters were seen as if thrust asunder by a microscopic vision that showed all the intermediate frivolities, all the suppressed egoism, all the struggling chaos of puerilities, meanness . . . from which human words and deeds emerge like leaflets covering a fermenting heap' (296). As with the Eccentric's 'mesmeric lucidity', the normal constraints of the senses have been intolerably removed, revealing other concealed worlds: 'It was like a preternaturally heightened sense of hearing, making audible to one a roar of sound where others find perfect stillness.' Into this clairvoyant nightmare enters the mysterious *femme fatale*, Bertha, desired despite her cynicism because she is the one person whose consciousness remains veiled. 'She was my oasis of mystery in the dreary desert of knowledge' (301). But the mystery is removed when, triggered by a portrait of Lucrezia Borgia in Vienna, his prevision gives him a brief glimpse of Bertha, now his wife, desiring his death. But this insight into her 'pitiless soul' (304) does not diminish his fascination with her in the present: 'The fear of poison is feeble against the sense of thirst' (305). In this stage of his nightmare there is a clear separation of the faculties which should normally work together. His prevision is guaranteed, and yet the passion for the (temporary) mystery remains.

This is George Eliot's version of the Faust legend for mid-Victorian England, based on a nightmarish dismantling of the cognitive process by means of paranormal phenomena. 'It is an old story, that men sell themselves to the tempter, and sign a bond with their blood, because it is only to take effect at a distant day, then rush on to snatch the cup their souls thirst after with no less savage an impulse because there is a dark shadow beside them for evermore' (306). The hypothesis of what might be the case is not supported or questioned by the facts in a continuing process of approximation, but confirmed absolutely and horrifyingly by prevision and insight; the present facts, on the contrary, by remaining opaque arouse his passion. He still has something to live for, thanks to his ignorance of Bertha in the present. In this, he is one with the reader, for it is this uncertainty which drives the plot of the story. Both are as self-consuming as *la peau de chagrin*:[83] Latimer's passion is leading him to dispel the ignorance in which his passion originates and which will lead him, as he foreknows, into hell; while the reader's desire to know will bring the inevitable closure to the story. Like Latimer, we know a lot but sufficient remains. To drive home the necessity of ignorance as a condition of life, he creates an imaginary dystopia within his own nightmare:

Conceive the condition of the human mind if all propositions whatsoever were self-evident except one, which was to become self-evident at the close of a summer's day, but in the mean time might be the subject of question, of hypothesis, of debate. Art and philosophy, literature and science would fasten like bees on that one proposition that had the honey of probability in it, and be the more eager because their enjoyment would end with sunset. (318)

This is the nature of George Eliot's current experiment. Interpretation by its nature implies a tension between illumination and concealment; but here is a world where the latter has virtually disappeared. Only the mysterious and sinister Bertha represents the honey of probability which is necessary for both life and narrative.

She is as absorbing to Latimer 'as a single hypothetic proposition to remain problematic till sunset'. Between the hypothesis and the facts there is still a gap – Bertha, uncertainty, life. The hints she drops act upon him like 'hashish': 'Out of the subtlest web of scarcely perceptible signs she set [him] weaving the fancy' that she really loved him (319). With her alone he weaves the web, instead of seeing through it, admitting that 'no matter how empty the adytum, so that the veil be thick enough' (318). And the life-sustaining mystery continues into their marriage.

Confirmation of his prevision comes at last, however, at his father's death when his passion for Bertha is for once 'completely neutralized' (322) and he experiences the 'terrible moment of complete illumination'. 'I saw all round the narrow room of this woman's soul.' Without his sustaining ignorance the narrator's own identity dissolves: 'I saw myself in Bertha's thought as she lifted her cutting grey eyes and looked at me: a miserable ghost-seer' (323). Seeing through everything, he is himself seen through. Latimer's life is now really over, *la peau de chagrin* consumed. 'Towards my own destiny I had become entirely passive; for my one ardent desire had spent itself, and impulse no longer predominated over knowledge' (325). With this final illumination, Latimer rejects all the mediations of life, the signs and hypotheses through which we negotiate with the world. The autobiographer rejects language, with the other social conventions, as a means of masking and deferring the reality of which the knowledge makes life impossible. 'We learn *words* by rote, but not their meaning; *that* must be paid for with our life-blood, and printed in the subtle fibres of our nerves' (326).

Latimer withdraws into himself and, as he begins to suffer a gradual death, his accursed gifts lose their power. But there is a final Gothic twist to his story as he awaits death. Through a friend's scientific experiment, his wife's maid is briefly resuscitated from death and reveals that Bertha is plotting to poison him. The final veil, that of death, has now been lifted: 'Good God! Is this what it is to live again . . . to wake up with our unstilled thirst upon us, with our unuttered curses rising to our lips, with our muscles ready to act out their half-committed sins' (339). Life-in-death simply confirms the narrator's experience of death-in-life. Now he not only knows what death is like, but also the perfect double-bind his life has become: his growing ignorance of Bertha's thoughts had made life possible, but all the time that ignorance was concealing the inevitable death at her hand. The honey of probability simply conceals poisoned knowledge. In the final paragraph Latimer writes down the present date in his journal which is the date, he knows, of his death to which we have circled back from the first page of the story. Knowledge, death, and closure finally coincide.

All three writers, then, are created out of the dismantling of the working hypothesis, the means by which we interpret and make sense of the world. The component parts of the hypothesis, idea and experience, are separated and thereby accentuated in an alarming way. With the Eccentric and Such, their malaise finds fragmentary expression in two forms – satirical observation and occasional glimpses of wholeness. The most vivid of these are of the creative artistic activity which they are denied. With Latimer, the normal constraints of human perception are tampered with even more radically, as the veils are lifted one by one. Only the last lingering hypotheses about his wife's feelings and then the nature of his death keep him alive; when they are dispelled, the only choice remaining is between life-in-death and death-in-life. Taken together, the three characters, all of whom have become their posthumous texts, embody different aspects of the writer's dilemma, the high cost of their charter to write. Latimer's story in particular explores the darker side of creativity: prevision and insight are the dangerous gifts *par excellence* of the novelist which are here blocked in a nightmare of perception, and which result in the narrator's one story, his own bitter obituary. Interpretation, as we have seen, embodies a tension between illumination and concealment. When that is lost, it is no longer possible to make sense of the world; the result is malaise and death. Such extreme dilemmas are a useful corrective to a too positive reading of George Eliot's description of her novels as 'experiments in life'. Experiments entail uncertainty and risk as they probe the unknown; and the fine balance of qualities required by scientist, philosopher, and writer is a precarious one. But the difficulties of the search pale before the horrors of life without these constraints. Life is only possible through ignorance, says George Eliot quoting Mackay, 'the eyelid through which [the soul] gradually opens itself to the truth, admitting no more than it can for the time support, and, as through a veil, learning to support its lustre'.

What emerges from the crisis of interpretation which finds expression in George Eliot's letters, essays, reviews, and translations, is a view of life deprived of orthodox certainties. Both origin and telos are unknowable. Instead, there is a dynamic model which, implicitly and explicitly, informs her thinking about life and its processes. What drives this model is the search for meaning, and life at all levels is envisaged as a never-ending interpretative quest to fit together idea and experience, part and whole, into ever-larger unities. The quest originates in the discrepancy between idea and experience, between theory and practice, and proceeds through a series of temporary harmonies and incoherences, continually driven on by the desire for a totality of meaning. The clearest form of this model is the hypothesis – in science, religion, art – where an idea is tested against the data which modifies it and is modified in its turn. Because the search is continuous – the hermeneutic circle never stops turning – the most that can be gained at each stage is a fresh and conditional awareness of unity and meaning. In this sense, the model is both dialectical and organic.

This dynamic model has implications at all levels of George Eliot's thinking. It explains cognition and interpretation in their most everyday sense. It provides a kind of master-plot for the individual life both in its questing forward and its continual recuperation. It is also a means of explaining the progress of the intellect through its various historical phases. Above all, in terms of fiction, the model provides the dynamics for the author to write her imaginative experiments in life, for the protagonists to search for coherence in their careers, and for the reader to formulate and re-formulate the hypotheses which eventually turn into an understanding of the novels' plots, structures, and meanings. But it is worth stressing again the provisional, open-ended nature of the view of life implied in this model. Knowledge and ignorance work together in a dangerously precarious balance which can easily be put in jeopardy: then hypothesis lapses into dogma, coherence into fragments. There is a dark side to the hermeneutic quest, especially apparent in the inevitable attempts to short-circuit the delicate process which leads, at best, to partial understanding. But it is only the uncertain gap between the known and the unknown which makes both life and narrative possible.

What follows is a reading of George Eliot's fiction which draws on the insights of modern hermeneutics in order to place the novels in the context of what I have called a crisis of interpretation. Special attention will be paid to the way in which the narrative drive of the novels articulates and forces this crisis to a climactic confrontation. It should be stressed that this study is not an attempt to trace the influence upon the fiction of all the various branches of knowledge in which this crisis manifested itself and in which George Eliot was formidably learned. Even when one focuses upon fictional hermeneutics, it will be realised that this crisis has implications at all levels: the reader interprets the narrator who interprets the characters who interpret the world and each other, and so on. The phrase 'double hermeneutic' captures some of this complexity. It is used by the sociologist Anthony Giddens to acknowledge the fact that the social sciences are seeking to interpret a universe which is already interpreted, 'already constituted within frames of meaning by social actors themselves'.[84] George Eliot's representation of a complex world where this double and reciprocal process is constantly at work is the distinctive mark of her fiction.

To make my discussion manageable, each chapter focuses on a central aspect of her hermeneutic mode as it develops novel by novel through George Eliot's career. Different novels emphasise different phases of the master-plot, that interpretative drive for meaning and coherence. The chapter on *Adam Bede*, for example, examines the depiction and dismantling of a series of pastoral theodicies in a world which ignores suffering. That on *The Mill on the Floss* discusses Tom and Maggie as hybrids seeking to construct a coherent world-view which is by definition denied them. After *Silas Marner*, which explores the minimal intelligibility necessary for life *ex nihilo* in a cataleptic weaver, George Eliot applies her dynamic model to a critique of Renaissance culture and its resurgent, competing myths at a turning-point of European history. On several occasions, the novelist achieves distance from the crisis of interpretation in the present by setting several of her fictions at critical historical moments in the past: the period of the First Reform Bill, for example, provides the unstable context for *Felix Holt* and *Middlemarch*, in which the condition of England can be re-examined in muted apocalyptic terms, as the ground shifts beneath all the political, social, and religious orthodoxies. What sustaining myth, creed, or world-view constitutes a viable mediation between the 'hungry, shivering self' and the expanding worlds of the later novels? As the answers to this question become increasingly uncertain, George Eliot carries out a withering diagnosis of contemporaneous British society in *Daniel Deronda* by juxtaposing it with that most hermeneutical of all cultures, Judaism, from which she seeks a redemptive vision of coherence and unity. There is a corollary to my argument which will become apparent in the chapters which follow. In the course of her career, George Eliot submits the major sub-genres of Victorian fiction – pastoral, *Bildungsroman*, legendary tale, the historical, political, and prophetic novel – to critical redefinition. These established forms, the literary *a priori*, must also be subjected to the hermeneutical pressures of an age of crisis.

CHAPTER I

Scenes of Clerical Life: familiar types and symbols

If stable character is based upon a coherent view of the world, then the clergyman protagonists of *Scenes of Clerical Life*, living in English provincial society during the first half of the nineteenth century, are at risk. They all embody radical discontinuities in communities which are themselves seriously divided. These gaps are ultimately bridged not by religious faith in any orthodox sense but by faith redirected to certain human continuities. The cost, however, is high: new life only emerges from pain, suffering, and death. That final discontinuity has to be experienced in each case before coherence in character and community can be achieved. These are George Eliot's most theological stories, engaged as they are in questioning, displacing, and then recovering the language of biblical hermeneutics for her own humanistic purposes.

'Amos Barton' is a bleak story whose bleakness is a reflection of its pervasive fragmentariness. It begins with the description of a gap of twenty-five years. On the far side of the gap is Shepperton church as it was in all its old quaintness and heterogeneity; on this side is the efficiently renovated church of the present. The crucial feature of the old church was the mysteriousness of the statues and the escutcheons, and the drama of the church service. To the imagination of the narrator's childhood self they provided 'inexhaustible possibilities of meaning' because, though more or less unintelligible, they allowed all kinds of emotions to be acted out through their traditional communal forms. On this side of the gap is the world of the mature narrator and the reader, the world created by the modern 'well-regulated mind'. The bleakness of the present is caused by the elimination of imaginative space and time: efficiency 'will yield diagrams, plans, elevations, and sections, but alas! no picture'. Form, function and meaning coincide to create a blank limbo in which 'with a dreary absence of contrast and mystery' one can 'see every thing at all moments'.[1] It is a familiar Victorian contrast but George Eliot views it from a characteristically interpretative angle. A world without gaps is as incoherent as one with unbridgeable ones. The childhood world is cherished because its mysteries prompted the imagination to the act of interpretation; without discontinuities and difference, however, history is banished and chiaroscuro eliminated to create a uniform space, the product of the rational mind. It is into this twenty-five year gap between the two worlds that George Eliot inserts the story of the Reverend Amos Barton, the man who effected the renovation of the church. This is a story about various forms of discontinuity.

The first gap to be bridged is that between narrator and reader. The narrator, whose life incorporates the change from old to new, is constantly reaching out with a mixture of coercion, familiarity, and jocularity to a readership distant in time and place. The reader may lack knowledge ('a miserable town-bred reader') or entertain false expectations ('to whom tragedy means ermine tippets, adultery, and murder') but, whatever it is, a radical re-orientation is required if the following narrative is to be appreciated. This can only be achieved initially by an act of faith: 'Depend upon it, you would gain unspeakably if you would learn with me to see some of the poetry and the pathos, the tragedy and the comedy, lying in the experience of a human soul that looks out through dull gray eyes, and that speaks in a voice of quite ordinary tones' (42). The character and career of Amos Barton, the impoverished curate, provide a rigorous test-case: not only have readers to revise their literary terminology but also to activate their imaginations about a man who has eliminated the imaginative world of Shepperton church. Described almost entirely in negatives, he seems to offer no purchase to the imagination: 'a narrow face of no particular complexion . . . with features of no particular shape, and an eye of no particular expression' (18). Persistently, the reader's conventional expectations are foiled as they seek to fill out the indeterminacies of what is being narrated. This Scene consists of a series of misguided interpretations by both readers and community which put at risk, as they enliven, the prosaic career of this provincial clergyman.

The community itself is fragmented into mutually unintelligible groups: the well-to-do inhabitants invited to Mrs Patten's farmhouse, the clergy at their monthly clerical meeting, and the group of grotesques in the workhouse. As the story moves sideways from one to the other with little forward movement, the sense of dislocation is accentuated. The larger world outside Shepperton is also impinging in a confusing way, adding to the sense of change and confusion: 'for over and above the rustic stupidity furnished by the farm-labourers, the miners brought obstreperous animalism, and the weavers an acrid Radicalism and Dissent'. The Church's only response has been to engage in its own theological controversy, but this has now waned and two years after Barton has taken over the parish 'the religious life of Shepperton was falling back towards low-water mark' (24). It is a harsh and bleak picture – especially when measured against the two subsequent Scenes – of a community which has both lost the traditional consensus of Mr Gilfil's day and is incapable of the vital conflict of the Reverend Tryan's ministry. It is a world of discontinuities which Barton epitomises.

He is unable to act effectively as pastor or mediator because he is a compendium of all the conflicting doctrines, values, and assumptions which are disturbing the community. The narrator suggests that he might have been, like his father before him, 'an excellent cabinet-maker and deacon of an Independent church', but, unfortunately, Barton is a man with 'opinions'. He flirts bewilderingly with anything that appeals to him. 'He preached Low-Church doctrine – as evangelical as any thing to be heard in the Independent Chapel; and he made a High-Church assertion of ecclesiastical powers and functions' (18). It is upon these contradictions and incoherences that George Eliot structures his wilful and muddled character in elaborate detail. The result is that he manages to confuse all sections of the community, despite his good intentions. The clergy are bemused: 'He was like an onion that has been rubbed with spices; the strong original odour was blended with something new and foreign. The Low-Church onion still offended refined High-Church nostrils, and the new spice was unwelcome to the palate of the genuine onion-eater' (30). Because he confuses all their categories he is gossiped about and ridiculed.

Similarly, he bewilders the well-to-do churchgoers by denying them their traditional rituals, substituting Dissenting innovations, and then antithetically threatening them with the High-Church ecclesiastical courts. And at the lowest level of the parish among the inmates of the workhouse, the final futility of Barton's ministry is spelled out. Preaching of 'blood as a medium of reconciliation' he uses the unleavened bread from Exodus chapter twelve as his example to the bewildered congregation. Here George Eliot is precise about the exact nature of the gap between Barton and the listeners which he fails to bridge by his use of 'familiar types and symbols': he 'succeeded in carrying the pauper imagination to the dough-tub, but unfortunately was not able to carry it upwards from that well-known object to the unknown truths which it was intended to shadow forth'. The gap between type and antitype, signifier and signified, is too great and Barton's 'geographical, chronological, exegetical mind' is, says the narrator, 'not apparently the medium through which Christian doctrine will distil as welcome dew on withered souls' (27). And, having preached reconciliation, Barton immediately threatens some of the recalcitrant inmates with the punishments of an angry deity. This parody of biblical typology points to one of the underlying purposes of George Eliot's choice of clerical life – to redefine and reconstruct a hermeneutic based upon communal experience.

The test George Eliot has set herself is to convert this character into an object of sympathy to both the reader and the community. She seeks the reader's sympathy by acknowledging that he is 'unmistakably commonplace', like most people 'neither extraordinarily silly, nor extraordinarily wicked, nor extraordinarily wise; their eyes are neither deep and liquid with sentiment, nor sparkling with suppressed witticisms; they have probably had no hairbreadth escapes or thrilling adventures' (42). In other words, nothing worth telling a story about. 'His very faults were middling . . . It was not in his nature to be superlative in anything; unless, indeed, he was superlatively middling, the quintessential extract of mediocrity' (45). The question then is, how do you show 'the poetry and pathos' of such a life so that it becomes significant in the world in which it is placed? The answer, as we have seen, is to make Barton representative of all the discontinuities and conflicts at work in Shepperton so that as well as being middling and mediocre he is also 'a mongrel' (19), a hybrid whose mixed origins can be disentangled. This is Barton's significance. He is the open space where competing social and religious forces meet without interacting and without resolution. This is the reason why, though middling to the nth degree, he fails as a 'medium' between conflicting ideas and conflicting social groups in the community. All the warring elements are present in his character in suspension and so he remains inchoate, without identity. In fact, the whole story can be seen as a play on the words 'middling', 'medium', 'mediocrity', with Barton's conversion conducting him from middlingness to mediation. In his *imitatio Christi*, however, he is not the 'one mediator between God and men' (I Timothy 2.5) but between the people of Shepperton.

Barton has no coherent character since he is unintelligible both to himself and to others. Not only is he 'unspeakably commonplace' and only definable by negatives, but the opinions and forces he embodies are not contained within anything larger than themselves. The other clergymen who attend the clerical meetings are not noticeable for their effectiveness or consistency, but they are intelligible; even Mr Ely who acts as moderator and host because 'he is a man who seems to listen well, and is an excellent amalgam of dissimilar ingredients' (51), functions adequately in his parish. Barton fails to amalgamate his dissimilar ingredients but insists on acting upon all of them: 'For though Amos thought himself strong, he did not *feel* himself strong. Nature had given him the opinion, but not the sensation' (24). This central discontinuity prevents him becoming the kind of comic 'character' George Eliot's more conventional readers are hoping for, but whose naive expectations are firmly dealt with. The story is full of such briefly typical characters, ranging from the doctor to the gallery of grotesques in the workhouse, but Barton is not allowed to congeal into such an intelligible mould. Is there any way in which he can become coherent to himself and intelligible to the bewildered community?

The 'mongrel' is married to a 'madonna' who represents everything missing from Barton's fragmentary, contradictory life of projects, bustle, and fads. She is a character in a different mode, one in which her 'gentle womanhood . . . supersedes all acquisitions, all accomplishments . . . You would even perhaps have been rather scandalized if she had descended from the serene dignity of *being* to the assiduous unrest of *doing*' (19). Yet amidst the bleakness of Shepperton she has to rise early to darn the socks of their six children and use her magical skills in 'metamorphosing boots and shoes' into new creations. In contrast to Barton, his wife transforms and redeems everything she touches into objects of use and beauty. The central irony of the story is that by protecting him from the realities of life by her support, her love, and practical skills – all the qualities he lacks – she deprives him of the means of achieving an identity, the quality of stable being. She makes it possible for him to ignore the radical discontinuities of which his life is made up, most pointedly in the matter of money, the management of which underpins the plot. This is announced early in the story as the problem much more intractable than biblical exegesis: 'By what process of division can the sum of eighty pounds per annum be made to yield a quotient which will cover that man's weekly expenses?' (10). Undercutting all the sermons, clerical meetings, and theological niceties are these persistent reminders of other things needful – money, clothes, food. Milly's attempts to bridge this gap combined with her persistent childbearing have worn her down; the additional burden of a non-paying guest and the premature birth of her seventh child – that other physical reality – finally destroy her. Barton, in other words, kills his guardian angel in his muddled way so that he can finally be redeemed by her death. He is forced by this ultimate discontinuity to grasp the 'being' she represented.

The precarious position of the Barton family within the community is finally undermined by the arrival in distress of a bogus countess whose predicament provides an analogy with Barton's. She too is a mixture of contradictions and, like Barton, is in the process of losing her chief support, the half-brother she undervalues. The two aliens flatter and encourage each other, and as the people of Shepperton draw the worst conclusions the Barton family is abandoned by the community to its own devices. With this mutual loss of faith, mediation is no longer possible. The narrator acknowledges that such misunderstandings are inevitable, that human relations are necessarily discontinuous, and that it is fortunate we are not in a position to compare our own view of our actions 'with the picture they make on the mental retina of [our] neighbours'. If we could, the narrator sceptically imagines, the 'very capacity for good would go out of us'. But, at the same time, there must be some overlap between the two (partial) interpretations to make life possible:

That is a deep and wide saying, that no miracle can be wrought without faith – without the worker's faith in himself, as well as the recipient's faith in him. And the greater part of the worker's faith in himself is made up of the faith that others believe in him.

This is a characteristically dialectical, Feuerbachian account of faith and *Scenes of Clerical Life* is full of such secular redefinitions: it moves from self to other, from other to self, and finishes with the reciprocal validation of I and Thou.[2] And integral to this definition of faith is its complement, 'illusion':

Thank heaven, then, that a little illusion is left to us . . . that the world is not made of looking-glass, to show us just the figure we are making, and just what is going on behind our backs! By the help of dear friendly illusion . . . we are able to dream that we are doing much good – and we do a little. (17)

This is a low-key, working definition of faith, bracketed between the two undesirable extremes of a looking-glass world of complete self-knowledge and a world of solipsistic fantasy, both of which preclude the 'miracles' of imaginative understanding. Faith is a kind of tentative hypothesis.

When faith is lost in the community, people make up stories to bridge life's discontinuities. Since these arise out of uncertainty and suspicion they express the community's lowest common denominator in the form of gossip and calumny. In this instance, the unlikely countess has to be provided with a narrative based on the 'premiss' that she is different and therefore objectionable – in order to exclude her from the community. But the gossip begins to blacken the Bartons themselves when her visit is prolonged. As we have seen, the narrator's version of events has constantly to be defended against other versions which criss-cross its surface: these are prompted either by the reader's conventional expectations ('ermine tippets and adultery') or the narrator's prosaic and unnarratable alternatives (Barton as cabinet-maker) or by the countess's aristocratic fantasies (her 'plot' to rescue the 'martyr' Barton and the 'dear saint' Milly by transplanting them to a rich living). All these potential, displaced narratives act as commentaries on the authorised kernel of events.

Now virtually everyone in Shepperton turns against the Bartons, with even the clerics encouraging rumours of indiscretion and adultery as they sharpen their exegetical skills. Mr Fellowes reports the gossip that Barton 'dines alone with the Countess at six, while Mrs Barton is in the kitchen acting as cook'. Mr Ely questions the source of the gossip as 'rather an apocryphal authority'; but it is left to Mr Cleeves, 'the true parish priest', to quash it good-humouredly with his own interpretation: 'depend upon it that is a corrupt version. The original text is, that they all dined together *with* six – meaning six children – and that Mrs Barton is an excellent cook' (54). Cleeves retains his faith and so refuses to encourage scandalous stories which simultaneously explain and reject Barton. His hermeneutic is unexciting: 'Depend upon it . . . there is some simple explanation of the whole affair, if we only happened to know it' (55). The narrator agrees – 'Depend upon it' expresses his faith too – and provides the explanation. The countess's long visit is simply the result of a shortage of money. Like her analogue, Barton, she has 'checkmated herself' (57) by walking out on her half-brother to whom she now sheepishly returns after being routed by the Barton's servant, the *deus ex machina* in the crisis, who turns the local gossip into the means of expelling her from the household. This is a comic version of Barton's tragic fate. In both cases, the community's defence mechanism against the unintelligible achieves its purpose.

The scandalous stories are over and the reader is returned to the authorised narrative of their after-effects: the premature birth, the death of Milly and her baby, and then the rallying of the community as the scandals are painfully exorcised. For this to happen, Barton has to be transformed from the bewildering agent of confusion to a suffering object who can be understood unmistakably in terms of his outward grief. Then faith can be re-established in Shepperton for in this role he generates neither anxiety nor further narratives. His grief at the funeral is an expression of his belated ability to interpret the basic human master-story, 'to decipher that terrible handwriting of human destiny, illness and death' (67). Such an understanding only comes with a full grasp of Milly's absence, the 'being' who made life possible and prevented him from understanding it. Her absence finally provides the continuity and the repetition to bind his life together:

The burial was over . . . and Amos, for the first time, felt that he was alone – that day after day, month after month, year after year, would have to be lived through without Milly's love. Spring would come, and she would not be there; summer, and she would not be there; and he would never have her again with him by the fireside in the long evenings. The seasons all seemed irksome to his thoughts; and how dreary the sunshiny days that would be sure to come! She was gone from him; and he could never show her his love any more, never make up for omissions in the past by filling future days with tenderness. (67–8)

The painful awareness of omissions in the past finally and paradoxically makes his life a continuum. Only after her sacrificial death does the saint take on her true significance. This is both the punishment and the redemption through which Barton gains possession of his life and achieves an identity, though this is tested by further discontinuities when he is forced to leave a sympathetic Shepperton and its 'material links between his mind and past' (69). His departure, another 'image of death', coincides ironically with the re-opening of the renovated church, that break with the past caused by his meddling plans. But in the Conclusion to the story, Barton experiences a kind of placid after-life with the daughter who most strongly resembles Milly.

After all the false stories, scandals, and misinterpretations have been cleared away in this virtually plotless narrative, we can begin to see why George Eliot chose to situate it in provincial clerical life. She is seeking to carry out, first of all, a thorough re-definition of theology as an interpretative system and, by extension, the role of the clergy. At a superficial level this is suggested by the parodic application of doctrinal terms to mundane matters, to Barton's 'baldness and supererogatory soap', for example, and his need for 'a hat which shows no symptom of taking to the hideous doctrine of expediency'. Another form of this is provided by the clergy themselves when they parody their own exegetical skills as they apply them to the local gossip. But as well as making fun of the absurd gap between theology and its application in the community, George Eliot is also redefining certain key religious terms and experiences. This is achieved in the process of converting Barton from an amalgam of conflicting opinions and doctrines into a suffering victim with whom the community can sympathise. In the narrator's deceptively simple terms, 'Amos failed to touch the springs of goodness by his sermons, but he touched it effectually by his sorrows' (70).

His sorrows, which belatedly unify his life, are the unwitting expression in his personal life of the doctrines preached in his absurdly erudite and unsuitable sermons. For example, when he speaks to the bemused workhouse inmates of 'Israel and its sins, of chosen vessels, of the Paschal lamb, of blood as a medium of reconciliation' (27), he is preparing the terms of his own and Milly's sacrificial role in the community. He becomes, in fact, the incarnation – the topic of another of his bound sermons – of the beliefs he has been preaching in his ineffectual way to the parish. And, in the course of the conflicts which this generates, other key terms such as 'faith', 'miracle', 'mediation', 'consecration', 'martyr', and 'saint' are all redefined as expressions of human relations within the family and the community. At the conclusion of the story there is no further need for the pedagogy of 'familiar types and symbols', no danger 'that the interest or comprehension of your hearers may stop short precisely at the point where your spiritual interpretation begins' (27). In achieving an identity, in becoming a character, Barton himself is transformed into a type of suffering, and shadows forth his own truth. Human and divine are conflated. Through the loss of Milly, 'that sacred human soul . . . the divinest thing God had given [him] to know' (68), he is ordained into the priesthood of suffering. When his parishioners 'saw him following the coffin, pale and haggard, he was consecrated anew by his great sorrow, and they looked at him with respectful pity' (67).

Barton has by the end become both martyr and scapegoat of the community, the pastor turned sacrificial lamb. In the beginning he brings confusion and conflict, embodying all the contradictory opinions and doctrines at large in society. Pastor and community reflect each other's incoherence. Then in its self-defensive attempt to render him intelligible, Shepperton helps him destroy his madonna, thus converting him into a recognisable type of suffering. As scapegoat, he reconciles all the conflicting elements in the community whose vindictiveness is now exorcised. In the process, doctrines and opinions become meaningful and experience transparent. It is a process which parallels that of the novelist who ten years later was to describe 'the severe effort of trying to make certain ideas thoroughly incarnate, as if they had revealed themselves to me first in the flesh and not in the spirit'.[3]

If 'Amos Barton' begins in discontinuity and division, 'Mr Gilfil's Love-Story', in contrast, begins with the communal solidarity of the vicar's funeral commemorating his forty-year ministry. All agree that the vicar was fully assimilated into the community: he spoke like them, he didn't tax them with theology, his sermons were always brief, he sided with the parishioners against the landowners, and he never solicited money. 'He belonged to the course of nature, like markets and toll-gates and dirty bank-notes' (77). It is because his life had been so thoroughly ritualised that he, like his endlessly repeated sermons, has had such a profound effect on the community for, as the narrator explains, 'to minds on the Shepperton level it is repetition, not novelty, that produces the strongest effect, and phrases, like tunes, are a long time making themselves at home in the brain' (80–1).

For the narrative to begin, however, repetition has to give way to difference and Gilfil has to be separated from the community. The 'superficial observer' who would see little to differentiate the pastor from his flock is replaced by a narrator observant of finer discriminations and in search of a narrative. If society is 'incarnate history', in George Eliot's earlier phrase, then so is the individual: 'I, at least, hardly ever look at a bent old man, or a wizened old woman, but I see also, with my mind's eye, that Past of which they are the shrunken remnant' (83). And when interpretative pressure is applied to the fine discriminations, then all kinds of hidden narratives are revealed. This is the Wordsworthian starting-point for 'Mr Gilfil's Love-Story' which will tease out and interpret the full significance of this slight difference. As in 'Simon Lee', the conventional reader is to be re-educated into the state of mind in which 'you would find / A tale in everything'.[4] In this case, interpretative pressure uncovers a Gothic melodrama which articulates and dismembers the very process of making sense in the secure world in which the story begins.

The key to Mr Gilfil's earlier history, his 'antecedent romance' (82), is quite literally the key to the locked room, full of the relics of his dead wife, about which the narrator is explicit: it is 'a sort of visible symbol of the secret chamber in his heart, where he had long turned the key on early hopes and early sorrows, shutting up for ever all the passion and the poetry of his life' (84). Can these relics provide an explanation or generate a narrative? Communal folk memory in the shape of Mrs Patten, the 'great source of oral tradition in Shepperton', can only provide formulaic responses to people who 'put old questions . . . for the sake of getting the old answers' (85). At this point the narrator is forced to take over. To gain a proper purchase on this love story he has to go even further back into the past – from a retrospect of thirty years to Gilfil's funeral, then a further forty years of his ministry, and now to 1788 and an abrupt change to a different social world and a different fictional mode. Gilfil's past contains a Gothic romance which George Eliot uses to deconstruct the communal solidarity of his latter years. At the centre of this romance is the clash between Sir Christopher Cheverel and Caterina, Gilfil's patron and future wife respectively. Sir Christopher is the semi-divine figure ruling over the manor-house he has reconstructed in the advanced and florid pointed Gothic style, creating a world of oppressive splendour. Everyone and everything is permanently posed for the portrait and landscape-painter; emotion is excluded. The manor-house is a place of worship and self-congratulation for the Cheverel dynasty, whose portraits cover its walls and whose lineage goes back to the Conquest and forward in Sir Christopher's imagination to his yet-unborn grand-nephew whom he expects to see in possession before he dies. In this

world, space is architectural and time is genealogical; and everything
is required to 'dovetail with his plans' (113). His nephew, Captain
Wybrow, will be his heir and in the meanwhile he is to be encouraged
to fall in love with a suitably wealthy heiress. Sir Christopher is a Sir
Thomas Bertram with a passion for the Gothic, and this Scene bears
several resemblances to *Mansfield Park*.

Within this benevolently ordered world there is, however, an
anomaly, the 'gypsy changeling' (99), Tina. The narrative has to
make another regression of fifteen years, to 1773, to account for the
presence of this epitome of Latin passion whom the Cheverels rescued
from poverty and Papism on a grand tour of Italy so that she could be
properly brought up at the manor. The contrast which is being
established is suggested by the common element in the protagonists'
pasts, Milan Cathedral. For Sir Christopher, it is the 'marble Gothic
miracle' which will supply him with the designs and inspiration for his
renovations; for Tina, the cathedral houses the pathetic tinsel
madonna which, during her father's absences, acts as the symbol of
maternal love and miraculous security for the motherless child. These
two miraculous demands, the aesthetic and emotional, which the
cathedral fulfils become increasingly separated over the succeeding
years. The architectural designs are methodically and at great
expense turned into the reality of the restored manor, but unlike the
building, 'Caterina's development was the result of no systematic or
careful appliances' (110). She is simply a curio, a pet to be pampered
so long as she doesn't displease her patrons; and eventually she is to be
married off to the chaplain, Gilfil, as part of the management of the
estate. She does, however, qualify for a place in the drawing-room of
this palace of art when it is discovered she has a fine voice. Otherwise,
she is petted and ignored. This is the fatal neglect which will finally
destroy Sir Christopher's world, for over the years her passionate
Latin temperament – this is the cliché George Eliot is seeking to
animate – develops unchecked its 'fierce resistance to any discipline
that had a harsh or unloving aspect' (109).

Just as Sir Christopher unilaterally imposes his will upon the world,
so Tina seeks to impose her passionate emotions. We are conducted
through all the permutations of the pathetic fallacy as Tina finds relief
by dissolving her passions in the moonlight or the rain, before
stumbling inevitably over the unaccommodating reality of the manor
or the inexorable workings of 'the great clock-work of nature' (115).
She is a pathological study of an emotional nature 'whose thoughts

are no more than the fleeting shadows cast by feeling' (132). She becomes her palpitations, which only music can articulate and control. Her large, blank inexpressive eyes plus the plant and animal imagery in which she is described, indicate that she has reached no social accommodation with the world, that she is not fully human. But the form of life she distils, 'lighter than the smallest centre of quivering life in the water-drop', is an essential ingredient in the cosmic scheme of things described in an extended passage which ends with the question: 'What were our little Tina and her trouble in the mighty torrent, rushing from one awful unknown to another?' (126). The same question is asked about Gwendolen Harleth twenty years later.

Situated between these opposing realities at Cheverel Manor is the prosaic world of the servants, similar in its assumptions to Gilfil's parishioners in the frame of the narrative. They are loyal to both Sir Christopher and Tina, but they look with suspicion on any kind of foreign innovation and provide a running critique of the Gothic mode and all its assumptions. Their traditional rituals centre on the housekeeper's hearth with its 'low brick altar' and the firelight flickering in the shadows: 'what a space of chiaroscuro for the imagination to revel in!' (105). Unlike the Gothic confection, this is massive, primitive, comfortable, and ill-defined. Ensconced here, the servants celebrate 'the happy monotony' (109) of their lives, the evening culminating with Mr Bates giving a 'remarkably *staccato* rendering of "Roy's Wife of Aldivalloch"'. As a corrective to Gluck's lament over Eurydice to be heard in the drawing-room, this song celebrates the ability of Roy's wife to 'chate' her husband. Its appeal is based upon its 'excessive iteration' and its repeated choruses, not upon its narrative possibilities – why did she cheat her husband? – which remain 'an agreeable mystery' (108). From this position, the melodrama of the Italian orphan in the Gothic manor which is about to unfold is viewed with suspicion and apprehension. Mrs Sharp's comment is definitive: 'I'd rather hear a good old song like that, nor all the fine 'talian toodlin'' (107).

Within the aristocratic world, the conflict of values begins when Tina falls passionately in love with Sir Christopher's heir who is supposed to marry the suitably statuesque and wealthy Miss Assher. Captain Wybrow, as both heir and lover, is caught in the middle. From one point of view he is a suitable inheritor of the beautiful manor-house for he is as handsome as an Olympian god with a cameo-like profile, and he is dutiful towards Sir Christopher who intimidates him. But he also has romantic leanings and enjoys flirting with Tina who appeals to his imagination, 'an agreeable sensation, comparable to smoking the finest Latakia' (114). He represents the shakily decadent stage of transition between an eighteenth-century aristocratic world and the romantic future, with the French Revolution rumbling in the background. His languid self-interest 'had guarded him from the liability to a strong emotion', yet he is in an exposed position. He is an artefact with a weak heart and liable to palpitations. The realistic colouring George Eliot adds to her Gothic romance ensures that Wybrow is not the 'reckless libertine' (114) which his decadent languor and attar-of-roses might suggest to his rival Gilfil, just as Sir Christopher is not as tyrannically autocratic nor Tina as beautiful and innocent as the literary conventions demand. As the irreconcilable demands upon Wybrow escalate, he feebly tries to extricate himself by disclaiming responsibility to both parties: 'Confound it Beatrice! you'll drive me mad. Can a fellow help a girl's falling in love with him?' (134). With his military slang, his growing fear of these 'plaguy perverse' women (127), his palpitations, his awe of Sir Christopher, and his desire to 'go off to some lotos-eating place or other' (138), he is the feckless Bertie Wooster of Cheverel Manor who really wants everyone to be happy. As he glides from one crisis to the next, his balancing act becomes more and more precarious, until in a final flurry of trying to please everyone his weak heart gives out in the rookery and he goes to his lotos-eating place sooner than anyone expects.

Wybrow sees himself justifiably as a passive victim, killed off by Sir Christopher and Tina as they project upon him their conflicting desires which he can neither fulfil nor reconcile. He is cast into incompatible leading roles in the narratives through which they interpret their lives at the manor. He is simply the reflector of these stronger agents: incapable of the intense emotion his beauty elicits from Tina, and without the will Sir Christopher inflexibly focuses upon him. The best reconciliation he can manage – as a precursor of Arthur Donnithorne and Tito Melema – is that he 'always did the thing easiest and most agreeable to him from a sense of duty' (114), as he flits between the two opposed realities of the novella. On the one hand, there are the fixed rituals of daily routine, timed precisely by the great clock in the courtyard, which firmly control any aberrations from decorum. On the other hand, there is a growing turmoil in Tina's emotions which can only find release in the drawing-room through the arias from Gluck's *Eurydice* in which 'the singer pours out his yearning after his lost love'. Then, briefly, one of the rituals at the manor is infused with unusual feeling. At the beginning of this romance, the intensity of Tina's outpourings seems to bring into magical existence what she most desires: either the faithless Wybrow glides to her side at the harpsichord or joins her in the moonlight among the other 'heterogeneous objects' (97) the Cheverels have collected on their travels. She conjures her lover magically into existence, 'as if a miracle had happened in her little world of feeling' (128).

These opportunities have, however, to be seized in the interstices of the aristocratic rituals. The impassioned operatic outpourings are firmly inserted each evening precisely between dinner and cards, and as the last note is dying away, Sir Christopher issues his instructions promptly: 'There's a clever black-eyed monkey. Now bring out the table for picquet.' Wybrow and Gilfil pick up their books 'and there was perfect silence in the room which, ten minutes before, was vibrating to the passionate tones of Caterina' (97–8). It is finely observed, the way the English upper-classes deal with the emotions, before getting down to a serious game of cards. Gongs and bells are constantly calling wayward feelings to order. Not only is emotion deprecated, it is also converted by British empiricism as quickly as possible into the forms of domestic materialism. Whenever Tina's inner turmoil makes her cheek paler or her eyes blacker than usual, she is bombarded with vinaigrettes, camomile tea, a volume of Tillotson's sermons, or forcibly put to bed and dosed with bitters. But this carefully ritualised world in which the emotions enjoy diminishing opportunities is also in its own way an illusion. The gongs and bells are Sir Christopher's magic for preserving an aristocratic fiction which, deprived of emotion, lacks substance but which, created by his strong will, no one is allowed to question.

Tina's fiction, in contrast, is a passionate drama oscillating from intense moment to intense moment as her feelings are reflected or denied by her milieu. She seeks to dematerialise the architectural and genealogical world in accord with her feelings, restlessly exercising her pathetic fallacy in the moonlight, the woods, and the gardens. As Sir Christopher's plans develop, these fluctuations become increasingly frustrated and violent, converting her need to love into hatred. This melodrama of unmediated passion is expressed through the suitably Gothic metaphor of poisoning. In her response to Wybrow,

Tina is now convinced that he has wilfully 'given her the poison that seemed so sweet while she was drinking it, and now it was in her blood, and she was helpless' (140). This is her only possible explanation of her violent palpitations: 'I don't feel the ground under me; I only feel my head and heart beating, and it seems as if I must do something dreadful' (142). The 'hidden crystal dews of trust' (144) have gradually distilled into the poison that maddens: 'With the poisoned garment upon him, the victim writhes under the torture' (149). But this is as much an oversimplification as Sir Christopher's official narrative. Wybrow has collaborated rather fecklessly with both of them by simply reflecting their wishes and so allowing the protagonists to frustrate each other. Tina has provided her own poison, as Wybrow points out in his complaint that despite his best efforts 'all the comfort I get is to have . . . venom spirted at me from women's tongues' (138). Emotion can be converted into poison or camomile tea.

The sudden death of Wybrow is so devastating because it occurs, inevitably, at the moment when Sir Christopher and Tina have each withdrawn most completely into their own partial worlds and when their conflicting demands upon him are at their most extreme. As a character he becomes incoherent and dies. Convinced that she has been cruelly betrayed, Tina seeks revenge before his poison can destroy her: 'Her heart throbs as if it would burst her bosom – as if every next leap must be its last. Wait, wait, O heart! – till she has done this one deed' (155–6). The imagery of domestic animals gives way to the predatory, as George Eliot resorts to her most Gothic pastiche to express this moment of romantic agony. Character is subsumed in allegorical purpose: 'Those gleaming eyes, those bloodless lips, that swift silent tread, make her look like the incarnation of a fierce purpose, rather than a woman' (155). She becomes her passion for vengeance, just as Sir Christopher becomes the manor-house which is to be his mausoleum. Single-minded and isolated in their solipsistic worlds, they both achieve a different kind of incarnation from the one offered by the community.

Tina finds Wybrow dead in the rookery, and the fantasy of her revenge seems to have become an unmediated reality. In the later words of Gwendolen Harleth, Tina sees her wish outside herself; romantic passion in the Gothic mode is a form of magic in which the world is an extension of desire. 'But when I meant to do it', Tina confesses to Gilfil later, 'it was as bad as if I had done it' (179). In her horror she rushes back to the manor to her protector, Sir Christopher, whose heir she is convinced she has murdered, and who is just congratulating himself on the imminent fulfilment of his plans. He is ready to step complacently into his portrait and hand the dynasty over to posterity: 'it really is a remarkable thing that I never in my life laid a plan, and failed to carry it out . . . A strong will is the only magic' (156). Both he and Tina believe that their wishes are the final, magical authority: she is shattered when she sees the result of her magic, he when his magic fails him for the first time. In the world of Gothic melodrama to which their fantasies belong, it seems as if her magic has defeated the magic of the man who would not allow her to marry his heir. In fact, they have combined unwittingly to terrorise Wybrow into a heart attack, and the chapter ends with the baronet kneeling beside the body of his heir. With this frozen, melodramatic tableau, the Gothic romance comes to an end.

The next chapter opens with the description of someone regaining consciousness. It is not clear whether it is Wybrow who is not dead after all or Tina who had fainted after delivering her message. Perhaps she had been mistaken about Wybrow, for even as he stoops over his heir Sir Christopher can't believe he is dead. In the terms of the melodrama, the question is, has Tina killed him or can Sir Christopher bring him back to life? Whose magic is the stronger? Or, more philosophically, what is the true relationship between inner desire and outward fact? The uncertain pause is the finest effect in the whole narrative. The description of returning consciousness which creates the doubt also seeks to define an answer to both questions. As the melodrama comes to a sudden end, this description re-establishes the essential relationship between consciousness and the world which the melodrama has short-circuited:

It is a wonderful moment, the first time we stand by one who has fainted, and witness the fresh birth of consciousness spreading itself over the blank features, like the rising sunlight on the alpine summits that lay ghastly and dead under the leaden twilight. A slight shudder, and the frost-bound eyes recover their liquid light; for an instant they show the inward semi-consciousness of an infant's; then, with a little start, they open wider and begin to *look*; the present is visible, but only as a strange writing, and the interpreter Memory is not yet there. (158–9)

As with Amos Barton, the dialectic of life in which the self and world are constituted is re-activated through pain, suffering and death. Consciousness and the world interact to enable memory to interpret and make sense of experience in what is the master-plot of George Eliot's fiction. Tina regains consciousness – the passage refers to her – in a more complex and ambiguous world from which her own and Sir Christopher's fantasies have been violently dispelled. The reality they divided between them has now to be put together again.

At this point, Gilfil enters belatedly into his own love story. Up to now he has played second string to Wybrow, repeating his roles in a more everyday, Anglo-Saxon mode: he loves Tina like a sister and has been chosen by Sir Christopher to be both his chaplain – 'that domestic appendage' (113) – and her eventual husband. Unlike Wybrow, however, he is a mediator rather than a cause of conflict. Now, he steps into his rival's shoes and seeks to transform the triangle of self-interest into a more secure structure. Tina returns to consciousness in a world where the external is now too persistently present as she accepts responsibility for Wybrow's death. For Sir Christopher, in contrast, the secure, architectural solidity of his world has dissolved in the play of fierce emotions of which he has only just become aware: 'I thought I saw everything, and was stone-blind all the while' (170). The miraculous demands of both characters, originating in Milan cathedral, have now deconstructed each other as their full implications have become apparent.

Once he has ministered to his patron, Gilfil must act the large-calved Orpheus to Tina's Eurydice in order to bring her into a stable relationship with the world. This cannot be achieved at the manor. Tina has run away to her old maid Dorcas, retreating into childhood and the domestic pastoralism in which the story ends and where Gilfil will spend the rest of his life. The element of parody is strong as Dorcas's husband, that 'most awful messenger from the land of shades', comes to announce that Tina has been found: 'an so I've rode twenty mile upo' Blackbird, as thinks all the while he's a ploughin', an' turns sharp roun', ivery thirty yards, as if he was at the end of a furrow. I've had a sore time wi' him, I can tell you, sir' (173). In the face of this persistent repetition, the narrative is forced to slow down in preparation for closure, as Gilfil's love now offers security in a world accommodated to human needs, an architecture of use not ornament, where the kitchen is 'handsomely tapestried with flitches of bacon, and the ceiling ornamented with pendant hams' (175). It is in this world that Tina regains consciousness, has to be reborn, become a child again, then a little girl, and finally an adult. It is a second upbringing in which the separate segments of her life are all fitted together in the security of Gilfil's love. The dramatic oscillations and discontinuities of the previous narrative are now replaced by an omniscient loving perspective which can dispel Tina's guilt, as Gilfil explains:

'Our thoughts are often worse than we are, just as they are often better than we are. And God sees us as we are altogether, not in separate feelings or actions, as our fellow-men see us. We are always doing each other injustice, and thinking better or worse of each other than we deserve, because we only hear and see separate words and actions. We don't see each other's whole natures. But God sees that you could not have committed that crime.' (179)

The act of faith which transcends all discontinuities is, of course, Gilfil's, and it provides the basis for a full acceptance, understanding, and interpretation of the individual. It is a crystallisation of the hermeneutic circle in which parts and whole, actions and character, fit together as they do in Mr Gilfil's Shepperton. With this the story circles back to the non-narratable, the communal repetition with which it opened. But Tina cannot become part of this world. Her second upbringing is completed when she sings *Che farò* once again as an act of recuperation, briefly achieves an identity, but then dies in childbirth, living on in the repeated traditions of Shepperton gossip as a voice and a pair of black eyes, or in the relics in Gilfil's locked chamber, from which the narrative was released in the first place.

In *The Melodramatic Imagination*, Peter Brooks suggests that the nineteenth-century novel – he is writing especially of Balzac and James – needed the theatricality of melodrama 'to get its meaning across, to invest in its renderings of life a sense of memorability and significance'. This is elicited by the narrator putting pressure on the banal surface of reality: 'The narrative voice, with its grandiose questions and hypotheses, leads us in a movement through and beyond the surface of things to what lies behind, to the spiritual reality which is the true scene of the highly colored drama to be played out in the novel'.[5] This reality is made up of conflicting, bipolar, psychic forces which act out an intense Manichean drama in a fully expressive form. This analysis is helpful in locating George Eliot's purpose in this pastiche of Gothic melodrama and its expression in her later fiction. In the frame of the story, the narrator self-consciously exerts pressure on the uneventful texture of Mr Gilfil's life in the community in order to uncover, through a series of historical regressions, the intense drama of Cheverel Manor. This, however, is not a Manichean confrontation of good and evil which we experience in conventional melodrama. Instead, George Eliot deploys the Gothic as a means of dismembering prosaic reality into the components of consciousness, of will and passion, of the external and the internal, of the Anglo-Saxon and the Latin, and their expression in architecture and music. In separation, these contraries cannot make sense, as their proponents exemplify in their denial of each other: Sir Christopher's vision of Italian Gothic turns him 'stone-blind', while Tina's single-minded passion is distilled as poison. In their denial of the dialectic, both drive towards death and the destruction of what they desire. But in that desire to change the world in accordance with their wishes, it is worth pointing out, they not only polarise it into a dramatic confrontation but also create high art in the form of Sir Christopher's Gothicised manor-house and Tina's operatic arias.

In contrast, the provincial frame of the Scene consists of repetition, recurrence, and community, which find expression in gossip, folk-memory, and choric songs. But the values of this world are validated by Gilfil's Gothic experience – his 'antecedent romance' – which he carries with him to Shepperton and which has revealed, at least to him, the precarious unity of life which appears so solid and permanent to the locals. By his faith he rescues Tina from the narrative of desire in which she is guilty, and expiates her sins through his vision of coherence and wholeness. This is the vision which he has subsequently brought into existence during his forty-year ministry in Shepperton where communal solidarity and extreme eccentricity, part and whole, co-exist harmoniously. But the melodrama is an essential device for the novelist, as we shall find repeatedly, to articulate the constituent elements of that vision.

If 'Mr Gilfil's Love-Story' is a Gothic pastiche, then 'Janet's Repentance' can be seen as a reworking of the temperance tract. In both of these Scenes George Eliot relies heavily on the melodrama integral to the genres she is redefining, even as she discounts the simplified categories upon which that melodrama is based. The method of achieving this is to begin in the mundane present – either in Shepperton or Milby – and then to scrutinise the texture of life in retrospect, by analysis, and careful discrimination. Out of this interpretative strategy there emerges conflict which was latent all the time but, when teased out in this way by the commentary, quickly escalates in the narrative into confrontation, crisis, and a resolution which returns us to the mundane reality which we now understand and which understands itself. Both individuals and the community have to pass through the hermeneutic of suspicion to the hermeneutic of restoration, an experience which is a painful articulation of the elements which go to make up the act of cognition, understanding, and interpretation. Then the dialectic essential to each of these can begin again.

The sense that the novelist has to rely upon a melodramatic mode which falsifies experience comes through most strongly in 'Janet's Repentance'. In the previous Scenes there was a repeated acknowledgement of the unreliability of narrative – generated either by gossips or readers – in contrast to the solid world of repetition, routine, and acceptance. Polish countesses and Gothic romances are routed by the lower orders who ridicule or parody these fantasies. In 'Janet's Repentance' the target is different. Here, there is a persistent, at times shrill, campaign by the narrator against all kinds of theory and doctrine; and it is from doctrinal differences that narrative conflict is generated. It is worth looking first at this running critique of a certain kind of hermeneutic in the commentary before examining how it is carried on at a different level in the narrative.

The method of explanation, interpretation, and judgment which the narrator persistently attacks is that of deduction, any kind of inference from the general to the particular. It is a wide-ranging attack on a view of the world diametrically opposed to that of the sensitive hypothesis which seeks to define reality as it is modified by it. This comment on the hero of the story, the Rev. Edgar Tryan, is typical: 'To persons possessing a great deal of that facile psychology which prejudges individuals by means of formulae, and casts them, without further trouble, into duly lettered pigeon-holes, the Evangelical curate might seem to be doing simply what all other men like to do' (246). The act of classification becomes a form of moral turpitude from which both characters and readers have to be rescued. A later comment brings out the absolute contrast between the onlookers who 'are coldly discussing a man's career . . . and labelling his opinions – "Evangelical and narrow", or "Latitudinarian and Pantheistic", or "Anglican and supercilious"' – and the man himself who 'in his solitude, is perhaps shedding hot tears' (248). As one can see, there is a great deal of moral energy and coercion invested in this contrast between two ways of looking at things – cold and hot, public and private, general and particular.

The most extensive of these critiques occurs at the climax of the public dispute: Tryan's victimisation and martyrdom, it is made clear, are the result of his being labelled and pigeon-holed more persistently than anyone else in the story. This is the interpretative violence he is subjected to and from which the narrator is careful to dissociate himself: '"One of the Evangelical clergy, a disciple of Venn," says the critic from his bird's-eye station. "Not a remarkable specimen; the anatomy and habits of his species have been determined long ago."' Unlike the critic, the narrator 'is not poised at that lofty height. I am on the level and in the press with him, as he struggles his way along the stony road through the crowd of unloving fellow-men.' Out of this comes a different mode of understanding and interpretation: 'Yet surely, surely the only true knowledge of our fellow-men is that which enables us to feel with him – which gives us a fine ear for the heart-pulses that are beating under the mere clothes of circumstance and opinion.' The passage switches from distant seeing to close hearing, from species to individual, from circumstantial to essential, and ends by seeking to synthesise these into the definition of a genuine hypothesis: 'Our subtlest analysis of schools and sects must miss the essential truth, unless it be lit up by the love that sees in all forms of human thought and work the life and death struggles of separate human beings' (257). This is, of course, a common refrain in the novels, and it points to a central interpretative dilemma: if the scrutiny of schools and sects turns them into separate human beings then they are no longer schools and sects. Somehow, the analysis of the general and the love of the particular have, in this moralising of the hypothesis, to be held in tension.

As the story develops, this alternative to deductive pigeon-holing is defined with more subtlety and validated by further scientific analogies. 'Do not philosophic doctors tell us that we are unable to discern so much as a tree, except by an unconscious cunning which combines many past and separate sensations; that no one sense is independent of another, so that in the dark we can hardly taste a fricassee, or tell whether our pipe is alight or not.' This is a more elaborate and dialectical model of interpretation which is then used to put the moral onus on the reader: 'If so, it is easy to understand that our discernment of men's motives must depend on the completeness of the elements we can bring from our own susceptibility and our own experience.' And, then, even this more complex perceptual model based on pre-understanding is deconstructed as subject and object become inseparable: 'The keenest eye will not serve, unless you have the delicate fingers, with their subtle nerve filaments, which elude scientific lenses, and lose themselves in the invisible world of human sensations' (258–9). Finally and invisibly, sensation responds to sensation, and further analogies are both unavailable and unnecessary. It may seem a long and complicated detour to arrive eventually at this definition of mutual sympathy, but this is the method of *Scenes of Clerical Life*. In the narrative itself we can see how the final transparency and immediacy of human relationships is only achieved after the deductions and the labelling have been experienced and discarded.

It is not only the role of the clergy which is being examined in Milby. All the professions, those vital organs of the community – and each with its own hermeneutic for interpreting symptoms, evidence, confession – have become rigidified and self-perpetuating systems, utilising their own esoteric codes and rituals for the purpose of retaining power and making money. These men in black – the priest, the doctor, the lawyer – are the professional listeners of people's secrets and, according to Balzac, in mourning for the death of all virtue and illusion.[6] In medicine, for example, the rival doctors quite happily divide the town between them, only co-operating to rout any medical interlopers and rivals. And by dividing their patients they rule them: Pratt refers every disease to 'debility' and Pilgrim to 'plethora' and the citizens fight over the merits of these magical labels. As the doctors practise their spells, the actual curing of sickness is not only lost sight of but is positively deprecated. The function of the patients is to be ill and pay their fees. Ends and means are reversed in such a society: the man becomes his profession and the patients his necessary means of support, as George Eliot's wordplay repeatedly suggests. 'A good inflammation fired [Dr Pilgrim's] enthusiasm, and a lingering dropsy dissolved him into charity' (203–4). The doctor's diagnosis deconstructs his own integrity. The lawyers operate in a similar way. Instead of safeguarding the social fabric, they are the keenest predators in the jungle of Milby life, utilising their inside information for their own material interests. They are encouraged in their unscrupulousness by their clients, until they too find themselves exploited, their bankrupt estates snapped up by their own lawyers. In the absence of a living social medium, law like medicine becomes the opposite of itself; both fix society in their own categories and exploit it at leisure.

The church in Milby has failed to challenge this materialism, for it too has degenerated into vested interests and empty forms. Church services have become pagan celebrations of wealth, booty, and status by means of which a 'distinguished aristocratic minority' defends its position by ridiculing publicly and by satire – that characteristic Milby mode – the dress and demeanour of the rest of the congregation. Even Dissent has succumbed to laxity, indifference, and materialism, and the *status quo* seems secure against any kind of criticism, especially as all the branches of Christianity are principally engaged in ridiculing their doctrinal rivals. As the community degenerates, a perverse ethic comes into operation. Since people are most comfortable when they 'look down a little on their fellow-creatures', the first commandment of Milby morality is, Don't pretend to be better than your neighbours. This makes good works difficult, for any attempt to help others implies your own superiority. Good works must, therefore, be performed clandestinely – or perhaps even better, show your solidarity by not performing them at all. You might even go further and practise 'an ingenuous vice or two' so as to provide everyone with the satisfaction of looking down on you. In the absence of faith, this is what happens to good works, and the only kind of spirit at work is the 'very abundant supply of stimulants' (197) imbibed by the citizens in their degeneracy.

The crucial sign of this division and degeneracy within the community is its readiness to label and categorise, in order to control or discount. So when the new Evangelical curate arrives to challenge Milby's values, the defence of the *status quo* by his opponents in the first chapter takes the form of a frenzy of labelling. He is, in turn, 'methodistical', 'Presbyterian', 'sectarian', 'antinomian', 'anabaptist', and a 'Jesuit'. The community's difficulty, as these labels suggest, is in grasping the meaning of the faith and spirituality which he brings to the town. The rigid organism sees living faith as a disease, 'the asinine virus of Dissent', and like other diseases mysterious into the bargain: 'the disease had been imported', says the narrator, 'when the parishioners were expecting it as little as the innocent Red Indian expected smallpox' (206). Behind their bluster and bullying, the indignant ratepayers of Milby feel helpless to deal with a phenomenon which evades their fixed categories; they can only interpret the new religion as a more devious form of self-interest. There is, however, another aspect to the life of the town which is only belatedly acknowledged. What 'at first seemed a dismal mixture of griping worldliness, vanity, ostrich feathers, and the fumes of brandy: looking closer, you found some purity, gentleness, and unselfishness' (202). Evangelicalism is welcomed by the blue-stockings of the town in a scene in which they catalogue the religious novels for Tryan's lending library – novels of which 'Janet's Repentance' is both a pastiche and a revision – in a finely managed contrast with the opening scene of aggressive masculine bonhomie in the Red Lion. It is this support which leads eventually to the public conflict of Tryanites against anti-Tryanites. As in the parallel commentary, the unilateral imposition of categories of interpretation has first to be challenged before it can be transcended and dissolved.

As the new influence begins to make itself felt, the opponents in the struggle exaggerate and allegorise the conflict. The ladies see lawyer Dempster, the defender of the establishment, as the agent of the devil, while Tryan accuses the vicar of wilfully throwing away the souls of his parishioners by not allowing him his Sunday lecture. From the other side come the traditional insults directed at the excesses of faith: 'Tell a man he is not to be saved by his works,' says Dempster, 'and you open the floodgates of all immorality' (194). The new influence is seen repeatedly as an insidious disease which has crept into Milby because it cannot be labelled and thereby excluded by the existing categories. Evangelicalism was 'a murrain or blight all the more terrible, because its nature was but dimly conjectured' (206). It is a virus, an infection, a miasma, against which the citizens respond in their customary way at the Red Lion: brandy has to be drunk as an inoculation against the onset of this unfamiliar spirit which is threatening the health of the *status quo*. And the first battle is won by the anti-Tryanites who carefully stage a spontaneous demonstration, exploiting the public forms of petition, assembly, and consensus, to defend their own interests. But Tryan appeals successfully to the Bishop, and the final confrontation occurs at his first Sunday lecture when the anti-Tryanites appear with their satirical playbills ridiculing Mr All-grace No-works, Mr Elect-and-Chosen Apewell, who is about to play his part in a piece entitled 'The Wolf in Sheep's Clothing' (250). Tryan's supporters are also ridiculed as his performing animals doing their unnatural tricks. But the crisis forces them, as they draw analogies with the persecution of Cranmer, Ridley, and Latimer, into a public confession of their faith; and despite the provincial absurdities of the episode, the reader is asked to sympathise with the clergyman as he brings the gospel into one of the 'dead an' dark place[s]' (244) of the earth.

This Bunyanesque allegorisation is the most extreme expression of false categorisation in action in the community, the attempt to control by a hermeneutic of suspicion, by the satire which declares the Evangelicals to be the opposite of what they profess. But once faith has made its stand it can no longer be ignored, and the vital interaction of stifled faith and rigid public forms can begin again. 'Evangelicalism was making its way in Milby, and gradually diffusing its subtle odour into chambers that were bolted and barred against it' (255). It has shaken Milby into an awareness of the idea of duty, which, says the narrator, is 'to the moral life what the addition of a great central ganglion is to animal life'. The primitive hierarchies of self-interest are replaced by a genuine 'principle of subordination', which makes a person 'no longer a mere bundle of impressions, desires, and impulses' (255). Categories are replaced by organic analogies which translate the subtle hermeneutic defined in the commentary into communal terms. Form and spirit are interdependent and inseparable. The decay of the social organism has been arrested through open conflict which has revived the dialectic upon which growth is based. And so, after the melodrama of the religious conflict, Tryan's success is dispersed tamely but pervasively into the texture of Milby's life, modified, supported, and transmitted, by the day-to-day habits of the community: 'convenience, that admirable branch system from the main line of self-interest, makes us all fellow-helpers in spite of adverse resolutions' (253). Milby has reconstituted itself but it has not returned to its original state of innocence, embodied in the character of the elderly Mr Jerome who represents an idea of community before the current religious and industrial upheavals. He is an anachronism who reconciles in his person most of the conflicts of contemporary Milby. Faith and good works are inseparable to his nonpolemical mind: he helps people because he has faith in their ability to help themselves. He is a Dissenter of a kind extinct 'in these days, when opinion has got far ahead of feeling' (242), and his garden at the White House is an image of the undissociated life.

Once Milby has become its own 'incarnate history' in this way, the question in the second half of the story is whether Janet Dempster can be reconstituted as a character. She is a victim of the darkness of Milby and, in particular, of her marriage to Dempster: she is the 'gypsy' who has become the 'crazy Jane', the spirited wife who has become the alcoholic. Will she be destroyed by her defeated lawyer husband – the 'dempster' or doomster[7] – or saved by the trustful clergyman, ridiculed as Mr Try-it-on? In the private conflict, the more obvious public contrasts are subtilised. Despite their natural antipathy, Dempster and Tryan inevitably have a good deal in common as they combine unwittingly to redeem Janet. They are both domineering characters seeking to impose their values on the town and refusing to tolerate opposition. Dempster's drunken aggression and Tryan's high-minded Rechabitism both result from their thwarted purposes; they are suppressing their human affections as they strive to impose, respectively, law and gospel upon the community. (St Paul's Epistle to the Romans is a sub-text to the story.) In his suicidal drive towards death Dempster almost destroys his wife, so that Tryan can save her before he kills himself by his pastoral exertions. The manner in which the influence of one man gives way to the other is the central melodrama of the private as it was of the public story. Janet is the site of this conflict and she becomes its memorial.

Dempster's career is a crescendo of bullying aggression as he rejects, one by one, his human ties – his friends, his servants, his clients, his coachman, and finally his wife – and seeks to control his world by the public forms and laws of society.[8] Alcohol is his antidote to any qualms of feeling and conscience. As he becomes more and more sadistic, Janet becomes desperate, but her pride provides the challenge Dempster needs. Alcohol induces in her, in contrast, the passive indifference and oblivion which enable her to survive. But after his public defeat, the recalcitrance of the world incenses Dempster to a fury, epitomised in his horsewhipping as he rejects all restraints. The only person now left upon whom he can exercise his will is Janet, for marriage, like the other institutions of unregenerate Milby, has become a means of exploitation within the security of the law. Each of her capitulations leads to further indignities. When she finally rebels, it was as if 'she had defied a wild beast within the four walls of his den' (273). Dempster must suppress this rebellion by an even more complete humiliation as he becomes, allegorically, 'this huge crushing force, armed with savage will' (274). Having reduced her from sentimental heroine to wife, to servant, to slave, he now ejects her from the house in the middle of the night, confident that she will creep back in utter humility and re-assume the clothes she has left behind and which he has locked in a closet to prevent anyone knowing what has happened. But in the surrealistic world into which the story is moving, he feels he has Janet's public self, his property – the only form of the self he acknowledges – locked up under perfect control. This is the final bizarre solution to the absolute control he needs. But, of course, he has achieved nothing, or less than nothing: for in the limbo to which she has been consigned, her rescue is about to begin under the influence of his public enemy, Tryan.

The final stage of Dempster's insane attempt to control his world is introduced by the inevitable accident when, whipping his horse, he is pitched out of his gig. Helpless on his deathbed, he is now haunted by visions which exaggerate to nightmare the illogicality of the will's pursuit of power. Janet's unique act of rebellion is final shocking proof that his world is no longer manageable even as he still tries to whip it into submission – but now in his delirium he is not whipping his coachman or his horse but his bedclothes, himself, to which the world has been reduced. This delirium is a remarkable dramatisation of the pathology of the will in its terminal phase, the end of his attempt to interpret, stabilise, and control reality on his own terms. Once the dialectical tension between the self and the world is lost, then each polarity seeks to become absolute, but in doing so becomes increasingly unstable until it turns, paradoxically, into its opposite. In these few surrealistic paragraphs of delirium, Dempster acts and re-enacts this reversal as he switches from victim to victimiser and back again.

When Janet discovers him raving on his sickbed, he is watching in terror the iron closet in which he has locked the clothes she was to re-assume in complete submission. But now it is he who is helpless. He sees Janet coming from the closet as a terrifying corpse – the servants are sure he has murdered her – a witch with Medusa hair, a siren intent on the fearful constriction of suffocation by drowning. The world, no longer kept in check by the force of his will, has been inundated, the floodgates have burst open, and his black-haired 'gypsy queen', whom he turned into a helpless 'crazy Jane', has finally become a vengeful siren rising from the flood. In a bewildering way, his actions have converted the old submissive Janet into this terrifying creature; in the world of power she must be either drudge or siren. Even when she says she forgives him, he is sure she is trying to make him confess so that his various crimes can be used against him. 'Do your worst! I've got the law on my side . . . I know the law' (308). He imagines he is in a court of law but now as the accused; judgment is impending but he will admit nothing. She must have learned this duplicity – at one moment submissive, the next rebellious – from the Evangelicals, the 'damned psalm-singing maggots', who defeated him in public life. He will destroy these insects which are eating away the solid structure of law and order from within: 'I'll make a fire under you, and smoke off the whole pack of you . . . I'll sweep you up . . . I'll grind you to powder . . . small powder.' But at this moment – a moment central to the dialectic – when he has in his nightmare pulverised his enemies to powder, they, like Janet, slip from his grasp in another alarming metamorphosis: 'powder on the bed-clothes . . . running about . . . black lice . . . they are coming in swarms.' Rage gives way again to terror, for by grinding them down he has made them more frighteningly unmanageable. He entreats and threatens the appalled Janet, but he is by now completely isolated, demented, mad: 'his sins had made a hard crust round his soul' (308).

In these final stages, as his guilt rises to the surface of his mind, he is convinced that the law itself will be turned against him in an accusation of Janet's murder. He is in the dock, subjected to his own juridical hermeneutic, and judgment is pending. He must prove that Janet is alive, but he is trapped by the law which he has practised and perverted, for the clothes he must produce as evidence appear before his eyes as lengthening serpents, ready to drag him down into the cold water. If she is dead he is guilty; if alive she is coming for vengeance. In his terror he whips himself along, overtaking the Evangelicals whom he will convict of witchcraft out of their own mouths by making them say the Lord's prayer backwards. Then he will use it as a magic spell to hand these maggots over to the devil whom he now conjures in desperation: 'I'll pepper them so that the devil shall eat them raw' (309). Everything must be used to fix and control a world continually slipping from his grasp through bewildering metamorphoses into ever more uncontrollable shapes. Originally he had used the law, the *status quo*, public opinion, and the rituals of Milby life, to achieve his purposes; these are all now revealed for what they are – spells and incantations to defeat a whole bestiary of threatening demons. (The satirical playbills depicting Tryan and his supporters as performing animals was the public version of this psychomachia.) His delirium has been a collage of phrases and images drawn from his legal career through which he has tried and, at his moment of death, failed to make sense of his life.

The central irony of the narrative – the point again in the dialectic where things turn into their opposite – is that the Janet whom Dempster is metamorphosing into various threatening shapes has, in the three days between her ejection and re-appearance, her death and resurrection, undergone a transformation of a different kind at the hands of Tryan. This is the crux of the story: as the influence of one man supersedes the other, we recognise that they are working together to bring about Janet's repentance. In this scene of clerical life George Eliot is providing her own version of the Pauline paradox of law and gospel, of form and feeling: the law destroys man's pride to show him in his sinfulness that he needs the gospel. Dempster embodies one half of the paradox, Tryan the other. But before she comes under the clergyman's influence, Janet as outcast enters a deathlike limbo in which the self, unrelated to the world, begins to disintegrate. The chapter which describes this scene reads like an episode from *The Scarlet Letter*: 'The stony street, the bitter north-east wind and darkness – and in the midst of them a tender woman thrust out from her husband's home' (275). The church clock strikes, the clouds part, and the dim light of the stars is 'like a cruel finger pointing her out in her wretchedness and humiliation' (277). She tries to interpret this judgment on her life but rejects, in turn, her mother's explanation, the answers of orthodox religion, and her own earlier hopeful assumptions – they 'served only to darken the riddle of her life' (276). It is the moment of non-meaning.

It is also another frozen melodramatic tableau which, like the death of Wybrow, has somehow to be re-integrated into the narrative. Janet is isolated and lost 'with the door shut upon her past life, and the future black and unshapen before her as the night' (275). Such moments, as we saw in the two previous Scenes, can only be depicted by death or an image of death.

The drowning man, urged by the supreme agony, lives in an instant through all his happy and unhappy past: when the dark flood has fallen like a curtain, memory, in a single moment, sees the drama acted over again. And even in those earlier crises, which are but types of death – when we are cut off abruptly from the life we have known, when we can no longer expect to-morrow to resemble yesterday, and find ourselves by some sudden shock on the confines of the unknown – there is often the same sort of lightning-flash through the dark and unfrequented chambers of memory. (275)

In the typology of death this is both a fleetingly brief 'single moment' as the lightning flashes and the curtain falls, and also a moment of plenitude which contains the whole of life. It is the sudden end but also the closure which allows recapitulation. If, as Walter Benjamin says, the obituary is the only completely satisfactory story, then this seems to offer such an opportunity.[9] But there are different kinds of end times. Both Dempster's death and Tryan's are yet to come in the narrative, though we have already seen how the former's death agony is certainly not a rounded summing up, but rather a panic-stricken attempt to avoid judgment – that final categorisation – in a court-of-law. Tryan's, as we shall see, is very different. Here, Janet's sudden 'death' by its very nature does not make sense; she is completely alone, with 'no faith, no trust'. In memory, she runs through the crucial scenes of her life but, since they don't provide a meaningful narrative, she, the product of the scenes, cannot claim them as her own. She 'sat staring fixedly into the darkness, while inwardly she gazed at her own past, almost losing the sense that it was her own, or that she was any thing more than a spectator at a strange and dreadful play' (276). In the next paragraph, the 'spectator' becomes a 'spectre' when she imagines her mother's horror at seeing her in this plight. She fragments under this double incoherence.

This is the moment towards which all of George Eliot's narratives, in one way or another, move. She described it in her letter of 1848 as 'the state of prostration – the self-abnegation through which the soul must go', in which the self is experienced only as a 'miserable agglomeration of atoms'. Here, it is dwelt on at great length in chapters fifteen and sixteen, even though it is not amenable to interpretation. The reason is that it represents the moment of non-meaning, the break, the gap at the climax of 'Janet's Repentance' which disconfirms her life-story as well as the two poles of law and gospel between which she is in transition. All the normal hermeneutic strategies – memory, narrative sequence, God as teacher, God as heavenly Father – fail to provide an interpretation. This is 'death' as a form of extreme unintelligibility. Far from articulating the meaning of her life, this 'supreme agony' is a moment of fission which disarticulates the elements of which life consists. The self only takes shape in its way of giving shape to the world, but she has become simply a spectator of her own life and a spectre to others. Even her thoughts become 'external existences, that thrust themselves imperiously upon her like haunting visions' (279), and then in the morning the world of chairs and tables also disengages itself from her life to be revealed as the 'naked prose', the opposite of those 'poetic' moments of synthesis. Dempster's task has now been completed: 'there was a darker shadow over her life than the dread of her husband – it was the shadow of self-despair' (281).

At this pivotal moment, which the elaborate structure of the novella has isolated and represented in detail, Janet suddenly remembers Tryan as a man supposedly 'fond of great sinners' (282) who might try to help her not merely by the 'barren exhortation' of good works, which she sees as another kind of legalism ('Do right . . . and God will reward you'). Now the mode changes from juridical to confessional. She narrates to him the story of her life with her growing addiction to the demon drink. She needs more than resolve and will, she tells him, in a paraphrase of Romans 7.15: 'It seemed as if there was a demon in me always making me rush to do what I longed not to do' (286). What the narrator calls this 'impulse to confession' (282) – I am divided against myself – is the crucial way out of the impasse into which the story has led. The narrative of confession leads out of isolation and despair, first of all, by the very fact of being told to a sympathetic listener. Secondly and by definition, the confession acknowledges the discrepancy between deeds and intentions which is no longer an occasion for satire, but for a recognition of human weakness. In other words, confession articulates a lapse and simultaneously makes an act of faith. And thirdly, the confessor interprets the incoherent narrative by placing it in a larger context of meaning. Whereas Dempster's terrified exegesis simply creates two contradictory images, Janet as drudge and destroyer, Tryan tentatively provides a plot to her story which links them: 'How can you tell but that the hardest trials you have known have been only the road by which [God] was leading you to that complete sense of your own sin and helplessness, without which you would never have renounced all other hopes, and trusted in His love alone?' (288).

Tryan knows, however, that this gloss on Janet's life can only be validated by his own confession, by telling her the story of how he came into his own faith. This turns out to be a conventional account of a betrayal of a young woman, loss of belief, sense of sin, and the recovery of faith through a friend to whom Tryan in his turn had confessed everything. Confession is discovered to be the model of human relationships: 'it is because sympathy is but a living again through our own past in a new form, that confession often prompts a response of confession' (288). The power of confession – the significance of which can hardly be exaggerated in George Eliot's fiction – is based on its appeal to the master-plot which underpins mutual sympathy. This master-plot is generated by the discrepancy, the difference between intentions and deeds, law and gospel, theory and evidence, God and man, all signs of the fallen world. For George Eliot, the confession which acknowledges this is also the act of faith which overcomes it, a form of *imitatio Christi*. Dempster had boasted that he would make Tryan cry '*peccavi*' before he did (236), and in one sense he has succeeded through the despair of his own wife, Janet, whom the curate is now seeking to save. For himself, the lawyer vigorously eschews confession and so in place of Tryan's chastened autobiography we have the tormented nightmare of his deathbed where fragments of suspicious evidence from his past float to the surface to be contradicted and denied. He cannot acknowledge that he is divided against himself, and so the dialectic of self and the world oscillates out of control. Tryan can acknowledge this through an ordered narrative which links the saintly clergyman to his sinful past. But however it happens, both men, to fulfil their roles in the repentance of Janet, have to recapitulate their lives and die so that she can witness these two versions of the master-plot: the confession and gradual death through consumption contrasted with the nightmarish self-defence of Dempster's final apoplexy. Each provides its own hermeneutic, that of faith and that of law which turns into demon-worship; while Janet subsumes both in her encompassing story.

In the theological terms upon which George Eliot is dependent throughout the story, Tryan has substituted for the judicial God of good works the forgiving, suffering Christ. This is the justification by faith which he has brought to Milby, and though he speaks the language of Evangelicalism, he stresses – and this is how the novelist separates him from his strict religious beliefs – the crucial importance of human mediation. And the narrator's description of this mediation goes further, offering it as the immediate, transparent form of mutual understanding, 'not calculable by algebra, not deducible by logic':

Blessed influence of one true loving soul on another! . . . Ideas are often poor ghosts; our sun-filled eyes cannot discern them; they pass athwart us in thin vapour; and cannot make themselves felt. But sometimes they are made flesh; they breathe upon us with warm breath, they touch us with soft responsive hands, they look at us with sad sincere eyes, and speak to us in appealing tones; they are clothed in a living human soul, with all its conflicts, its faith, and its love. Then their presence is a power, then they shake us like a passion, and we are drawn after them with a gentle compulsion, as flame is drawn to flame. (293)

Medium and message, emotion and ideas have become inseparable. This is George Eliot's own form of incarnationalism, the task 'to make ideas thoroughly incarnate' that she set herself in her fiction. She gently applies her own hermeneutic of suspicion to Tryan's evangelical beliefs in order to redefine them by her own hermeneutic of restoration. As with Deronda later, Tryan is the Christ-like mentor who in his incarnation – his confession reveals him to be in possession of his own life – creates a person out of Janet's disarticulated self. This can only occur when – as in the case of the scientific model of perception George Eliot employs in the commentary – subject and object, priest and confessor, transcend their roles and through mutual confession validate each other as human beings. Then the demon of indifference, epitomised in alcohol, can be replaced by the spirit of true submission, and, in the language of the temperance tract, the final choice is embodied in the pun on the word 'spirit'. Dempster has planted in her the demon of self-will which Tryan exorcises by the more powerful spirit of faith and submission. Janet's salvation is located precisely between the two meanings of the temperance-tract pun; it is neither spiritual nor material, but their reconciliation.

As in the public dispute, the open conflict is followed by a less dramatic period of consolidation as the stark dialectic of Janet's crisis is absorbed into the diurnal rhythms of life. The nature of this consolidation is demonstrated when Janet is tempted into a momentary relapse by the hidden bottle of brandy. It is as if Dempster is bewitching her from the grave by this magic elixir. But she now has the means of salvation. She deliberately re-activates the story of her life by rehearsing the conflict between Dempster and Tryan. First, she sits by her husband's grave 'to lash the demon out of her soul with the stinging memories of the bygone misery' (320), and then once again confesses to Tryan. As the allegorical drama of her repentance is absorbed in this way, it becomes a learned inner discipline, a kind of spiritual exercise whose form is not imposed but derived from her personal history which it articulates. This is her own version of the master-plot which now acts as the hermeneutic key to her life. She has now taken possession of her own narrative; and the two men, who had to recuperate their own lives to make this possible, become irrelevant as is usual in such triadic structures. In all three cases, sin is a form of narrative which has to be confessed (or not) and exorcised, so as to become part of the non-narratable life of the community.[10] Tryan, in a final ironic twist, does glimpse the possibility of wholeness for himself through his growing love for Janet. It comes too late to save him from the consumption caused by his self-mortification, but he achieves a gentle after-life in Janet's memory, in contrast to the hell into which the apoplectic Dempster sinks, dying without human recognition.

In this way, Janet becomes the story's and the community's 'incarnate history', the embodiment and resumé of the dialectic of life which is defined by the hypothetical method, the component parts of which have in this case become separated. First, theories, categories, laws are imposed. Then, the particular, the individual, the emotions rebel. Out of this confrontation there emerges a new synthesis, and life regains its interrupted rhythm. It is a sequence of crucial significance which George Eliot repeatedly expresses through the religious, more particularly, the trinitarian language of her clerical scenes and in her later fiction. Law is fulfilled and superseded by gospel which in turn, through the continuing presence of Tryan in Janet's and the community's memory, is completed by the work of the spirit. The two poles between which the narrative moves may be suggested by two phrases from George Eliot's commentary. The first is 'the serene air of pure intellect', that realm where 'individuals really exist for no other purpose than that abstractions may be drawn from them' (301). The second, in opposition, is the 'serene freedom from the importunities of opinion', which is used to describe the life of the sick chamber where there are 'no self-questionings, no casuistry, no assent to propositions, no weighing of consequences' (310). The narrative, with its discontinuities and conflicting interpretations, moves between these two serenities, neither of which is itself narratable. The first serenity is that of pure ideas, the second that of their complete incarnation.

CHAPTER 2

Adam Bede: pastoral theodicies

Anamorphosis is a term from art history which refers to a drawing or painting so executed as to give a distorted image of the object represented but which, if viewed from a certain point, or reflected in a curved mirror, shows the object in true proportion.[1] One of the best known examples in Britain is the distorted skull in Holbein's painting, *The Ambassadors*, in the National Gallery in London. It is a device which, I believe, can help us to understand some of the curious ambiguities of George Eliot's pastoral novel, *Adam Bede*, that most pictorial of her works over which there has been a good deal of critical dispute in recent years.

In one sense, the novel appears to be the most static and stable of all her fictions, with its descriptive set-pieces itemised in the chapter-headings: 'The Workshop', 'The Preaching', 'The Rector', 'The Dairy', 'The Games', 'The Dance', and so on. The perspective within which these locations and characters are described also seems reassuringly normative. But when it comes to matters of representation and interpretation, George Eliot's reassurances are often disingenuous. Her refusal, for example, to improve the facts of her story for the benefit of her more refined readers in chapter seventeen ('In Which the Story Pauses a Little') is a characteristic trope: she will 'give a faithful account of men and things as they have mirrored themselves in [her] mind'. But characteristic also is the *caveat* which follows: 'The mirror is doubtless defective; the outlines will sometimes be disturbed, the reflection faint or confused; but I feel as much bound to tell you precisely as I can what that reflection is, as if I were in the witness-box narrating my experience on oath.'[2] This recalls the first sentence of the novel, where the narrator compares himself not to a witness in the dock – not itself always the most reliable source of truth, as the novel demonstrates – but to someone much more mysterious. 'With a single drop of ink for a mirror, the Egyptian sorcerer undertakes to reveal to any chance comer far-reaching visions of the past.' What this sorcerer reveals, certainly at the beginning of the novel, are 'faithful pictures of monotonous homely existence' after the Dutch model – but with a difference. And this is where anamorphism comes in.

In *Adam Bede* the reader's attention is drawn several times to objects, characters, attitudes, and values which will not fit into the conventional perspective the novel seems to assume.[3] They are premised upon some other reality. One of the most striking examples, an image of the Cross, has to be imported from a continental landscape into Hayslope:

It has stood perhaps by the clustering apple-blossoms, or in the broad sunshine by the cornfield, or at a turning by the wood where a clear brook was gurgling below; and surely, if there came a traveller to the world who knew nothing of the story of man's life upon it, this image of agony would seem to him strangely out of place in the midst of this joyous nature. (II.112)

Concealed in the landscape, the passage continues, there might well be 'a human heart beating heavily with anguish', but to perceive it – and the Cross – clearly, the onlooker has to adopt a different, a negative perspective to bring it into focus. And as the anamorphosis assumes a clear shape, the solid pastoral landscape becomes blurred and dissolves. This effect is sometimes presented through the recognisable literary convention of *Et in Arcadia ego*,[4] as when Adam and Seth carry one of their father's coffins to Broxton: 'It was a strangely-mingled picture – the fresh youth of the summer morning, with its Eden-like peace and loveliness, the stalwart strength of the two brothers in their rusty working clothes, and the long coffin of their shoulders' (I.73). Or it might be presented as an hallucinatory merging of one apparently precise image with another. The question implied in all of these vignettes is, what angle of vision, if any, will enable the reader and the characters to perceive clearly and simultaneously both the anomalies and the norm, the figure and the ground? Several Victorian critics saw 'no reason why a picture of village character and village humour should be made so painful as it is by the introduction into the foreground of the startling horrors of rustic reality'. More recent critics see the difficulty of achieving such a focus as an indication of George Eliot's uncertainty about the kind of novel she was writing, a pastoral tale or a moral drama. What is highly significant is that in all cases the critics themselves employ the language of optics, perspective, and focus.⁵ My argument is that, far from being a dislocation, this is the central hermeneutic issue in *Adam Bede*.

The anomalies in the pastoral world which the inhabitants of Hayslope seek to exclude are of two extreme kinds: one, as my examples suggest, is the reality of sin, suffering, and death; the other is erotic desire. Both threaten the *status quo*, within which all the characters have, in one way or another, constructed world-views which provide them with stability and coherence in the community. They have established their own pastoral realities. After the sharply focused intensities of *Scenes of Clerical Life*, one of the most striking features of *Adam Bede* is the leisurely parade of these characters and their worlds, as the community is mapped out in preparation for the narrative which is slowly generated as the established perspective on life is challenged. It is in the presentation of these various figures, some major but most minor, that one can witness George Eliot developing what I called in the introduction her essentially hermeneutic view of character: each is presented in terms of a way of making sense of the world in which he or she lives. This skill was widely appreciated by the Victorian reviewers, those connoisseurs of character study. The critic of the *Saturday Review*, for example, noted, in terms which George Eliot would have approved, that it consists of more than simply recording distinct characteristics: 'There must be something that answers to the hypothesis in experimental inquiry – something that comes from the observer, not the observed – a general key to the character which the drawer of the character assumes at first, and then proves by elaborating it.'⁶ The author makes sense of the characters as they seek to make sense of their world. And since this is a traditional, pastoral world, their world-views are best described as theodicies, justifications of the ways of God to man, with its attendant question: *Si Deus justus – unde malum?*⁷ But before examining their responses to this question, I wish to look at the two interlopers in Hayslope who seek to subvert the apparently stable middle-ground, populated by the other characters, by insisting that their own anamorphic perspectives are the only valid ones.

The two interlopers are the orphans, Hetty Sorrel and Dinah Morris, the nieces of Mr and Mrs Poyser respectively. If Dinah strives towards a selfless, spiritual identification with suffering humanity, alien to the very nature of Hayslope, Hetty represents the opposite moral pole. She is the natural, instinctive self seeking its own pleasure, the quintessence of the golden world of pastoral, nature in all its 'self-engrossed loveliness'. The two women are juxtaposed and contrasted in the novel in various ways, some stylised, some less obvious; and it is worth recalling that their meeting in the prison was the episode that prompted George Eliot to write the novel in the first place.[8] The narrative of *Adam Bede* records the process of bringing them and what they represent together – indistinguishable in the darkness – at the climax of the novel. At first, one is simply aware of the striking contrast between the spirituality of the ascetic Methodist preacher and the hedonistic amorality of the dairymaid. In conventional terms, they represent nature and grace, madonna and magdalene. Dinah's selflessness is so extreme that she appears as a pale, disembodied spirit living through other people and their troubles, while Hetty is a pleasure-seeking animal untouched by anything outside her immediate desires. The contrast is enforced in a variety of ways – in the two bedroom scenes, for example, in Hetty disguising herself as Dinah, and in Dinah substituting herself for Hetty in Adam's dream. But as polar opposites they have a good deal in common, each avoiding the full complexity of life in the community, and each radically subversive of the *status quo*. Female spirituality challenges pastoral reality from without, just as female sexuality challenges it from within.

Dinah's radical challenge is expressed at greatest length in her sermon to the unresponsive onlookers in Hayslope at the beginning of the novel. She brings the Cross into Arcadia and beseeches her congregation to see the world differently in consequence. With her 'belief in visible manifestations of Jesus, which is common among the Methodists', says the narrator, she appeals to them to *see* afresh: 'see where our blessed Lord stands and weeps, and stretches out his arms towards you . . . See the print of the nails on his dear hands and feet' (1.40). Hidden within the pastoral landscape is the reality the true shepherd seeks to reveal to them, as her 'mild loving eyes took an expression of appalled pity, as if she had suddenly discerned a destroying angel hovering over the heads of the people' (1.37). It is a form of typology, indicating that this is the reality they have to recognise and live out in the present, whatever their own assumptions might be. Life can only be interpreted in the terms into which everything must eventually resolve itself and be fulfilled. The lesson she provides for the startled Bessy Cranage, whose fate is a caricature of Hetty's, is that of the vain young girl who 'one day when she put her new cap on and looked in the glass, she saw a bleeding Face crowned with thorns' (1.42). Such a radical change of perspective challenges the conventions of fictional verisimilitude – that other kind of mirror – apparently favoured by the narrator as well as by the inhabitants of Hayslope.

The new vision Dinah is offering is explained by the story upon which her sermon is based – a concise version of the whole biblical narrative. First, there is the awareness of God through creation and design: 'We know very well we are altogether in the hands of God . . . the daylight, and the wind, and the corn, and the cows to give us milk – everything we have comes from God.' But then, questions arise about the bad harvests, pain and suffering: 'For our life is full of trouble, and if God sends us good, he seems to send bad too. How is it? how is it?' The answer to this question (*Unde malum?*) which is asked repeatedly in the novel is provided by the gospel: 'Then Dinah told how the good news had been brought, and how the mind of God towards the poor had been made manifest in the life of Jesus, dwelling on its lowliness and its acts of mercy' (1.33–4). In this way Dinah's dissenting sermon also challenges the social hierarchies of Hayslope as well as its other normative assumptions. Jesus, through his incarnation, 'has showed us what God's heart is, what are his feelings towards us' (1.36). But the climax of her salvation story is the appeal to sinners through the events of the passion – the betrayal, Gethsemane, the scourging, the crucifixion, the cry of dereliction, his forgiveness. Dinah acts out the whole drama before them; she sees the events and becomes the crucified Christ ('Ah! what pain!') offering through her love the salvation they, the villagers, reject as they sink 'into a dark bottomless pit' (1.42). The diminuendo of her conclusion is an account of 'the joys that were in store for the penitent' when 'heaven is begun upon earth, because no cloud passes between the soul and God' (1.43), and no further mediation or explanation is needed.

The whole sermon is a lengthy and vivid pastiche which asserts the claims of the Christian master-plot in the rural Arcadia of Hayslope. George Eliot is careful to distance herself from its intensities by means of its stylised language, and by handing over the narrative point of view to an anonymous stranger; but his scepticism about women preachers and Methodists is gradually overcome as he listens to her impassioned sermon 'as if it had been the development of a drama'

(1.44). He reappears at the end of the novel – he is the governor of the prison – when the fulfilment of this drama reaches its climax. The sermon is both a drama which uses the whole gamut of preaching methods – prayer, biblical quotation, redaction, direct appeals, personal experiences, exemplary anecdotes – to present the reality of sin and salvation, and it is also an elaborate exercise in hermeneutics. Dinah interprets, for example, the meaning of the passion story as she dramatises it; at another level, she explains the meaning of Jesus's own teaching ministry; she also sketches out the significance of the whole biblical narrative from Genesis to Revelation. But at its most general level, the sermon is about making sense of life by reconciling meaning and event, and at the centre of Dinah's exegesis is the Incarnation, that mediation between God and man, or, in Feuerbach's terms, between the noumenal and the phenomenal, abstraction and perception.[9] What exactly the Incarnation signifies in *Adam Bede* depends on how the biblical narrative is displaced into and interrogated by the novel.

Dinah, however, exists on the periphery of Hayslope life, only bringing her message of sin, suffering, and redemption during brief visits or through her letters. She must always return to the poor and needy of Stonyshire in order not to be tempted from the creator to his creatures. It is through these repeated withdrawals that George Eliot suggests Dinah's limitations. She has been called to minister to others, not to have any joys or sorrows of her own (1.48); but, as Mrs Poyser points out in frustration, this makes reciprocal relations impossible: 'if everybody was to do like you, the world must come to a standstill . . . Everybody 'ud be wanting everybody else to preach to 'em, istead o' bringing up their families and laying by against a bad harvest' (1.113–14). She objects to Dinah's placid disengagement from the world in which she herself is so embroiled, and to her refusal to listen to commonsense arguments. 'When there's a bigger maggot than usual in your head you call it "direction": and then nothing can stir you – you look like the statty o' the outside o' Treddles'on church, a-starin' and a-smilin' whether it's fair weather or foul. I hanna common patience with you' (1.115). Mrs Poyser translates Dinah's interpretative principle of 'direction' into a 'maggot' or a whim. This is not simply pique. Mrs Poyser, in her busy unease, has constant forebodings that Dinah's help is needed in Hayslope, and that her rejection of this role is a form of self-indulgence: 'as I told her, she went clean again' the Scriptur', for that says, "love your neighbour as yourself"; "but," I said, "if you loved your neighbour no better nor you do yourself, Dinah, it's little enough you'd do for him. You'd be thinking he might do well enough on a half-empty stomach"' (1.286–7). In other words, Mrs Poyser, a central figure in Hayslope, wittily and anxiously deconstructs Dinah's otherworldliness, just as Mrs Cadwallader does with Dorothea in *Middlemarch*. It is a matter of expression as well as of values. When, for example, Mrs Poyser comments on her sister Judith, who brought up the motherless Dinah, that 'she'd bear a pound weight any day, to save anybody else carrying a ounce', Dinah placidly translates the sentiment into her own stylised discourse: 'She was a blessed woman . . . God had given her a loving, self-forgetting nature, and he perfected it by grace' (1.111–12). The racy, proverbial style gives way to the impersonal and emblematic which sees the world in abstract typological terms.

In one sense, Dinah is living in a dream world, cut off by her selflessness from the reality around her. She has no roots and will make no plans for the future. Whether she is suffering the anguish of creation groaning and travailing, or reposing in her more contemplative moments, she is invariably absorbed 'in thoughts that had no connection with the present moment or with her own personality' (1.45). Her hold on the external world is tenuous. She is a channel for God's spirit, she tells the sceptical Anglican Irvine, and therefore must wait passively, though she is aware of the dangers: 'for when I'm not greatly wrought upon, I'm too much given to sit still and keep by myself: it seems as if I could sit silent all day long with the thoughts of God overflowing my soul – as the pebbles lie bathed in the Willow Brook . . . and it's my besetment to forget where I am and everything about me, and lose myself in thoughts that I could give no account of' (1.131). Such self-abnegation becomes a self-indulgent dream. Without selfhood, she cannot relate to individuals in their temporal immediacy; she has first to place them in the perspective of her timeless vision of suffering humanity. As she tells the mystified Hetty, it is only when she is alone that Dinah fully experiences the presence of the people she has known: 'I hear their voices and see them look and move almost plainer than I ever did when they were really with me so as I could touch them'. Only then can she 'feel their lot as if it was my own' (1.211). But this form of translation can be circuitous and belated as we see later when Dinah, sensing that Hetty is in trouble, is unable to read the obvious clues and act upon them. Instead, she is granted a glimpse of Hetty's ultimate fate *sub specie aeternitatis* as an antitype of the lamb or scapegoat: 'her imagination had created a thorny thicket of sin and sorrow, in which she saw the poor thing struggling torn and bleeding, looking with tears for rescue and finding none' (I.236). Even then, she must verify her vision against a random opening of the Bible before she dare approach Hetty, and then the opportunity is wasted because she is unable to speak personally and directly.

Dinah is vividly aware of a world of suffering and the master-plot of salvation, but is imperceptive about its particular manifestations in time and place. She occupies simultaneously a spiritually timeless world and the immediate present – 'It's good to live only a moment at a time' (I.51), she says – but not the temporal middle ground, as it were, in which the normal rules of perspective apply and in which development takes place and selfhood is achieved. She is cut off from this world and, like her fellow Methodists, relies for her understanding of it on inner promptings, the drawing of lots, revelations by dreams and visions, and opening the Bible at hazard (I.52–3). But the received wisdom of Hayslope provides a resistant medium to her visions. Only when they lose their confident grasp of their rustic reality does she take on substance for them. Lizbeth Bede, for example, alienated from the familiar by the loss of her husband, is brought to a new acceptance of life and death by Dinah who, materialising 'like the shadow on the wall' (I.162), gets down to the practical business of cleaning the house and preparing the food. In a scene of suffering, her typological vision meshes with and gives meaning to the immediate reality: 'But now, dear friend, drink this other cup of tea and eat a little more' (I.165). But as soon as grief is relieved, she melts away, back to the ascetic milieu of Stonyshire, to what Mrs Poyser calls 'that bare heap o' stones as the very crows fly over an' won't stop at' (II.283). Dinah embodies a suffering vision of the world, but without a life of her own she does not suffer.

Hetty, in contrast, appears to be fully in harmony with pastoral Hayslope. Her beauty is perfectly natural and in the Poyser's dairy she performs the bucolic rites of Arcadia, but like Dinah, she never really belongs to the community. She is the daughter of Mr Poyser's dead sister who married the wastrel Sorrel and who has never been forgiven by the family. She is an interloper whose beauty questions Hayslope values, as much as Dinah's asceticism, because the villagers can't interpret it in terms of character or morality. Hetty is completely natural in her amorality, and her career in the novel acts out the implications of this. Just as the community is unsympathetic to

Dinah's preaching, so they drive Hetty away when she acts out her natural hedonism. Like Dinah, she is not fully human, as her frequent comparison to animals, birds, and plants suggests: the moral life can only arise from the self's reciprocal interaction with others, and Hetty and the community are mutually incoherent. The complexity of the presentation of the two cousins in the novel depends on their alternation and juxtaposition, as the world expands to Dinah's selflessness or contracts to Hetty's self-absorption, the disconnected systole and diastole of the moral life.

Hetty's world is also a dream but in her case, of the self. It has taken on a new intensity with the appearance of Arthur Donnithorne, the means of fulfilling ambitions which are not simply pastoral. This new influence is

vague, atmospheric, shaping itself into no self-confessed hopes or prospects, but producing a pleasant narcotic effect, making her tread the ground and go about her work in a sort of dream, unconscious of weight or effort, and showing her all things through a soft, liquid veil, as if she were living not in this solid world of brick and stone, but in a beatified world, such as the sun lights up for us in the waters. (1.146)

Again, the solid world dissolves, this time through the lucid veil of Hetty's romantic fantasies where life is conducted in a watery, unstable medium of wish-fulfilment. At the height of her dreams Hetty, like Dinah, has no more sense of her physical self than if she had been a water-lily – but in her case it is because of the intensity of her desire for Arthur who eventually becomes for her 'a river-god, who might any time take her to his wondrous halls below a watery heaven' (1.202) for her consummation in a pagan world of luxury. It is a vision which in its single focus is, like Dinah's, proof against the ironies – at first comic, later tragic – that Arthur is the callow young squire in the regimentals of the Loamshire militia. It moulds the world to its desire through its own kind of pagan typology, that of Ovidian metamorphosis. The Fir-tree Grove of their secret meetings is haunted by the nymphs: 'you see their white sunlit limbs gleaming athwart the boughs . . . you hear their soft liquid laughter – but if you look with a too curious sacrilegious eye, they vanish behind the silvery beeches, they make you believe that their voice was only a running brooklet, perhaps they metamorphose themselves into a tawny squirrel' (1.192). Like Christian typology, this classical vision requires a special angle of perception; without it the shapes and sounds, the weeping and the laughter, dissolve back into nature. From the extreme of either imaginative vision, the apparently solid world is infinitely malleable and can be dissolved, diffused, and dissipated, in order to be re-created according to the observer's beliefs. Stability is only achieved through the delicate tension of self and other, or in optical terms between the eye and its object. In their visions, however, space becomes watery and hallucinatory, and time disintegrates into timeless moment as they achieve transcendence through their own typologies. When Arthur kisses Hetty ('and for a long moment time has vanished') they are metamorphosed into the antitype of the classical world: 'He may be a shepherd in Arcadia for ought he knows, he may be the first youth kissing the first maiden, he may be Eros himself, sipping the lips of Psyche – it is all one' (1.204).

Hetty's dream of desire discounts, by its nature, everything which fails to conform to its wishes. And again it is Mrs Poyser who delivers the sharpest critique: 'She's no better than a peacock, as 'ud strut about on the wall, and spread its tail when the sun shone if all the folks i' the parish was dying.' Her 'heart's as hard as a pebble' (1.232–3), not submerged like Dinah in thoughts of God, but in her private desires. She is a cherry with a hard stone (not a maggot) inside it, and 'things take no more hold on her than if she was a dried pea' (II.75). She has no roots in the community and is unconcerned about its day-to-day life, 'isolated from all appeals by a barrier of dreams – by invisible looks and impalpable arms' (1.147), by the looks and arms of her Olympian god, Arthur, rather than those of Christ crucified, but they create a similar state of abstraction from the present. Arthur is only the occasion for her fantasies; her true object of worship is herself, before whose image in the mirror she practises her 'religious rites' (1.223). She needs other people only for their approval or as agents of her desire, and when they fail to conform they elicit either annoyance or that most rudimentary of the moral senses, shame. Her 'vision of consequences' has the obtuseness of a felicific calculus, 'at no time more than a narrow fantastic calculation of her own probable pleasures and pains' (II.76). Like Dinah's, her vision dissolves the solid shapes of rustic reality, and the *status quo* is no constraint to her calculus in which the young squire is required to play his part.

There is one further quality Dinah and Hetty, these moral antinomies, have in common. In their exclusive focus they both become their opposites. We have seen how Dinah's selflessness appears to be, when viewed from the middle-ground of the community, a form of self-indulgence. Similarly, Hetty's self-engrossed beauty becomes an impersonal symbol transcending her selfishness with which it appears to have no correlation. This is why everyone is both fascinated and baffled by it, as even Mrs Poyser confesses to her husband, for 'the naughtier the little huzzy behaved, the prettier she looked' (1.121). It is all part of George Eliot's interrogation of the pastoral convention, the pathetic fallacy, the argument from design, upon all of which she plays many variations. 'Nature has her language, and she is not unveracious; but we don't know all the intricacies of her syntax yet, and in a hasty reading we may happen to extract the very opposite of her real meaning' (1.229). So Hetty's beauty, freed from any moral significance, becomes a universal symbol, another form of typology, to which the nobler characters in the novel respond: 'There are faces which nature charges with a meaning and pathos not belonging to the single human soul that flutters beneath them, but speaking the joys and sorrows of foregone generations' (1.430).

Both Dinah and Hetty, then, have their agendas – the narrative of salvation and the narrative of desire – which they hope to see fulfilled in Hayslope. Their radical visions are based on contrasting typologies, one Christian, one classical and pagan, by means of which the pastoral norm is dismembered, even as their own exclusive perspectives are shown to be in their disjunction radically unstable. The other theodicies of Hayslope are defined and assessed within these two extremes.

The inhabitants of Hayslope are the embodiment of world-views which seek to reconcile and moderate in a variety of ways the extremes represented by Dinah and Hetty. Unlike the two interlopers, they all appear to be at one with the world through their roles in the community, a stability expressed through and confirmed by the idioms derived directly from their social status, class, and function. These characters are immediately recognisable as types – the village carpenter, the rector, the schoolmaster, the farmer's wife – but this is a typology of a different kind. Rather than the biblical or classical typology of anticipation and fulfilment, these are social types apparently secure in the community: the way they interpret the world and the way in which the world interprets them reflect each other.

This is the pastoral of character of *Adam Bede* which finds expression in a series of carefully graduated modes: there is the upper-class pastoralism of the Squire, his heir, the Rector, and his mother; then there is the pastoralism of the established farmers like the Poysers; next that of the skilled artisans like the Bedes; and finally the pastoralism of the farmworkers, the Hayslope version of the classical Tityrus and Meliboeus (II.348), seen and heard best at a distance. The social hierarchy establishes their differences but, at first sight, they all seem to enjoy an enviable permanence and security within a community which is accepted as a fact of nature. Things seem to fit together symmetrically in a pattern of mutual self-interest which is controlled by the rhythm of the seasons and the festivals which punctuate them. The disturbing presence of Dinah and Hetty, however, whose imaginative visions question the *status quo*, quickly uncovers the discrepancies between public forms and private feelings which the narrative ironically exploits. The complex time-scheme of the novel repeatedly undercuts the public celebrations with private agony: Arthur's inheritance of the estate, for example, coincides with the death of his unknown child.[10] But even before the narrative subversion gets under way, the reader senses in Hayslope a sharpness of comment, an acerbity of temper, an intolerance of anything failing to conform to its *mores*, which indicate an unease, a lack of trust which shouldn't be mistaken for the vivid and crusty rustic realism, much praised by George Eliot's reviewers. It is the purpose of *Adam Bede* to revise radically that idea of pastoral verisimilitude.

What these pastoral theodicies refuse to accept is the inevitability of the personal experience of sin and suffering (*Unde malum?*). If Dinah and Hetty embody extreme, almost impersonal visions of life – the typology of suffering and that of desire – which cannot be viewed in one perspective, then each of the characters in the community embody, as it were, this anamorphism within themselves. In the phrase from *Childe Harold* used to describe Mr Poyser, they are all 'antithetically mixed'.[11] The stability of the pastoral types, those mediations between the self and the world, proves to be illusory, as it must, given the assumption that life in George Eliot's terms is a never-ending series of hypotheses, testings, and partial resolutions. World-views which deny this are either radically exclusive or contradictory.

At the top of the social scale, there is the Squire and Mrs Irwine, the Rector's mother, who occupy their superior positions by divine right. The bejewelled old lady, 'as erect in her comely embonpoint as a statue of Ceres' (1.79), exercises a sharp sarcasm with which to check any infringements on her position, and a shrewdness of observation which is given strong pagan, magical qualities. She deploys these powers most regally at the birthday-feast, when she presides at the prize-giving like an unfeeling senior goddess. But her shrewdness is based on a simple and exclusive Platonism. Despite her son's objections, she insists that her sharp, long-sighted eyes are all that she needs to decipher the world: 'Nature never makes a ferret in the shape of a mastiff. You'll never persuade me that I can't tell what men are by their outsides' (1.93). Perception is very definitely a form of interpretation. And ugliness is excluded, whenever possible, from the vistas of the estate. It is an ethos George Eliot frequently embodies in a neo-classical, stylised eighteenth-century landscape, where the perspective is cunningly arranged to enhance what is socially and aesthetically acceptable. It is a world of externals which, in this case, dispenses with the presence of Mrs Irwine's faded daughters, 'inartistic figures crowding the canvass of life without adequate effect' (1.96). It is a world in which the débâcle of Arthur's fall from grace cannot be mentioned, even when Mrs Irwine herself acknowledges, with unwitting irony, that Hetty does seem an anomaly in this Platonic universe: 'What a pity such beauty as that should be thrown away among the farmers, when it's wanted so terribly among the good families without fortune!' (1.413).

Her moral obtuseness is shared by her godson, Arthur, who sympathises with her views on Hetty but is less rigid about the responsibilities of his social position. Arthur's view of the world incorporates an awareness both of self and others but, as with many inhabitants of Hayslope, these are combined in a limited and finally contradictory way. In his desire to create a harmonious Arcadia without pain or suffering, he enjoys performing deeds of kindness which, says the narrator, 'were the common issue of his weakness and good qualities, of his egoism and his sympathy (11.33). The self and other are combined, as with Hetty, in a felicific calculus. The ego is seeking pleasure, and deeds of kindness prompt other people to provide the approbation Arthur needs. He especially enjoys bestowing favours in the community – like the promotion of Adam – which bring him approval and which also advance his own interests. These are the little dramas, Irwine comments, 'in which friend Arthur piques himself on having a pretty part to play' (1.38), complacently creating an identity for himself out of his tenant-audience's goodwill.

But this identity is only secure so long as Arthur's pleasures and other people's approval coincide. When they don't, as in the seduction of Hetty, he has to conceal his actions, thereby cutting his impression-able nature off from the source of its moral constraints. When the lovers are discovered by the irate Adam, for example, Arthur's self-approbation and his identity are simultaneously shattered, but he is not prepared to abandon his calculus in the face of a single error. Circumstances are malleable in accordance with the pleasure principle and he will tell Adam what he would like to hear. Suffering cannot be acknowledged. So begins what the narrator calls 'this vitiating effect of an offence against his own sentiment of right', expressed once again in terms of angles of vision, perspective, and forms of perception. Actions which before commission were seen clearly, are 'looked at afterwards with the lens of apologetic ingenuity' (II.37) and their consequences discounted. And once Adam has been reassured, Arthur feels he has dealt with the problem. He will certainly look after Hetty's interests in the future to repay her for any disappointment, and the aristocratic pastoral will be re-established: 'So good comes out of evil. Such is the beautiful arrangement of things!' (II.36).

As Arthur's mentor, it is the Rector's task to suggest that life is less harmonious than his pupil had assumed. At first sight, Irwine seems hardly equipped to do this. He shares some of his mother's epicurean fastidiousness and his 'mental palate, indeed, was rather pagan, and found a savouriness in a quotation from Sophocles or Theocritus that was quite absent from any text in Isaiah or Amos' (I.99–100). He is a pastor, comments the narrator, who 'somehow harmonised extremely well with that peaceful landscape' (I.101) of Loamshire, believing that 'live and let live' is the best response to the spiritual challenge of the Methodists. And he provides his congregation with the weekly reassurance which they all, like Mrs Poyser, value: 'it makes you think the world's comfortable-like'. But there is another, contrasting side to Irwine's character which is also part of his classicism. He has a strong sense of the irrevocable nemesis of wrongdoing. This is the awareness he tries to convey to Arthur, who is seeking to discount actions performed in uncharacteristic moods. But the moods are part of his nature, replies Irwine, who shares the strict determinism of the farmers: 'A man can never do anything at variance with his own nature.' Potentially unpleasant consequences must be kept in the mind's eye as a warning against temptation, as 'a sort of smoked glass through which you may look at the resplendent fair one and discern her true outline'. This will pre-empt the need for the 'lens of apologetic ingenuity' after the event. Irwine acknowledges in his tolerant way that 'the smoked glass is apt to be missing just at the moment it is most wanted' (1.257), but if so, he adds: 'Consequences are unpitying. Our deeds carry their terrible consequences, quite apart from any fluctuations that went before – consequences that are hardly ever confined to ourselves.' The more a person struggles against temptation before succumbing, the more he will experience 'the inward suffering which is the worst form of Nemesis' (1.258).

Irwine fails, however, as Arthur's mentor through his excessive fastidiousness. The reason is that he is another of the antithetically mixed characters in Hayslope. In his case, this is not the result of an attempt to deny the existence of suffering. His unyielding doctrine of consequences is an explanation of suffering and the way it spreads uncontrollably; this is what gives him his 'subtle moral fibre'. But this doctrine is combined with an easy-going epicureanism which subtly undercuts the lesson he is trying to convey. That very different pastor, Dinah, provides the clue to Irwine's ineffectiveness when she tells him, in her forthright way, that she has noticed in villages like Hayslope 'a strange deadness to the Word' (1.134). His doctrine of consequences and nemesis carries a warning without offering any means of repentance and redemption, no possibility of the transmutation of pain into sympathy. On the one hand, there is the irrevocableness of consequences, on the other, an epicurean enjoyment of life; the two fit together as a calculus, without synthesising into a redemptive vision. Like all George Eliot's pupils, Arthur seeks to reconcile these elements of his mentor's world-view in a more felicific manner by his own theory of life. There, Nemesis becomes Providence, and the epicureanism less fastidious. So, however much the narrator seeks to extenuate Irwine, the shepherd of the pastoral world, the aged Adam has to admit retrospectively that he 'didn't go into deep speritial experience': 'There's things go on in the soul, and times when feelings come into you like a rushing mighty wind, as the Scripture says, and part your life in two a'most, so as you look back on yourself as if you was somebody else' (1.274). But the pentecostal experience has initially no place in Hayslope.

George Eliot ranges through the various classes of the community eliciting the same pattern in a variety of forms, an inner equilibrium without genuine synthesis. Lacking a view of the world in which suffering is integral, they exclude, often harshly, those elements which don't conform to the nature of things. This often finds expression in an apparent incongruity of character such as Mr Poyser's harshness. His mild contentment with life is coterminous with the stable assumptions of the farming community; but if any of these are transgressed – by lackadaisical farmers or his niece Hetty – his anger is implacable and dismissive. Such hardness seems endemic to Hayslope, in George Eliot's harsh critique; it is the price paid for pastoral equilibrium. The most extreme example of this potential instability is Mrs Poyser who occupies a position in the novel midway between the extremes of her two nieces, both of whom she criticises and is fascinated by. In this role she is shrewd and authoritative, but she fails to replace the dangers of the two extremes with a vision which reconciles and synthesises. One side of her character is at ease in Hayslope. She rejoices in the lush countryside of Loamshire and in the Hall Farm which she runs efficiently, comparing it favourably with the starved acres of Stonyshire from where she originates. She is respectful to the gentry, maintains the old traditions, and is appalled that her Methodist niece has been seen preaching in the village. She also shares the villagers' confidence in their ability to see through appearances to reality: 'Some cheeses are made o' skimmed milk and some o' new milk, and it's no matter what you call 'em, you may tell which is which by the look and the smell' (1.138). This, in turn, confirms her sense of determinism and dogmatic judgments: Thias Bede is best dead because he was a troublemaker.

There is, in juxtaposition to this, a very different side to her character which reminds us that she is related to Dinah, that she suffers from a recurrent illness, and comes from Stonyshire. She has bouts of anxiety in which she becomes very aware of the suffering and evil inherent in the solid pastoral comfortableness of Hayslope. Whatever the situation, however apparently favourable, Mrs Poyser can discern a lurking menace. Her fears gather an accumulative force through the novel. The pleasures of the birthday feast, for example, present themselves to her simply as an opportunity for the forces of evil to take over the farm: 'and they all collogue together, them tramps, as it's a mercy they hanna come and pisoned the dogs and murdered us all in our beds afore we knowed, some Friday night when we'n got the money in the house to pay the men'. The basis for her fear comes at the end: 'for if Old Harry wants any work done, you may be sure he'll find the means' (1.379). She expresses her conviction that the devil is at work everywhere in a series of apocalyptic visions. Loamshire might be the land of Goshen but, when the Squire threatens their tenancy of the farm, she ripostes that any new tenant won't like 'a house wi' all the plagues o' Egypt in't – wi' the cellar full o' water, and frogs and toads hoppin' up the steps by dozens – and the floors rotten, and the rats and mice gnawing every bit o' cheese, and runnin' over our heads as we lie i' bed till we expect 'em to eat us up alive – as it's a mercy they hanna eat the children long ago'. In this mood she abandons her appreciation of Hayslope and her respect for the *status quo*, becoming as subversive as her nieces. In particular, she attacks the Squire when she feels he is trying to outmanoeuvre them, telling him he has 'Old Harry' as his friend (ii.88–9), and although it jeopardises their tenancy she can't help herself, she must 'have her say out'. Thus, like the other inhabitants, she has a double vision of the world which leads her into contradiction and self-defeat.

Mrs Poyser is central to the novel because of her keen awareness of each side of the contradiction, and her ability to express them both so sharply. Though she criticises Dinah and Hetty, she responds to each of them in turn, and in her sharp visions domesticates their typologies into her own vivid vernacular. This is the significance of the episode of the dropped beer mugs when Hetty parodies Dinah's Methodist dress and demeanour: 'The thought of Dinah's pale grave face and mild grey eyes, which the sight of the gown and cap brought with it, made it a laughable surprise enough to see them replaced by Hetty's rosy cheeks and coquettish dark eyes' (1.343). Dinah in Hayslope is already an anomaly, but Dinah imitated by Hetty is a double anamorphosis. They all enjoy the joke except Mrs Poyser who, at the centre of the scene, is disturbed by the ambiguous apparition. It is as if she knows that the incongruous image is prophetic, that the contradictory dimensions of reality of which she especially is vividly aware have finally to be brought together, and that this reconciliation will only come through the suffering of a genuine apocalypse. She quickly quells the laughter with another of her imaginary scenarios: 'an' I know one thing, as if trouble was to come, an' I was to be laid up i' my bed, an' the children was to die – as there's no knowing but what they will – an' the murrain was to come among the cattle again, an' everything went to rack an' ruin – I say we might be glad to get sight o' Dinah's cap again, wi' her own face under it' (1.344). Her Manichean world is the expression of the antithetical mixture of her character. And this is the basis for her set-piece attack on Bartle Massey, the epitome of male complacency with its belief in rationality.

Finally, there is the Bede family. Here George Eliot relates four other world-views in the form of an hereditary diagram of forces, in a way which will be developed further in *The Mill on the Floss*. It is a family in which – by definition, the author implies – there is tension and conflict held in precarious pastoral balance. 'Nature, that great tragic dramatist, knits us together by bone and muscle, and divides us by the subtler web of our brains; blends yearning and repulsion; and ties us by our heartstrings to the beings that jar us at every moment' (1.55). The Bedes are trapped, in the phrase from Aeschylus, within the 'unloving love' (1.386–7), that central contradiction in the novel, by which Irwine answers Arthur's baffled question: why does his grandfather leave him all his money even though he appears to hate him? This is a crucial expression of the unresolved tensions between individual and communal values in the pastoral world which finds various expressions. The father of the family, Thias, for example, is a skilled carpenter from Stonyshire with a mild, passive disposition, who has turned to alcohol as an escape from his wife who is a mixture of opposites – 'at once patient and complaining, self-renouncing and exacting' – and with 'no joy but in the happiness of the loved ones whom she contributed to make uncomfortable' (1.60). Her love, especially for Adam, is 'idolatrous'. Seeing her sons as part of her own life, she is unable to free them into a genuinely loving relationship. As with all these contradictory world-views, she defeats herself: her love is so intense, so close, so perceptive, that she is compelled to alienate them. With nagging querulousness she criticises one son for his pride and the other for his humility, but the one thing unthinkable is life without them; even life-after-death can only be envisaged as a continuation of family togetherness: 'I'll ne'er rest i' my grave if I donna see thee i' the churchyard of a Sunday' (1.179), she tells Adam. It is an unflinching exposure of the contradictions of maternal love through which Lisbeth Bede interprets the world.

The sons are compounds of their parents' qualities. Seth combines his mother's self-renouncing love with his father's passivity and escapism. The result is a characterless man who paradoxically seeks fulfilment through the self-denial of his love for Dinah, recommending himself to her on the grounds that he won't interfere in her life in any way. This is his own self-defeating felicific calculus, the only way he can bring together the two sides of his character. Without a clear identity, he fades from the novel after Dinah rejects him, acknowledging as his religious faith falters that his love for her is in its own way idolatrous: 'Perhaps I feel more for you than I ought to feel for any creature' (1.50). Seth is in sharp contrast to Adam who has inherited his father's skills and his mother's exacting sense of duty and practicality. At the centre of the novel, poised between Dinah's sense of the divine and Hetty's sense of self, he is the most integrated of its inhabitants, with values and a philosophy of life which seem proof against any emergency, a character out of Samuel Smiles. He is also at the centre of Hayslope society, enjoying established relationships with the gentry, the Poysers, the schoolmaster, the clergyman, and exercising a firm but fair control of his workmen. He is almost universally respected and admired – a kind of Nostromo of the community – and consequently the testing of his values is the most critical for the pastoral ethos as a whole.

Adam's moral universe consists essentially of God and his own conscience, both of which are defined through the idiom of his carpentry. He walks into the novel singing Bishop Ken's morning hymn, recommending a 'conscience clear' beneath 'God's all-seeing eye' (1.4). The two fit together in the divine plan. The effect is to give Adam a trust in the divine order which he feels it improper to question, and a keen self-sufficiency in the world where he is master of his trade. But the narrator elicits the incongruities that make up this self-sufficiency: 'he had that mental combination which is at once humble in the region of mystery, and keen in the region of knowledge'; he is 'at once penetrating and credulous'; he 'had the blood of the peasant in him as well as of the artisan' (1.70); and, finally, he is both Saxon and Celt. He is a composite character whose confidence in his own integrity and identity issues in a form of spiritual pride which he himself is half-aware of at the beginning of the novel. In other words, he is another version of the pastoralism of character in which the self and the universe seem to fit together harmoniously. The crucial faculty in Adam's calculus is the conscience. This is the mechanism which guides him and makes wrongdoing pointless, as he says to Arthur: 'It takes the taste out o' my mouth for things, when I know I should have a heavy conscience after 'em . . . It's like a bit o' bad workmanship – you never see th'end o' the mischief it'll do' (1.250). Society works on the same principle of mutual self-interest, as he says in his speech of thanks at the birthday-feast. So while Arthur and Adam appear to be contradictory in their views and behaviour, they are both versions of pastoral: the former believes that things are licit if pleasurable, while the latter moralises this naive pastoralism into the form of pleasing if licit. In literary terms it is a version of the famous dispute between Tasso and Guarini.[12] In religious terms all the various world-views of Hayslope can be grouped around the two major solutions to the problem of theodicy (*unde malum?*): on the one hand, the dualistic or Manichean conception of a conflict between good and evil principles, on the other, the monistic conception in which only the good exists and evil, a form of non-being, simply serves the good.

Since the laws of this world are self-evident, Adam asserts the claims of God over the gospel, and the claims of the conscience over the unhealthy spirituality of the Methodists. In contrast to Dinah's master-plot, his account of life sees no need for a suffering Saviour as mediator. When Adam becomes convinced of a proposition about the world, 'it took the form of a principle in his mind: it was knowledge to be acted on, as much as the knowledge that damp will cause rust'. Whereas Seth accepts weakness and suffering with placid disengagement, Adam acts is if it could be eradicated by brisk application. This is how his strength becomes hardness, as his attitude to his father demonstrates: 'he had too little fellow-feeling with the weakness that errs in spite of foreseen consequences'. And it is the death of Thias Bede which begins to teach Adam at least 'the alphabet' (1.316) if not the language of suffering, and the inadequacy of his own theory of life. In his pride and sense of duty he misreads the mysterious tap of the willow-wand – and Thias drowns in the brook. As Adam acknowledges at the funeral, 'the devil *will* be having his finger in what we call our duties as well as our sins' (1.330). This sudden death challenges his calculus by teaching him the lesson that 'there's no real making amends in this world' (1.304), but he has to experience it more directly through Hetty. And it is from this point in the novel that he begins to cultivate more romantic dreams about her, quite out of keeping with his public character. As his stoical determinism hardens – 'the natur o' things doesn't change . . . The square o' four is sixteen' (1.171) – he must seek relief in the 'margin of dreams' (11.303) which he creates out of his wilful misreading of Hetty's actions and which will lead ultimately to despair and the destruction of that stoicism – and, after that, to the fusion of his reverence and independence, his humility and pride, the Saxon and the Celt.

Many of Adam's attitudes to life have been derived from his mentor, Bartle Massey the schoolteacher, who defines the antinomies that his pupil has to reconcile in his own way. Massey's view is the harshest in the pastoral world, and results from his lameness and his bitter but concealed relations with women in the past. (This past is one of several concealed narratives in *Adam Bede*.) He is a soft-centred Gradgrind, anxious to equip his bucolic pupils for the world by means of mensuration, spelling, writing, and reading. He considers that the only way to deal with life, this painful interim between birth and death, is to rationalise it as far as possible, and this entails the exclusion of both women and emotion. When his favourite pupil Adam – seeking a more comprehensive view than his teacher – suggests that women may belong to the scheme of things, he is incensed. Eve might have been the proper companion of the first Adam in Paradise, 'But it's an impious, unscriptural opinion to say a woman's a blessing to a man now; you might as well say adders and wasps, and foxes and wild beasts, are a blessing when they're only the evils that belong to this state o' probation, which it's lawful for a man to keep as clear of as he can in this life, hoping to get quit of 'em for ever in another' (1.361). Like Irwine, that other bachelor mentor, he fails his pupil in this regard – Hetty is the stumbling block in each case – and this is why Massey responds so harshly in his misogyny when the infanticide becomes known. Hetty is as dispensable as the adders and the wasps sent to plague rational man in his state of probation, for it is crucial to note that, although Massey acknowledges the world as a place of travail, the suffering is probationary and not redemptive. His conflict with Mrs Poyser, which rumbles through the novel and culminates in their public debate, reflects the symmetry of their attitudes to the opposite sex. Massey seeks a world without the confusions of feminine irrationality; Mrs Poyser seeks one without the complacent male obtuseness which ignores the uncertainties of life. Their conflict underlines the fact that the pastoral theodicies are categorised by gender as well as by class.

In the relatively static world of Hayslope, one feels at times that these characters constitute a gallery of representative types, a leisurely display which underlines the economy of the later novels. But it is essential to recognise that they are depicted by George Eliot as types in the limiting sense that they are products of a pastoral community which turns away from the reality of suffering. Their latent instability, the symptom of this, surfaces when the typological visions of the two Poyser nieces begin to be disturbingly and simultaneously realised in Hayslope. This leads to the crisis of the novel which demands that the pastoral world-views be reconstituted. That reconstitution can only be understood in the light of the developing relationship between the two women.

The two women meet only three times in the novel. They come together first just after they have parted from their respective suitors in chapter fourteen. Dinah has finally freed herself from the love of the creature, Seth, preparatory to returning to Stonyshire to serve the creator; while Hetty is becoming more and more entangled with Arthur. Dinah tries unsuccessfully to understand Hetty's happiness, while the latter finds Dinah a 'riddle' she is unable to comprehend. Both are in a state of abstraction from the present – Dinah in a trance of sympathy, Hetty back in the woods with Arthur. This lack of understanding is carried over to their second meeting on the same evening in the stylised diptych of the two bed-chambers, each with its own perspective. Hetty is worshipping her own beauty in the mirror, while Dinah looks out into the night thinking of the people of Hayslope before closing her eyes, 'that she might feel more intensely the presence of a Love and Sympathy deeper and more tender than was breathed from the earth and sky' (1.235). Both are locked into their own visions. Then, the noise of the falling looking-glass forces an immediate awareness of Hetty into Dinah's abstraction: 'her imagination had created a thorny thicket of sin and sorrow, in which she saw the poor thing struggling torn and bleeding, looking with tears for rescue and finding none' (1.236). Abstract and concrete come together in a prophetic vision in which Hetty is seen clearly in the role the community requires her to play, that of the scapegoat. Dinah obtains typological confirmation of this vision from the Bible before tapping on Hetty's door, when they both emerge, still under the influence of their respective visions: Hetty with 'her cheeks flushed and her eyes glistening from her imaginary drama', and Dinah 'almost like a lovely corpse into which the soul has returned charged with sublimer secrets and a sublimer love' (1.238). Again, they both – nature and grace, body and soul – fail to understand each other; and the narrator is anxious to apportion the blame equally. The 'higher nature [too] has to learn this comprehension, as we learn the art of vision, by a good deal of hard experience, often with bruises and gashes incurred in taking things up by the wrong end, and fancying our space wider than it is' (1.240). The art of vision is the acknowledgement that one's own perspective is limited.

This meeting occurs in the first book of the novel and Dinah doesn't reappear in person until the fifth book, in the climactic prison-scene at Stoniton. But midway between these we have her letter to Seth which is juxtaposed with Arthur's letter of rejection to Hetty. The first expresses an identification with suffering humanity, while the second is the sign that the narrow circle of Hetty's fantasies is contracting suddenly and decisively. The epistolary form gives Dinah an even more ghostly reality as she writes about 'the outward light' fading and 'the inward light' shining the brighter, as if she was 'out of the body and could feel no want for evermore'. She experiences 'all the anguish of the children of men ... [which] I can bear with a willing pain, as if I was sharing the Redeemer's cross'. And out of this comes her central belief in the Crucifixion – 'infinite love is suffering too' – which challenges all the theodicies of Hayslope:

> that is a blind self-seeking which wants to be freed from the sorrow wherewith the whole creation groaneth and travaileth. Surely it is not true blessedness to be free from sorrow, while there is sorrow and sin in the world: sorrow is then a part of love, and love does not seek to throw it off. (II.59)

The intensity of her vision of sin and suffering provides her with a further premonition of imminent sorrow at the Hall Farm, but its nature remains obscure. This is, however, clarified for the reader in the second letter, a different kind of love letter, which Hetty is reading in her bedroom. Whereas the first, Pauline-like epistle to Hayslope is seeking to strengthen the community of the 'children of God' which 'can never more be sundered, though the hills may lie between' (II.61), this letter is severing a relationship of mutual self-interest: 'we must try not to feel like lovers any more' (II.65). In her disappointment, Hetty's reaction is to hate everything that frustrates her desires, even Arthur its object: 'She hated the writer of that letter – hated him for the very reason that she hung upon him with all her love – all the girlish passion and vanity that made up her love' (II.68). In this extreme form of 'unloving love', she turns within the narrow circle of her own imagination to herself – to her own weeping image in the mirror awaiting its own crown of thorns – aware that outside are the Poysers and the community at large where she will only discover her own shame and no sympathy. Dinah's vision of the scapegoat is being realised: Hetty can only think of the community's response 'as the sick and weary prisoner might think of the possible pillory'. Her rudimentary moral sense only registers shame, 'and shame was torture' (II.71).

Hetty's journey, initiated shortly afterwards, is the beginning of her move towards Dinah – at first in pretence, eventually in desperation, and finally in confession. It begins in anxiety with her 'seeing nothing in this wide world but the little history of her own pleasures and pains' (II.121), and develops through hope and despair in the inevitable working out of this felicific calculus. The contradictions have been there from the start in that Hetty craves the glamour of Arthur's love but knows she can't enjoy it publicly; his gift of jewellery has to be hidden. The same is true, of course, of her pregnancy and finally of her baby which, in her agony, she conceals and then partly uncovers. It is the journey which strips bare in plain, matter-of-fact prose the illusions and contradictions of a self seeking to escape to the last the suffering of the world which Dinah embraces. After discovering at Windsor that Arthur is in Ireland, she becomes a 'corpse' (II.131), her hopes die, and she enters as scapegoat the 'borders of a new wilderness' (II.135). In her despair she begins to think of Dinah as the only person who does not belong to the Hayslope 'whose glance she dreaded like scorching fire' (II.139). But first, Hetty's calculus has to grapple with the temptation of suicide – the self fulfilling its desire in self-destruction. By now, the underwater world of pastoral delight has become the black pool under the darkening sky, the arcadian images have turned into the poisoned garment of Nessus, Hetty's childish prettiness into 'that wondrous Medusa-face, with the passionate, passionless lips' (II.145). But as food alleviates her pain she glimpses again life's pleasures, relieved to find she is still alive. The self-contradictions are defining themselves more and more sharply: 'She felt a strange contrasting wretchedness and exultation: wretchedness, that she did not dare to face death; exultation, that she was still in life' (II.148). She oscillates between the desire for life and the desire for death, until these become indistinguishable: 'the poor soul, driven to and fro between two equal terrors' (II.149). At this point, when 'Life.. . was as full of dread as of death' (II.152), the narrative of Hetty's journey breaks off. The final stalemate in this primitive conflict of interpretations comes to centre, after a gap in the story, on the death of her child.

These final events of the journey are eventually described through the eyes of the two witnesses at the trial, where the contest between interpretations takes on its public form: the first witness maintains that Hetty is innocent, the second that she is guilty. From these plain, factual but incomplete testimonies the law is satisfied that Hetty abandoned her child which subsequently died, and that on returning to the scene of the crime she was taken into custody. She is found guilty of infanticide and condemned to be hanged. This is the supreme moment of her isolation and despair to which her pastoral fantasy has led. Her shame has prevented her speaking at the trial; the world is too hostile and condemning. To the spectators in court, her appearance confirms the verdict: 'she looked as if some demon had cast a blighting glance upon her, withered up the woman's soul in her, and left only a hard despairing obstinacy' (II.216). When her sentence is declared, Hetty shrieks and Adam vainly reaches out to her, but 'there was a deep horror, like a great gulf, between them' (II.224–5). This is Adam's supreme experience of the irrevocableness of suffering under the law, and through him it is experienced in the community. It is the end of the journey in which Hetty is simultaneously criminal and scapegoat, carrying the sins of the community to their extreme of harshness and despair where she sinks finally into the great gulf of complete isolation. Her isolation is complete because the law has now confirmed her terror of the world; no one has access to the state of mind in which Hetty allowed her baby to die. This is the secret (anamorphic) agony implicit in the pastoral world, the full knowledge of which is still denied to Hayslope and the reader. It is the cul-de-sac of her journey, in which life and death have become indistinguishable. Only a confession can break the isolation of the self, but the community only confirms her exclusion.

This is the situation in which the final meeting of Hetty and Dinah takes place, that origin of the novel towards which the narrative has been moving. On one level the two cousins have been withdrawing more and more completely into their respective worlds; and yet George Eliot has prepared us for their final coming together by a series of incongruous juxtapositions of their images, memories, and now their names which are recorded in Hetty's notebook when she is arrested. In her self-imprisonment she refuses to say which name is hers. Now, when she joins her in the dark cell, Dinah repeats their names in a form of incantation: 'Hetty . . . it's Dinah'; 'Hetty . . . Dinah is come to you'; 'Don't you know me, Hetty? Don't you remember Dinah?' At this moment the two women are still emblematically opposed: 'The two pale faces were looking at each other: one with a

wild hard despair in it, the other full of sad yearning love.' Though she
now turns to Dinah, Hetty 'was not the less sinking into the dark gulf'
(1.240–2). Her only hope is her ghostly cousin to whom she now clings,
their faces gradually becoming indistinguishable as they sink together
into the darkness. This is the extreme point at which their roles
culminate in a complete loss of their identities: as Hetty reaches the
isolation of self-despair, Dinah attains a sympathy with the whole of
creation which groaneth and travaileth. Hetty is able to move
towards Dinah because the latter has no social identity, no links with
Hayslope, is not a character in the way the other people are. Dinah's
abstraction from life, previously a limitation, suddenly takes on a new
reality when life is stripped to its fundamental typological forms of
pain and suffering. Event and meaning come together in the
simplicity of melodrama.

Dinah first asks Hetty to confess 'the sin you have been guilty of
against your heavenly Father'. When Hetty appeals to her ('I can't
feel anything like you . . . my heart is hard'), Dinah makes her own
confession of faith to the Son: 'Jesus, thou present Saviour! Thou hast
known the depths of all sorrow; thou hast entered the black darkness
where God is not, and hast uttered the cry of the forsaken' (11.245).
Dinah identifies Hetty with the cry of dereliction, abandoning her
own already ghostly self in the love of the Saviour: 'What is *my* love
or *my* pleading? It is quenched in thine. I can only clasp her in my
weak arms, and urge her with my weak pity.' Then, finally, she
appeals to the third person of the Trinity to inspire Hetty to confess
her sins; 'breathe upon her thy life-giving Spirit, and put a new fear
within her – the fear of her sin. Make her dread to keep the accursed
thing within her soul.' Dinah appeals in these trinitarian terms as the
final means of achieving the only hope of Hetty's rescue, confession.
The Spirit is the final agency: 'Thou – thou wilt breathe on the dead
soul, and it shall arise from the unanswerable sleep of death' (11.246).
And yet, of course, it is Dinah in her selflessness who is the crucial
human mediator leading Hetty to her redemption. At this, the climax
of the novel, George Eliot is dramatising in this prayer (and the
confession which follows) the coming together of the two cousins in the
symbolic re-enactment of the crucifixion and resurrection of Christ.
The contrasting trajectories of their lives have finally merged in the
darkness of the prison, where Hetty's despair and forsakenness are
identified with Christ's agony, while Dinah's selfless compassion is
Christ's love which redeems, transforming through the Spirit the pain

into sympathy: 'Yea, Lord, I see thee, coming through the darkness, coming like the morning, with healing on thy wings. The marks of thy agony are upon thee – I see, I see thou art able and willing to save – thou wilt not let her perish forever' (ii.246). This is the promise of the master-plot within the narrative, that the two extreme moral dimensions of the novel may finally come together as love and suffering are shown to be identical. All the qualities which had before distanced Dinah from Hayslope – her abstractedness, her lack of identity, her selflessness, her apocalyptic visions – now become strengths. By means of her vivid, almost hallucinatory vision of Christ, she seeks to fit together the two partial lives, her own and Hetty's, in the Passion and so reunify the moral universe. Only in this way can the great gulf be bridged, as Hetty reaches out from her suffering to love and Dinah reaches out from her love to suffering. This is the context in which the hard heart may be melted, the darkness pierced, and Hetty by her confession enabled to break through to the world of others by describing the death of her soul. As so often in the novels, the character in despair will now tell her own story to a sympathetic listener. We move from the biblical type – the hermeneutic paradigm – to the personal history which it will interpret and be realised by.

Hetty's pathetic confession – repeatedly deferred through the six chapters of the search, the spreading of the news, and the trial – completes the narrative of her journey, filling in the blanks left by the other witnesses, and leading the reader and Dinah to the centre of the negative world of the novel. Her story continues to articulate and focus the impossible double-binds of the position in which the narrative left her: she wants, for example, to seek Dinah 'for I didn't think you'd be cross wi' me, and cry shame on me', but she daren't because 'then the other folks 'ud come to know it at last, and I couldn't bear that' (ii.248). Every event has two possible meanings which cancel each other out. Then the baby is born and the conflict intensified, for it comes to epitomise the struggle between Hetty's life-wish (her love for the child) and her death-wish (her sense of shame). Throughout this dramatic monologue, George Eliot is implicitly castigating the community which could create a sense of shame so intense that it equals and cancels Hetty's natural love for her child, 'that completest type of the life in another which is the essence of real human love' (ii.216). In order to break the intolerable deadlock, Hetty is forced to make a choice, and it is shame which predominates as she looks for a place, a ditch or a pond, in which to hide the baby. 'I seemed to hate it – it was like a heavy weight hanging round my neck; and yet its crying went through me' (II.249). The echo of *The Ancient Mariner* picks up an earlier reference to the poem and suggests how the original act of nature has turned into a crime against nature. Then Hetty sees 'a hole under the nut-tree, like a little grave' (II.250); this is the place to which her world finally narrows. She covers the child in the hole, but a vestige of love prevents her hiding it completely.

In the end, the moral conflict resolves itself simply into the two actions of moving away from and moving back towards the baby; as in Gwendolen's jump at the climax of *Daniel Deronda*, the two actions are indistinguishable and inseparable. This is why the legal trial comes first, makes its judgment, and is then superseded by the agony of Hetty's confession, upon which no judgment is possible since she is completely divided in her thoughts and actions. Having placed the baby in the hole, she runs away but has to return because she can hear it crying everywhere she goes, and yet she is 'frightened to death' (II.251) as she does so. Approaching the hole she imagines she hears the crying again, but by now the oscillations of emotion have led to equilibrium: 'I don't know whether I was frightened or glad.' When she sees the baby has gone, she knows the irrevocable has happened, but her response is again completely ambivalent: 'when I'd put it there, I thought I should like somebody to find it, and save it from dying; but when I saw it was gone, I was struck like a stone with fear.' The baby has gone and therefore may be alive; but since it has gone, people will know of her shame and she will be condemned. Then the soul, torn by this unloving love, dies. 'My heart went like a stone . . . it seemed as if I should stay there for ever, and nothing 'ud ever change' (II.252). But people do come to her; only to take her away and condemn her to be hanged.

Hetty's belated narrative is irrelevant as far as her legal guilt or innocence is concerned, but what George Eliot articulates here in the most fundamental way is the inner contradiction of the felicific calculus in all the various forms in which it is practised in Hayslope. This is why Hetty is both the representative of the community as well as its scapegoat. And the result of her self-seeking actions confirms this contradiction: she is both condemned to death by the world she has tried to placate and she loses her child. This moment of negation, to which Hetty has been led in her confession by Dinah, is one in which all moral imperatives are opposed and frozen. The central opposition underpinning everything else is that between suffering and love. In the final sentence of her confession, Hetty expresses this with supreme pathos: 'Dinah, do you think God will take away that crying and the place in the wood, now I've told you everything?' (II.252). Each element has been defined as the tortured symbol of suffering and love: the crying signifies simultaneously that the baby is alive but that people will come to know of her disgrace; the hole in the wood is the baby's grave but, since it was not fully concealed, it held the hope of discovery. Hetty's final state, her heart petrified like a stone, is that of a paralysis in which suffering and love remain opposed, incapable of being transformed into the higher state – the *coincidentia oppositorum* – which Dinah has described in her opening sermon.

This is the reason why Hetty's confession is the supreme statement of moral contradiction and death in the novel, which she has to re-enact and articulate in response to Dinah's own confession of faith, so that the master-plot of salvation may become effective. This re-enactment forces upon Hetty the unresolvable choice through which she becomes in her agony a moral being. All the antinomies of the novel are encapsulated here in the simplest, barest language in what seems to be an irremediable impasse. But at the negative dead centre of this impasse, which is now at last revealed to the reader, the redemption has already begun in the very fact of Hetty's confession, made in response to Dinah's vision of the suffering, loving Saviour. By means of her confession, Hetty breaks out of her deathly isolation where love and shame, self and community, are in frozen contradiction. The extreme moral polarities of the novel are finally brought together, as type and antitype, in the form of these complementary confessional narratives which interpret and realise each other.

As far as Hetty's guilt or innocence is concerned, legal hermeneutics have been superseded by George Eliot's own kind of biblical and fictional hermeneutics as the means of interpreting her actions. In the absence of any confession at the trial, the law has had to reach its verdict on circumstantial evidence. In this, *Adam Bede* shows significant similarities with Scott's *The Heart of Midlothian*, a story of two half-sisters in which a trial for infanticide occupies a central place.[13] In both trials the saintly 'sisters', Dinah and Jeanie, intervene decisively in the fates of the magdalenes, and, in both, legal hermeneutics are shown to be inadequate to penetrate the complexity of human guilt. As the prosecutor says at Effie Dean's trial: 'It was the very purpose of the statute to substitute a certain chain of presumptive evidence in place of a probation, which, in such cases, it was peculiarly

difficult to obtain'.[14] In *Adam Bede*, the complex and uncertain
transmission of Hetty's story through the community, as well as from
the historical past to the reader's present, is an essential aspect of this
interpretative uncertainty.[15] As the narrator acknowledges, 'no story
is the same to us after a lapse of time; or rather, we who read it are no
longer the same interpreters' (II.364). At the climax of the novel there
remains the central indeterminacy: Hetty moves away from and then
towards her child without any resolution of her motives, her love and
shame predominating in turn. As Irwine says, when asked about
Hetty's and Arthur's guilt: 'That perhaps can never be known with
certainty, Adam . . . It is not for us men to apportion the shares of
moral guilt and retribution . . . and the problem how far a man is to be
held responsible for the unforeseen consequences of his own deed, is
one that might well make us tremble to look into' (II.204). Who is to
blame? Who is to judge? Hetty is both criminal and scapegoat.
Pastoral theodicy has now to come to terms with this indeterminacy.

Once the polar moral dimensions of life have interacted decisively
through the passion narrative re-enacted by Dinah and Hetty, all the
fixed pastoral compromises of Hayslope are put at risk. Through its
scapegoat, the community has been forced to experience the 'deep
unspeakable suffering' (II.209) it previously evaded or discounted.
And as the antinomies of life, previously held in precarious balance,
begin to interact dialectically in their lives, the characters respond
according to their previous beliefs. One reaction, the more common,
is anguish at the irrevocability of the evil committed; the other
emphasises the need to lessen the evil consequences of wrongdoing.
These correspond to the pastoral of duty and the pastoral of pleasure;
so that, even though suffering is now accepted, it is viewed from
different perspectives which still have to be reconciled.

The major exponents of these opposing views in the final chapters
are Adam and Arthur. Adam has to accept the fact that the evil can
never be undone, but then his fatalism only confirms and increases his
anguish: he feels himself 'powerless to contemplate irremediable evil
and suffering'. Slowly, through his own 'baptism of fire' (II.208–9), he
begins to modify his attitude to suffering but, until late in the novel, he
is still rejecting bitterly any suggestion that the irrevocable nature of
evil and suffering can be transformed. When Massey suggests that
good may come out of the tragedy, Adam ripostes: 'That doesn't alter
the evil; *her* ruin can't be undone. I hate that talk o' people as if there
was a way o' making amends for everything' (II.258). The opposite

reaction springs from the pastoral of pleasure. Arthur believes that amends can always be made to recoup past mistakes, and even when he undergoes his own symbolic death on discovering Hetty's tragedy, it is he who rides romantically hard for the victim's reprieve. He, like Adam, shares Hetty's suffering acutely, but whereas Adam is vividly aware that a moral law has been broken and nothing can cancel the wrong, Arthur is anxious to mitigate the spreading effects of the evil consequences. Both eventually gain a new sense of the community to which they are forced to turn: Adam through sharing the burden of suffering, Arthur through the desire to alleviate it.

Each response is, however, still partial. Adam has to be shown that pain can be transformed, while Arthur has to be shown that the consequence of evil actions cannot be cancelled, whatever his wishes to the contrary. No calculus must be allowed to discount the suffering which has destabilised the community and its pastoral theodicies. In other words, their two positions, which were previously complementary in the economy of Hayslope, are now opposed and have to be reconciled. This reconciliation takes place in the wood, where they recapitulate their earlier conversations which have gradually elicited and sharpened an original difference into this critical confrontation. The two men appear as 'spectres' (II.266) with the marks of suffering upon them. Arthur asks Adam to help him 'lessen the evil consequences of the past' (II.268), which the latter immediately condemns as 'that notion of compensation for irretrievable wrong, that self-soothing attempt to make evil bear the same fruits as good, which most of all roused his indignation' (II.269–70). The two force their views on each other: Adam insists on the irrevocableness of Arthur's wrong-doing, while Arthur shows to Adam his own unrelenting hardness. Finally, Adam relents – 'I've no right to be hard towards them as have done wrong and repent' – and Arthur, correspondingly, acknowledges the irrevocable results of his own actions: 'I'd give my life if I could undo it' (II.274).

The final phase of the transformation of pain into sympathy, as it spreads through Hayslope, is dramatised in the new relationship between Adam and Dinah. Adam has by now moved into a general, selfless awareness of others, with 'the sense of our lives having visible and invisible relations beyond any of which either our present or prospective self is the centre' (II.302). He has changed places, as it were, with the earlier Dinah who is now very self-consciously aware of her love for him. For them to be brought together, both have to undergo their symbolic deaths and resurrections, the several antitypes of the climactic prison-scene, itself an antitype of the Passion. When he finally acknowledges his love, Adam becomes 'not quite conscious of where he was' and then experiences 'a resurrection of his dead joy' (II.322). In her turn, Dinah dies – 'Her hands were as cold as death between Adam's' (II.332) – and then undergoes a metamorphosis in the direction of her pastoral cousin: 'the grey eyes, usually so mild and grave, had the bright uneasy glance which accompanies suppressed agitation, and the slight flush in her cheeks . . . was heightened to a deep rose-colour. She looked as if she were only sister to Dinah' (II.297). This is Dinah's 'trial' (II.310) and she resists strenuously the onset of her own emotions. She has, however, to accept the vulnerability of this love to become, in the novel's terms, fully human and so disprove Mrs Poyser's final comment: 'She'll never marry anybody, if he isn't a Methodist and a cripple' (II.339). But the clinching argument comes from Adam who applies to her resistance what he has learnt about sorrow from her. To the preacher of Christ's suffering, he says: 'for it seems to me it's the same with love and happiness as with sorrow – the more we know of it the better we can feel what other people's lives are or might be, and so we shall only be more tender to 'em, and wishful to help 'em' (II.335–6). And if this is irrefutably true of sorrow, then it must be true of love, for Dinah has taught that they are, in the last resort, inseparable. She finally accepts this when Adam's voice, in an acceptably disembodied form, calls her down from her spiritual isolation on the hill at Stoniton into the human community of Hayslope.

In whatever terms it is expressed, George Eliot reiterates, at times diagramatically in *Adam Bede*, that there is no world-view, theodicy, calculus, or theory, which can explain away that central discontinuity of life which is registered as suffering. Pastoral in all its forms is the attempt to do this. When it is fundamentally challenged by the novelist's version of the Passion story – the suffering at the heart of life – then the fixed compromises of its theodicies eventually rediscover a dialectical vitality which becomes merged in the continuing life of the transformed community. The final autumnal and apocalyptic vision of Loamshire, as the harvest is brought in, confirms that the incongruous image of the Cross has been assimilated into a new kind of pastoral. Instead of the clashing perspectives of anamorphosis with which the novel opened, we now have forms merging and being transformed (morphologically) into each other: 'Let us rather be thankful', says the narrator, 'that our sorrow lives in us as an indestructible force, only changing its form, as forces do, and passing from pain into sympathy' (II.302). With the cottage windows 'a-flame with a glory beyond that of amber or amethyst', Adam feels that he is 'in a great temple, and that the distant chant was a sacred song', but its tone is both celebratory and elegiac. This is a Golden Age with a difference, one in which Adam acknowledges the central discontinuities of life through an organic metaphor: 'there's a parting at the root of all our joys' (II.344).

CHAPTER 3

The Mill on the Floss: growing up in St Ogg's

In both *Adam Bede* and *The Mill on the Floss*, George Eliot interrupts her narrative to deliver a lengthy apologia for the kind of novel she is writing. It is prompted in each case by what appears to be an anomaly. In *Adam Bede*, the vicar of Hayslope fails as Christian mentor and appears to a putative reader as 'little better than a pagan'. Chapter seventeen which follows is the famous aesthetic justification based on a contrast between the 'secret of proportion' of classical art and 'the secret of deep human sympathy' of Dutch realism. Only sympathy can understand and interpret the human anomalies who fail to measure up to the conventional types and contrasts of high art. The apologia in *The Mill on the Floss* is very different. This is again prompted by an apparent conflict between Christian and pagan values. Mr Tulliver, though a regular church-goer, has just recorded his desire for vengeance against one of his enemies on the fly-leaf of the family Bible. The chapter which follows, 'A Variation of Protestantism Unknown to Bossuet', defines the strategies which this novel has adopted to interpret such heretical behaviour.

Once again a contrast is established between two forms of life, symbolised on this occasion by the ruins of the Rhine and the Rhône. The former represent a time of romance when moral categories were clear and antithetical, when the great cathedrals were built and the known world was intelligible through the world-shattering opposition of Christian and pagan values: 'did not great emperors leave their Western palaces to die before the infidel strongholds in the sacred East?'[1] This is George Eliot's version of Ruskin's 'The Nature of Gothic', a brief re-creation of a dramatically coherent world in which art and religion reflect each other. That such coherence has been lost in the world of *The Mill on the Floss* is clear from the anomalous action of Mr Tulliver which confuses these clear categories. His provincial world is more fittingly symbolised by the ruins on the Rhône, the remnants of a 'narrow, ugly, grovelling existence, which even calamity does not elevate' (237) and which can only be understood by careful investigation and interpretation, not through simple contrast and literary convention. But what is going on here, and 'by hundreds of obscure hearths' cannot be ignored. It too belongs to the 'historical advance of mankind' but it needs a different approach to understand it: 'we need not shrink from this comparison of small things with great; for does not science tell us that its highest striving is after the ascertainment of a unity which shall bind the smallest things with the greatest?' This is a different kind of hermeneutical language from that used in *Adam Bede*. Here the narrator is not evoking 'the secret of deep human sympathy', but recommending a scientific examination of the 'theory of life' of the Dodsons and Tullivers. His justification follows: 'In natural science, I have understood, there is nothing petty to the mind that has a large vision of relations, and to which every single object suggests a vast sum of conditions. It is surely the same with the observation of human life' (238). This explains why *The Mill on the Floss*, as it traces the natural history of these provincial families and their strange tribal customs, is the most anthropological of George Eliot's novels. It deploys also a wide range of analogies and metaphors from classical literature and the natural sciences, but it does so ironically, as if to establish its own fictional mode in the territory between, traditionally that of the folklorist and anthropologist.

The remainder of the chapter puts the method vividly into practice. The theory of life of the Dodsons and Tullivers is too specific and eccentric 'to be arrived at deductively, from the statement that they were part of the Protestant population of Great Britain' (238–9). The 'large vision' and the 'single object' must be held in a flexible, dialectical relationship. Where the theologians fail, the trained folklorist is more likely to succeed: 'If, in the maiden days of the Dodson sisters, their Bibles opened more easily at some parts than others, it was because of dried tulip-petals, which had been distributed quite impartially, without preference for the historical, devotional, or doctrinal.' Such practices belong to the 'eternal fitness of things' (239), in the same way as the mutton-bone Mrs Glegg carries in her pocket protects her against cramp (105). By representing such esoteric customs and elaborate rituals, George Eliot both distances the world of the novel and then, through the children, brings it close as she uncovers its assumptions and values. What is being uncovered is – in that crucial term – a world-view. In other words, the narrator as anthropologist is interpreting this way of life itself as an interpretative grid, a collage of pagan and Christian elements, which mediates between the families and their conditions. His careful fieldwork will eventually elicit the founding myth of the society to which they belong. At the end of this apologia, the narrator assumes that the reader will no longer be surprised by Mr Tulliver's action.

Such a narrative stance, which predominates in the childhood half of the novel, foregrounds the problems of interpretation in quite a different way from *Adam Bede*, where Hayslope at the turn of the century is presented through pastoral norms and types. In *The Mill on the Floss*, by contrast, the narrator allies himself with the cultivated reader in the difficult task of decoding this oppressively narrow and eccentric form of provincial life in the more recent past (1829–39). And there is a second feature of the novel which foregrounds interpretation in a decisive way. *The Mill on the Floss* is a critical adaptation of the *Bildungsroman*[2] and, as such, shows Tom and Maggie struggling to adapt their inherited world-view to the conditions in which they are growing up – 'in the onward tendency of human things that have risen above the mental level of the generation before them, to which they have been nevertheless tied by the strongest fibres of their hearts' (238). What epitomises this most clearly is their desire – expressed as a refrain in the novel – for a 'key' to 'the painful riddle of this world' (316). As their dilemmas crowd in upon the children, these two dimensions of the novel are seen to be inseparable: the family world-view they have inherited (which requires the skills of the anthropologist to interpret) is both the origin and the obstacle to their own search for an interpretative key to life. This chapter will examine first the lives of the Tullivers and Dodsons, George Eliot's most detailed piece of ethnography, and then the struggles of Tom and Maggie for a coherent view of the world.

The co-ordinates of the children's world are the respective codes of their parents' families, the Dodsons and Tullivers. Other Victorian writers are fond of binary oppositions in their definitions of culture: Hebraism and Hellenism (Arnold), mechanical and organic (Carlyle), Gothic and classical (Ruskin), or, as we have seen, Christian and pagan. George Eliot domesticates with sustained irony her fundamental binary opposition in these two provincial families, so that the values and assumptions of the Dodsons and Tullivers become the building blocks out of which Tom and Maggie have to construct their world-views. From a distance, provincial life may appear uniformly and oppressively narrow; on a closer look, crucial differences emerge. As these are investigated by the narrator, he uncovers two quite different logics, each of which seeks and fails to control the uncertainties of life.

For Mr Tulliver, the mill is the centre of his emotional and imaginative life. It links his present existence directly to that prelapsarian state when he was a child within the security of the family, bound by the kind of close personal relationships he still maintains with his sister Gritty. One of his earliest memories is of the completion of the malthouse and his childhood anticipation of a future replete with plum puddings. But this future never materialised, and the more confusing life becomes, the more his mind harks back to that time of simple, unquestioned verities before the devil, in the shape of the lawyers, began to interfere in the affairs of the world. The puzzling world in which he now finds himself can only be explained by his increasingly 'rampant Manichaeism' which tells him that 'rats, weevils, and lawyers were created by Old Harry' (14), and somehow these have gained access to his Eden. The lawyers are particularly dangerous because the prelapsarian identification of words and things, signifiers and signifieds, has been fractured: 'Not but what, if the world had been left as God made it, I could ha' seen my way, and held my own wi' the best of 'em; but things have got so twisted round and wrapped up i' unreasonable words, as aren't a bit like 'em, as I'm clean at fault, often an' often.' In this gap, the lawyers machinate. 'Everything winds about so – the more straightforward you are, the more you're puzzled' (18). And this is the fallen world for which Tom is to be prepared – according to Tulliver's muddled plans – by knowing 'a good lot o' words as don't mean much, so as you can't lay hold of 'em i' law' (11).

Mr Tulliver is vulnerable because the mill is not only the centre of his emotional life, it is also a piece of mortgaged property. And it is here, in the public domain, in that other reality made up of laws, money, debts, and interest rates, that he appears so deficient and his enemies so cunning. He is a man of ends not means; of metaphoric identification ('water is water') not of metonymic accretion. The more he identifies himself with the absolutes of water, land, and mill, the more unintelligible the contemporaneous, changing, provincial world becomes. He has to keep creating in explanation new enemies: 'his entanglements in this puzzling world . . . required the hypothesis of a very active diabolical agency to explain them' (216). Anyone who challenges his predominance is quickly placed in the devilish half of his Manichean universe – lawyers, Dodsons, Pivart, Papists, even Tom and Maggie at different times. When he becomes sufficiently incensed by his enemies' effrontery, he has no choice but to make an aggressive foray to defend his possessions, for they are 'part of his life, part of himself' (229). As the novel opens, he has just made what is to be his last successful skirmish over his irrigation rights; from this point his attacks become increasingly rash and intemperate and the destructive rhythm of his life is accentuated. A violent counter-attack on his encircling enemies is followed, after the inevitable defeat, by a retreat to the security of the mill and its memories based on the inalienable values of the land, river, and water-power, in a world of pastoral equipoise. As these oscillations become increasingly violent during the first half of the novel, the mill becomes more and more necessary to Tulliver as a refuge, but also more and more vulnerable in the public domain where his Manicheism prevents him dealing with the simplest problems. He even revokes the Dodson loan in one of his rages. Finally, the public domain in the person of his enemy Wakem gets control of the mortgage to the mill and then the prising apart of the world and what it signifies is complete. The centre of his emotional life has been invaded and possessed by the evil principle.

Tulliver is by his very nature unable to accept this contradiction inherent in his theory of life. His paralysis is the sign of this impasse from which family memories briefly revive him, only to be superseded by the rages which conjure up further devilish enemies and return him to his living death. As he gradually recovers, he is forced by his wife to come to terms with financial reality; it was she who in the first place provided Wakem with the opportunity of causing Tulliver this 'most deadly mortification' (220). The Dodson and Tulliver principles, though complementary, are in their partiality in deadly opposition, as Mrs Tulliver discovers to her cost during the bankruptcy. Now, Tulliver is faced with an impossible choice, the kind of choice which the dialectical narrative of *The Mill on the Floss* repeatedly generates to challenge every fixed world-view. He can stay at the mill, the only place where his life has continuity and meaning, if he is prepared to work for Wakem's wages, thereby humbling his pride and sacrificing his independence. The alternative is to salvage his pride (as Tom wishes) by leaving the mill and handing it over to the evil principle. In either direction lies renunciation, and like Wordsworth's Michael, which this part of the novel movingly recalls, he chooses to stay at the mill sustained by the memories of his forefathers, but truncated – 'a tree as is broke' (232) – in the present. He is defeated, but the god of his Manichean world will not allow him to forgive his enemies, as he records in the Bible: 'I'll serve him honest, I wish evil may befall him' (233). This is an animus the commercial Dodsons do not understand, but Tulliver keeps it alive until the moment when all his debts are paid off, a remnant of his pride returns, and then he is empowered to attack once again. His physical assault on Wakem is the final violent oscillation in his life's rhythm as he tries to rout the devil, is frustrated by Maggie, and dies still hating his enemies.

At the very end, however, in the most moving phase of Mr Tulliver's confused life, there is a suggestion that he transcends briefly the rigid dichotomy of the Manichean world which has betrayed him. It is Maggie who prompts this awareness: she had protected the defenceless Wakem and now, as her father is dying, she asks him if he forgives his enemy. He can't love a rascal, he replies, but she prompts in him a final question. While '[h]is hands moved uneasily, as if he wanted them to remove some obstruction that weighed upon him', he asks, 'Does God forgive raskills? . . . but if He does, He won't be hard wi' me' (315). At the last, Tulliver struggles hesitantly out of the constraints of his world and dimly acknowledges the possibility of a god who might conceivably forgive the devil's party which, for the moment, comes to share the same puzzling human reality as himself. It is the briefest moment of puzzled transcendence, but it re-enacts that crucial paradigm in George Eliot's fiction in its fundamental form: the claims of the two Manichean interpretative schemes are perfectly balanced in a moment of equipoise. Can they turn into a dialectic out of which a new vision of life will come? Or, in Mr Tulliver's terms, is there a god able to forgive both himself and rascals in his divided world?

The contrasting world of the Dodsons is experienced by the children through their mother and her three sisters who live in the nearby town of St Ogg's. This contrast, as it shows itself within the family, is dramatised in the opening conversation of the novel between Mr and Mrs Tulliver. He is seeking to outflank his enemies by sending Tom, his agent, away to school for a superior education. To each of his muddled arguments his wife simply responds with a practical suggestion – to kill a couple of fowl, to wash Tom's clothes, to air the sheets for the best bed. The husband plans, the wife translates the plans into objects. Ends – the ultimate defeat of his enemies – are instantly reduced to means, to objects in a world which the Dodsons know how to control and in which Mr Tulliver has little interest. In contrast to the rashness, generosity, and emotional warmth of the Tullivers, the Dodson theory of life is cautious, ritualised, and impersonal. Any account of it rapidly turns into a list of objects, sacred and profane:

A Dodson would not be taxed with the omission of anything that was becoming, or that belonged to the eternal fitness of things which was plainly indicated in the practice of the most substantial parishioners, and in the family traditions – such as, obedience to parents, faithfulness to kindred, industry, rigid honesty, thrift, the thorough scouring of wooden and copper utensils, the hoarding of coins likely to disappear from the currency, the production of first-rate commodities for the market, and the general preference for whatever was home-made. (239)

It is an ethic expressed in negative and precautionary terms, in the avoidance of omission: 'it was necessary to be baptized, else one could not be buried in the churchyard, and to take the sacrament before death as a security against more dimly understood perils' (239). But their world is not full of enemies. More Augustinian than Manichean, evil for them consists in the absence of good.

The concern with objects is, of course, common to both families, but there are crucial differences. For Mr Tulliver the mill, the water, and the land are co-extensive with his emotional life. He has remained in the pre-industrialised, pre-commercial rural world, expressed most vividly in the novel as the pastoral of childhood, 'where objects became dear to us before we had known the labour of choice, and where the outer world seemed only an extension of our own personality: we accepted and loved it as we accepted our own sense of existence and our own limbs' (133). This is very different from the facticity of the Dodsons. Their spontaneous, inner life has all gone into their objects – the teaspoons, the teapots, their bonnets – and congealed there. Consequently, they are able to manipulate these objects adeptly, according to their family rituals and without emotional complications. Within the family they communicate with each other, expressing their firmly controlled feeling, in a sign system which almost precludes the use of words. Its main purpose is keeping errant members of the family up to the mark. 'So if Mrs Glegg's front to-day was more fuzzy and lax than usual, she had a design under it: she intended the most pointed and cutting allusion to Mrs Tulliver's bunches of blond curls, separated from each other by a due wave of smoothness on each side of the parting' (47). In contrast to Mr Tulliver's intemperate outbursts, Dodson emotion is expressed through subtle deviations from the norm which can only be properly analysed by the skilled anthropologist, as we see when sister Pullet seeks to express her grief: 'From the sorrow of a Hottentot to that of a woman in large buckram sleeves, with several bracelets on each arm, an architectural bonnet, and delicate ribbon-strings – what a long series of gradations!' Grief checked by ritual 'produces a composition of forces' (50) which only a Dodson can decode.

All the sisters, with the exception of Mrs Tulliver, are firmly linked to the commercial world of St Ogg's through their successful husbands, so that they see even their marriages as important business deals. They have invested so many years of their lives, plus their hand-embroidered tablecloths, in return for the legacies they anticipate at their husbands' deaths. Mrs Glegg, for example, is quickly reconciled to her husband after one of their rows at the thought of the 'testamentary tenderness' (111) she is sure will be forthcoming. This is the reverse side of the Dodson solidarity, loyalty, and sense of duty. Personal relations must take second place to the laws of exchange, legacies, and interest rates. Tenderness is testamentary. This is harshly demonstrated at the Tulliver bankruptcy when the Dodson sisters refuse to recover their sister's precious objects – her 'teraphim or household gods' – and, apart from a few things they need themselves, allow everything to be sold. Affection must not interfere with the judgment expressed through the ineluctable workings of the market: as Mrs Glegg says, 'The disgrace is, for one o' the family to ha' married a man as has brought her to beggary. The disgrace is, as they're to be sold up. We can't hinder the country from knowing that' (187). Unlike the good-natured Tulliver who lends money for sentimental reasons and creates the impression that he is 'a much more substantial man than he really was' (67), the Dodsons through their careful and relentless hoarding of money turn means once again into ends. The purpose of life becomes 'an ingenious process of nibbling out one's livelihood without leaving any perceptible deficit' (107). And it is the money market which determines the Dodson attitude to time: they are constantly anticipating the maturing of their investments and the regular payments of interest. Unlike Mr Tulliver, fearful of the future 'when the country would become utterly the prey of Papists and Radicals' (65), they look ahead confidently to a time when all preparations in the form of tablecloths, clothes, even burial sheets, have been made in advance – and their account with life closed. Then, they are forced willy-nilly to contemplate death.

Here, means become ends in the most striking way. Compared to the Tullivers, the Dodsons are practical people with great skills of survival in their changing provincial world. But death is their constant concern and topic of conversation. It is the final contingency they are all seeking to prepare for, control, and survive. At the beginning of the novel, Mrs Tulliver reassures her husband that if he were to die tomorrow the laying-out sheets are 'mangled beautiful' and ready for use (10). 'Funerals were always conducted with peculiar propriety in the Dodson family' (38), we are told. But these careful preparations for death seek to deny its reality through the assumption that the dead Dodson will be present to enjoy her triumph. When Mrs Glegg's will is read out, no one must be able to say 'that she had not divided her money with perfect fairness among her own kin' (113). Preparations are made for the final settlement, death is jumped over, and the deceased Dodsons will still be there commenting on their own wills, their laying-out sheets, and their superior lace. The practical preparations for death become ends in themselves. In a world of solid, valuable objects death has no place. All the proprieties will have been observed and death will have become so much a part of the public domain that it will not be experienced as a personal, private experience. If their possessions survive, they will too. Mr Tulliver's failure was his inability to recognise a public world independent of himself; the Dodson failure is the opposite – the inability to acknowledge the end of the self which has become so completely ritualised and objectified in the public domain.

George Eliot plays several variations on the self-confident Dodsons' ritualised attempts to defeat that final end which their means seek to pre-empt. Aunt Pullet's constant topic of conversation is illness and its remedies, and the pills and medicines with which she keeps death at bay. But, in a characteristic Dodson reversal, the remedies – or at least their containers – become themselves the justification of the life they are seeking to extend. Mr Pullet, she announces, keeps all her old medicine bottles, and her only concern is that 'I may go before I've made up the dozen o' these last sizes' (83). The aim of life becomes the collection of medicine bottles, and the sorrow of death lies in the failure to collect enough. Similarly, the awesome viewing of aunt Pullet's new bonnet becomes the opposite of what is intended. The imagined triumph turns to ashes as she realises that a death in the family would prevent her wearing her masterpiece until it was out of fashion. The hidden keys, the darkened corridors and rooms, all become pointless as time triumphs again, and the shrouds turn the furniture into 'corpses', the solemnity becomes 'funereal', and the shrine a mausoleum. The alternative strategy of stockpiling clothes regardless of fashion is practised by aunt Glegg, but this also defeats itself. She becomes walking testimony to time's decay as she uncovers the next ancient stratum of clothes to wear: her gowns, covered in damp spots, give off 'a mouldy odour' (48), while at one especially awe-inspiring moment she appears at a family crisis in 'garments which appeared to have had a recent resurrection from a rather creasy form of burial' (181).

The Dodsons don't only value material objects. Their clan is a network of human relationships within which they have clear obligations: 'The right thing must always be done towards kindred' (240). But these obligations have been externalised to such an extent that the only relations which have any validity are guaranteed blood relationships. The result is a clan system with virtually no emotional validation: 'And it is remarkable that while no individual Dodson was satisfied with any other individual Dodson, each was satisfied, not only with him or her self, but with the Dodsons collectively' (38). What is lacking, of course, is an infusion of the Tulliver spontaneity and warmth. Their only concern is public disgrace. Theirs is no Manichean world: if someone fails, they deserve it. And Mrs Tulliver herself movingly accepts this view, as 'her old self' in the shape of her precious objects 'which had made the world quite comprehensible to her for a quarter of a century' (242) is sold off. Mr Tulliver's final baffled question was, why should evil triumph? His wife asks, what have I done wrong? In her 'helpless imbecility' (242), bewildered and cut off from the security of her own clan, Mrs Tulliver makes a feeble and pathetic attempt to break through the Dodson constraints. She turns away at the end of the novel from the externals of respectability, away even from Tom – that true Dodson – to the previously despised Maggie, to the life of personal affection discovered through her suffering. In the valley of his humiliation, Mr Tulliver similarly reversed his natural tendency in a desperate attempt to come to terms with the world which had destroyed him, becoming increasingly attached to Tom as the only person likely to re-establish the family fortunes. But it is too late for either husband or wife to rescue the wholeness of the worlds they have lost.

The answer to both their perplexed questions is that they have married each other. Dodsons and Tullivers embody vital but partial truths which, when they meet within the family, proceed to destroy each other. Mr Tulliver's imaginary battles with the evil principle astonish her, while his wife's appeals to Dodson traditions enrage him: 'Mrs Tulliver had lived fourteen years with her husband, yet she retained in all the freshness of her early married life a facility of saying things which drove him in the opposite direction to the one she desired' (66). The plotting of the first half of the novel demonstrates this mutual destruction which culminates in the bankruptcy. Mrs Tulliver's fatal interference results in the loss of the mill and her husband's 'deadly mortification' in being forced to work for the devil's wages, a tragedy dismissed by the Dodsons as 'but a feeling in Mr Tulliver's mind' (222). But it works the other way also. He brings upon his wife her most 'deadly mortification' with the financial disgrace and the loss of her household gods. With remorseless logic, the two theories of life probe, interrogate, undermine, and finally destroy each other.

What, finally, are the controlling myths which underpin these contrasting, complementary, and fallible theories? Both seek worlds beyond the reach of time, either before the narrative began or after it has ended. Tulliver is sustained by the prelapsarian world of his childhood to which things will return once he has defeated the evil principle and its agents, whereas the Dodsons look beyond the final contingency of death, to a time when all their accounts will have been settled, their wills read, and all the proprieties observed. Then, they will be able to enter into full enjoyment of their possessions, safe from the anxieties of the moths that consume and the thieves that break in. Death itself has been elided in both scenarios but, unfortunately, the eternal verities embodied in the mill and the Dodson household gods prove not to be inalienable. At the climax of the novel, Tom and Maggie subsume both of these family myths – pre- and post-lapsarian – in their final reconciliation.

The general ambience in which the children grow up, then, is one in which life, 'a painful riddle', is lived in 'the maze of this puzzling world' (61) without any obvious key. And the narrator, as ironic anthropologist, frequently expresses this through the bewildered natives' attempts to make sense of things. Mr Glegg, for example, in his retirement has two hermeneutic obsessions. First, he has noticed remarkable but unexplained coincidences between 'zoological phenomena' in his garden and 'the great events of that time', such as the burning of York Minster. A parody of the narrator, he too is seeking that 'unity which shall bind the smallest things with greatest'. And secondly, he is bewildered by the fact that Mrs Glegg – 'a creature made . . . out of a man's rib' – should be in a state of permanent contradictoriness. This 'was a mystery in the scheme of things to which he had often in vain sought a clue in the early chapters of Genesis' (106). St Ogg's, it is clear, is an ethos very different from Hayslope and its confident theodicies, one in which the search for keys, clues, and origins is never ending and never satisfied. It is, in fact, a community in transition between the verities of Tulliver's rural traditionalism ('water is water') and the new commercial capitalism (bringing steam-power to the mill) which has produced the Dodsons. The result is a fragmentation of values into sects, schisms and, as we have seen, families: 'Public spirit was not held in high esteem at St Ogg's' (104).

The fragmented world of the present contains within it, however, evidences of the founding faith of the original community. This is 'a town which carries the traces of its long growth and history like a millenial tree' (101), and the narrator turned antiquarian is able to decipher these traces of mainly architectural evidence. The old Norman hall incorporating the older half-timbered banqueting-hall is still in use, comments the narrator, but is itself pre-dated by a piece of wall in the parish church, 'said to be a remnant of the original chapel dedicated to St Ogg, the patron saint of this ancient town, of whose history I possess several manuscript versions' (102). Reading the evidence of the stones in this way, the narrator cautiously arrives at the founding myth in manuscript form and then relates its briefest version – commenting with ironic pedantry that, 'since, if it should not be wholly true, it is at least likely to contain the least falsehood' – the legend of Ogg ferrying the woman in rags and her child across the river. Revealing herself to be the Blessed Virgin, the woman sanctifies Ogg and blesses his boat; 'thou didst not question and wrangle with the heart's need, but wast smitten with pity, and didst straightway relieve the same' (102). It is a complex historical account in which the narrative moves back to an uncertain legend, forward to the time of narration, and then back again thirty years to the Dodsons and Gleggs, deciphering the layers of history like a palimpsest. But the interpretative pressure exerted brings to light the crucial foundational story. This, by definition, needs no interpretation ('didst not question . . . straightway relieve'). But it has been forgotten, for 'the days were gone when people could be greatly wrought upon by their faith, still less change it'. The churches of all denominations are either lax or schismatic. It is a diagnosis confirmed by Dr Kenn at the end of the novel in accounting to Maggie for the absence of a shared ethic in the community.

By planting this kernel of the legend of origins in the first book of the novel in this way, George Eliot is sketching a possible closure to *The Mill on the Floss*. Is it possible, the narrative implies, for the neglected type – like Dinah's opening sermon in *Adam Bede* – still to foreshadow and be fulfilled by its antitype in the present? In the puzzling world of St Ogg's, made up as it were from the fragments of this primal ethic – and of which the Dodsons and Tullivers are schismatic elements – is it possible to reconstitute, however briefly and circuitously, a world of transparent ethical meaning?

Tom and Maggie are hybrids born into a world which believes in the fixity of species. Their dilemma, representative in one sense, is acute because of the comprehensive opposition between their parents' theories of life; the sisters agree 'that the Tulliver blood did not mix well with the Dodson blood' (53). The problem the novel examines in its brilliant first phase is, how do they begin to create their own world-views from these opposing elements out of which they are constituted?

The children's growth into self-consciousness is measured nostalgically against the unified world of the pastoral of childhood, that 'Eden before the seasons were divided, and when the starry blossoms grew side by side with the ripening peach' (163). A world without time is also a world 'where objects became dear to us before we had known the labour of choice, and where the outer world seemed only an extension of our own personality' (133). This is an absolute reality when a view of the world is, by definition, impossible. The world is the self, and the self is the world: 'the pattern of the rug and the grate and the fire-irons were "first ideas" that it was no more possible to criticize than the solidity and extension of matter' (133). It is a world so identical with itself that it can only be described in philosophical terms which have no relevance to it. It is, in fact, a pre-linguistic world where the physical, natural objects of flowers, fields, and hedgerows form a fully semiotic system: 'such things as these are the mother tongue of our imagination, the language that is laden with all the subtle inextricable associations the fleeting hours of our childhood left behind them' (36). It is also a non-narratable world which can only be glimpsed during pauses in the narrative, or before the narrative begins, and after it ends, as in the prelude to the novel. Here, in a scene of equipoise – river and sea, town and country, seed and harvest, man and nature – Maggie is transfixed in a timeless moment, 'rapt' as she watches the mill-wheel turning in 'dreamy deafness' and cut off by 'a great curtain of sound . . . from the world beyond' (7). In its fine balance between stillness and motion, the episode recalls a Words-worthian 'spot of time' when the child, suddenly stationary, experiences the earth rolling 'With visible motion her diurnal round'.[3] It is a moment safe from narrative temporality, cut off in its circularity not only by the curtain of sound but also by a time-gap of thirty years which the narrator's memory suddenly bridges.

This is the reality which the Dodsons and Tullivers have divided between them and, as soon as the narrative proper begins, Maggie is summoned into the house where her parents are quarrelling. Even this moment by the mill-wheel, at the age of nine, proves to be already a recovery of an earlier state, a brief ekstasis from the problems of her world which arise initially from the fact that both children are perceived as anomalies, mistakes of nature, by the two families. The Dodsons decide early that Tom belongs to their species – 'in liking salt and eating beans' (39) – while Mr Tulliver constantly sees his mother and sister in Maggie. The first difficulty with this is that the Dodson–Tulliver classification contradicts classification by gender. Dodson values are supposed to be transmitted through the women, Tulliver values through the men. Mrs Tulliver, therefore, wants a Dodson daughter as neat, pretty, and docile as her niece Lucy; while Mr Tulliver wants a son with the skills necessary to run rings round the lawyers – someone like himself, he imagines, with a little more education. Both are disappointed. Even the fixity of species can no longer be relied on in this puzzling world, concludes Mr Tulliver: 'That's the worst on't wi' the crossing o' breeds, you can never justly calkilate what'll come on't' (11).

Nevertheless, the two families don't give up easily. Maggie is tortured in various Dodson ways when she refuses to conform – 'Little gells as cut their own hair', announces aunt Glegg, 'should be whipped and fed on bread-and-water' (59) – while Tom is sent off to school to his ordeal by Latin grammar, a teaching device compared by the narrator to 'that ingenious instrument the thumb-screw' (149). Both regimens achieve the opposite of what they intend. The more Maggie is forced into the Dodson mould, the more her Tulliver characteristics of spontaneity and rebellion assert themselves; 'the small demons who had taken possession of Maggie's soul' become so strong that her actions become unintelligible to her mother. Similarly with Tom. His confident Dodson sense of the factual and the physical is undermined by the conventional and highly abstract education provided by the Rev. Stelling. As a manuscript deletion expressed it at this point, Tom's brain could 'mov[e] with much vigour and ability among things themselves, but [was] helpless among the signs and definitions of things' (122). His nature is emasculated. The perversity of the children's treatment is dramatised when Maggie visits Tom at his school and to everyone's surprise – considering the universal and 'superficial cleverness' (132) of young girls – moves with vigour and ability among the signs and definitions of things in her own imaginative way. She has learnt, like her father, that there is no singular relationship between words and things, that a word, as she explains to a sceptical Tom, 'may mean several things – almost every word does' (127).[4] This is a linguistic discovery sadly confirmed by the narrator when he questions Aristotle's praise of metaphorical speech – that ubiquitous tendency of 'so seldom declar[ing] what a thing is, except by saying it is something else' (123).

With the family bankruptcy, any hope of the children reconciling the opposing sides of their natures in a satisfactory way is lost. Tom leaves school, puts aside the dreams and ambitions linking him with his father, and hands himself over to the Dodson side of the family to be fitted into the world of commerce. The pragmatic language of the self-made Mr Deane drastically reduces life's possibilities: 'If you want to slip into a round hole, you must make ball of yourself – that's where it is' (201). And to find out 'what the world is made of', Tom has to 'learn the smell of things' (202) in the warehouse. Now it is the Dodsons' turn to educate him according to their lights into the role of the Industrious Apprentice (272) – this part of *The Mill on the Floss* is a critique of that influential Victorian genre – but again the children

evade this simple dualism. Tom does submit himself to learning the
ways of the mercantile world of St Ogg's, yet his underlying single
motive is eventually to re-possess the mill, the charged symbol of his
father's life, and wipe out the family disgrace. The Dodsons never
understand how this can take precedence over the accumulation of
capital. As Tom excludes more and more from his life in order to
achieve this end, his career becomes a slow and undramatic suicide.
From the opposing elements he has inherited, circumstances have
required him to combine his strong Tulliver pride with his pragmatic
Dodson sense of fact into a formidable combination, binding 'together
his integrity, his pride, his family regrets, and his personal ambition'
(272). The two complementary but restricted sides of his nature fit
together, denying him the obvious satisfactions of either the Dodsons
or the Tullivers.

Maggie's career provides a very different model of the *Bildungsroman*. Cut off abruptly by the bankruptcy from her previous
memories and satisfactions, Maggie's 'conflict between the inward
impulse and outward fact, which is the lot of every imaginative and
passionate nature' (241) is exacerbated. Instead of Tom's concentration of purpose, there is increasing instability and oscillation. This is
her long suicide. In many ways, the rhythm of her life is similar to her
father's – a destructive oscillation between moods of emotional
aggrandisement and fulfilment in which reality conforms briefly to
the demands of the self, followed by moods of despair and fury when
these demands are thwarted by an unmalleable world. When the
disenchantments occur, something like her father's uncontrollable
fury takes over: fits of 'anger and hatred . . . would flow out over her
affections and conscience like a lava stream, and frighten her with a
sense that it was not difficult for her to become a demon' (251). But
hers cannot be a simple repetition of her father's Manichean struggle.
With her passionate Tulliver nature there is combined a strong sense
of external obligations, characteristic of the Dodsons, which denies
her any clear-cut victories over the evil principle. The result is that
whereas Tom fits together, through abstinence and self-denial,
elements from the two families into a limited but unified purpose,
Maggie embodies the more positive qualities – Tulliver spontaneous
affection and Dodson sense of loyalty – in a life of increasing
oscillation. These two versions of the *Bildungsroman*, masculine and
feminine, constitute *The Mill on the Floss* even as they deconstruct each
other.

We can now see that the conflict between their parents' families, which bankrupts and destroys the family at the mill, is internalised in the children's careers. This is what creates the powerful sense of unity and development in the novel, both organic and dialectical. In the background of the children's struggles are the shadowy paradigms of Dodson and Tulliver which are now being re-enacted in more complex permutations. For Tom and Maggie, this is both an opportunity and a premonition; it is, says the narrator, the situation of each generation which seeks within the dialectic of the family 'to rise above the level of the preceding generation'. But in this case the terms have been too rigidly established. What happens, therefore, between brother and sister is a new and more extreme – because more intimately personal – polarisation than the original Dodson and Tulliver conflict. It is also more anguished because their relationship inevitably contains all the components of their family inheritance; it recalls that holistic unity of childhood, lost before the novel begins, but present in their memories. Both the Dodsons' and Tullivers' 'theory of life had its core of soundness' (239) despite their inner contradictions, but the children never establish such a core. Tom's self-willed denials create a united but truncated life, while Maggie's character is continually decentered by the oscillations of clashing elements. Because of these differences, they quarrel with increasing violence, and yet they know that they need each other, that growth into a fuller life from their abbreviated childhood cannot be achieved separately.[5] It is this which controls the pattern of their later lives, as it did their childhood: again and again they drift apart in alienation and misunderstanding, only to be re-united with increasing desperation and relief. Each character represents a discrete phase of a complete dialectical movement: Maggie's response to life is the prolonged and unresolvable oscillation of antinomies, Tom's is a premature and drawn-out synthesis. Her world is subject to a dramatic catastrophism spinning out of control; his is controlled by an undramatic gradualism slowly running down.

The title of the novel underlines both the similarity and conflict in the children's careers. Both are seeking to recover the mill which has been lost. Tom is intent on re-possessing it as a piece of property, free of debt, to restore the family's pride; Maggie is seeking to recover the state of unified consciousness which the mill has symbolised since childhood. The plotting of the novel shows their aims becoming increasingly antagonistic as their quests intensify: Tom becomes more single-minded than any Dodson, while Maggie's inner conflicts are more turbulent than even her father's puzzlement. As this occurs, each comes to represent and force on the other what they have rejected from their combined inheritance.

To achieve his purpose, Tom submits himself completely and at great emotional cost to the commercial system which defeated his father. Maggie, in contrast, seeks to recover everything that he has rejected – the dreams and demands of the self reconciled to the world through a reciprocated love – all fused into the unified consciousness of childhood at the mill. After each attempt and failure to achieve this – her childhood flight to the gypsies establishes the pattern – she must return to the mill for security and recuperation. Only from there can she start again. After Mr Tulliver's death, these departures and returns take the form of quarrels and reconciliations with Tom. If the present can't provide the key to the unity she is seeking, then her brother, her complementary half, is the means to the pastoral holism of childhood. The first separation occurs when Tom goes away to school and ends with the bankruptcy: the 'two poor things clung closer to each other' (166). They drift apart again and are brought together by their father's death: '"Tom, forgive me – let us always love each other"', says Maggie, 'and they clung and wept together' (316). Each time they move further apart as they seek their own fulfilments – each time it requires a more serious crisis to bring them together, until only the final catastrophe of the flood can achieve this. The progression of both their careers is, in their contrasting ways, back to the mill and what it symbolises – their interdependence and alienation.

From his position of self-denial, Tom sceptically observes and judges Maggie's erratic career. Until the very last, she refuses to accept the truth of the novel's realism that there is always a discrepancy between the inner desire and the outward fact. This can be denied, regretted, ignored in various ways; the Dodsons sought to circumvent it by curtailing the inner life, Tulliver by outmanoeuvring the devil's party which was gaining control of the world. Maggie uses both methods in various forms, unwilling to accept the impossibility of complete fulfilment. This unacceptable truth, which she has to win through to (and transform) at the end of her suffering, is stated early in her career by Thomas à Kempis: 'for in everything somewhat will be wanting, and in every place there will be some that will cross thee.' (252). But characteristically, Maggie deploys the *Imitation of Christ* to satisfy separately both sides of her nature, so turning the message of renunciation into a precarious means of satisfaction.[6] The Dodson belief in external obligation, and the determinism which accompanies this, are spiritualised into the ability 'of taking her stand out of herself, and looking at her own life as an insignificant part of a divinely-guided whole' (254). In parallel fashion, the Tulliver conviction that the world is really co-extensive with the self converts this form of self-abnegation into a creation of her own mind: 'Here, then, was a secret of life that would enable her to renounce all other secrets – here was a sublime height to be reached without the help of outward things – here was insight, and strength, and conquest, to be won by means entirely within her own soul, where a supreme Teacher was waiting to be heard' (254). In this way, the conflicting claims of the self and the world are reconciled, not through genuine renunciation, but through satisfying both sides of her divided nature in a temporary truce. 'Yet', says the narrator, 'one has a sense of uneasiness in looking at her – a sense of opposing elements, of which a fierce collision is imminent' (263).

Unlike Tom, what Maggie has not grasped is that 'renunciation remains sorrow'. She was 'still panting for happiness, and was in ecstasy because she had found the key to it' (254). The *Imitation*, she eventually discovers, offers a 'clue' to a life to be lived rather than a 'key' to be applied, a pattern or type to be fulfilled rather than a formula to be copied. These are two forms of repetition and imitation which the climax of the novel holds in tension. But the crucial importance of Thomas à Kempis's work – the most extensive example of intertextuality in George Eliot's fiction – lies in Maggie's persistent misinterpretations, mistranslations, and evasions of its real meaning – a meaning redefined, in her own way, by the novelist. The text is presented as a voice which speaks quietly but persistently through the novel, its crucial truths marked in the margins by 'the quiet hand' (252) which indicates their importance to Maggie. This is the kind of interpretative mediation George Eliot is so aware of: the *Imitation*, itself a (translated) collage of biblical texts, is subjected to the marginal selection by an unknown hand in a copy sympathetically handed on to Maggie by Bob Jakin. And it is through Thomas à Kempis that her definition of ekstasis begins, from wish-fulfilment to 'an emphatic belief', a genuine 'enthusiasm' – 'something, clearly, that lies outside personal desires, that includes resignation for ourselves and active love for what is not ourselves' (255).

Maggie is now seventeen, and this particular state of equilibrium can only be maintained by suppressing the full demands of her nature. Philip, on his re-appearance, makes her realise this – 'Stupefaction is not resignation' (288) – as he gradually insinuates his own claims and appeal into her life. As a result, 'a doublenes' (267) creeps between her family loyalty and her friendship with the son of the man her father has cursed. Philip's attraction is that he seems to reconcile in his character the elements previously opposed in her life, the attachment to her brother and the desire for emotional and artistic fulfilment. As well as his intellectual and artistic interests, he is gentle, sympathetic, and understanding. He would be an ideal replacement for Tom: 'You would have loved me well enough to bear with me, and forgive me everything. That was what I always longed that Tom should do' (288). But although Philip offers a seductive synthesis, she tells him she cannot reject Tom. 'Maggie felt a great relief in adjourning the decision. She was free now to enjoy the minutes of companionship' (268). It is in these moments of adjournment, through a kind of psychological legerdemain, that Maggie characteristically achieves a brief fulfilment by acknowledging and suspending the discrepancies in her life – until Tom forces upon her the necessity of choice.

These choices, under which Maggie 'writhes' (302), become increasingly unacceptable and anguished because she accepts both the truth and the incompleteness of Tom's position. Whereas Tom acknowledges no disparity between conduct and feeling, Maggie stresses the inability of the former to express the latter: 'sometimes when I have done wrong, it has been because I have feelings that you would be better for, if you had them' (304). But Tom's reply contains a 'demonstrable truth' which he has lived by in the other half of this double *Bildungsroman*: 'if your feelings are so much better than mine, let me see you show them in some other way than by conduct that's likely to disgrace us all – than by ridiculous flights first into one extreme and then into another' (305). The language of this bitter confrontation echoes that of George Eliot's essay on Sophocles' *Antigone* which defines that 'antagonism between valid claims' in which neither side can be exonerated as 'blameless martyr' or condemned as 'hypocritical tyrant'.[7] Here, they have been domesticated into an extreme form of 'that family repulsion which spoils the most sacred relations of our lives' (285). These are the unpalatable truths that the brother and sister force on each other, and on this occasion it takes the death of their father to bring them together again.

After three years of teaching and submission, Maggie returns to St Ogg's for the final phase of her struggle and temptation. Coming under the influence of Stephen Guest, the 'negative peace' of her life is disturbed irrevocably as she glimpses again the 'brighter aërial world' (338) of her hopes. Again, she is seeking to balance in a state of unresolved equipoise her loyalty to Tom and her affection for Philip, each compensating for the other's deficiencies and so creating for herself a world without the labour of choice. (The earlier Philip who had seemed to reconcile her previous conflict has now become one antinomy in this next stage of the dialectic.) Tom's demands enable her to keep at bay Philip's emotional claims, while Philip provides her with the affection Tom denies. While the two men neutralise each other in this way, other appetites which they do not include assail and get possession of Maggie. Stephen's impact is so powerful because he not only brings the new element of sexual attraction, but he also duplicates, subsumes, and reconciles in his character the conflicting qualities of Tom and Philip. He is strong, influential, and decisive in the world of men, business, and action – the world, for example, where the future of the mill will be determined – and, as the son of the firm, he has achieved his position without the grinding effort which has stunted Tom. At the same time, he represents like Philip the world of art and intellect – as well as being an amateur geologist – but without Philip's uncertainty and physical disability. Stephen's presence, of course, briefly neutralises rather than resolves the others' claims, so that he becomes simply the next stage in the destructive dialectic of Maggie's career.

In this final stage, the concealed desires of both Maggie and Stephen are so intense, and yet their public obligations so clear, that they have to consign their feelings to the twilight world below the level of conduct and action where they can allow their minds to deceive themselves that nothing is happening. It is another form of the 'adjournment' of decision and choice at which Maggie has become so expert. The growth of their intimacy is a wonderfully dramatised piece of self-deception, as they continually assert their obligations to others while at the same time drifting together, like sleep-walkers in a timeless world without memory or choice. Stephen, like Maggie, 'wilfully abstained from self-questioning, and would not admit to himself that he felt an influence which was to have any determining effect on his conduct' (354). It is here, in the gap between feeling and conduct, words and actions, that their infatuation is allowed to develop. And it can do so the more easily because Maggie's commitment to Philip is an unspoken one, while Stephen and Lucy are in 'that stage of courtship . . . when each is sure of the other's love, but no formal declaration has been made' (322). What George Eliot captures so compellingly is the involuntary nature of their deepening attraction, once the earlier decision not to make decisions has been made. They become monomaniacs in a dream of their own emotions, out of contact with the external world which, paradoxically therefore, when it does impinge controls them helplessly and effortlessly. Afterwards it is possible to plead, as Stephen does, that their actions were determined for them, that their love was not of their own choosing.

Of special appeal to Maggie is the fact that this man, who apparently reconciles the clashing polarities of her previous life, is not only attracted by her – he is submissive. When he offers her his arm it is as if, at last, the unmodifiable empirical world of fact is amenable to her desire: 'the help is not wanted physically at that moment, but the sense of help – the presence of strength that is outside them and yet theirs – meets a continual want of the imagination' (358). In other words, it is another of those moments of ekstasis which provide Maggie with the outside standing-ground from which all conflicts can be reconciled and lifted to a higher unity. The dialectic of her life is punctuated by such moments, as we have seen, all of which are repetitions, anti-types of the holistic experience of childhood, symbolised by the trance in the presence of the mill-wheel: 'the presence of strength that is outside them and yet theirs'. But far from returning her to an earlier simplicity, these moments compound her conflicting loyalties when she has to return to the world of time and choice.

Stephen, in contrast, is fascinated by the alternations in Maggie's moods as she switches from her opium dream to resistance when her sense of duty re-asserts itself, and back again. This unpredictability, so different from Lucy's docility, captivates and challenges: 'such eyes – defying and deprecating, contradictory and clinging, imperious and beseeching – full of delicious opposites. To see such a creature subdued by love for one would be a lot worth having' (359). There is a considerable distance from this provincial infatuation to Grand-court's sinister and sadistic subduing of Gwendolen's 'iridescence', but in both cases George Eliot juxtaposes male power and female plenitude. The delicious opposites represent possibilities as well as a challenge to masculine values; in their oscillations they articulate a vital spark which the men – Tom, Philip, Stephen – seek to appropriate and subdue. In other words, Maggie's search for, and inability to find, a 'key' to this puzzling world is now recognised as an inability to categorise her. If character is world-view, then this is inevitable; unable to impose a coherent interpretation upon the world, she is herself uninterpretable. Everyone knows where they stand with Tom, 'a character at unity with itself' (272), whereas they find Maggie baffling. For Stephen she is a 'dark-eyed nymph' with 'an alarming amount of devil' (330–1); while for Lucy her wide learning 'always seemed to me witchcraft before – part of your general uncanniness' (340).[8] These are more sophisticated versions of Maggie's hybrid nature as a child, which baffled the family, and they develop the premonitory hints of the inevitable end to which such an innocent witch will come.

She bewilders and fascinates the fashionable and snobbish provincial world of St Ogg's in the same way. She challenges, as we have seen, the categories upon which its view of the world is constructed, and succeeds in confusing all her friends. As Stephen, for example, struggles against his betrayal of Lucy, fluctuating between his love for Maggie and his attempt to suppress and conceal it, his conduct comes to appear to Philip hypocritical. But this is a falsification: 'The conduct that issues from a moral conflict has often so close a resemblance to vice, that the distinction escapes all outward judgments, founded on a mere comparison of actions.' This is the ambiguous terrain into which Maggie is leading her friends and St Ogg's in general. Stephen, we are assured, was not a hypocrite, 'capable of deliberate doubleness for a selfish end' (381), yet his response to Maggie can only be construed in these terms. The final phase of the novel is constructed to demonstrate the unreliability of this mode of interpretation and judgment. The signs are increasingly misread. Tom, Philip, and Lucy misconstrue the relationship between Maggie and Stephen, and unwittingly bring them closer together. As the world of feelings and motives drifts away from the world of actions and consequences, we seem to be entering a realm of experience where inner and outer bear only a fortuitous relation to each other. But Maggie is not prepared to abandon the idea of meaningful action. As Stephen forces his love upon her, she begins to articulate the problems and paradoxes that have bedevilled her life. One side of her nature agrees that their love is 'natural – it has taken hold of me in spite of every effort I have made to resist it' (394), but she opposes to this her sense of faithfulness and duty. So that when Stephen pleads he was not officially engaged to Lucy anyway, Maggie replies that 'the real tie lies in the feelings and expectations we have raised in other minds' (394). Dodson and Tulliver values are being synthesised belatedly into a more coherent world-view: the former provides the crucial significance of temporal priorities, the latter charges this with feeling. What reconciles them is the renunciation which Tom has been demonstrating in his parallel career and which has just enabled him to recover the mill.

As the structure of their careers suggests, Tom's character has become focused most narrowly and rigidly just as Maggie's conflict between the two sides of her nature is most unstable. She has begun to formulate a theory of renunciation, a restatement of Thomas à Kempis, but to put it into practice she has to resist the hypnotic fascination of Stephen. Renunciation must begin now 'when something like that fulness of existence – love, wealth, ease, refinement, all that her nature craved – was brought within her reach' (402). It is, of course, too late as the boating episode proves. Stephen seems to offer a momentary reconciliation of the previously competing elements of her life. She knows it will cut across and compound her existing obligations, but, when he presents himself, she is prepared once again to adjourn her moral dilemmas. It is another moment of false ekstasis as she stands outside her own life and allows the embodiment and reconciler of her inner conflicts to take control. 'Maggie felt that she was being led down the garden among the roses . . . all by this stronger presence that seemed to bear her along without any act of her own will, like the added self which comes with the sudden exalting influence of a strong tonic – and she felt nothing else. Memory was excluded' (407). The puzzling world, now in the shape of Stephen, at last seems amenable and submissive, and suddenly circumstances have combined to make their final meeting possible, perhaps inevitable. In this fatal moment of adjournment, they persuade themselves that everything is being determined by forces outside their control. It is another misapplication of Thomas à Kempis ('Forsake thyself, resign thyself, and thou shalt enjoy much inward peace') through which Maggie still seeks the atemporal world of childhood.

The drifting on the river is a fine expression of this adjournment in which, inevitably, decisions are being made by their apparent postponement.

The more the factitious ekstasis excludes, the more devastating and problematic is the backlash of conscience. Up to now Maggie has tried to keep separate the legitimate, though narrow, claims of her family from the more attractive ones which corresponded to her own desires. But just when – here, on the drifting boat – she realises she has betrayed the former and is prompted to renounce the latter, she becomes aware of Stephen's own suffering. Suddenly the categories dissolve and merge: 'This yielding to the idea of Stephen's suffering was more fatal than the other yielding, because it was less distinguishable from that sense of others' claims which was the moral basis of her resistance' (409). Once the temporal priority of moral claims has been ignored, then subsequent claims begin to establish their own validity. But equally, as events force upon Maggie the consequences of her actions, the two sides of her nature – desire and duty – are being revealed as only artificially separated. The implications of this discovery, however, here at the end of Maggie's day of wish-fulfilment on the river with Stephen, are again adjourned: 'then came food, and then quiet reclining on the cushions, with the sense that no new resolution *could* be taken that day. Everything must wait till to-morrow' (411).

Between falling asleep in the sunset and waking to reality in the dawn, Maggie experiences a complex dream. Throughout the novel, as her dilemmas have multiplied, she has repeatedly longed to 'wake back' (418) into an earlier time before fatal choices had to be made. In the dream there is a double return into the past. First, the myth of St Ogg's is re-created with Tom, Lucy, and Philip acting out its foundational ethic from which she and Stephen are excluded as their boat turns over and they begin to sink, clutched in each other's arms. Such an isolated and alienated future for the lovers is one possible ending of the novel. The second part of the dream into which Maggie 'wakes' from this nightmare is a return, not to the mythic, but to the familial past: 'she was a child again in the parlour at evening twilight, and Tom was not really angry'. This is another possible, though increasingly unlikely, ending. When she awakes properly, however, it is to a realisation that neither of these dream solutions is permissible; while, on the one hand, the 'irrevocable wrong that must blot her life had been committed', alienating her from family and friends, on the other, 'her soul, though betrayed, beguiled, ensnared, could never deliberately consent to a choice of the lower'. She is in limbo. She has 'rent the ties that had given meaning to duty, and had made herself an outlawed soul', but thanks to the other side of her nature, 'the consequences of such a fall had come before the outward act was completed' (413). She is neither able to go forward into an alienated future with Stephen or back into the past to rejoin her betrayed family and friends. And yet as always with Maggie, the nature of her impossible dilemma also defines the possibilities of her character. Can the mythic and familial be synthesised?

Through this dilemma, she comes finally to a true understanding of the meaning of renunciation: 'she had thought it was quiet ecstasy; she saw it face to face now – that sad patient loving strength which holds the clue to life – and saw that the thorns were for ever pressing on its brow' (413). Now, in her genuine *imitatio Christi*, suffering is accepted not as the key to life but simply as a 'clue' – and it is a clue to the fact that there is no final interpretative key, that there is always a discrepancy between inner and outer, and that this form of suffering is the meaning of renunciation. The crucifixion image expresses the genuine ekstasis which transforms, without adjourning or abandoning, the conflict between desire and duty. This, like her father's final puzzled questioning of his Manichean world, is a move to a genuine synthesis which gives her the strength and confidence to rebut Stephen's renewed arguments the next morning. She rejects his antithesis between natural law and outward ties, and in doing so moves beyond the Dodson–Tulliver conflict, which has bedevilled her life, towards a genuine reconciliation. Outward ties, she now sees, are not merely ritualised (Dodson) bonds; she redefines them as an acknowledgement of 'the reliance others have in us'. In other words, they must be transformed by an infusion of Tulliver emotion and fellow-feeling. She now begins to formulate a creed in which claims and feeling define and reinforce each other: 'if I had been better, nobler, those claims would have been so strongly present with me – I should have felt them pressing on my heart so continually, just as they do now and in the moments when my conscience is awake – that the opposite feeling would never have grown in me, as it has done: it would have been quenched at once' (417). Maggie is only enabled to say this because she has both fallen, and resisted the fall, into temptation; the drifting with the tide, followed by the refusal to complete the outward act, are the correlatives of this.

The temporary fall from grace has provided Maggie with a true glimpse of the meaning of renunciation. Duty and desire can be grasped simultaneously and, as they come together, they change their natures: outward claims become inner faithfulness, while emotional desires become loving sympathy. This accounts for the poignancy of her rejection of Stephen. Just as she has gained a new sense of the outer claims which she will now seek to honour, so her wish-fulfilling desire for Stephen is transformed into a loving sympathy with its own valid claims. Painful renunciation lies either way; each course of action both fulfils and denies legitimate claims, each victory is simultaneously a defeat. Only her idealism tells her that she must try to attain once more – this time through the rejection of all subsequent claims – the simplicity and unity of her childhood relationship. What view of the world does this finally represent? It is a martyrdom in which the full possibilities of life – those 'delicious opposites' – have been given full expression until, in the limbo where all categories have dissolved and merged into each other, Maggie has grasped the genuine clue of renunciation, the crown of thorns, which underpins and holds together all the antinomies in conflict. George Eliot redefines martyrdom, most publicly in the life of Savonarola, not as a witnessing to some accepted truth, but as the acting out of the 'antagonism of valid claims'. The martyr embodies this antagonism, out of which the conflict of interpretation arises.

The question now is, how will the moral conundrum of Maggie's renunciation be interpreted? As we have seen, in reaching it she has revealed the inadequacy of all criteria except for that moral intuition of which her whole life is the culmination. She has grasped the clue that there is no key to life, only the renunciation upon which her actions are finally based. How will such an interpretation be interpreted? The final book of *The Mill on the Floss* is occupied with this question in the same way that the final phase of *Adam Bede* shows Hayslope trying to come to terms with Hetty's infanticide. This is Maggie's trial and it consists of a series of interpretations (followed by judgments) of Maggie's rejection of Stephen and her return to St Ogg's, the action which has confounded everyone's expectations.

The first and crucial reaction is Tom's. Not only is it essential for Maggie to re-establish their relationship, but her return to the mill is a sign of her new submission, 'to submit in patient silence to that harsh disapproving judgment against which she had so often rebelled' (425). In a limited sense Tom has been all along the embodiment of the renunciation she has at last discovered, as he indicates when she pleads with him: 'You struggled with your feelings, you say. Yes! *I* have had feelings to struggle with; but I conquered them' (427). This reminds us again that the novel is a double *Bildungsroman* and that Tom has been making hard choices which have just resulted in the recovery of the mill, the mill which Maggie now needs as an emotional symbol of her new life. He interprets her liaison with Stephen in the harshest light as another attempt to sabotage his hard-won success. By turning her away from the mill, Tom now sabotages, in turn, her planned life of belated renunciation, for she needs him as 'a mind that we can never mould ourselves upon, and yet that we cannot endure to alienate from us' (425). In this penultimate meeting, they represent a confrontation between two contradictory forms of renunciation, the only possible theories of life to come out of their hybrid natures. Tom's career of grinding endeavour and self-denial began in renunciation and has apparently succeeded in its ultimate aim; in reality, his residence at the mill is the conclusion of a long suicide which has withered all feeling and sympathy. He has recovered the family home in order to turn his sister away in her need. In contrast, Maggie has refused the hard choices of life and allowed the oscillations of her character to end in repeated defeats; in reality, her failures have led to the final discovery of true renunciation which the symmetrical paradoxes of the novel define as success. The irony of Tom's rejection is that it springs from the same source as Maggie's need: his repulsion towards her 'derived its very intensity from their early childish love in the time when they had clasped tiny fingers together, and their later sense of nearness in a common duty and a common sorrow' (439). By his lights he has remained true to that early love, so that the logic of his life of renunciation is now to reject her in her betrayal of it. The logic of Maggie's oscillating life is leading her to the discovery of a very different kind of renunciation. Her rejection by Tom prevents her putting into practice her sacrifice of expiation. This is the stalemate their lives have reached before the flood.

The next attempt to interpret Maggie's actions is made by public opinion or, more specifically, 'the world's wife' (431) in the chapter entitled 'St Ogg's Passes Judgment'. It is striking how many times and in different ways the boating episode is scrutinised and its ambiguities interpreted according to different keys. St Ogg's interprets by results – 'how else? – not knowing the process by which results are arrived at' (431) – and we are provided with two contrasting assessments of Maggie's behaviour, the first on the assumption that she would return to the town as Mrs Stephen Guest, the second in the knowledge that she 'had returned without a *trousseau*, without a husband' (431). The favourable, though hypocritical, extenuation of the first version is replaced by the harsh, equally hypocritical, re-interpretation of the second. As examples of a utilitarian calculus, both are rejected by the novel out of hand. Having shown how the dialectic of Maggie's life deconstructs all criteria, George Eliot becomes incensed in her satire when anyone seeks to judge her heroine. One is reminded of that intemperate paragraph in the Finale of *Middlemarch* which the novelist felt obliged to revise.

Even by the calculus of results, Maggie is condemned either way: if she came back married she could be looked down on in her lapse, if unmarried then she must have failed in her scheming. As she comes to be the scapegoat upon which St Ogg's heaps its hypocrisies, we are reminded of the story Maggie herself recounts at the beginning of the novel from Defoe's *The History of the Devil*: 'That old woman in the water's a witch – they've put her in to find out whether she's a witch or no, and if she swims she's a witch, and if she's drowned – and killed, you know – she's innocent, and not a witch, but only a poor silly old woman. But what good would it do her then, you know, when she was drowned?' (16). The inadequacy of such a hermeneutic is analysed most explicitly by Dr Kenn, the author's voice at this point and the next interpreter of Maggie's choice. He considers her desire to come back to St Ogg's, 'to remain where all the ties of your life have been formed – is a true prompting' to which the Church, representing the community, should respond by receiving the penitent with open arms. But, because 'the ideas of discipline and Christian fraternity . . . can hardly be said to exist in the public mind' (435), he lacks the confidence to advise her either to stay or leave. And the way in which the parish turns against him in his continuing support of the scapegoat confirms his diagnosis; he is tarnished and bewildered – like generations of readers[9] – by the ambiguities she embodies. In the absence of a coherent community, all he can conclude is that 'her conscience must not be tampered with: the principle on which she had acted was a safer guide than any balancing of consequences' (437).

The principle Dr Kenn recommends is, of course, a denial of

principle, a moral intuition not a general idea. As the narrator makes clear at the end of the chapter, in rejecting 'the men of maxims' with their 'general rules' and 'ready-made patent method' in favour of the maligned casuists: 'their perverted spirit of minute discrimination was the shadow of a truth to which eyes and hearts are too often fatally sealed – the truth, that moral judgments must remain false and hollow, unless they are checked and enlightened by a perpetual reference to the special circumstances that mark the individual lot' (437–8). This is casuistry seen in terms of the hypothetical method – tentative, dialectical, never finalised. But not only does it reject general rules, it seems unwilling in Maggie's case to formulate a tentative hypothesis: 'the question whether the moment has come in which a man has fallen below the possibility of a renunciation that will carry any efficacy, and must accept the sway of a passion against which he had struggled as a trespass, is one for which we have no master-key that will fit all cases' (437). Indeed, if you are able to 'apprehend' the problem, says the narrator, you are unable *ipso facto* to propose a solution. This exegesis is, of course, what Maggie, the exegete of her own life, had already discovered.

Judging by results is crass, the balancing of consequences is dangerous, general rules are reductive, and even casuistry hesitates to formulate a specific hypothesis. In effect, the final isolated phase of Maggie's career consists of a series of responses and reports, a kind of forensic commentary made up of conflicting opinions on her conduct. They alternate between support and rejection. Mrs Glegg is prepared to stand by her kin according to the Dodson ethic, which echoes Kenn's words in schismatic form: 'it was not for her own friends . . . to cast her out from family shelter to the scorn of the outer world, until she had become unequivocally a family disgrace' (438). But she is unable to overcome the stronger opposition of Tom. Next, Maggie receives a letter from Philip who has witnessed her martyrdom and through it been transformed: his own search for personal ekstasis has been succeeded by an 'enlarged life which grows and grows by appropriating the life of others' (443). But opposition and rumours of further scandal about Maggie spread through St Ogg's, so that the Miss Guests are in no doubt she must be prevented from ever marrying their brother (447). The scales are tipped again when Lucy visits Maggie and expresses her belief in her, but then in the final chapter Stephen's letter of reproach arrives and the oscillations intensify with Maggie 'battling with the old shadowy enemies that were for ever slain and rising again' (449). The 'long penance of life' in which she might change 'that passionate error into a new force of unselfish human love' (449) now seems increasingly unattainable.

All of these reactions, these voices, reflect publicly the inner conflict Maggie has been unable to resolve, frustrated by Tom's final rejection which is the expression of his own impasse. As she sits in the darkness alone, this plethora of interpretations is reduced to two, those of Stephen and of Thomas à Kempis, texts which become alternate voices speaking through her. 'The words that were marked by the quiet hand in the little old book . . . rushed even to her lips . . . "I have received the Cross, I have received it from Thy hand: I will bear it, and bear it till death, as Thou has laid it upon me"' (453). But equally strongly come Stephen's pleadings in his letter to which she can only beg forgiveness. There is no resolution to Maggie's dark night of the soul, only the 'cry of self-despair', her cry of dereliction: 'Am I to struggle and fall and repent again?' But then out of her despair comes again a movement towards the renunciation and self-abnegation she had glimpsed before Tom's rejection: 'O God, if my life is to be long, let me live to bless and comfort –' (453). Here, effectively, Maggie's unresolvable conflict ends and with it the novel. 'At that moment' the water rises, Maggie sets off on her rescue attempt, and verisimilitude is suspended: 'The whole thing had been so rapid – so dream-like – that the threads of ordinary association were broken' (455). The typology of the imitation of Christ is being fulfilled. After Gethsemane and the trial, after the crucifixion and the cry of dereliction, the final episode of the novel represents a brief resurrection: 'In the first moments Maggie felt nothing, thought of nothing, but that she had suddenly passed away from that life which she had been dreading: it was the transition of death, without its agony – and she was alone in the darkness with God' (455). As with *Adam Bede*, the whole narrative has been driving towards this point of uninterpretability – in that case, Dinah and Hetty sink in the darkness and come together in prayer and confession, here Maggie enters the darkness to be released from her intolerable struggle. She is allowed to begin life again, to emerge out of the darkness – her first memory was holding hands with Tom by the side of the Floss, 'everything before that is dark to me' (270) – and be reconciled with her brother, not by expiation, but through the self-sacrifice of redemption. This is the form her resurrection takes because her faith ('Let me live to bless and comfort') has remained inviolate.

Maggie's conflict, dramatised in the earlier boating episode, could not be resolved, interpreted, or judged according to any principle or maxim. As the narrative became clogged with commentary, the heroine's dilemma became more and more intractable. Now, suddenly, narrative is transformed into simple story: the flood rises, Maggie rescues Tom from the mill, and they are drowned in each other's arms. These events take place in a world without introspection or prevarication, a world where 'we are all one with each other in primitive mortal needs' (456). 'Maggie knew it was the flood' and there is 'great calm in her' as she acts 'without a moment's shudder of fear'. 'In the first moments Maggie felt nothing, thought of nothing, but that she had suddenly passed away from that life which she had been dreading.' When she becomes aware of her situation on the water she remembers her old home: 'Her whole soul was strained now on that thought.' As she sets out to rescue Tom, she is 'hardly conscious of any bodily sensations – except a sensation of strength, inspired by mighty emotion', and, despite the obvious dangers, 'there was no choice of course, no room for hesitation' (455–6). There is no gap here between conduct and motive, actions and feeling; everything is in the present and response is immediate ('now . . . now . . . now . . .'). Even at the very end when sister and brother are in the boat together, the triumph of Maggie's martyrdom over Tom's comes without commentary or interrogation: 'It came with so overpowering a force – it was such a new revelation to his spirit, of the depths in life, that had lain beyond his vision which he had fancied so keen and clear – that he was unable to ask a question' (458).

What is this new reality where actions are so intuitive and transparent that they need neither justification nor interpretation? A reality where all the premises of George Eliot's realism – that character is not destiny, that words cannot say what they mean, that motives are never simple – are in abeyance? Where the flood is immediately recognised as 'that awful visitation of God' (455), and where Maggie's whole being is directed towards a single end in 'a story of almost divinely-protected effort'? And where characters return to their primary roles of brother and sister, expressing their deepest feelings through simple nomination: 'It is I, Tom – Maggie.' To which Tom need only reply, 'Magsie!' (458). It is, of course, the world of melodrama which has emerged finally from the complex hermeneutics of her fiction. Though it appears to share the logic of a dream, George Eliot is keen to contrast it with that other boating episode which was described in dream-like terms and where the self was passive. Here, Maggie rows strenuously against the tide to achieve fulfilment through self-sacrifice. What validates the action of the melodrama is myth, in this case the legend of St Ogg's, the foundation myth which the town has lost sight of. As Peter Brooks has suggested, melodrama is 'the repository of the fragmentary and desacralized remnants of sacred myth'.[10] Maggie 'wakes back', not only into childhood to recover her unity with Tom, their atonement, but also into the mythic reality of the original social contract.[11] Her action combines the two dreams which, separated and contradictory in the first boating episode, now coalesce: she responds, like Ogg, to human need as well as 'waking back' into her childhood with Tom. From this coalescence some critics choose to emphasise the former, some the latter. As in *Adam Bede*, the melodrama is a form of typology: there, Dinah's sermon and prayers defined the type which the final meeting in the prison fulfilled, while here the early account of St Ogg and his response to need is the type of which Maggie's and Tom's self-sacrifice is the antitype. In both cases, the novels present the long and circuitous process of hermeneutic restoration through which the world of transparent meaning returns. St Ogg's 'inherited a long past without thinking of it, and had no eyes for the spirits that walk the streets' (106), but these are now given substance again by Maggie and Tom in their mutual need and its fulfilment.

The first boating episode was so problematic because, dramatising Maggie's contradictory motives as it did, it frustrated all the hermeneutic codes applied to it. In this second episode her motives are intuitive, unified, and unquestioned: 'the threads of ordinary association were broken' and she is disentangled from the complications of the web-like circumstance of George Eliot's fictional realism. This, however, does not mean that the final action itself is without ambiguity, as generations of critics have reminded us. The flood, as its description makes clear, is simultaneously both destruction and creation, both that of Noah and of Genesis. Maggie's action is both the ekstasis she has been searching for and the culminating example of those adjournments of her conflict which have punctuated the novel. Each victory can still be seen as a defeat. It has even been suggested that Tom would have been safe if he had stayed in the mill – 'the house stood firm' (457) – and not been lured into the boat.[12] And, though Tom and Maggie by accepting each other's renunciation 'wake back' to their childhood love before renunciation was necessary, they die and, as Maggie commented in recounting the story of the drowned witch – 'what good would it do her then?' And, finally, though Tom and Maggie re-validate the myth of St Ogg's, it is in a severely reduced, demythologised form: a sister tries to rescue a brother before they both drown. Even their epitaph – 'In their death they were not divided' (460) – has different meanings depending on whether the emphasis falls on 'death' or 'divided'.

Such ambiguities should not surprise us as the pressure of the whole novel is working against any clear-cut moral. For while their motives are at the last clear to themselves – they incarnate them in their final embrace – the double martyrdom of Tom and Maggie is acted out in a world without generally shared beliefs which will make of the drowning what it will. Maggie cannot be suddenly transformed from scapegoat and witch into martyr, saint, and prodigal; nor, in his different way, can Tom. The ambiguities of the novel as a whole remain. But the final episode is written in a different mode from the fictional, that of story, in Walter Benjamin's terms, which descends from and is taken up into legend and which eschews motivation and explanation. The ambiguity and the tension rest finally between two kinds of narrative, that of the logic of cause-and-effect based on observation and past experience, and that of typology which looks to the future and is based on faith, hope, and vision.[13] In the former, repetition can lead only to frustration and disillusionment: the final reunion of Tom and Maggie is, therefore, a defeated and incestuous regression to childhood. In the latter, repetition is a fulfilment of the apocalyptic promise to 'make all things new', a forward-looking vision of the possible: the final reunion is then a repetition of their earliest unity lifted to a mythical level. In *The Mill on the Floss* we have, as it were, both narrative logics so that the novel and its legendary, melodramatic ending remain in tension. The novel can be read as a long digression between the childhood union of Tom and Maggie, fleetingly hinted at the beginning, and its fulfilment in their death; or more sceptically, as a piece of fictional realism which casts doubt both on the pastoral unified world of childhood which predates the novel and on their ecstatic reunion after the novel proper has ended. As the history of its reception shows, it has not been easy to read *The Mill on the Floss* in both ways at the same time.

CHAPTER 4

Silas Marner: rustic hermeneutics

From the discussion of the early fiction so far it will be clear that there is a doubleness in George Eliot's writing. On the one hand, there is the strong emphasis on life as a kind of muddling through, in which any attempt to articulate a coherent world-view is bound to fail of its very nature. The idea, she says disparagingly in *The Mill on the Floss*, that 'men usually act and speak from distinct motives, with a consciously proposed end in view . . . [is] nowhere abundant but in the world of the dramatist'. 'We live', she continues, 'from hand to mouth, most of us, with a small family of immediate desires' (22). As a result, the narrative becomes increasingly enmeshed in interpretation as motives proliferate, contradict one another, and escape the constraints of any kind of maxim. But, on the other hand, there is a persistent narrative drive in the fiction towards the simplicity of myth, fable, and melodrama, the need to discover a world where motives are, however briefly, distinct and direct and acted upon. Such motives and actions do not need interpreting, for though they are dramatised in a variety of ways – Janet Dempster in her husband's sick-room, Hetty and Dinah in the prison, Maggie and Tom in the flood – they all take place in milieus where, as she writes in *Scenes of Clerical Life*, 'the moral relation of man to man is reduced to its utmost clearness and simplicity: bigotry cannot confuse it, theory cannot pervert it, passion, awed into quiescence, can neither pollute nor perturb it' (310). The first mode of writing retards the narrative, the second accelerates it, while the tension between them produces George Eliot's characteristic fictions.

It has been suggested in the introduction that a crucial expression of this tension in George Eliot's thinking is the hypothesis, in which an idea or concept is tested against a complex of circumstance and evidence. In the fiction the clear idea is frequently represented as a narrative kernel – the myth of St Ogg's, for example – which is seeking recuperation and realisation in the present; while the circumstances which are testing and retarding this realisation are the complications of the puzzling modern world where the action is located. One way of discriminating between these two fictional modes is by recalling Walter Benjamin's distinction between the story and the novel, referred to briefly at the end of the last chapter. It is, he writes in his essay 'The Storyteller', 'half the art of storytelling to keep a story free from explanation as one reproduces it . . . The most extraordinary things, marvellous things, are related with the greatest accuracy, but the psychological connection of the events is not forced on the reader. It is left up to him to interpret things the way he understands them.' In this way, the story 'does not expend itself. It preserves and concentrates its strength and is capable of releasing it even after a long time'. In contrast to this, 'In the midst of life's fullness, and through the representation of this fullness, the novel gives evidence of the profound perplexity of the living'.[1] Because time is constitutive of the novel – Benjamin is here quoting Lukács – then 'meaning and life, and thus the essential and the temporal, [are] separated'. The contrast can be encapsulated in two phrases, the 'meaning of life' and the 'moral of the story': 'with these slogans novel and story confront each other, and from them the totally different historical co-ordinates of these art forms may be discerned'.[2] If we take these as two tendencies rather than as two distinct genres, they help to define the tension in George Eliot's fiction between the desire for the self-explanatory story and the need to comment and interpret. When these co-exist in the one literary work they both, of course, change their natures.

Nowhere is this twin impulse more apparent than in *Silas Marner*. The novelist herself describes the origin of the story in these terms in her well-known comment to John Blackwood in February 1861:

It came to me first of all, quite suddenly, as a sort of legendary tale, suggested by my recollection of having once, in early childhood, seen a linen-weaver with a bag on his back; but, as my mind dwelt on the subject, I became inclined to a more realistic treatment.[3]

The tale is displaced into the novel but the reader is constantly being reminded that amidst the fictional complexity there is a simple story with its own narrative logic. The most succinct version of this story is Silas's, 'My money's gone, I don't know where – and [the child] is come from I don't know where',[4] which shortly afterwards is translated into the logic of fairy tale: 'that the child was come instead of the gold – that the gold had turned into the child' (188). And, true to this logic, the climax of the novel poses the question: since Silas has recovered his gold, should he hand back the child? This is the narrative kernel which is turned this way and that in *Silas Marner*, commented on, interpreted, puzzled over by the community and each of the characters in turn. What is of crucial significance is that the legendary tale, the story with its own simple moral, is never finally dissolved, demythologised or fully displaced into the novel, which is searching in its own way for the meaning of life. The reader, like the characters, has to learn to accept this tension and what it signifies in a sharper form than in any of the later fiction. As Richard Holt Hutton, the perceptive Victorian critic, said in a review in the *Economist*: 'One of the most striking features in this striking tale is the strong intellectual impress which the author contrives to give to a story of which the main elements are altogether unintellectual, without the smallest injury to the verisimilitude of the tale.'[5] In *The Mill on the Floss*, as we have seen, the legend of St Ogg was recovered from the past in order to be revived in schismatic form in the present; the type is partially fulfilled by the antitype in the puzzling modern world. Here, however, in *Silas Marner* the novelist seeks to show how a legend originates in a remote farming community at the turn of the century. In her next novel, *Romola*, for which she was already preparing, George Eliot turns to an analysis of the origins of European culture in the Florentine Renaissance. How does this parochial tale of the rustics of Raveloe articulate one of the author's most subtle hermeneutic explorations?

What impressed the reviewers on the appearance of *Silas Marner* was something we have learned to take for granted. George Eliot knew how to depict the life of the poor in a strikingly new way. In most of the tales of country life now being written, said the *Saturday Review*, the poor are always looked at from the point of view of the rich: 'They live in order to take tracts and broth.' In such fictions, however detailed and concerned, the poor remain 'a distinct race': 'What they think of and do when they are not being improved and helped, remains a blank.'[6] George Eliot occupies this 'virgin soil' by means of two special skills, according to the *Westminster Review*. Everything is so carefully and vividly contextualised that 'It is impossible to dissociate any of the characters from the village in which they were born and bred – they form an organic whole with Raveloe'. And secondly, by her sympathetic insight the novelist revivifies that world of fifty years ago: 'There is nothing so difficult to a cultivated intellect as to enter into the mental states of the ignorant and uniformed, it is an accomplishment of genius alone, the minutest analysis, and the most comprehensive inductions are but tools and helps in such a task.'[7] This is the conventional critical response of the time – the reviewer is, in fact, paraphrasing the novelist's own commentary (61–2) – and similar in many ways to the reception of the two previous novels, but it does indicate the general recognition that here was a new development in fiction and that its originality consisted of the ability to enter unfamiliar worlds and world-views – and then, like the anthropologist, stand back and decipher them. The originality of George Eliot's achievement can be appreciated in the indebtedness of, say, Hardy's Wessex to her explorations; the denizens of Little Hintock and their world in *The Woodlanders*, for example, are a natural development from those of Raveloe. The comparison makes George Eliot's economy of method at this stage of her career even more striking, as the opening paragraph of *Silas Marner* demonstrates.

The most revealing way to elicit the values and assumptions of any family, community, or society, the novelist had discovered in her earliest fiction, was by the introduction of an anomaly, an alien. As in scientific experiment, this has then to be assimilated by a readjustment of the accepted paradigm. In *Scenes of Clerical Life* the aliens are the clergymen Barton and Tryan; in *Adam Bede* Hetty and Dinah enter the community as interlopers; while in *The Mill on the Floss* Tom and Maggie appear as the hybrids offending against conventional wisdom and mores. In an even more extreme way, the opening of *Silas Marner* describes the rustic mind trying to come to terms with the phenomenon of the weavers, 'alien-looking men' who appear unexpectedly in the countryside like 'the remnants of a disinherited race'. Everything about them is either mysterious or eccentric: their appearance, their trade, their origin. The anthropologist narrator draws the horizon of belief and understanding firmly and narrowly around such a community, 'never reached by the vibrations of the coach-horn, or of public opinion' (7), in which George Eliot's current fictional experiment is being carried out.

Beyond the horizon is perplexity and fear: 'To the peasants of old times, the world outside their own direct experience was a region of vagueness and mystery' (4).

The final sentence of the first paragraph then takes a characteristic interpretative turn. 'In this way it came to pass that those scattered linen weavers – emigrants from the town into the country – were to the last regarded as aliens by their rustic neighbours, and usually contracted the eccentric habits which belong to a state of loneliness' (4–5). Not only has the narrator to uncover the world-view of the remote rustics, but the aliens in this remoteness have also to be understood as they respond to their sense of isolation. This effects the transition to the career of Marner in Raveloe in the next paragraph which brings out sharply the discrepancy between the way he is seen and the way he, in his naivety, sees. Not only is he a weaver, he also suffers from cataleptic fits, and this double mystery taxes the rustic mind. In a parody of intellectual exegesis frequently repeated in the novel, various theories are put forward to explain Marner's trances: he must die and come to life again, it is a fit or a stroke, his soul leaves his body to acquire forbidden knowledge. But these diagnoses are according to Raveloe assumptions. To understand Marner fully we must also seek to uncover his 'inward life' which 'had been a history and metamorphosis, as that of every fervid nature must be when it has fled, or been condemned to solitude'. In a kind of infinite regress of interpretation, this leads us back to the place from which he has been disinherited, that 'little hidden world' (10) of Lantern Yard where he was once at home. This too, of course, contains its unexplained mysteries.

With great skill the narrative opens up worlds within worlds in this way, according to the double imperative of life: interpret and be interpreted. Characters can be explained from the outside, they can only be understood from within. Here, in *Silas Marner*, the essential dialectic of George Eliot's hermeneutics is sharpened and tested in various ways more fundamental than the later explorations of the world-views of her more sophisticated characters. There are several features of life in Raveloe which bring out this fundamentalism. First of all, the communities described are remote in time and space, providing the narrator – and the Victorian amateur folklorist – with vestiges and remnants of an even more distant past to be deciphered: 'Such strange lingering echoes of the old demon-worship might perhaps even now be caught by the diligent listener among the grey-haired peasantry' (6). And, beyond these echoes, analogies hint at an even more remote, mythical past with which the events of the novel link up: 'In the early ages of the world, we know, it was believed that each territory was inhabited and ruled by its own divinities.' And Marner, we are told, 'was vaguely conscious of something not unlike the feeling of primitive men.' (22). Part of George Eliot's purpose, as a natural historian of religion, is to explore the origins of folk myth and its continuity with more sophisticated belief, as the network of biblical allusions implies.[8] The narrator reminds us repeatedly that these origins are the foundations upon which we still rely: 'The gods of the hearth exist for us still; and let all new faith be tolerant of that fetishism, lest it bruise its own roots' (212).

Secondly, it is a world full of mysterious gaps and uncertainties. Beyond Raveloe is an inexplicable world from which strangers manifest themselves like apparitions or into which people disappear without explanation. Some things come (a child), other things go (the gold). A dominant image is that of light, a candle, surrounded by an encroaching darkness which the characters are unwilling to penetrate. As a result, they are frequently confronted by unexplained events which test their exegetical skills to the utmost. Within the community, too, there are social gaps between the landed parishioners and their tenants which are accepted as unbridgeable and eternal, 'the Raveloe imagination having never ventured back to that fearful blank when there were no Osgoods' (32). And this particular mystery is sharpened significantly by a new development in George Eliot's fiction, the double plot of Silas and Godfrey Cass which reflects these social divisions and in which the interconnections are minimal and mysterious, but of crucial importance. This device, which was anticipated in 'Janet's Repentance', and is to become a central feature of her novels, creates a gap in the fictional structure itself. This is of great problematic significance to both characters and readers as they seek to interpret the relationship between parts and whole. A second gap is the narrative hiatus of sixteen years between the two parts of the novel, the significance of which only becomes fully apparent in the climactic debate.

In addition, as if to underline unmistakably the indeterminacies in this particular fictional world, George Eliot endows the central character with catalepsy, 'the chasm in his consciousness' (169), which baffles both the brethren of Lantern Yard and the rustics. This is another radical challenge to the novelist's experiment in the basic logic of human world-making. In a hostile comment in *The Times*, E. S. Dallas wondered what was the point of writing a story about such 'a singularly unaccountable being' as Silas, since 'the pleasure of fiction depends mainly on our being able to count upon the elements of human character and to calculate results'.[9] The answer is that George Eliot is raising the stakes to show how the very unaccountableness of the world at all levels highlights the crucial interpretative strategies by which people make sense of their lives. This, in other words, is the opposite dilemma to that faced by the protagonist of that other case history, 'The Lifted Veil', as the veils of experience were lifted one by one. Here, the question posed is: how do the characters begin to make sense of a world of gaps, to bridge over such chasms in their lives?[10]

There is a third reason which sharpens this question as far as the major characters, Silas and Godfrey, are concerned. Whereas the community relies on its shared beliefs, that mixture of superstition and religion which finds expression in their public rituals – the Sunday church service, the New Year's dance, the discussions in the Rainbow – the protagonists experience a series of sudden dislocations which makes them reject and revise their ways of looking at the world. This combination of development with disruption, gradualism with catastrophism, is an essential feature of the evolution of world-views in all George Eliot's fiction. Here, however, the discontinuities are so marked that the phrase used of Marner can be applied to all the major figures: their 'inward life had been a history and a metamorphosis' (10) as inexplicable events impinge upon them. The history belongs to fictional narrative as it traces causes and effects, the metamorphosis to legendary story; *Silas Marner* seeks to embody both in such a way that they will articulate and illuminate each other. The reason for George Eliot's interest in such dislocations can be seen in the following comment on Marner's move to Raveloe:

Even people whose lives have been made various by learning, sometimes find it hard to keep a fast hold on their habitual views of life, on their faith in the Invisible, nay, on the sense that their past joys and sorrows are a real experience, when they are suddenly transported to a new land, where the beings around them know nothing of their history, and share none of their ideas – where their mother earth shows another lap, and human life has other forms than those on which their souls have been nourished. (20)

One world-view is dismantled and an alternative has to be created. The novelist goes on to describe the whole symbolic system which had made Silas's previous life meaningful – referred to here as 'habitual views of life', 'faith', 'sense' of reality, and 'forms' of human life – and the effect of his transplanting to a world where he neither knows nor is known. The fictionalised 'legendary tale' is the means of reconciling metamorphosis and history.

These, then, are the features of *Silas Marner* which enable the novelist to carry out her most fundamental experiment into what constitutes a minimally coherent world-view. And the narrative commentary draws its analogies from even more extreme situations. Silas's desperate weaving, for example, is explained in these terms:

Have not men, shut up in solitary imprisonment, found an interest in marking the moments by straight strokes of a certain length on the wall, until the growth of the sum of straight strokes, arranged in triangles, has become a mastering purpose? Do we not wile away moments of inanity or fatigued waiting by repeating some trivial movement or sound, until the repetition has bred a want, which is incipient habit? (27)

Silas, the prisoner in solitary confinement, the author, and the reader, are all brought together in the inescapable need to create sense and purpose through repetition and habit.[11] But, under the narrator's later dialectical scrutiny, even repetition and habit are shown to be, of necessity, insecure in a temporal world:

The sense of security more frequently springs from habit than from conviction, and for this reason it often subsists after such a change in the conditions as might have been expected to suggest alarm. The lapse of time during which a given event has not happened, is, in this logic of habit, constantly alleged as a reason why the event should never happen, even when the lapse of time is precisely the added condition which makes the event imminent. (60)

This is the kind of commentary, analysing in abstract terms the various logics of life and their instabilities, in which the legendary tale is embedded. One of its primary functions, as these quotations show, is to hold together the cause and effect of realistic narrative with the inexplicable events, the metamorphoses, of legend. The best place to examine the relationship between these fundamental logics is in the communities of believers untouched by the hermeneutic of suspicion: 'To people accustomed to reason about the forms in which their religious feeling has incorporated itself, it is difficult to enter into that simple, untaught state of mind in which the form and the feeling have never been severed by an act of reflection' (18). To see how the novelist separates form and feeling – and then re-unites them – in order to examine their relationship, it is necessary to turn to the careers of the two major characters.

The parallel careers of Silas and Godfrey Cass, out of which the novel is constructed, originate in contrasting systems of belief, each of which is shown to be insecure in its response to the unpredictable. This inadequacy is deftly dramatised in *Silas Marner* through the simple groupings of a few characters.

In response to 'the currents of industrial energy and Puritan earnestness', the narrow religious sect of Lantern Yard has developed its own form of Calvinistic Dissent. Its nature is revealed on the occasion of the youthful Silas Marner's first cataleptic fit during a prayer meeting. In the absence of medical explanations, two competing interpretations seek to account for his 'suspension of consciousness'. One is that he has been divinely 'selected for a peculiar discipline': the other, put forward by his rival and one-time friend William Dane, is that it is 'more like a visitation of Satan'. There is no way of adjudicating between these two contrasting interpretations which, George Eliot implies, are both generated by their common supernatural premise: the belief in justification by faith alone and the need for the assurances of salvation to which that leads. The first interpretation, based on simple religious trust, is accepted cautiously by the 'impressible' Silas. The other, based on his arrogant confidence in the 'unshaken assurance' (11–13) of his own salvation, is put forward by the jealous and 'imperative' Dane. The original friendship of the two men – known by the brethren as David and Jonathan – is based on the polarity of their characters, which defines the vulnerability of the religion of Lantern Yard. Assurance and trust, active and passive, have become separated. This is subsequently demonstrated by the ensuing scandal over the theft of church money of which Silas is accused. Dane has, in fact, exploited one of Silas's catalepsies in order to convert what had been seen as evidence of salvation into evidence of guilt, in the knowledge that neither legal measures nor the examination of the circumstances of the theft will be resorted to. Instead, in the first of the two trials in the novel, the brethren pray and draw lots as a means of eliciting 'immediate divine interference'. When the lots declare Silas guilty, he blasphemes in his despair against 'a God of lies, that bears witness against the innocent' (17), and leaves Lantern Yard as the true meaning of the evidence becomes clear to him. In the search for a hermeneutic of absolute assurance, things, as so often in George Eliot, have become their opposites: the certainty of immediate divine intervention finds expression in the randomness of the drawing of lots. In such an interpretative community, duplicity easily, almost inevitably, exploits innocence.

Not only does Silas lose his faith, his rationale of life, but he also moves to the contrasting rural and easy-going world of Raveloe where excessive spirituality is as unwelcome as too-regular churchgoing (133). Here, in exile, he has to begin again, trying to make sense in a state of despair which is 'little short of madness' (18). As with Mr Tulliver's 'mortification' on the loss of the mill, George Eliot's prose quickens when a character is disinherited of the place in which his world-view is grounded, where its coherence makes objects meaningful and their facticity gives it substance. Its painful loss elicits the strongest sense of its reality. What follows is exile, that limbo 'in which the past becomes dreamy because its symbols have all vanished, and the present too is dreamy because it is linked with no memories' (20). This blank must – and it is one of George Eliot's imperatives – be filled with some minimal coherence if Silas is to continue as a character. This is perhaps the closest the novelist comes in her fiction to the complete deconstruction of one of her characters. With the chasm in his consciousness within and the meaningless world of Raveloe without, he has to be reconstructed virtually *ex nihilo*.

All he carries with him into exile is his skill in weaving, and around this a new coherence is created as he weaves himself into existence, as it were, enacting a miniature creation myth.[12] The stages are carefully defined. First, with both past and future cancelled, it is the act of weaving itself which begins to fill the gap in his life, the threads crisscrossing its emptiness. 'He seemed to weave, like the spider, from pure impulse, without reflection. Every man's work, pursued steadily, tends in this way to become an end in itself, and so to bridge over the loveless chasms of his life' (23). The commentary provides the application for the educated reader. Then, the gold that he earns becomes, in the absence of all other purposes, an aim in life: 'that habit of looking towards the money and grasping it with a sense of fulfilled effort made a loam that was deep enough for the seeds of desire' (24). Out of the 'immediate sensations' of weaving, Silas's new world-view is beginning to form. Time acquires a structure and a meaning: 'the money had come to mark off his weaving into periods, and the money not only grew, but it remained with him' (27). Although it is in a cramped and isolated form, with 'his life narrowing and hardening itself more and more into a mere pulsation of desire and satisfaction that had no relation to any other being', past, present, and future are being linked meaningfully together. Then, as the gold pieces begin to provide the continuity in his life, Silas comes to love them as 'his familiars' and 'to enjoy their companionship' (28). And, finally, out of his single-minded activity he creates the ritual, his Midas-like 'revelry', which expresses and celebrates this vivid fetishism.[13] At night he locks his doors and closes his shutters, bringing out the golden guineas – the sacraments of his belief – for his love and worship.[14] 'He spread them out in heaps and bathed his hands in them; then he counted them and set them up in regular piles . . . and thought fondly of the guineas that were only half-earned by the work in his loom, as if they had been unborn children – thought of the guineas that were coming slowly through the coming years, through all his life, which spread far away before him, the end quite hidden by countless days of weaving' (30–1). From the mechanical and minimal rhythm of his weaving, he has created a world of meaning which appears to fulfil all his needs and give coherence to the rest of his life. One contemporaneous reviewer perceptively compared Silas to Job, but at this stage of his career Silas has effected some kind of restoration in defiance of the lament of the man of Uz: 'My days are swifter than a weaver's shuttle, and are spent without hope.'[15]

Through this account of Silas's early life and his fifteen-year exile, George Eliot is establishing the basic rhythm of the novel, the metamorphosis of one world-view into its opposite: in this case, absolute trust in the divine is replaced by fetishism, the miraculous by the materialistic, trust by self-dependence, the believing community by a world of solitary utility. As Gillian Beer has written, 'Metamorphosis emphasises abrupt disconnection, the apparent fissuring of past and present', and quotes Cassirer to the effect that 'the mythic consciousness does not see human personality as something fixed and unchanging, but conceives every *phase* of a man's life as a new personality, a new self'.[16] In neither phase, George Eliot implies, is Silas fully human. In Lantern Yard, he is defenceless, naive, and with his 'deer-like gaze' (12) disengaged from the world. Now, in contrast, in his embittered reaction he simply becomes the energy that drives his loom in the workaday world as his physique changes and his 'face and figure shrank and bent themselves into a constant mechanical relation to the objects of his life'. Though the phases are not completely exclusive – the narrator is at pains to remind us that his 'sap of affection was not all gone' (29) – these are the sharp antinomies which the dialectic has to move beyond. At this point, the career of Godfrey Cass in the other half of the novel first impinges upon Silas in the theft of his gold.

Having lost his god, Silas has turned himself into a machine (that 'great art of adapting means to ends', in Carlyle's phrase)[17] for making gold, and, like Midas, he becomes what he believes in. Now, with his gold mysteriously snatched away, he teeters again on the edge of madness and meaninglessness as he utters 'the cry of desolation' (64). He begins to work again, 'but the bright treasure in the hole under his feet was gone . . . the evening had no phantasm of delight to still the poor soul's craving'. Again, a 'sudden chasm' has opened up in his life but now he can only '[fill] up the blank with grief' (117). How can he begin to make sense once more in his dereliction? '*Was* it a thief who had taken the bags? or was it a cruel power that no hands could reach, which had delighted in making him a second time desolate?' (65). This is the question that Silas, in his helplessness, is now forced to carry into the community where he finds no clear answers.

There follows George Eliot's lengthy pastiche of the hermeneutics of juridical evidence. By what theories of evidence, motive, and circumstance is crime explained and guilt established? Unlike the prompt trial at Lantern Yard, this case is embraced by the whole Raveloe community which discusses it endlessly but no conclusion is reached, not even by Justice Malam, 'a man of capacious mind' who 'could draw much wider conclusions without evidence than could be expected of his neighbours' (114). In the process, which she clearly relishes describing, George Eliot gently parodies the contemporaneous debates in theology and history as to the nature of evidence and its interpretation. As R. H. Hutton commented, 'The turn given to the conversation of the peasants . . . has almost always a distinct relation to the intellectual forms of the same questions as discussed in moden times by the educated classes'.[18] Even the establishment of the simplest facts is shown to be fraught with difficulty. For example, it is considered important at one stage of the inquiry to establish if a pedlar, a possible suspect, wore ear-rings when he passed through the village. The response is immediate. 'Of course, every one who heard the question, not having any distinct image of the pedlar as *without* ear-rings, immediately had an image of him *with* ear-rings, larger or smaller as the case might be' (94). And the testimony to the size and the incriminating nature of the ear-rings escalates rapidly. But finally, as interest peters out, the debate divides characteristically into two irreconcilable schools of thought, both of which the community accommodates: 'the balance continued to waver between the rational explanation founded on the tinder-box, and the theory of an impenetrable mystery that mocked investigation' (115–16). Every act of interpretation is shown, with persistent irony, to be the expression of a particular world-view to the extent that the one crucial fact in this case, the simultaneous disappearance of Dunstan, is never linked to the robbery in this semi-feudal world of Raveloe. 'I doubt whether a combination so injurious to the prescriptive respectability of a family with a mural monument and venerable tankards' – says the narrator in a judicial manner – 'would not have been suppressed as of unsound tendency' (115).

It is in this context of indeterminacy that Silas begins the third phase of his career, the final stage of the dialectic. No longer 'utterly forsaken' (117), he is initiated by his Raveloe 'comforters' (133) into a way of looking at his afflictions very different from the assurances of salvation sought so urgently in Lantern Yard. Mr Macey first tells him that his loss may be all for the best, because 'there's windings i' things as they may carry you to the fur end o' the prayer-book afore you get back to 'em' (120). Dolly Winthrop develops this mystery in a more benign direction with 'her simple Raveloe theology', which combines 'trust i' Them as knows better nor we do' (128) with good works. Certainly, 'left groping in darkness, with his prop utterly gone', Silas now knows 'that if any help came to him it must come from without' (124). Prompted by their rustic theology, this is why on New Year's Eve he is waiting expectantly with his door open when he is again arrested 'by the invisible wand of catalepsy, and stood like a graven image ... powerless to resist either the good or evil that might enter there' (169). The second impingement of the Cass family upon Silas's life then occurs. This can be seen as either good or evil: out in the snow Godfrey's opium-addicted wife dies and the child enters his cottage. As the most sudden metamorphosis in the novel happens – his gold is transubstantiated into Eppie's curls before his eyes – Silas begins to evolve his third world-view to explain these events.

With nothing left, Silas has been prepared for this catalepsy and what it brings. Into the chasm in his consciousness something will enter – 'there was really something on the road coming towards him' (169) – and the crucial concern is his response. As with Job, the question is, what has survived his afflictions? First, as the gold changes into a child, he remembers his dead sister and then Lantern Yard, as if the child were a messenger from his past: 'it stirred fibres that had never been moved in Raveloe – old quiverings of tenderness – old impressions of awe at the presentiment of some Power presiding over his life' (171). But from the mystery of the otherworldly he is recalled to the immediate present by concern for the child who is 'happily occupied with the primary mystery of her own toes, inviting Silas, with much chuckling, to consider the mystery too' (172). He is forced now to address the 'ordinary natural means by which the event could have been brought about' (170). In other words, his response to the child brings rapidly together his family memories, his original faith, and his this-worldly concerns into a new synthesis. What has made this possible is the persistence of the 'sap of affection'. This is confirmed as he claims the right to keep the child, when 'his speech, uttered under a strong sudden impulse, was almost like a revelation to himself: a minute before, he had no distinct intention about the child' (177). George Eliot holds in skilful tension the suddenness of metamorphosis with the development of character. Silas's response to the child, his act of faith – a revelation, at last – subsumes and transforms both the search for salvation in Lantern Yard and the hoarded treasure of his life at Raveloe.

The belief he now begins to articulate is based on this simple act of faith: 'My money's gone, I don't know where – and this is come from I don't know where. I know nothing – I'm partly mazed' (181). Dolly Winthrop, echoing God's covenant with Noah,[19] encourages him to see this as the vital rhythm of life itself: 'it's like the night and the morning, and the sleeping and the waking, and the rain and the harvest – one goes and the other comes, and we know nothing how nor where' (186). This encourages Silas to formulate the inner logic of the legend, his reversal of the Midas story: 'Thought and feeling were so confused within him, that if he had tried to give them utterance, he could only have said that the child was come instead of the gold – that the gold had turned into the child' (188). Each of these minimal interpretations is a confession of faith out of which the legend is finally constructed. But even after sixteen years, by which time he has, through Eppie, 'come to appropriate the forms of custom and belief which were the mould of Raveloe life' (213), Silas is still seeking the deeper meaning of these events. He recapitulates his earlier life to Dolly for her guidance and, as with the other fundamentalist aspects of *Silas Marner*, this is hermeneutics at its most basic: 'The communication was necessarily a slow and difficult process, for Silas's meagre power of explanation was not aided by any readiness of interpretation in Dolly, whose narrow outward experience gave her no key to strange customs, and made every novelty a source of wonder that arrested them at every step of the narrative' (214). It is a kind of *mise-en-abîme* of interpretation: the reader interprets the narrator who interprets Dolly's interpretation of Silas's fragmentary account of his mysterious experience.

Dolly is at first baffled but then, at certain moments when she is helping people in need, she is given insight. There is no master key, the puzzle remains, but there is a clue: 'And all as we've got to do is to trusten, Master Marner – to do the right thing as fur as we know, and to trusten. For if us as knows so little can see a bit o' good and rights, we may be sure as there's a good and a rights bigger nor what we can know – I feel it i' my own inside as it must be so' (217). The dialect forms help to effect, and keep in tension, the transition from God is Love to Love is God, in a paraphrase of Feuerbach.[20] It is crucially important that Dolly's confession of faith arises out of the experience of helping others, for it acknowledges the inseparability of faith and works, those two dimensions of her Raveloe theology which had been fatally separated in the first two stages of Silas's career – the Calvinism of Lantern Yard and the utility of his isolated weaving – but which have now been joined. He acknowledges this in another minimal statement of belief: 'That drawing o' the lots is dark; but the child was sent to me: there's dealings with us – there's dealings' (218). And, as Q. D. Leavis has suggested, faith and works are held together in the community at large by means of the concept of deserved good luck.[21] It is in these terms that Raveloe eventually comes to understand the meaning of the legend, 'Silas Marner's strange history', with its 'conclusion that he had brought a blessing on himself by acting like a father to a lone motherless child' (272). It is worth emphasising that its meaning can only be expressed in the legendary narrative evolved and validated in the community. In Lantern Yard the narrative came to a halt in the randomness of the drawing of lots; while Silas's solitary weaving was a form of non-narratable re-iteration, 'the monotony of his loom and the repetition of his web' (184). Through the mediation of Eppie, in contrast, Silas establishes a covenant with the world, as her biblical name implies,[22] through which faith and works vitalise each other, bringing together continuity and change in the developing narrative of his life.

In the other half of the novel, the career of Godfrey Cass undergoes its own metamorphoses, not as sharply as Silas's for this is the more realistically contextualised part of the story, but according to a similar rhythm. This again traces the origins, the self-contradictions, and the re-establishment of world-views. The context here is the aimless, indulgent, and bored life of the rural landowners whose repetitive rituals are – in a compelling phrase – their only means of 'annulling vacancy' (46).

As with Lantern Yard, George Eliot sketches and analyses the ethos of the Cass family by a simple arrangement of characters, a genealogy of world-views. The family is ruled over by Squire Cass, a widower, who in the semi-feudal but easy-going world of Raveloe, combines in an unpredictable way the qualities of indulgence and harshness. His two sons have responded in contrasting ways and have become, like Silas and Dane, polar opposites dangerously separated. The good-natured but irresolute Godfrey hopes for the best in this uncertain world, developing his own minimal strategies of coherence. 'He fled to his usual refuge, that of hoping for some unforeseen turn of fortune, some favourable chance which would save him from unpleasant consequences' (126). And George Eliot again shows how such a self-justifying belief becomes its opposite: in Lantern Yard divine omniscience found expression in the drawing of lots, while here favourable Chance itself becomes 'the god of all men who follow their own devices instead of obeying a law they believe in'. This part of the novel also seeks to negotiate between the extremes of determinism and randomness, both fatal to the development of narrative, by insisting on 'the orderly sequence by which the seed brings forth a crop after its kind' (113).

In contrast to the passive Godfrey, the decisive Dunstan doesn't believe in chance but in his own good luck, which he actively pursues with 'diabolical cunning' (45) in a Raveloe version of William Dane's assurances of salvation. Dunstan seems to have all the necessary

156   George Eliot and the conflict of interpretations

qualities for survival under the erratic rule of his father which his older
brother, who he is intending to supplant as heir, lacks. And this is why
Godfrey has to use him repeatedly as his agent and intermediary – in
his clandestine marriage (into which Dunstan trapped him in the first
place), in the settling of his debts, and the selling of his horse. Relying
on him more and more, Godfrey becomes increasingly vulnerable to
his blackmail, as their opening conversation in the novel skilfully
dramatises, one frustrated and blustering, the other sarcastic and
manipulative. As his agent, Dunstan expresses his brother's illicit
desires, his wish to marry the desirable Nancy, his 'good angel', with
its accompanying darker corollary, the wish for the death of 'demonic'
Molly. Their interdependence is expressed in their mutual recrimina-
tions, their reciprocal threats to tell all to the squire, their shifting of
responsibility on to the italicised other: 'It's *you* have got to pay
Fowler's money; it's none of my business' (42). Both, also, are in fear of
the Squire who shows occasional but startling insight into their
characters. They are complementary characters who seek to survive
in a haphazard world by using and blaming each other; their
doppelgänger relationship[23] – dramatised in more detail than that of
Silas and Dane – points ahead to Bulstrode and his blackmailing
agent Raffles in *Middlemarch*. In this way, by means of a simple,
legendary-like genealogy, a tyrannical father with one good son and
one bad, George Eliot defines three world-views: an unstable original
which splits into two hostile polar opposites which undermine each
other. The stable world of the rustics, based on their belief in deserved
good luck, is here dismantled by their betters into a reliance on chance
or a cunning self-interest. Separate from each other, faith and works
are again shown to be corrupting and self-defeating.

    From this perspective, those mysterious interventions in Silas's life
are explicable as successive expressions of the Cass world-view – the
loss of gold becomes theft, the arrival of Eppie becomes her
abandonment by her parents. When Dunstan sets off, therefore, to sell
Godfrey's horse and subsequently, after its death, to steal the gold, we
are repeatedly reminded that he is acting as his brother's agent. In
their world of chance, Dunstan embodies the need to improvise. It is a
darkening world: the winter afternoon wanes, the mist gathers, and
self-interest loses contact with reality. 'A dull mind, once arriving at
an inference that flatters a desire, is rarely able to retain the
impression that the notion from which the inference started was
purely problematic' (57). In this narrowing world, Dunstan steals the

gold and then, with a bag in each hand, confidently 'stepped forward into the darkness' (59). The darkness into which he steps is the epitome of all the other gaps of unintelligibility in the novel. It is, for one thing, a gap in the narrative – the chapter ends here – which isn't explained to characters or readers until the end of the novel. It is also the acting out of all those metaphors of entering 'the cold darkness' (41) of negation and vacancy we have seen in both halves of the novel. Most suggestively, at the beginning of the next chapter, Silas's devastation at his loss is compared to that of 'a man falling into dark waters [who] seeks a momentary footing even on sliding stones' (64). The black hole of predatory self-interest turns into that of innocent despair: both thief and victim have narrowed their worlds to the gold.

Though he is now freed from his familiar, his dark shadow, Godfrey is still vulnerable to the consequences of his worship of chance, still 'visited by cruel wishes, that seemed to enter, and depart, and enter again, like demons who had found in him a ready-garnished home' (47). The biblical allusion[24] emphasises that this is another kind of covenant, and points ahead to Godfrey's vulnerability later when his wife and child are found. First, he hopes that his wife is dead; it is as if Molly's death-wish through opium, 'the familiar demon in her bosom' (165), has transferred itself to Godfrey as the fulfilment of Dunstan's earlier prophecy. Then, having received the 'demon', he rejects, or rather fails to claim, the 'angel' (210), his own child, at the crucial pause in the narrative which is to determine its conclusion. 'The wide-open blue eyes looked up at Godfrey's without any uneasiness or sign of recognition: the child could make no visible [or] audible claim on its father; and the father felt a strange mixture of feelings, a conflict of regret and joy ... when the blue eyes turned away from him slowly, and fixed themselves on the weaver's queer face' (181). As with Silas's catalepsies, such a hiatus acquires meaning from the response it elicits. Event is interpretation. What Godfrey thinks mistakenly is the 'deliverance from his long bondage' (179) is, in reality, Silas's: the first is simply a passive reliance on events, the second a positive prompting which leads to salvation.

At this moment, Godfrey is about to initiate his second, fifteen-year phase, the reverse of the first, as Silas's rescue from his fifteen-year isolation begins. Godfrey's marriage to Nancy is both his salvation and his nemesis. The Lammeter family, as the other main landowners in Raveloe, represent a countervailing tendency to the Casses, as their names suggest.[25] Again, George Eliot sketches their world-view in the form of a simple genealogy: the sober, strong-minded and orderly widower, with his two contrasting daughters. Nancy's sense of propriety, conventionalism, and exactitude is complemented by Priscilla's rough, plain-speaking independence. After the fifteen-year gap in the novel, we see that Nancy has transformed Godfrey's view of the world. Chance has given way to routine, order, and accountability. But amid this ordered life there is one omission, described variously as a 'blank' or a 'void' (237–8), which corresponds to the gap in the text for the reader. This is their childlessness. Godfrey seeks to repair the omission through the adoption of Eppie, but Nancy's providentialism denies him this compensation. Their lack both unites and separates them. Over the years Godfrey has come to see their childlessness as a retribution, which Nancy is at a loss to understand. And just before the discovery of Dunstan's body which precipitates the denouement of the novel, we see Nancy applying her theory of life to this mystery. It is a kind of displaced theological exegesis. She sits with her Bible open and begins to think about her marriage. 'She was not theologically instructed enough to discern very clearly the relation between the sacred documents of the past which she opened without method, and her own obscure, simple life', but she is rigorous in her self-scrutiny with its 'excessive rumination and self-questioning' (231). As with the Casses, George Eliot dialectically uncovers the contradictions within this rigidly ordered Lammeter world: it is based on its own kind of superstitious belief in coincidence (217), the belief she has, paradoxically, rescued Godfrey from. Now, without making her revise 'her unalterable little code' according to which 'to adopt a child . . . was to try and choose your lot in spite of Providence' (234), she has been forced to try and see things from her husband's point of view. '*Had* she done everything in her power to lighten Godfrey's privation?' (233). This lack of accord, this tension centred on the gap in their marriage, has defined their relationship of fifteen years, changing both of them in the process. Godfrey, we are told, 'was kept in a certain awe of this gentle wife who watched his looks with a yearning to obey them' (238).

This is the long preparation, running parallel to Silas's fostering of Eppie in the time-gap allowed by legend,[26] which culminates in the discovery of Dunstan's body at the climax of the novel. It is, like so much else in the story, both sudden and carefully prepared, initiated in the plot by Godfrey's longstanding concern over Nancy which has prompted him to drain the stone-pits to make a dairy. With this discovery Godfrey's growing sense of order and retribution now turns into a full confession and acceptance of an omniscient divine power: 'Everything comes to light, Nancy, sooner or later. When God Almighty wills it, our secrets are found out' (243). They find they have misinterpreted each other. Her shock is followed by Godfrey's surprise when she replies: 'Do you think I'd have refused to take her in, if I'd known she was yours?' (244). This mutual and finely prepared misjudgment is an essential part of the mild nemesis of the story. But now, having fully reversed his earlier belief in chance, Godfrey is ready to accept his full responsibilities in an ordered universe; and the representatives of the Cass and Lammeter families, those pillars of the community, are of one mind as they go to claim their daughter. As with the earlier novels, the climactic events release a flood of interpretation and re-interpretation. Not only do Godfrey and Nancy re-examine their positions, but also Silas, Eppie, Dolly, and the rustics all state their views on what has happened.

The first trial scene in *Silas Marner* was concerned with the theft of money at Lantern Yard, the second is about the ownership of Eppie. In the weaver's cottage the 'contest' (256), as it is called, takes place between the two fathers with the recovered gold on the table. The legendary nature of the story prompts us to ask, who will get which? Or, according to the logic of metamorphosis, for whom will the gold turn into the child and for whom will the child turn into the gold? Underpinning this logic, as we have seen, George Eliot has developed a complex hermeneutic of contrasting and juxtaposed world-views. As the views of Silas and Godfrey come into direct confrontation, the question prompted by this aspect of the novel is, what interpretative principle or key will settle this semi-legal contest of a paternity suit?

The reader has been well prepared for the difficulties attending the assessment of evidence upon which truth-claims can be based. The divided structure of the novel has guaranteed that all the major events are ambivalent – someone's loss is another's gain – while, in addition, the precise interpretation of these events is determined by particular world-views. It is this psychological contextualisation which has turned the legend into the novel. As one would expect, a good deal of this interpretative gloss is assigned to the narrative commentary, though all the major characters have been seen performing acts of exegesis. There is, however, one chapter in which George Eliot carries out, through the rustics of Raveloe, a full-scale rehearsal of the problems attending any act of interpretation. The conversation in the bar of the Rainbow in chapter four is a brilliant tour-de-force which dramatises the paradigm upon which the true meaning of the legend of Silas Marner will be based. It is as if, before finally abandoning her rural fictions, George Eliot intends to show that all the hermeneutic complexities she is concerned with can be expressed quite adequately through rustic dialogue.[27]

There are essentially three topics of conversation, and each dramatises the impossibility of finding a single key of interpretation. First, there is an argument about a cow between the aggressive farrier and the mild butcher, each of whom views the cow from his own incontrovertible, professional point of view beyond which he refuses to go, leaving it to the pacific landlord, secure in his own profession ('but this I say, as the Rainbow's the Rainbow'), to draw the only conclusion: 'The truth lies atween you: you're both right and both wrong, as I allays say' (70). A variation is played on this theme when the argument switches to the singing of the village choir. This in turn is defused by that other arbiter, the parish clerk, Mr Macey, on similar grounds: 'there's allays two 'pinions; there's the 'pinion a man has of himsen, and there's the 'pinion other folk have on him' (72). In this way, some of the basic modes of interpretative conflict are set out before the ritualised conversation moves on to the strange marriage ceremony of Nancy's parents, but only after the raconteur Mr Macey has issued a warning against premature interpretations. He then tells the story of how the vicar, who had taken too much brandy, put the crucial questions of acceptance to the bride and groom the wrong way round, 'by the rule of contrary, like', and nobody noticed. As parish-clerk, Mr Macey experienced a kind of hermeneutical vertigo:

'why, I was all of a tremble; it was as if I'd been a coat pulled by the two tails, like; for I couldn't stop the parson – I couldn't take upon me to do that; and yet I said to myself, I says, "Suppose they shouldn't be fast married, cause the words are contrairy?" and my head went working like a mill, for I was allays uncommon for turning things over and seeing all round 'em; and I says to myself, "Is't the meanin' or the words as makes folk fast i' wedlock?" For the parson meant right, and the bride and bridegroom meant right. But then, when I come to think on it, meanin' goes but a little way i' most things, for you may mean to stick things together and your glue may be bad, and then where are you? And so I says to mysen, "It isn't the meanin', it's the glue".'
(76)

With both public testimony and private intentions shown to be fallible, Mr Macey was left with only his analogical and mysterious 'glue'. The vicar, however, quickly came to his assistance and identified the glue as the medium through which both public and private find expression; 'it's neither the meaning nor the words – it's the re*ges*ter does it – that's the glue' (77).

With the gap between words and meaning, signifiers and signifieds, closed for the time being – the anecdote, like the whole discussion, has to be regularly repeated – the conversation turns from the validation of human relationships to a more theological topic, the existence of ghosts at the Warrens. How does one test the evidence? Old Mr Macey provides the traditional account of the mysterious sights and sounds at the old house, but the sceptical farrier, 'the negative spirit in the company' and an uncompromising materialist, rejects his supernatural interpretation. He is ready to wager ten pounds with anyone who will go with him that they neither hear nor see anything. Someone points out the weakness of the experiment: 'You might as well bet a man as he wouldn't catch the rheumatise if he stood up to 's neck in the pool of a frosty night.' As an alternative, let the farrier go and stand in the dark by himself, suggests Mr Macey cunningly, 'and then he can let the parish'ners know if they're wrong'. He agrees to these conditions until the butcher points out the snag: 'Ah, but who's to watch you, Dowlas, and see you do it?' At this point, the landlord again seeks to pacify his customers with a more subjectivist view of the truth. Just as his wife can't smell the strongest cheese, there are some people, he believes, who 'can't see ghos'es, not if they stood as plain as a pike-staff before 'em . . . And so, I'm for holding with both sides; for, as I says, the truth lies between 'em.' But the farrier rejects this shilly-shallying 'analogical argument' and insists that the ghosts must meet his own positivist criteria: 'If ghos'es want me to believe in 'em, let 'em leave off skulking i' the dark and i' lonely places – let 'em come where there's company and candles.' His annoyance has led him to concede the premise, which the parish clerk seizes upon in a final dismissive deconstruction: '"As if ghos'es 'ud want to be believed in by anybody so ignirant!" said Mr Macey, in deep disgust at the farrier's crass incompetence to apprehend the conditions of ghostly phenomena' (78–82).

It is highly significant that George Eliot translates these hermeneutic principles into the idiom of the folk. The discussion on ghosts, for example, runs through several different kinds of arguments – from historical evidence, experience, experiment, analogy, belief – and ritually deconstructs each in turn. The village consensus, expressed through the parish clerk and the landlord, is that that there are always two opinions and 'they've only got to split the difference and make themselves even' (73). As with Hardy, this pervasive and cautious irony of the rustics is the communal context in which the landowning protagonists seek and fail to establish their more unilateral world-views, expressed through pairs of contrasting characters. The folk hermeneutic expresses through dialogue, debate, argument, disagreement, and reconciliation, the mode of the community's trust and survival. The name of the inn itself, where Silas failed to find his pot of gold, points to the covenant of the community. And it is within the covenant of this interpretative community that the story of Silas's life will be validated as legend.

The conversation at the Rainbow was broken off by the arrival of Silas, bereft of his gold. Now at the climax of the novel, these rustic hermeneutics are recalled as Silas refers back to that moment of desolation, as the Casses arrive to assert their legal claim on Eppie. The two worlds of the novel confront each other. On what principle will the ownership of Eppie be decided? Silas has passed from the otherworldliness of Lantern Yard through the machine-like world of his weaving to their synthesis and sublation in his life with Eppie. Now that the gold has been found, he is in his moment of 'transfiguration' (247) in possession of his whole life, and is beginning to understand its meaning. This interpretation is what he is about to articulate and defend. He is just telling Eppie that if he lost her, if she were turned back into the gold, he would feel in his forsakenness that 'it was a curse come again' (248). Godfrey, on the other hand, having fully accepted the Lammeter version of a divinely ordered cosmos in which everything comes to light, is now intent on claiming Eppie as the 'blessing' denied his marriage and so putting to rights his sixteen years of secrecy and irresponsibility, impatient of any obstacles to 'his virtuous resolves' (254).

The climactic trial-scene of claim and counter-claim is finely observed, especially the nuances of class-conflict which become a decisive factor. First, Godfrey and Nancy offer to adopt Eppie in order to 'make her a lady'. When she rejects this, Godfrey asserts his real claim: 'It's my duty, Marner, to own Eppie as my child, and provide for her. She's my own child; her mother was my wife. I've a natural claim on her that must stand before every other' (254). As for Nancy, too, 'her code allowed no question that a father by blood must have a claim above that of any foster-father' (233). But even though it combines arguments from legality, duty, and nature, we know from the problematic climax of *The Mill on the Floss* that any such claim is vulnerable to counter-claims based on 'the special circumstances that mark the individual lot'. Silas immediately invokes these circumstances by asking, 'Then, sir, why didn't you say so sixteen years ago, and claim her before I'd come to love her?' And later, 'Your coming now and saying "I'm her father" doesn't alter the feelings inside us. It's me she's been calling her father ever since she could say the word' (255).

This – the proof is in the naming – is the basis of Silas's claim, and he is now ready to articulate the theology he has evolved out of his experiences. In one sense, he has come to accept the Raveloe belief in earned good luck, but Godfrey's challenge pushes him beyond this to a more comprehensive statement of his faith which is a synthesis of all his experiences both in Lantern Yard and Raveloe. We are alerted to this by 'his accent of bitterness' which recalls his moment of youthful blasphemy. He fears that he is going to be tricked again. The difference is, however, that he is now in a position to justify his claim by an interpretation of events which finally exorcises his earlier blasphemy, combining as it does the language of Lantern Yard with what he has learned in Raveloe: 'God gave her to me because you turned your back upon her, and He looks upon her as mine: you've no right to her! When a man turns a blessing from his door, it falls to them as take it in' (254). What was before a simple sequence – gold, child – now becomes a more complex statement of cause and effect, a kind of teleology, since Silas, unlike the rustics, knows at last how the two halves of the novel fit together. Secure in the community, in possession of his past, this expression of his belief announces the completion of his becoming fully human. His 'transfiguration' at this point is the final metamorphosis of his career.

The final decision, the judgment in the trial, however, is not left to the principals or to any external authority, but to Eppie, the living result of that sixteen-year time-gap in the novel and the confirmation of one man's blessing and the other's retribution. The princess in exile chooses to stay with her foster-father by re-affirming the covenant Silas had made in adopting her as a child, and she expresses it in the same balanced biblical rhythms used by Dolly Winthrop and, more recently, by Silas to articulate their beliefs. First comes the negative version ('he'd nobody i' the world till I was sent to him, and he'd have

nothing when I was gone') and then the fulfilment of the covenant:
'And he's took care of me and loved me from the first, and I'll cleave to
him as long as he lives, and nobody shall ever come between him and
me' (258). The circumstantial and social context out of which this
statement comes is repeatedly emphasised, as Silas and Eppie, vividly
conscious of each other, touch and hold hands in their cottage. It is a
complex and moving scene which recuperates the whole of the double
narrative: the world-views of the Lammeter and Cass families, now
united, confront Silas's theology, evolved through his painful career.
The trial dramatises the irreconcilable conflict of interpretations to
which George Eliot's fictions invariably lead. There is no key of
interpretation, as Maggie discovered in her dilemma, only a
breakthrough into another kind of action, discourse, confession. On
this occasion, the breakthrough is into the sixteen-year gap in the
novel during which Eppie has become the incarnate history of Silas's
love. With great simplicity Eppie cites this as the evidence which
ensures the fulfilment of Silas's covenant.

   Though the life of 'the poor who are born poor' (257) is
unintelligible to Godfrey and Nancy, they accept Eppie's decision
and Silas's judgment, and through this rejection Godfrey is forced, in
turn, to move on. He now begins to reconcile the passive reliance on
chance of his early life with its opposite, his belief in a fixed order and
nemesis, neither of which have brought him his daughter. The sad
acceptance is expressed in terms of organic growth: 'While I've been
putting off and putting off, the trees have been growing – it's too late
now' (262). This is the darker side of the belief in earned good luck.
Neither he nor Silas are allowed to go back into the past, pay off their
debts, clear up the mystery, and start again – for even Lantern Yard
has disappeared when Silas returns there at the end of the novel. In
this way, there is no final clarification of the events of the novel. Silas's
interpretation, as it is validated by the community, remains
authoritative, a belief in order based on trust, an expression of the
inseparability of faith and good works.

In a recent essay on *The Ancient Mariner*, Jerome McGann has
suggested that the poem can be read as an expression of Coleridge's
reformulation of the Higher Critical approaches to the Bible with
which he was familiar. Central to these – and crucially to the
transmission of the gospels – is the belief that all event is, in the first
place, interpretation and that inevitably, therefore, 'the Scriptures

grew by accretion and interpolation over an extended period of time',
by which they were constantly validated within the Christian
community. In this perspective, McGann sees *The Ancient Mariner* as
'a poem which illustrates a special theory of the historical interpretation of texts' with its 'four clear layers of development' – the original
mariner's tale, the ballad narrative of that story, the editorial gloss,
and Coleridge's own controlling perspective. 'The "events" treated in
the poem actually represent interpretations of events carried out in
terms of certain fragmentary "systems" of human thought',[28] each in
its own way part of the continuing process of spiritual revelation.

The whole essay is suggestive in the discussion of the hermeneutics
of *Silas Marner*, profoundly influenced as both authors were by biblical
Higher Criticism. In the novel, as in the poem, there are a few crucial
fabular events – the theft of the money, the drawing of the lots, the
theft of the gold, the arrival of a child, the recovery of the gold – all of
which are subjected to layers of interpretation. Instead of different
textual levels, we have in the fiction different levels of discourse. At the
primary level there are those crucial spontaneous reactions, analo-
gous to the blessing and cursing of the albatross and the water-snakes.
These reactions are shown in turn to be interpretations based on
developed world-views which are confirmed or challenged. In the
course of the protagonists' careers, George Eliot depicts dialectically a
range of 'fragmentary systems of human thought' all with their
contemporaneous analogies – Calvinistic Dissent, Utilitarianism,
Chance, Providentialism – which are all taken up into the resolution
of the novel. The two essential poles of the dialectic are chance and
order, both of which are shown to be superstitious if pursued
unilaterally, and neither of which is able to create by itself a coherent
narrative. Such a narrative only emerges as Silas (and belatedly
Godfrey) begin to scrutinise the events of their lives retrospectively
and, secure in some kind of love and community, combine chance and
order into a sequence which acknowledges both. The next layer is that
of the believing community of Raveloe which both guides and
validates Silas's recovery of his life as he grows into fellowship. And,
acting as a bridge between the characters and the reader, there is
finally the narrator's commentary which elucidates, generalises, and
interprets the events of the rural community at the turn of the century
into the language of the Victorian educated reader, who is thus
invited to become a member of the believing community. But there
really is no final layer of interpretation. As the critical tradition

demonstrates with regard to both poem and novel, the discussion of the precise symbolic significance of the patterning of character and event continues. As McGann writes, in language applicable to *Silas Marner*, 'In Coleridge's terms, the symbolically grounded interpretations are acts of witness rather than definitions, human events which dramatically testify to the desire to know and continuously create the truth that has always set men free'.[29] In George Eliot's case, it is the tension and interaction between the legend and the novel which make that creation and re-creation not only possible but necessary.

CHAPTER 5

Romola: duplicity, doubleness, and sacred rebellion

After the anthropology of the first three novels, George Eliot turns to historical reconstruction in *Romola*, a work of extraordinary scope and ambition. We have seen how the novelist sketched a variety of alternative world-views in the theodicies of Hayslope, and then in *The Mill on the Floss* focused on the process by which a family of world-views was formed and destroyed. These can now be read as adumbrations of the far more ambitious work which follows: *Romola* extends and recasts this range of world-views into a comprehensive history of European civilisation. As such, it dramatises the formidable task of hermeneutics to re-possess the past in those belated Victorian times, beset by a keen awareness of the discrepancy between inherited forms and the contemporary spirit, a state of mind embodied most vividly in Dorothea Brooke's anguish as she confronts in bewilderment the 'stupendous fragmentariness' of a Rome which should have been 'the spiritual centre and interpreter of the world'. How can one recover the past as a living presence? Or, in the words of *Middlemarch* again, how does one acquire 'the quickening power of a knowledge which breathes a growing soul into all historic shapes, and traces out the suppressed transitions which unite all contrasts'?[1] This is the task to which *Romola* explicitly and urgently addresses itself.

There were many hermeneutic metaphors or models available to describe the interpretation and recovery of the Victorian past. In his opening remarks to *The Ring and the Book* (1868), Browning, for instance, runs through several possible analogies for his re-creation of a seventeenth-century Roman murder trial – painting a landscape, conducting an electrical experiment, reconstructing a column from a fragment of stone. But the controlling metaphor is that of the poet as metal-worker. To the pure gold of the trial record, the Old Yellow Book, he has added the alloy of his imagination to make it malleable, meaningful, and recoverable. It is, significantly, an action which

167

avoids either the embalming of a dead past or creating something out of nothing; the former would be idolatrous, the latter sacrilegious. The writer must 'project his surplusage of soul' into the dead body of the past and so achieve 'Mimic creation, galvanism for life' – 'Creates, no, but resuscitates, perhaps'.[2] Beginning with the proem to *Romola*, George Eliot, too, becomes more explicit about her interpretative aims and problems. In *Felix Holt* she will introduce these through the device of the coach ride, and in *Middlemarch* by means of a saint's life; here, at the beginning of *Romola*, she performs her own act of resuscitation as a way of expressing the hermeneutic task.

The angel of the dawn sweeps in Ruskinian fashion[3] eastwards from the Levant to the Pillars of Hercules in the spring of 1492, announcing the epic scope of *Romola* as he pauses, not over a Gothic cathedral, but over Renaissance Florence at the time when Columbus is waiting for the ships which will carry European civilisation further westwards. From this lofty perspective, it is 'the broad sameness of the human lot' which reminds us 'that we still resemble the men of the past more than we differ from them'.[4] And, to test this theory, the narrator summons from the shades 'the spirit of a Florentine citizen' who died earlier that year and invites him to scrutinise the city from the hill of San Miniato in the Victorian present.[5] Initially, the spirit confirms that 'the sense of familiarity is so much stronger than the perception of change' (1.3). But then differences become apparent and he begins to query certain architectural details – the new spires, the demolished towers, the closed gates. His questions become more difficult to answer, especially when they focus upon the political life of the community. Who is in power? Who is out? To understand his questions it is necessary to interpret the interpreter, to locate him in his own Florence of 350 years earlier, to provide a detailed *curriculum vitae*, and to uncover his assumptions in order to fit together his world and his world-view. The result dispels any simplistic ideas that the past is easily accessible.

Our resuscitated Spirit was not a pagan philosopher, nor a philosophising pagan poet, but a man of the fifteenth century, inheriting its strange web of belief and unbelief; of Epicurean levity and fetichistic dread; of pedantic impossible ethics uttered by rote, and crude passions acted out with childish impulsiveness; of inclination towards a self-indulgent paganism, and inevitable subjection to that human conscience which, in the unrest of a new growth, was filling the air with strange prophecies and presentiments. (1.9)

Though the mixture is antithetical, it is, like the spirit's eventful career, comprehensive. The 'strange web of belief and unbelief' is

accommodated by Renaissance tolerance: 'For the human soul is
hospitable, and will entertain conflicting sentiments and contradictory opinions with much impartiality' (1.7). But can such a mind
understand the Florence of the Victorian present? It is as if
Browning's bishop had been resuscitated from his tomb and is now
asking, 'How has it all turned out?' (1.10).

As the spirit is about to descend to the city to find out, the narrator
delivers a warning: 'Go not down, good Spirit! for the changes are
great and the speech of Florentines would sound as a riddle in your
ears' (1.11). The figure from the past cannot go forward into the future
and rejoin his old community: if he could, he would no longer be a
spirit. It is doubly impossible in his case because he died just as the
Florentine amalgam was about to fragment, with Lorenzo de'Medici
in his final illness and Savonarola beginning his denunciations from
the pulpit of San Lorenzo. If he insists on trying, the narrator advises
him to look selectively at the things which have not changed – the
sunlight, the shadows, the children, the churches, and their worshippers – as sights more suitable for the half-life of a revenant. But if he is
unable to come forward into the present, the novelist can go back to
1492, understand both sameness and difference, and so fill the 350-
year gap for her Victorian readers. Indeed, she has already begun to
do so by her act of resuscitation. The point which these complicated
temporal shifts are making is that the past, especially the Florentine
Renaissance past which has made us, can and must be re-possessed
through memory, imagination, and interpretation. But the plight of
the spirit – a world-view without a world – dramatises the difficulties
of the task. Time is continually moving on: 'For the Pope Angelico is
not come yet' (1.12).

In this way, George Eliot initiates the formidable task of historical
retrieval and reconstruction in which she displays all her intellectual
credentials for the first time. As Felicia Bonaparte has suggested in
impressive detail, George Eliot was seeking to write 'the first distinctly
modern epic' in the tradition of Homer, Virgil, and Dante, 'a
prospectus for the future progress of Western civilization'.[6] The
extraordinary scholarly preparation, the notebooks of accumulated
erudition, the recurrent attacks – acute even by her standards – of
psychosomatic illness, Lewes's fear that she was compiling an
encyclopedia rather than writing a novel, and her conviction that it
turned her into an old woman – all these signal the turning-point that
Romola represents in her career. In one way, it can be seen as her

fictional response to those Victorian synthetic philosophies, gathering up the past and projecting the future, with which she was intimately and cautiously familiar. To achieve this, the original model – the master plot articulating 'the fate of poor mortals' – has to be expanded in various ways to accommodate a history of European culture, but it remains essentially the same. Various world-views are again formulated and subjected, in an enlarged sense of the phrase, to 'the varying experiments of Time' by which they are juxtaposed and tested to destruction, until there occurs the final impasse from which a new future has to be summoned into existence. It is no accident that in this novel 'a huge and ghastly image of Winged Time' himself appears, 'with his scythe and hour-glass, surrounded by his winged children, the Hours' (1.308). The new element that *Romola* introduces is the enormously problematic nature of historical recovery upon which a realistic future can be projected. As such, it truly reflects the novelist's own travails in the writing of her modern epic.

The novel begins on the day after the death of Lorenzo de'Medici which had been accompanied with suitably apocalyptic omens. The dismayed Florentines reassure each other with the report that their Christian Magnifico, 'at once lettered and devout' (1.11), *l'uomo universale*, finally requested Savonarola's blessing and at the last 'never took his eyes from the holy crucifix' (1.33). For George Eliot, the end of the precarious synthesis he symbolised is the pivotal moment of the Florentine Renaissance and by extension of European civilisation. A new dark epoch has immediately come to the city, says one of the characters: 'Lorenzo has left behind him an inheritance that is but like the alchemist's laboratory when the wisdom of the alchemist is gone' (1.111). Now, in this vacuum, each of the alchemical elements seeks to assert its own unique claims to the truth, to transmute everything, in Browning's phrase, into its own kind of 'mimic creation'. As the web of Florentine culture is unravelled in this way, the process of historical development is reversed and the past re-enacted in the rebirth of the founding myths of European culture.

The claims of the classical past in the form of pastoral hedonism are embodied in Tito Melema, who comes to consciousness on a Florentine pavement in a dehistoricised present 'with the startled gaze of a suddenly-awakened dreamer' (1.15). This enigmatical figure, with his bland, untroubled pagan beauty, baffles and fascinates the Florentines as they seek to accommodate him within their own world. His lineage is that of Heine's *The Gods in Exile*, of Hawthorne's *The Marble Faun*, or Pater's later *Denys l'Auxerrois*, where an amoral classical past bursts into the modern present with shattering results. With his hyacinthine locks and looking as if he has come 'straight from Olympus' (1.41), Tito is the apparent anomaly which Florence has to re-possess as part of its disrupted inheritance. He in turn projects his selective vision on the Florentine complexity, unravelling the strands the author is weaving together. He dismisses condescendingly the 'Christian barbarism' in their buildings, the 'hideous smoked Madonnas', 'fleshless saints in mosaic', and 'skin-clad skeletons hanging on crosses' (1.49), but congratulates them on the vital humanism of Ghiberti's baptistery doors. This is another form of the anamorphism, the extreme perspectivism of *Adam Bede*, which results in a limited but powerful interpretation of a complex reality with which, Tito is assured, others in Florence will sympathise. But when the Florentines talk of 'the gods awaking from their long sleep and making the woods and streams vital once more' (1.50), it is a piece of whimsy. Classical paganism is only one strand of their complex web. Tito, in contrast, has to create a life for himself in Florence with pagan good looks, charm, and classical learning, as his sole assets. This is the dramatic, dialectical view of the Renaissance that George Eliot presents in *Romola*: not only is Florence trying to re-possess the classical past at a time of cultural fragmentation, but also that reborn embodied past must adapt its ideas to the far-from classical, historical present. Parallel to this, *mutatis mutandis*, is the Victorians' intense, ongoing dialogue with the Renaissance with which they felt they had so much in common. One of George Eliot's aims is to deliver a caution against a too easy identification.

The elaborate episode in the barber's shop initiates the pagan god into Florentine life. In his impartiality, the barber Nello is an embodiment of all the different elements which constitute secular Florence, his shop an ironical mosaic of classical Renaissance culture. If Lorenzo was the Pericles of the Athens of Italy (1.44), he tells Tito, then his shop 'is a no less fitting haunt of the Muses, as you will acknowledge when you feel the sudden illumination of understanding and the serene vigour of inspiration that will come to you with a clear chin' (1.51). This is the mock domestication of the pagan god into the pastiche jumble of the neoclassical world – manuscripts, musical instruments, ancient masks, sketches – which Nello has enshrined in his adytum at the centre of which is a statue of Hermes, the messenger of the gods and the presiding deity of hermeneutics. *Romola* is noticeably full of such collections of heterogeneous objects which challenge any kind of unitary interpretation, collections which are a *topos* of Victorian representations of the Renaissance. Tito, undismayed, offers to decipher one of the objects, a sketch by Piero di Cosimo of a triptych of masks – Satyr, Magdalen, and Stoic – in the lap of a child which invites (and has attracted) interpretation. But the reader, like Tito, is cautioned by Nello: 'everybody has his own interpretation of that picture' (1.52). Tito is, however, now ready to begin his career at the Via de' Bardi where, on his arrival, the cloistered heroine's 'astonishment could hardly have been greater if the stranger had worn a panther-skin and carried a thyrsus' (1.89).

A second messenger arrives in Florence a few weeks later, not to be born but to die, and for the purpose of asserting the claims of the countervailing myth, that of an ascetic medieval Christianity. This is the Dominican Fra Luca, Romola's brother Dino, who delivers to his sister as he dies a warning that has been conveyed to him in a vision, 'in a low passionless tone, as of some spirit not human, speaking through dying human organs' (1.236). In contrast to Tito's disdainful commentary on Christian Florence, Dino warns Romola against the corruption and aridity of its pagan, classical culture by means of an allegory. 'And at last you came to a stony place where there was no water, and no trees or herbage; but instead of water, I saw written parchment unrolling itself everywhere, and instead of trees and herbage I saw men of bronze and marble springing up and crowding around you.' And at the centre of this nightmare of classical learning, says Dino, 'stood a man whose face I could not see. I looked and looked, and it was a blank to me, even as a painting effaced' (1.241). Just as Tito dismissed the spirituality of the churches as so much spasm and colic without entering them, so Dino imposes his obsessive typological vision upon the secular life of the city without being able to describe the figure (who has come to marry his sister) at the centre of its classical paganism. Each man's extreme perspective creates a blind spot which prevents them acknowledging in normal human terms their opposites.

The result is that though both men are seeking to influence Romola, one to captivate, the other to warn, they are passive and helpless when confronted by their opposites. The two 'apparitions' define themselves by their obtuseness. Dino, for example, as well as delivering his apocalyptic vision also carries a more prosaic message to Tito that his foster-father needs rescuing from slavery, but he ignores its human significance: 'The prevision that Fra Luca's words had imparted to Romola had been such as comes from the shadowy region where human souls seek wisdom apart from the human sympathies which are the very life and substance of our wisdom' (1.246). Not only does it prevent him from warning his sister about Tito, but its extreme nature – the indulgence George Eliot locates at the centre of asceticism – pushes her towards the tempter. Tito's obtuseness is of the opposite kind: in his pagan hedonism he is unable to engage with the basic moral concern, in this case of son for father, which has been challenged by Dino's message. In a sense, both characters come from different extremes of the same 'shadowy region', seeking wisdom apart from the sympathies which make us human. Romola, who responds to both, is their only tenuous connection.

The extreme perspectivism of the two men has obvious similarities with that of Hetty and Dinah in *Adam Bede* who personified the forces out of which Hayslope had been constituted. The difference here is that we are shown what motives have resuscitated the pagan god and the medieval ascetic (and their respective myths) in Renaissance Florence: both Tito and Dino are the products of the intense, single-minded quest of the previous generation for the roots of classical antiquity. In this most self-consciously textual of novels, the two men are the direct result of scholarly research. Tito's stepfather, Baldassarre, in fulfilling one of the crucial roles in the classical rebirth has risked his life travelling widely in Greece 'for the discovery of inscriptions and other traces of ancient civilisation' (1.96), at a time when the Turks are destroying the remaining records. This obsessive pursuit of origins through epigraphy seeks to recover classical learning in all its purity by placing it once again in its original context. This is an essential hermeneutic task, as Tito explains; 'my father . . . was of opinion that a new and more glorious era would open for learning when men should begin to look for their commentaries on ancient writers in the remains of cities and temples, nay, in the paths of the rivers and on the face of the valleys and the mountains' (1.99). But the dangerous quest for origins has become a sacrilegious end in itself; Baldassarre has been 'lost on a voyage he too rashly undertook to Delos' (1.93), the most sacred shrine of ancient Greece. When he returns he is possessed.

Baldassarre's plans have been thwarted in another way. Having rescued Tito from poverty, he subordinated him to his overriding purpose, turning him into an accomplished scholar whose memory is the only record now remaining of his stepfather's researches. But these stringent demands have been rejected by Tito in favour of a way of life to which the mission itself was directed: 'I have rested', he boasts, 'in the groves of Helicon, and tasted of the fountain Hippocrene' (1.102). He has chosen to live the life of a hedonistic pagan god, and so escape the demands made upon him. Out of the strenuous scholarly quest for the origins of classical antiquity has emerged its apparent opposite – the original pastoral vision which was, of course, one of its objects. It is the familiar ironic juxtaposition of 'Old learned, respectable bald heads' and the passionate texts they are editing and annotating: 'Lord, what would they say / Did their Catullus walk that way?'[7] For George Eliot it is also a dramatic version of the dangers of the unilateral, singleminded attempt to resurrect the past in an unmediated form. Baldassarre puts aside his humanity in the present to resuscitate a past which becomes a charming monster, embodying everything he has rejected, which then rejects him in turn. The subsequent relationship of the two men is a kind of Frankenstein version of the history of ideas. This rupture and betrayal is inherent in the search for origins, as we see again in *Middlemarch*.

The scholarly mission of Romola's father, Bardo, is equally singleminded and similarly frustrated. He has channelled the old family pride of the Bardi, in Renaissance fashion, into the editing of classical texts. Only the editor, he believes, can recover the texts in their original purity and so reveal 'the minds of the immortals who have reaped the great harvest and left us to glean in their furrows'. In the belated present, he tells his daughter, everything 'must depend on the manuscript over which we scholars have bent with that insight into the poet's meaning which is closely akin to the *mens divinior* of the poet himself'; if this is neglected, then 'the very fountain of Parnassus' will be turned 'into a deluge of poisonous mud'. With classical stoicism, energy, pride, and misogyny, he has cut himself off from the world in order to pursue this self-imposed and exclusive mission: 'it was with the great dead that I lived; while the living often seemed to me mere spectres – shadows dispossessed of true feeling and intelligence'. He, like Baldassarre, is punished for this unnatural, idolatrous, and bibliographical reversal: the historian loses his memory, the editor has lost his sight. As a result, 'that great work in which I had desired to gather, as into a firm web, all the threads that my research had laboriously disentangled' (1.76–7) is unfinished. Time entangles, the editors and historians seek to disentangle; but lacking genuine insight they become blind, without acquiring like Teiresias, in the story from Poliziano's *Miscellenea* that Bardo is misinterpreting to Romola, the compensatory gift of prophecy. And so on his first appearance in the novel he sits unseeing in his library, surrounded by his books and manuscripts, collating from memory a variety of authors – Nonnus, Plautus, Quintilian, Boccaccio, Petrarch, Homer, Callimachus, Epictetus, Horace, Zeno, Epicurus – in a scene of extraordinarily complex intertextuality, in order to justify his stoical pride and self-dependence. But the true copy-text is there beside him, acting as his despised amanuensis, Romola, whose hair is 'the only spot of bright colour in the room' (1.72) surrounded, as she is, by 'the lifeless objects around her – the parchment backs, the unchanging mutilated marble, the bits of obsolete bronze and clay' (1.79).[8]

Like Baldassarre, Bardo has been abandoned by his son Dino, the coadjutor upon whom he depended, who has left 'all liberal pursuits that he might lash himself and howl at midnight with besotted friars – that he might go wandering on pilgrimages befitting men who know of no past older than the missal and the crucifix' (1.80). This is again the extreme perspectivism of George Eliot's Florence where disagreement leads to total rejection in the form of parody, caricature, and ridicule. But like Tito, Dino has looked at the content as well as the text of the classical works he was editing and seen only 'worldly ambitions and fleshly lusts' (1.236) from which he turns in horror, aware of his own weaknesses from which the maxims of philosophy provide no release. But he also glimpses in the classics the possibility of 'a life of perfect love and purity for the soul', 'a foreshadowing of [the saint's] ecstasy'. 'For the same truth had penetrated even into pagan philosophy: that it is a bliss within the reach of man to die to mortal needs, and live in the life of God as the Unseen Perfectness' (1.237–8). This is the 'seed' which begins to grow, leading him to forsake his father, the world, and in his extreme asceticism the church, prompting him to live like a hermit and only returning to Florence, like Tito from the east, to deliver his visions and prompt his brethren to study oriental, as opposed to classical, languages.

In this family history of ideas, the son has again been led to a rebellion which is both a development and a betrayal. Dino has realised that his father's life is a contradiction. In his retreat into scholarship, Bardo had sought to fortify himself against the vicissitudes of Fortune and the temptations of Fame by means of stoical precepts. And yet his maxims are powerless to control the pride which, like his daughter's, makes large claims on life. Fame may be hollow, 'but not if it is the just meed of labour and a great purpose. I claim my right' (1.86). The stoic demands paradoxically that his work – or at least his library – shall be a monument to him so that the future will acknowledge its indebtedness. But in this way he puts at risk his peace of mind, his reputation, his immortality, among the very people he despises in his isolation. He even refuses to publish any of his work because, he argues, scholarship in the modern world has become 'a system of licensed robbery' (1.84). And yet, as he becomes his own obituary, he feels he has a right to be remembered. This is the stalemate his life has reached and which Dino seeks to supersede and sublate through his ascetic Christianity which resolves the contradiction between his father's worldly desire for immortality and his stoical detachment, granting the son the visions denied the father.

For both Baldassarre and Bardo, then, the obsessive attempt to recover the original purity of classical antiquity fails because of its non-dialectical nature. Their antiquarianism refuses to enter into a dialogue with the past which, in consequence, uncovers the contradictions in their lives. As these become apparent, their coadjutors resolve the contradictions in their own way, selecting from antiquity those strands which satisfy their own needs. There is a deep irony in this genealogy of ideas: Bardo needs his son's eyes and is offered his visions, while Baldassarre needs his stepson's memory and is offered pastoral forgetfulness. The younger men diverge in opposite directions, one towards hedonism, the other towards asceticism, according to the biases of their mentors. So out of the common rebirth of classical learning spring these two contrasting forces, the whole process being dramatised in terms of father-son relationships which are both a process of development and a break between generations. But in Florence, as the Renaissance synthesis fragments, it is the violent disruption that is emphasised as fathers and sons pronounce 'anathemas' (1.82) on each other.

The forces released into Florence in this way, as the past erupts into the present, are each seeking their own fulfilment, their paradise or world apart – the phrases are used repeatedly in the novel – either through an ecstasy of sensual fulfilment or through the spiritual ekstasis of asceticism. These are the absolute states the myths define. But both Tito and Dino are deflected from their quests by the heroine, whom they wish to rescue from their opposites and then appropriate to their own world-views. Having learned how to avoid appropriation by their fathers, these male-engendered characters now seek to appropriate Romola, the soul of Florence. Tito quickly gains access to the Bardi household because he is everything that the ascetic and anathematised Dino is not. As an intermediary with 'the alien world' (1.93) he is not only beautiful and charming but undemanding. He is a character in the pastoral mode of Theocritus (1.162) who seeks effortless assimilation to the world. 'He never jarred with what was immediately around him' (1.155). If this is the world, then the reclusive Bardo and his daughter feel they might come to terms with it as they project upon Tito their own feelings and ambitions. Romola, in particular, moralises his pagan aestheticism as the mutual appropriation proceeds: 'A girl of eighteen imagines the feelings behind the face that has moved her . . . as easily as primitive people imagined the humours of the gods in fair weather' (1.104). But this kind of response is not peculiar to the heroine. Through Tito, George Eliot is exploring a new kind of characterisation in her fiction, one in which there appears at first to be no interaction between the self and circumstance from which character is formed. His 'beautiful form represented a vitality so exquisitely poised and balanced that it could know no uneasy desires, no unrest' (1.152). Matthew Arnold called this the 'equipollency' of Hellenism.[9] Tito's eyes, with their 'unwearied breadth of gaze' and 'perfectly pellucid lenses' (89), offer no barrier to the traffic between inner and outer experience. This is the moment of the Hellenic ideal which Pater also captures memorably in his essay on Winckelmann (1867) in *Studies in the History of the Renaissance*, a work which reads at times like an extended commentary on *Romola*. It is symbolised, for Pater, in the *adorante* of the Berlin museum: 'Fresh, unperplexed, it is the image of a man as he springs first from the sleep of nature, his white light taking no colour from any one-sided experience. He is characterless, so far as *character* involves subjection to the accidental influences of life.'[10]

George Eliot characteristically interrogates the nature of this ideal by thrusting Tito into the modern reality of Renaissance Florence, from myth into history. What happens when the 'accidental influences of life' are allowed to impinge upon this ideal? How do the intense and worldly Florentines interpret him? 'Was it that Tito's face', asks the narrator, 'attracted or repelled according to the mental attitude of the observer? Was it a cypher with more than one key?' (1.156). In the intensely spiritual perspective of Dino, for example, such a character – bland, atemporal, amoral – can only register as a tempter with a blank face, 'a painting effaced'. Others respond differently, but it is always in accordance with what they bring to the encounter: 'The strong, unmistakable expression in his whole air and person was a negative one, and it was perfectly veracious' (1.156). His most successful relationship is with the contadina Tessa; 'he was simply a voice and a face to her, something come from Paradise into a world where most things seemed hard and angry' (1.163). She accepts him as an apparition, while he sees her condescendingly as a 'little loving ignorant soul [which] made a world apart' (1.223), without moral judgment. But in Florence proper he is faced with choice and decision. Confronted with the evidence about his stepfather, he is forced to form a hypothesis to justify his inaction and, though he has apparently done nothing decisive, this hypothesis becomes part of his characterless character. 'He had made it impossible that he should not from henceforth desire it to be the truth that his father was dead.' The next stage is to conceal the facts so that the hypothesis remains unchallenged: this is 'the contaminating effect of deeds' which leads to 'the consequent adjustment of our desires' (1.153). The final stage which comes later in the novel is to ensure that the desired hypothesis becomes fact. This is the process by which Tito, the figure from myth, is being transformed willy-nilly into a character, even through apparent inactivity, as his 'talent for concealment was being fast developed into something less neutral' (1.173). Later, he learns to deploy his apparent neutrality more actively, as he becomes all things to all men in Florence. Margaret Homans has examined in some detail the ways in which Tito achieves his own ends by repeatedly offering himself as the passive translator, the apparently uninvolved interpreter of other people's messages.[11] Hermes adapts himself in this way to the modern world.

Tito's motivation is his pagan hedonism: 'What, looked at closely, was the end of all life, but to extract the utmost sum of pleasure?' (1.175). He is Bacchus reborn and the justification of his hedonism – his interpretation of the myth he embodies – is presented as a powerful element in the modern world; and through this critique of the utilitarian felicific calculus, George Eliot is reminding her readers that they too are involved in the intense struggles in fifteenth-century

Florence. As Felicia Bonaparte comments, 'Bacchus proves to be the most thoroughly modern man'.[12] The oneness with the world which Tito seeks, precludes the feeling of dread, that contrasting strand of Greek thought, which George Eliot sees as the origin of the moral life: 'it is the initial recognition of a moral law restraining desire, and checks the hard bold scrutiny of imperfect thought into obligations which can never be proved to have any sanctity in the absence of feeling' (1.177). Without this dread – its importance as nemesis is represented in the novel by the Eumenides of Aeschylus – obligations are naturalised and disposed of; but the excluded dread is then externalised in Baldassarre's revenge from which there is no escape. Before that manifests itself, however, Tito's naturalisation of the world continues apace, stripping value, meaning, and significance from the highly charged culture of Florence as he subjects it to his calculus. The ultimate prize, of course, is Romola, the soul of Florence, who holds all its best qualities in vital suspension.[13] As he tries to aestheticise her moral grandeur, he finds himself unexpectedly under the influence of her 'noble womanhood which is perhaps something like the worship paid of old to a great nature-goddess . . . whose life and power were something deeper and more primordial than knowledge' (1.143-4). It is an experience which grants, uniquely to Tito before he becomes entangled in the Florentine labyrinth, a glimpse of Romola's true origins outside time from where she must begin her recuperation of the history of western civilisation. In this perspective, the heroine predates both the pagan god and the medieval ascetic.

The countervailing influence on Romola is that of her brother who seeks, in turn, to spiritualise the world. With his 'monkish aspect' and 'the far-off gaze of a revisiting spirit' (1.234-5), the contrast with Tito is extreme but it conceals certain similarities. The divine love which has 'sought' and 'penetrated' Dino has taken possession of him as 'a seed that wants room to grow' (1.237); in the same way, Tito sees his pastoral ideas as 'lively germs' sown in the fresh soil of his mind according to 'the order of nature' (1.175). These are moments of insemination, the creations of classical antiquity in new forms unsuspected by their mentors. And in Dino's case too, this new growth dissolves all previous human ties as 'fellow-beings' are metamorphosed into 'human souls related to the eternal unseen life' (1.238). By not engaging with the life of Florence in its human complexity, by seeking to realise their unmediated, mythic visions, both revenants manifest a similar passivity, the 'delicious languors' (1.277) of one balancing the spiritual abandonment of the other. In his spiritual decoding of the world, Dino discounts the self as much as Tito asserts it: 'For in the painful linking together of our waking thoughts we can never be sure that we have not mingled our own error with the light we have prayed for; but in visions and dreams we are passive, and our souls are as an instrument in the Divine hand' (1.239). His warning to Romola against marrying the tempter, 'delivered in his hour of supreme agony, like a sudden awful apparition from an invisible world' (1.243) and expressed in types and symbols, screens out entirely the natural forms of life. If Tito cancels time and glimpses Romola before the beginning of history, this apocalyptic vision projects her into the end-time – 'and the graves opened, and the dead in their shrouds rose and followed you like a bridal train' – as history comes to an end. But the warning is ignored, precipitating the heroine in reaction into the arms of Tito.

These two violently opposed views of life, two anamorphic perspectives, are now juxtaposed in Romola's experience. Can she combine them in a larger synthesis?

Strange, bewildering transition from those pale images of sorrow and death to this bright youthfulness, as of a sun-god who knew nothing of night! What thought could reconcile that worn anguish in her brother's face – that straining after something invisible – with this satisfied strength and beauty, and make it intelligible that they belonged to the same world? Or was there never any reconciling of them, but only a blind worship of clashing deities, first in mad joy and then in wailing?

This is one of those crucial hermeneutic moments in the careers of George Eliot's heroines. Which interpretation, which deity, makes sense of the world? It is the moment which may either bring the heroine into the fallen, problematic life of the realistic novel or finally take her out of it into some other reality. Here it is the former. 'Romola for the first time felt this questioning need like a sudden uneasy dizziness and want of something to grasp; it was an experience hardly longer than a sigh, for the eager theorising of ages is compressed, as in a seed, in the momentary want of a single mind' (1.274). The vertigo at such moments is familiar but, in this historical novel, it turns into a seed, a kind of annunciation, in which the future and her role as the Madonna is latent. It is an image which underlines the complex dialectical structure of the novel. Both Tito and Dino, faced with a similar conflict of forces in their mentors, glimpsed a seed of truth by which they could resolve the conflict and be reborn into a new life. These reborn forces, the polar opposites of the Renaissance, now confront Romola with an even more radical conflict: can she synthesise these antinomies in a larger vision without betraying the affiliations which have made her, the soul of Florence, what she is? The two mentors, both the result of classical insemination, now prompt in Romola through their opposition the need for a larger feminine synthesis, itself the seed of the future. This seed, the moment of equipoise and uncertainty, is potentially both the recuperation of the past and a new birth, both dialectical and organic. European civilisation pivots on this moment which is 'hardly longer than a sigh'.

It will be evident by now that *Romola* is not only George Eliot's historical reconstruction of fifteenth-century Florence and a comment on mid-Victorian England, but also a novel full of characters whose own *raison d'être* is the re-creation or re-interpretation of the past according to their own urgent needs, theories, and myths. In this sense, *Romola* is as much an historiographical and mythographical as it is an historical novel. The fathers, Bardo and Baldassarre, seek to recover the past through different kinds of scholarly research; the sons, Dino and Tito, reject their fathers in order to re-live the past in myth which that research has opened up to them. All four characters in their intense rivalry and enmity are each seeking to impose upon Renaissance Florence a theory of history or its denial which will determine its future development. There are many other characters with similar aims in the novel. But it is left to the heroine to recuperate the past as a living reality in the present, without compromising its historicity: in other words, she has to combine the historical recovery of the first generation with the resuscitated myths of the second.

In the absence of such a unifying vision, the life of the past becomes a collection of heterogeneous fragments. We have seen how this is an essential stage of George Eliot's ruling paradigm. In *Romola* she deploys collections of objects extensively, partly as a means of giving substance to the miscellaneousness of Florence but also, more importantly, as embodiments of Renaissance methods of preserving the past. As far as the first generation of scholars is concerned this is expressed through their antiquarianism in which such collections are invariably presented as fragments which have lost their significance in a museum of the dead. In Bardo's library, for example, a 'feminine torso', 'a headless statue . . . wielding a bladeless sword', 'infantine limbs severed from the trunk', Roman busts and Greek vases supplement his books and manuscripts. All are arranged 'in scrupulous order' (1.71-2) but forming no larger meaning in the absence of an informing vision, symbolised by the scholar's blindness. They are awaiting a rebirth which never comes, and after Bardo's death they are sold off by Tito. The collection is doubly metonymic: the fragments of limbs stand for the bodies which in turn stand for classical antiquity. And yet the dead fragments *are* brought back to life once – by Bardo's coadjutor, his despised son, but not in the way desired. In Dino's typological Christian vision, the fragments turn into demonic bronze and marble figures which taunt Romola as a warning against her pagan lover, himself the re-embodiment of the classical past (1.241-3).

Corresponding to this kind of classical museum is the Church of the Nunziata, where the multitude of worshippers is duplicated by 'another multitude' on the walls and ceilings – 'the crowd of votive waxen images, the effigies of great personages clothed in their habit as they lived', 'the exact doubles of the living', a kind of Madame Tussaud's resumé of Florentine history. 'And wedged in with all these were detached arms, legs, and other members', all awaiting a different kind of rebirth from the *disjecta membra* of classical antiquity: 'It was a perfect resurrection-swarm of remote mortals and fragments of mortals' (1.222) providing again a parody – this time of eternity, seen through Tito's sceptical eyes. In both cases, the reifications of the past, embodied metonymically, are only brought into a surreal kind of life through the alienated parodic vision which dismisses them as *simulacra*. In these forms, neither classical renaissance nor Christian resurrection offers that genuine recuperation and rebirth of the past which everyone – including the historical novelist – is seeking. That will come, not through the fragmentariness and contiguity of metonymy, but through the substitution and identification of metaphor. This has already been hinted at in Romola's momentary dizziness as she oscillates between the 'clashing deities' of paganism and Christianity – 'for the eager theorising of ages is compressed, as in a seed, in the momentary want of a single mind' (1.274). It is through this seed, rather than the preserved fragment, that rebirth will occur.

There are other collections of miscellaneous objects in the novel – Nello's barber's shop (1.51), Bratti's rags-and-bones (1.19), and the Pyramid of Vanities (II.195–6), for example – but the most comprehensive is that of the painter Piero di Cosimo, through whom George Eliot explores further the representation and recovery of the past.[14] The painter is a kind of bricoleur whose attitude to the past is neither antiquarian nor respectful. His studio, a 'heterogeneous still life' (1.284), is a lumber-room from which the novel itself is being constructed – marble fragments, sketches of satyrs and maenads, madonnas and saints, as well as living toads, pigeons and plants – and of which any unifying vision is impossible. Only God can achieve that, as Piero warns a bewildered Tito: 'don't be trying to see everything at once, like Messer Domeneddio' (1.285). The artist's empiricism eschews both philosophy and religion with their unitary abstract truths; and, in addition, he refuses to interpret his own works. To questions about his enigmatic sketch of the three masks, his ironical reply is always that 'his pictures are an appendix which Messer Domeneddio has been pleased to make to the universe, and if any man is in doubt what they mean, he had better inquire of Holy Church' (1.52). Art as appendix avoids both sacrilege and idolatry.

He never aspires, therefore, to the kind of unifying vision towards which the heroine is being conducted, even though he provides in his eclecticism the symbols for both Tito's pagan fantasy and Dino's apocalyptic warnings. But through his paintings he cautions against antiquarianism or any kind of selective historicism, implying as he does so a possible living unity which he never defines. His method is that of metamorphosis. For Piero there is no disjunction between past and present, history and myth, art and nature. When he needs a model for Ariadne, he says he will use a sketch of Antigone he has obtained from depicting Romola, and 'put the likeness into Ariadne'; and for Bacchus he will use a sketch of Tito and 'take the fright out it' (1.286). The archetypes of myth are continually changing into each other and into the characters of the novel; as Browning's Fra Lippo Lippi says, 'Like the Prior's niece . . . Saint Lucy, I would say'.[15] This kind of metamorphosis runs counter to the selective anamorphism of Tito and Dino through which they create their own selective coherences. The difference between the two kinds of morphology is, in fact, acted out in Tito's commission of a miniature of the triumph of Bacchus and Ariadne from Piero to celebrate his betrothal to Romola. Tito borrows a scene from Ovid's *Metamorphoses* but wants the myth modified to conform to his pastoral vision of what life might be (162). Piero complies, but in this most painterly of all George Eliot's novels it is he who once again challenges the fixed image, the false petrification. Character is a state of metamorphosis and can only be represented by the juxtaposition of opposites which imply a larger coherence: the painting of Tito's triumphant joy conjures up the vengeful Baldassarre for its maenadic completion. And it is Piero who prophetically hints at Romola's climactic role – when the clashing deities are reconciled – in his playful naming of her as 'Madonna Antigone'.

These, then, are different versions of the past and the uses to which it can be put. In her progress through the novel Romola is required to assimilate them all, without submitting to the falsification of any. How can the past be recovered as a living presence? In the words of *Middlemarch* again, how does one acquire 'the quickening power of a knowledge which breathes a growing soul into all historic shapes'? The scholars have recovered the 'historic shapes', while Piero the artist has demonstrated some of 'the suppressed transitions' through his metamorphoses. Romola has learnt from these but, in addition, she has to reconcile the deities, the vital forces from the past reborn into the present. She must pass through and beyond metonymy, synecdoche, and metaphor – three of the four master tropes of historical reconstruction, as they have been called – to the final trope of the dialectical,[16] and this grand, comprehensive recuperation must be experienced as a form of historical knowledge and development.

For this purpose George Eliot deploys that characteristic Victorian version of the eternal triangle she used in 'Janet's Repentance', where the heroine is first appropriated by her mentors and then appropriates them in her turn. In this scheme of things which so preoccupied the Victorians, the heroine represents a form of wholeness which the male characters seek to appropriate, coerce, or destroy. To such typical examples as *Jane Eyre* and *Tess of the d'Urbervilles* can be added *Felix Holt* and *Daniel Deronda*, as well as *Romola*. One of the most vivid versions of this is to be found in *Jane Eyre*, in the form of the female catechumen who rebels by providing her own answers to the male catechist. Romola, too, allows herself to be appropriated – by pagan god and Christian prophet – before rebelling and moving beyond them into the future. But there is a curious sense that the heroine comprehends these partial visions from the beginning within her inchoate and antithetical character, as we have seen: from Tito's point of view she is the nature goddess outside history whose reality he is trying to recover, while for Dino she lives beyond the end-time his apocalyptic vision re-creates. She represents a form of essential being which both predates and postdates Renaissance Florence, and upon which the forces of history act to elicit and articulate what is already there. This is the reason her opposition to these forces is so minimal, as George Levine points out in his fine essay on the novel: 'In fact, Romola has from the start a highly complex moral sensibility, and the education she undergoes is only growth in knowledge, which makes the sensibility richer, a working out of that sensibility's implications and possibilities'.[17]

Appropriation proceeds at both public and private levels, and Tito and Savonarola are involved in both, as the conflicting forces seeking to control Florence are polarised with the arrival of the French invaders. On the one hand, the city becomes the centre of a debased form of materialism in which Tito flourishes: it is 'a world in which lust and obscenity, lying and treachery, oppression and murder, were pleasant, useful, and when properly managed, not dangerous' (1.319). Against this corruption Savonarola pronounces his prophetic vision. 'From the midst of those smiling heavens he had seen a sword hanging – the sword of God's justice – which was speedily to descend with purifying punishment on the Church and the world.' As with Dino's warning vision, so Savonarola's prophecy reveals the eternal truths of biblical typology under 'that splendid masquerade of dignities sacred and secular': 'in the Sacred Book there was a record of the past in which might be seen as in a glass what would be in the days to come, and the book showed that when the wickedness of the chosen people, type of the Christian Church, had become crying, the judgments of God had descended on them' (1.319–20). Through this interpretation of events Savonarola declares 'that he had a mission like that of the Hebrew prophets, and that the Florentines . . . were in some sense a second chosen people' (1.317). It is this conflict between two versions of Florence that provides the religious and political context for Romola's education.

This education consists – as it does later for Esther Lyon and Gwendolen Harleth – of a double appropriation by Tito and by Savonarola (who has taken over Dino's role) to their competing visions of the world. These visions, it should be stressed, are not hypotheses to be tested and modified through experience. Their mythic origins define their unmediated nature: they are to be projected on to the world. For Tito, the image of what life should be is the painting of the triumph of Bacchus and Ariadne on the casket he presents to Romola at their betrothal; for Savonarola it is Dino's crucifix. These are not the metonymic fragments of the antiquarians but synecdoches, the part representing a whole vision of life. The impossible paradox for both men, however, is that in order to realise their visions they have to become more and more embroiled in the political present from which they are seeking a world apart. Tito applies his felicific calculus to life and concludes that 'the sentiment of society' is 'a mere tangle of anomalous traditions and opinions, which no wise man would take as a guide, except so far as his own comfort was concerned' (1.176). Explaining away all claims in this way, he seeks to strip value from the world, reducing it to objects which can be manipulated for his pleasure but which have no other significance. In aiming to respond freely and instinctively to any situation according to his self-interest, Tito is refusing to become a character with a moral identity. In contrast, Savonarola's attempt to fulfil his typological vision is the attempt to recover a world of transparent and comprehensive meaning. And he is continually being frustrated by matters of immediate expediency as he becomes embroiled in Florentine party politics. His natural tendency in this situation is to rely dangerously on the power of his prophetic visions and those of his more fanatical followers to achieve his aims.

From observing her two mentors, Romola begins to perceive the narrowness and doubleness upon which their projections are based. First, her marriage enables her to observe how the life of her joyful pagan god is constantly being threatened and darkened by the past he has denied, in the form of his enraged stepfather. Baldassarre represents that other dimension of the Greek world-view of which Tito is oblivious, 'the initial recognition of a moral law restraining desire', justice and nemesis. He becomes the threatening shadow in Tito's life, constantly compromising his success and forcing upon him the claims he rejects. The two men explain each other as they act out the Bacchic myth to which their singlemindedness consigns them. The clarity of Tito's pastoral perspective is blurred by this repeated (anamorphic) intrusion, so that he eventually accepts that he 'should be prepared to see this face rise up continually like the intermittent blotch that comes in diseased vision' (1.404). Baldassarre always appears at Tito's moments of political triumph, demonstrating the impossibility of his attempt to create a value-free world. And Tito is always shocked and unprepared for this apparition from a world he has rejected and yet upon which he has built his success. As a result, he refutes instinctively the claims made upon him, but each rejection embroils him further in plans to evade Baldassarre, and also by extension in the inevitable formation of his moral identity. 'Tito was experiencing that inexorable law of human souls, that we prepare ourselves for sudden deeds by the reiterated choice of good or evil which gradually determines character' (1.340). The individual is the product of history too, even though the felicific calculus seeks to deny it.

The most dramatic expression of the logic of the myth which Tito inhabits is the episode in the Rucellai Gardens. This is a fascinating incident from a hermeneutic point of view, for it shows the stepfather seeking to interpret himself back into existence through the classical texts to which he has devoted his life, so that he can revenge himself on his treacherous amanuensis. Tito's aim is to prevent his recovery from amnesia. The acts of reading and interpretation become the sources of selfhood and power, as Baldassarre realises that the black marks in the volume of Pausanias he is looking at have again become meaningful – 'they were the magic signs that conjure up a world'. He reads, translates, interprets, and applies the text to his own situation: 'That city, which had been a weary labyrinth, was material that he could subdue to his purposes now . . . he was once more a man . . . who felt the keen delight of holding all things in the grasp of language. Names! Images!' In this Renaissance moment, signifiers and signified, names and images, past and present, are rejoined as a source of power and control through the act of reading. This magical skill which brought the pagan revenant Tito into existence will now be used to destroy him as a sacrifice to the 'dark deity' (11.68) of justice whose agent Baldassarre has become. The sudden breakthrough is compared to 'that of the Maenad in the glorious amaze of her morning waking on the mountain-top' (11.70). And as the avenger circles round his prey, it seems that Tito too is preparing for the final Bacchic confrontation as he sings the maenad-chorus from Poliziano's *Orfeo*: 'Bacco, Bacco, evoé, evoé!' (11.89). But he is not ready yet to acknowledge that he is beholden to the past. The cognoscenti set the old scholar a literary context question from Homer as a test of his identity which he fails under the 'dizzy horror' of Tito's renewed rejection. The words become black marks again and Tito is briefly saved.[18]

By now, Romola has perceived the duplicity and contradictions in Tito's philosophy of life as he has tried to adapt it to the complexities of Florence. She resolves to leave both him and the city. But as an acknowledgement of the appropriation she is now refusing, she must reject him in his own terms. As she takes off her betrothal ring, 'the law of her affections' convinces her that she is justified in 'breaking an outward tie that no longer represented the inward bond of love' (II.46). In her rebellion she swings to the other clashing deity, disguises herself as a nun, recalls Dino's prophetic warning against her husband, and glimpses the meaning of 'the agonies of martyrdom' (II.53). But the rejection of one deity and the acceptance of its opposite is not to be as easy as this, as Savonarola points out when he intercepts her flight, reminds her of Dino's warning, and condemns her for breaking the bond of marriage: 'I say again, man cannot choose his duties' (II.105). This is the countervailing appropriation of the heroine for which a different symbol is offered, the crucifix: 'Conform your life to that image, my daughter; make your sorrow an offering' (II.106). She has misunderstood the nature of renunciation and is, in consequence, 'shaken by the suggestion in the Frate's words of a possible affinity between her own conduct and Tito's' (II.104). Her education cannot proceed by simply rebelling against one deity in its own terms and then embracing its opposite: instead of oscillation there must be dialectical progression. Though she is dressed like a nun and carrying a crucifix, she has neither understood nor is fitted for that role. Savonarola explains the true meaning of renunciation and sends her back to her husband in order to join in 'the great work by which Florence is to be regenerated and the world made holy' (II.107). As we have seen previously, the elements are already latent in the heroine's character. This new mentor simply articulates her latent feelings: 'his words had come to her as if they were an interpretation of that revulsion from self-satisfied ease, and of that new fellowship with suffering, which had already been awakened in her' (II.109). Her religious conversion from one clashing deity to the other is not simply a metamorphosis from one kind of ecstasy to another, from the image of the Ariadne to the image of the crucifix. There is growth as one form of rapture is subsumed in the other, as self-interest turns to the general good. The negation of Tito's influence preserves what it negates while transforming it, so that Romola's growth now includes both symbols which are placed side by side.

Though Romola returns to her husband, she has now been appropriated, in turn, by Savonarola's noble task of regeneration in which she achieves 'a new consciousness of the great drama of human existence in which her life was a part' (ii.148). This is the next stage of her complex, dialectical progress. All her other mentors – Bardo, Dino, Tito, Bernardo – have fiercely rejected aspects of life which failed to conform to their views, but now in her long recuperation of the drama of European civilisation Romola appears to have found a mentor whose vision embodies the wholeness she initially represented. But her progress which proceeds simultaneously on the mythical, historical, and domestic level is not over yet. As she glides through Florence, performing acts of charity in a rather detached manner, she again becomes beset by doubts, gently parodied by her cousin Monna Brigida. Savonarola has allowed political intrigue to confuse the simplicity and clarity of his prophetic vision. As he is compromised in this way, we observe his prophetic claims in the perspective of Romola's growing alarm, and his political embroilment in the perspective of Tito's cynical scheming. Then, the self and the larger purposes to which it is committed fall apart into another example of the inevitable 'doubleness' of character.

There are two reasons why Savonarola's oscillations between his vision and his politics are so anguished. First, the very breadth of his character which enables him to respond to both realities militates against their unification. 'Savonarola's nature was one of those in which opposing tendencies coexist in almost equal strength: the passionate sensibility which . . . tends towards contemplative ecstasy, alternated in him with a keen perception of outward facts and a vigorous practical judgment of men and things' (ii.357). These antithetical tendencies are forced into extreme conflict in the episode of the trial by fire, which lesser mortals see either as a divine test or a tactical, political move. Responsive to each, he fails on both counts. And, secondly, Savonarola is especially vulnerable because he is a rebel against the Church which he is trying to purify along with Florence. When the Church is envisaged as 'a living organism, instinct with Divine power to bless and to curse' (ii.255), the decision of exactly when duty turns into resistance must be an agonising one. As George Eliot commented in *The Mill on the Floss*, the answer to such a problem 'is clear to no man who is capable of apprehending it'.[19] The discrepancy between the outward law and the inner moral facts brings the individual to the extreme conflict of interpretations: this is the moment of isolation and freedom, as Romola realises when she

draws an analogy between her own eventual rejection of her
marriage, against Savonarola's advice, and his rejection of the
authority of the Church.

The law was sacred. Yes, but rebellion might be sacred too. It flashed upon
her mind that the problem before her was essentially the same as that which
had lain before Savonarola – the problem where the sacredness of obedience
ended, and where the sacredness of rebellion began. To her, as to him, there
had come one of those moments in life when the soul must dare to act on its
own warrant.

This is the key moment in the onward dialectic of life, the Antigone
moment, when the soul acts without precedent, not only 'without
external law to appeal to but in the face of a law which is not unarmed
with Divine lightnings' (II.273). And the 'sacred rebel', as the
oxymoron implies, can never rest in his rebellion.

Like Tito, Savonarola's dilemma intensifies as he becomes entangled in the web of Florentine life. Then, Romola's trust begins to
waver as the priest responds to political pressure with increased
fanaticism, a fanaticism expressed as 'that hard systematic judgment
of men which measures them by assents and denials quite superficial
to the manhood within them' (II.235). The crucial test comes when
she visits Savonarola to plead for her imprisoned godfather's life –
only to be told that in the last resort 'the death of five men . . . is a light
matter weighed against . . . the furthering of God's kingdom upon
earth, the end for which I live and am willing to die' (II.308–9). This is
where Savonarola's appropriation of the heroine to his vision of life
comes to an end. As with Tito's opposing vision, it has been tested to
destruction and it is now rejected in the terms Romola has again
learned from the mentor himself: 'I do not believe it! . . . God's
kingdom is something wider – else, let me stand outside it with the
beings that I love' (II.309). The irony, as we have seen, is that she
justifies her rebellion against the sacred rebel by discovering an
analogy between their situations. At her godfather's subsequent
execution, she has moved beyond the conflict of interpretations,
apparently beyond all her mentors, back to that intense primordial
experience before history articulated and divided it into separable
and opposing world-views: 'She felt that intensity of life which seems
to transcend both grief and joy – in which the mind seems to itself akin
to elder forces that wrought out existence before the birth of pleasure
and pain' (II.316). These elder forces precede the clashing deities and

their dialectic within the historical life of Florence. She must now leave the city and the constraints of verisimilitude, drifting away in her boat to seek freedom from the burden of choice.

As the historical focus comes increasingly to bear on Savonarola, George Eliot has used the continuing marital conflict between Romola's high ideals and Tito's cynical pragmatism as a means of access to the priest's dilemma. At this point in the narrative, for example, just after Romola has left, Tito visits Savonarola to trap his political opponent into an error which will be used in his overthrow; he is shown to his cell as the inner conflict of the 'sacred rebel' – 'the conflict was one that could not end' (II.360) – is modulating into the glow of the yet-to-be-fulfilled vision. It is this which makes him gullible and manageable as Tito obtains the incriminating letters that he needs. Like Romola, he too finds Savonarola inconsistent, but on the grounds of realpolitik, and he exploits this inconsistency later to trap him into the disastrous trial by fire which leads to his downfall. From Romola's point of view, Savonarola was discredited because his political ambitions vitiated his moral principles; Tito, and his friend Machiavelli, in contrast, are impressed by his political skills but can't understand the admixture of religious fanaticism which constantly frustrates those skills. With the downfall of Savonarola in the 'Masque of the Furies' (ch. 66) which he has helped to bring about, Tito too realises his life in Florence has come to an end, not because of moral conflict but because of his multiple deceits whose consequences it would require an unattainable 'omniscience' (II.350) to handle successfully. His conflict of interpretations, which has resulted from the persistent application of the felicific calculus, is a parody of Romola's high-minded balancing of values and responsibilities. This is how far he has travelled from his apparently innocent awakening in Florence exactly six years earlier. As his enemies unexpectedly catch up with him in the general riot, Tito jumps into the Arno, not drifting away like Romola, but swimming with the confidence that he can escape death and find a new life. This is not the abandonment of self, but its concentration in the act of survival at all costs.

Romola drifts out to sea in her boat, Tito jumps into the Arno, while in the final apocalyptic frenzy Savonarola is captured by his enemies, convinced that he is a failure as both visionary and politician: 'I am not worthy to be a martyr; the Truth shall prosper, but not by me' (II.382). All three of these intertwined episodes dramatise, in their different ways, the breakdown of the attempt to create and live out a coherent world-view in Renaissance Florence. These experiences of non-meaning or negative epiphanies are the final experiments in life the novelist practises upon her characters. This is the end of the line and the question is, where is meaning to be found as the world constituted with their world-views fragments in the climactic Masque of the Furies? We noticed how in *The Mill on the Floss* the narrative proper ended at this point and then moved into a different mode, that of mythic recapitulation in which everything becomes meaningful and in its own way perfectly coherent. The same is true in *Romola* as far as Tito and Romola are concerned. George Eliot acknowledged that the heroine's drifting away and the plague-stricken village 'were by deliberate forecast adopted as romantic and symbolical elements',[20] and the same terms can be applied to Tito's end. But the final assessment of the historical figure, Savonarola, is inevitably more complicated. They flee from Florence, the martyr remains. It will be best to examine first the flights of Tito and Romola and then bring their juxtaposition to bear upon the final estimate of Savonarola.

At the climax of his career Tito, the pagan god, must act out the true significance of the myth which he embodies and by which he has interpreted life in Florence. Since the myth is the limit of his understanding, his world-view, he is trapped within it, ignorant of its culmination. His life has been a sustained attempt to realise the dream of Bacchic pastoral bliss and rapture: the impossibility of this is announced, on one level, by the growing complexity of his chicanery which cannot be sustained, and on another, by the total myth which he is required to fulfil. These levels of action merge in the Masque of the Furies when Tito's sponsors see through his duplicity, his triple deceits, his multiple masks, and turn on him, preparing the way for the final *sparagmos* of the god which enacts his fragmentation into several selves. In Dolfo Spini's words, 'I should like to hang skins about him and set my hounds on him!' (II.384). That dismemberment comes paradoxically at the moment when Tito's life reaches the apex of concentrated self-interest: all his affiliations are cast off, he escapes the mob by throwing them his diamonds and gold, still confident that 'salvation' and 'deliverance' will come from his own efforts. But as he swims down the Arno the dismemberment is already beginning. The narrative refers to fleeting glimpses of Tito as 'the floating hair', 'the velvet tunic-sleeves', 'a pale olive face' floating on the water like a severed head. Then the current takes control and he drifts away:

'exhaustion was bringing on the dreamy state that precedes uncons-
ciousness' (II.392). He is lapsing into the dream from which he was
awakened on the first page of the novel, that atemporal world where
the myth will be completed. At this moment he floats into the vision of
the waiting Baldassarre as 'something dim, formless' (II.387) which
the latter conjures into distinct existence, so that the two men may
complete the maenadic ritual which they have been preparing
throughout the novel. As Tito loses control, Baldassarre once again
regains his wits and his strength: the dark shadow of nemesis
completes the pastoral ekstasis. And, as Baldassarre throttles his son,
the mutual recognition – desperately sought by one, so long denied by
the other – is completed in an eternity of betrayal and vengeance:

> Tito knew him; but he did not know whether it was life or death that had
> brought him into the presence of his injured father. It might be death – and
> death might mean this chill gloom with the face of the hideous past hanging
> over him for ever.

Baldassarre too dies, retaining his grip, prepared to 'follow the traitor
to hell that he might clutch him there' (II.394). The hideous past,
denied so strenuously, becomes on this occasion the Dantesque
judgment itself, the frozen *contrapasso*[21] of eternally throttling and
being throttled.

What is the significance of the climax to Romola's career as she too
commits herself to the waves, a career which has tried and failed to
synthesise the classical and pagan in the life of Florence? By what
myth are her drifting away (ch. 61) and waking on the plague-
stricken island (ch. 68), events which bracket the end of both Tito's
and Savonarola's careers, explained? As with the two men, these final
events are both a recapitulation and culmination. Before she embarks,
she recalls in her despair the contradictions she has discovered in her
mentors, Bacchic and Christian, which have led to the loss of belief in
her own 'better self' (II.323). The conflict of interpretations has led
again to this impasse, this need to free herself 'even from the burden of
choice', as she drifts 'orphaned in those wide spaces of sea and sky'
with a thirst for human sympathy that 'the Great Mother has no milk
to still' (II.326). She is doubly orphaned – from mother nature and, as
Felicia Bonaparte writes, 'there are no fathers now to act as her
teachers and heroes because in having relived in her life the history of
civilization Romola has at last caught up with the cultural heritage of
mankind'.[22] But as she drifts out to sea she remains a curious amalgam

of the values she has rejected: disguised as a nun yet seeking 'repose in mere sensation . . . fanc[ying] herself floating naiad-like in the waters' (II.323).

She had committed 'herself, sleeping, to destiny which would either bring death or else new necessities that might rouse a new life in her' (II.325). She awakes seven chapters later to a new reality, but the nature of this breakthrough is determined by the whole of her previous life – the troubled formation of her own moral tradition. In consequence, what follows is not an escape but, as in Tito's case, a judgment. The attempt to form a coherent world-view out of the interaction of idea and circumstance, has come to an end: now the character no longer interprets but acts out this predetermined 'new life' and not in the terms of her choice. It is neither a world of pastoral bliss nor a world of death to which she drifts, but a combination of the two. All the elements of her previous life are present in the plague-stricken village but in a simpler, clearer form to which she can respond directly. As she acknowledges in retrospect, the attempt to impose the myths of the European past on her life has failed in contradiction and confusion; the clashing deities, those coercive types, in cancelling each other out have prepared the way for her breakthrough into another form of life. In a crucial phrase, Romola acknowledges that her experience in the village 'had come to her with as strong an effect as that of the fresh seal on the dissolving wax' (II.412). The cancellation, the dissolution of the previous types has prepared the wax for the fresh seal, the new type, which is unmediated experience itself. And her sojourn in the village is, in effect, a speeded-up version of her whole career. First, in this novel of rebirths, the boat has become the 'cradle of a new life' and she is reborn as a child into 'mere passive existence', 'a bliss which is without memory and without desire'. Passing next through 'the afternoon dreams of her girlhood' she becomes aware of her surroundings and then memories of Florence re-assert themselves: 'Already oblivion was troubled' (II.398–9). Then, the cry of the child leads her back into the world of suffering, the horror of the plague. Her past experience returns to her now without complication or reservation but as knowledge to be acted upon: 'Romola's experience in the haunts of death and disease made thought and action prompt' (II.400). It was the same with Maggie as she set out to rescue Tom from the flood, that other visitation of God. The burden of choice has been removed not in a world of bliss but in one of immediate human need. And the villagers respond to their rescuer by seeing her first as 'the Holy Mother' (II.404) with 'the Hebrew baby' on her arm, before gradually transforming her 'supernatural form' into the reality of 'a substantial woman' (II.408–10).[23] This is the incarnational moment, anticipated in Romola's perplexed annunciation, when the conflict of interpretations is set aside, when ideas become flesh, and the heroine sees as she is seen. And out of such moments new myths are created, but ones which – the narrator is careful to add – contain their own interpretative key. 'Many legends were afterwards told in that valley about the blessed Lady who came over the sea, but they were legends by which all who heard might know that in times gone by a woman had done beautiful loving deeds there' (II.411).

This mythic episode doesn't, of course, resolve the conflicting loyalties of Florence to which she must now return. As she prepares to go back she finds herself re-living those conflicts: 'All minds, except such as are delivered from doubt by dullness of sensibility, must be subject to this recurring conflict where the many-twisted conditions of life have forbidden the fulfilment of a bond.' From the mythic simplicity of the village she is back in the complex world of the casuists praised in *The Mill on the Floss* but, unlike Maggie, Romola has to learn to live in that world. 'What if the life of Florence was a web of inconsistencies?' (II.415) she asks, and condemns herself for abandoning the city. The second test of her maturity now occurs. The first was her instinctive reaction to suffering in the village. Now she must come to terms with this apparent web of inconsistencies by seeking to interpret the life and death of Savonarola at the centre of the web. In one sense, the whole novel has been a long detour to get to this point: not only was the career of Savonarola the originating idea for the novel but Romola's recuperation of European history has prepared her for the final purpose of carrying out this interpretation of his character.

The assessment of Savonarola at the end of *Romola* must be seen as part of the Victorian obsession with the great figures of history. What is a hero? Who is the true martyr? In the epilogue of the novel the heroine defines different kinds of greatness to Tito's son, a question Villari also discusses in some detail in *La Storia di Girolamo Savonarola* (1859–61), one of the sources George Eliot cites in the novel.[24] He maintains that Savonarola's greatness and originality consisted of his anticipation, at the end of the Renaissance, of the modern age. 'The men of that time justly deserving the title of innovators were those who foresaw the progress of civilization towards a vaster synthesis of the human race, and felt drawn nearer to God . . . Theirs is the prophetic mind, the hero's heart, the martyr's fate.'[25] But though Savonarola sought to embody this synthesis, he possessed 'a dual nature, composed of two opposite individualities, and that whereas the one spurred him towards the future, the other almost chained him to the past'.[26] He was also, in Villari's view, the embodiment of a 'singular contrast' between the highest faculties and human weaknesses which was characteristic of the Renaissance, 'that rejuvescence of the human race [when] men's faculties were strained to a higher pitch'.[27] These antitheses are the conventional elements of the Victorian view of the Renaissance, here epitomised in Savonarola: such a man both embodies the antitheses and looks ahead to a new and future synthesis. The difficulty of interpreting the motives of such a person at the cutting edge of the dialectic of history is obvious. This is the task Romola has to perform at the end of the novel to show that her lengthy recuperation of European civilisation is completed.

Behind all the great martyrs of history there is, however, one supreme model which George Eliot deploys in the assessment of Savonarola, of whom he is the antitype and of whose life his own is the imitation. At first, Savonarola is the Hebrew prophet in whose typology Florence is a second Jerusalem, 'chosen city in the chosen land' (198) to which he offers the promise of the redemption of Italy, the Church, and the world. But as with Tito, the vision becomes hopelessly entangled in the complexities of Florentine politics, forcing upon Savonarola the full enactment of the biblical myth he invokes. If Tito finally becomes the dismembered Bacchus, Savonarola becomes the crucified Christ. He articulates the complete curve of his career in Florence through the biblical narrative of his sermon in the Duomo: the Shecinah in the sanctuary, its pollution by an unfaithful Israel, his own role as the Hebrew prophet, the call to repentance, the destruction of Jerusalem, and then Savonarola becomes the Christ offering the new covenant. This is the master-plot which culminates in his self-sacrifice: 'O Lord, thou knowest I am willing – I am ready. Take me, stretch me on the cross . . . let the thorns press upon my brow, and let my sweat be anguish – I desire to be made like thee in thy great love. But let me see the fruit of my travail – let this people be saved!' (1.350). In his imitation of Christ he, like all the martyrs, finally repeats the sequence of the Passion narrative – betrayal, arrest, trial, torture, and public execution. He, like his type, does not see the fruit of his travail in his lifetime, the kingdom does not come on earth, and even his martyrdom is problematic as we shall see in a moment.

In an indirect way, then, *Romola* can take its place alongside all those Victorian lives of Jesus which were engaged in the historical quest for the key to his character. These works raised all the hermeneutical questions in their acutest form. As an indication of their closeness to the issues raised in *Romola*, one may refer to Charles Hennell's *An Inquiry Concerning the Origin of Christianity* (1838), an early radical examination of the evidence which George Eliot knew well. In trying to sharpen 'the indistinctness of the image' of Jesus, Hennell focuses at the end of his study on the paradox of the messiah who is also a political leader, of a mind 'of that contemplative and imaginative cast, which appears too fine for the coarser turmoils of the world', being led 'to the adoption of views partly political'. His conclusion is that, as with all those historic figures 'leading men into any new domain of mind and heart', Jesus experienced uncertainty and oscillation: there is 'no absurdity in supposing that there was some fluctuation in the views of Jesus himself at this period, and that the enthusiasm of the multitude revived for a moment his own expectation of the approach of the kingdom; but that subsequent events forced him to recur to the anticipation of his death'.[28] E. S. Shaffer comments on this new form of the defence against rationalist attacks on the character of the religious reader: 'No longer superhuman, these men were, by virtue of being vessels of revelation, more fully aware of their personal inadequacy, their mendacity, their poverty of spirit.'[29] It is this ambiguous model that George Eliot uses for her final assessment of Savonarola, rather than the more orthodox one of the traditional imitation of Christ. Romola, in other words, practises a form of the Higher Criticism, since the despised amanuensis is by now the perfect interpreter of the direction European history is going to take: she is, after all, the daughter of a classical scholar, married to a pagan god, instructed by a prophet, and mythologised as the Madonna Antigone.

Her task is to decide if Savonarola is a genuine martyr, and her interpretation is based on the imprisoned priest's confession. The text is of doubtful authority: it was obtained under torture, it is an unofficial second edition printed after the first was withdrawn, and the digest of the confession was made by a corrupt notary. As she reads the evidence she also listens to the public reactions. The devout followers of Savonarola reject everything as false which doesn't conform to their faith in him, or as the narrator ironically puts it: they were convinced 'he had been tortured in proportion to the distress his confessions had created in the hearts of those who loved him' (II.427).

More worldly supporters accept the validity of the confession, despite possible transpositions and additions, and only disagree about the need for the death sentence. Romola accepts none of these. But how to explain both his claims and his rejection of those claims? Through 'her long meditations over that printed document' she becomes convinced that 'Savonarola's retractation of his prophetic claims was not merely a spasmodic effort to escape from torture'. How then to find 'some explanation of his lapses which would make it possible for her to believe that the main striving of his life had been pure and grand'? As she struggles to find a coherent interpretation in this way, she is repeating Savonarola's own struggle to retain the purity of his ideal in the complexities of Florentine life. She too has been a sacred rebel. The search for an interpretation is, in this way, an imitation of the priest's struggles which were in turn an imitation of Christ. And Romola's resolution of her own conflict supports this reading. Her final appeal is not to the reliability of the confession but to her own experience: when she rejected Savonarola she lost her best self in a discontent from which she now reacts with 'a sort of faith that has sprung up . . . out of the very depths of despair'. After the crucifixion comes the resurrection of her faith in this man 'who had been for her the incarnation of the highest motives'. The final reading depends on what has been transferred to the reader. It was, she now believes, 'impossible that it had not been a living spirit, and no hollow pretence, which had once breathed in the Frate's words, and kindled a new life within her' (II.429–30). This new life is that which she experienced in the village, the work of George Eliot's version of the Holy Spirit, bequeathed to Romola from that 'incarnation of the highest motives', Savonarola. His life, in its full trinitarian scope – the Father's prophetic voice, the Son's sacrifice, and now the Spirit's renewal – is validated and continued in the life of his disciples as they gather at his shrine at the end of the novel. The allusions in *Romola* to Joachim of Fiore suggest that George Eliot is adapting the three stages of his trinitarian theory of history to the career of Savonarola.[30]

In the last phase of her exegesis, Romola picks her way past 'erasures and interpolations' in the confession not in order to dismiss Savonarola's lapses and vacillations – his claim to prophetic inspiration, his retraction of that claim, and the retraction of the retraction – but to interpret them by means of her new faith. (It is the Holy Spirit rather than Hermes who is identified as the final interpreter.) They must be understood as a form of the inevitable doubleness which life exacts in different forms from everyone. Though there are 'moments of ecstatic contemplation, doubtless, [when] the sense of self melted in the sense of the Unspeakable', for the most part ideal and reality, the hypothesis and the facts, must always be in tension. 'And perhaps confession', Romola tentatively suggests, 'even when it described a doubleness that was conscious and deliberate, really implied no more than that wavering of belief concerning his own impressions and motives which most human beings who have not a stupid inflexibility of self-confidence must be liable to under a marked change of external conditions' (ii.432). This is especially true of the sacred rebel who, by definition, can appeal to no external sanction or achieve orthodox martyrdom by witnessing to an acknowledged truth. Yet Savonarola's final writings – here Romola examines the further textual evidence of his prison meditations – confirm the essential purity of his motives, the absence of 'the old vehement self-assertion' (ii.433), his penitence, and the acknowledge-ment of failure before God. But the clinching proof of his claim to the status of martyr is, paradoxically, that from his imprisonment to his death he never 'thought or spoke of himself as a martyr. The idea of martyrdom had been to him a passion dividing the dream of the future with the triumph of beholding his work achieved.' His self-sacrifice was directed to that end, to be succeeded now only by resignation. '*But therefore*', asserts the narrator in italics, '*he may the more fitly be called a martyr by his fellow-men for all time*' (ii.434). This is the nature of the sacred rebel who strives for a higher good which has no external validation and who dies acknowledging his own unworthi-ness, as his life fails to realise the vision for which the world is not yet ready. In George Eliot's redefinition, the martyr's life centres on this uncertain moment of the dialectic; only in retrospect can he be called a martyr. And this is why he endured – in the phrase Newman was to use in *The Dream of Gerontius* (1865) two years later[31] – 'a double agony: not only the reviling, and the torture, and the death-throe, but the agony of sinking from the vision of glorious achievement into that deep shadow where he could only say, "I count as nothing: darkness encompasses me: yet the light I saw was the true light"' (ii.435).[32]

Like Tito, Savonarola is trapped within the myth he seeks to live out, between the idea and the facts, between the vision and the world, but he refuses to compromise either for personal glory. His double agony reflects that refusal: he suffers both at the hands of the world and at the failure of his vision, but remains true to the dialectic which they constitute. This keeps alive 'the true light' of the future which briefly vitalises the heroine's new life in the village as a sign of that promise. In *Romola*, the major myths of European civilisation, dramatically reborn in the Florentine Renaissance, act out their ideals and the destruction to which their own inner contradictions consign them under the experiments of winged Time.[33] Each myth is part of the larger dialectic which is historical development. The lesser characters are consumed by their myths as they seek to realise their own partial ends; the great figures of history, in contrast, self-consciously dramatise the dialectic within their lives, acknowledging the incompatibility of the light and the darkness, but pointing forward to the true path of development, the larger synthesis of these incomplete mythologies. Romola, in her own grand recuperation, finally despairs of the endless reiteration of the dialectic, abandons Florence and history, and briefly acts out the humanistic myth towards which the struggles of Savonarola are pointing. It is his 'spirit', the motive force of these struggles, which has given her a proleptic glimpse of a world of suffering redeemed by love. It is an episode, then, out of time and out of sequence, which points beyond interpretation to a world where things are what they seem to be. But it is only after this experience of the hermeneutic of innocence that the heroine is able to return and make a definitive interpretation of Savonarola's martyrdom, overlaid as it is at the complex centre of the dialectics of history by the hermeneutic of suspicion.

CHAPTER 6

Felix Holt: commentaries on the apocalypse

After the epic recapitulation of European culture and mythology carried out in *Romola*, the scope of *Felix Holt* seems drastically curtailed. Indeed, the introductory chapter of this novel reads like a domesticated pastiche of the proem to *Romola*. Instead of the opening sweep across the contours of Europe we have a coach ride through the Midlands; instead of the angel of the dawn pausing meaningfully over Florence, the pivot of the Renaissance, we have the coachman gossiping about the towns and villages he passes through until his narrative focuses on Transome Court. But, even though the style of this 'modern Odyssey'[1] is ironic and mock-heroic, these are also disturbing times: as in Renaissance Florence, the old synthesis is fragmenting and, with the approach of the First Reform Bill, competing forces are laying claim to the nation's inheritance. The Masque of the Furies in *Romola* is replaced by an election riot. The coach ride is George Eliot's device for making a preliminary survey of these forces and interests, and also for introducing the reader to the interpretative problems they pose.

The mode of this introductory chapter to *Felix Holt* is essentially apocalyptic. Like her modernist successors who announced that human nature changed in 1910 or that the old world ended in 1915, George Eliot chose 1832 as her year of cosmic crisis after which things could never be the same again. And she was, of course, writing in the 1860s, with a repetition of that crisis in the offing with the Second Reform Bill about to be passed in 1867, the year after the novel was published. But the mode is also ironic. The novelist has assimilated the martyrdom of Savonarola and the world-shattering events at the climax of *Romola* into the texture of what can be seen as the beginning of her mature style. Apocalypse is, as it were, everywhere.[2] This is not surprising since a form of catastrophism was integral to the master-plot she described early in her career: each stage of life ends in the fragmentation of a world-view which gives coherence to life and is succeeded by the creation of a new world. With the writing of *Felix Holt* this catastrophism is ironically merged with her desire 'to show the gradual action of ordinary causes' in an exploration of the condition of England.

The coach ride is a brilliant device to bring out the hermeneutic implications of this apocalyptic and ironic vision. The stage-coach in which the reader is conducted through the Midlands in 1831 represents nostalgically for the Victorians that world lost to the railways, but to the elderly gentlemen in pony-chaises taking evasive action it embodies in its 'rolling swinging swiftness' (5) the onset of the destructively new. The coach ride effortlessly opens up this double, ironic perspective as it simultaneously makes accessible and disturbs a series of English locales. Each locale represents geographically and historically a separate world with its own world-view, which the narrator sketches quickly and succinctly as the coach and the natives impinge briefly on each other. The shepherd's earth-bound, cattle-bound reality, for example, can only acknowledge with difficulty a stage-coach which is as alien as 'the most out-lying nebula': 'his solar system was the parish; the master's temper and the casualties of the lambing-time were his region of storms' (6). George Eliot is conducting a series of small-scale experiments: into each of these self-contained worlds an anomalous element, the stage-coach, is introduced as a means of eliciting its true nature. In the prosperous, agricultural 'district of protuberant optimists, sure that old England was the best of all possible countries' (7) the reaction is very different from that of the population of the manufacturing towns which doesn't share that conviction.

The interpretative challenge is reciprocal. As the natives respond from their separate worlds, so the coach passengers try to make sense of what they see. And the task is increasingly difficult as the scenes become more kaleidoscopic and the contrasts more marked: 'In these midland districts the traveller passed rapidly from one phase of English life to another' (8). Any attempt to fit these phases into any kind of coherent unity seems impossible: 'it was easy for the traveller to conceive that town and country had no pulse in common' (8). The passengers, the readers, occupy briefly the role of a narrator who has not yet made sense of his panoramic novel, and it is this awareness of disjunction between the separate worlds, the impossibility of combining the fragments into a whole, which dramatises the impending apocalypse. But as the narrator edges the reader towards 1832 and the beginning of the novel proper, he acknowledges that the forces of change are universally at work – in Catholic emancipation, in 'rick-burners, trades-union, Nottingham riots, and in general whatever required the calling out of the yeomanry' (8) – and these forces, welcomed by some, totally rejected by others, are linking these locales in new ways.

At this point in the journey, the coachman is introduced as an additional means of interpretation, a 'commentator on the landscape' (9), whose role and analogues are carefully defined: 'he could tell the names of sites and persons, and explain the meaning of groups, as well as the shade of Virgil in a more memorable journey; he had as many stories about parishes, and the men and women in them, as the Wanderer in the "Excursion", only his style was different' (9). With him the apocalyptic overtones increase. A once genial man, he is embittered and confused by the arrival of the railways and 'now, as in a perpetual vision, saw the ruined country strewn with shattered limbs', and all the coaching inns closed: 'and at that word the coachman looked before him with the blank gaze of one who had driven his coach to the outermost edge of the universe, and saw his leaders plunging into the abyss' (9). This is the penultimate state of the world, and the journey which began in a pleasantly pastoral mood has turned into the final ride of the last coach through a devastated countryside of shattered limbs. Such a penultimate state of mind is inseparable from the difficulties of interpretation, as the coachman demonstrates when he 'relapse[s] from the high prophetic strain to the familiar one of narrative' (9). One of his stories – that of the innovating farmer, the parson, and the villagers – is a parody of biblical hermeneutics, complete with the provenance of the text, its exegesis and accommodation, and final confirmation (9).

As these stories come closer to the present, they become more problematic as the old certainties are eroded. The coachman is forced to acknowledge, for instance, the new distinction between Reformer and anti-Reformer in order to classify the landowners, with the added paradox 'that there were men of old family and large estate who voted for the Bill'. Such an anomaly is beyond his powers of interpretation: 'He did not grapple with the paradox; he let it pass, with all the discreetness of an experienced theologian or learned scholiast, preferring to point his whip at some object which could raise no questions' (10). The coachman reads the landscape like a difficult text, though when Transome Court finally comes into view his narrative takes on a confident specificity, presenting us with what amounts to a potted version of the aristocratic half of the novel. But here too he falters when he comes to the rights and wrongs of the family law-case, at which point he 'would screw his features into a grimace expressive of entire neutrality, and appear to aim his whip at a particular spot on the horse's flank'. The commentator runs out of comment, the interpreter is finally left to the several interpretations of his passengers: 'Some attributed this reticence to a wise incredulity, others to a want of memory, others to simple ignorance' (11).

Here, the coach ride ends in uncertainty, at which point the last two paragraphs of the introduction dip abruptly below the legal dispute, below the level of narrative itself to the hidden reality of suffering described darkly in terms of entail, progeny, and inheritance: 'some tragic mark of kinship in the one brief life to the far-stretching life that went before, and to the life that is to come after'. But the tragedy though Aristotelian – 'such as has raised the pity and terror of men ever since they began to discern between will and destiny' – is 'noiseless', 'unknown to the world', 'a mere whisper in the roar of hurrying existence'. It is virtually indecipherable since it is 'committed to no sound . . . seen in no writing . . . breathed into no human ear' (11). The only way to convey the tragedy and suffering is by the parable of Dante's 'dolorous enchanted forest' in the *Inferno* XIII, with human histories hidden in the thorn-bushes.[3]

The introduction as a whole, then, is a complex survey of the Midland counties – their politics, history, religion, economy, and world-views – preparatory to an examination of the condition of England.[4] But it is also a journey into uncertainty, moving from what the narrator calls 'picture' and 'aspects of earth and sky' through an increasing use of separate narratives to prophecy and then the final mystery of parable. At this penultimate moment of historical crisis, the question raised in all aspects of life is, what is the relationship between the *status quo* and social change, between conformity and rebellion, between will and destiny? Can the imminent apocalypse show them in their true colours? In *Romola*, Savonarola's martyrdom was presented as an heroic exploration of these questions. In *Felix Holt*, the idea of the sacred rebel is domesticated and generalised into the texture of the novel, and the apocalypse, as with *Middlemarch*, is both muted and secularised. But the relationship of will and destiny is formulated in essentially the same terms as those used in the earlier novel: 'the problem where the sacredness of obedience ended, and where the sacredness of rebellion began'. This is the interpretative crux which is to diagnose and ultimately determine the condition of England.

When the novel proper opens in September 1832, the Reform Bill has been passed but – as with the death of Lorenzo de'Medici – no apocalyptic vision has yet been granted. The old categories have simply been confused and the search for certainties become more problematic. In *Romola*, this situation was dramatised when figures from European myth stepped into the historical present of Florence in an attempt to direct the course of history. In *Felix Holt*, George Eliot introduces, more modestly, into the mixed conditions of Treby society three recognisably English characters who embody and are to act out the triangle of forces in the novel. Each of the male characters brings an invitation and a warning to the heroine who is again in a state of enchanted suspension, a sleeping beauty. All three are products of the complex forces they are seeking to understand: the aristocratic Harold surprisingly presents himself as a Radical in the first chapter, while Felix, the working-class Radical, turns out to be a conservative gradualist mistrustful of political change. In other words, they are anomalies, peculiar amalgams of the old and new, just as incongruous as Esther with her refinements and snobberies in Malthouse Yard. The two men are returning to Treby, having gone away to make their fortunes, in order to act upon the community, and when they first appear in the novel they have already decided confidently and ingenuously how they intend to do this. Because the social and political paradigms have shifted, the two men represent new, apparently paradoxical combinations; as a result they read the world differently and the world interprets them with difficulty.

From the beginning, as we have seen, character has been defined by George Eliot as the tension between contradictory forces, from the theodicies of Hayslope through the tragic hybrids of *The Mill on the Floss* to the various doublenesses and duplicities of *Romola*. With the growing sense of crisis, George Eliot's modernism expresses itself as an awareness of new, anomalous combinations coming into existence at all levels of life; and it is here that the process of character is linked to the questions of social and political change. First comes a new sense of unity. In the case of Treby Magna, it is the canal, the coal-mines, and the saline spring which are the 'new conditions' which complicate its relations with the rest of the world, 'gradually awakening in it that higher consciousness which is known to bring higher pains' (41). The old-fashioned market-town 'took on the more complex life brought by mines and manufactures, which belong more directly to the great circulating system of the nation than to the local system to which they have been superadded' (43). But with the greater sense of unity comes a more complex differentiation of the component parts, the individuals, which cannot be easily explained by the new labels. 'It so happened in that particular town that the Reformers were not all of them large-hearted patriots or ardent lovers of justice . . . Again, the Tories were far from being all oppressors, disposed to grind down the working classes into serfdom.' (44). At this time of ironic apocalypse the concord between labels and reality has broken down because the conditions of life are too mixed, too complex.[5]

This is a condition-of-England novel with a difference. Though it contains all the usual ingredients of such novels – working-class hero, aristocratic rival, heroine as heiress, election riot, and so on – *Felix Holt* is, like George Eliot's other novels, a critical examination of the genre to which it belongs.[6] This is carried out by means of a rigorous scrutiny of the phrase 'the conditions of life' and its implications. A great many variations are played on the phrase, but the predominant and most abstract meaning refers to that which must be present if something else is to take place or that on which anything else is contingent.[7] Its more restricted sense is the context or social milieu in which character and event exist. George Eliot's realism is, of course, partly dependent on her awareness of these contingencies, of the complex operation of ordinary causes, especially as they link private and public life. 'Even in that conservatory existence where the fair Camelia is sighed for by the noble young Pineapple . . . there is a nether apparatus of hot-water pipes liable to cool down on a strike of the gardeners or a scarcity of coal' (45). But the question of which are causes, effects, or simply conditions, has become increasingly difficult to answer in the troubled 1860s. The novelist had been especially preoccupied with this since May 1864 when she had the idea for *The Spanish Gypsy* while visiting Venice. She began to see her subject, she wrote, 'as a symbol of the part which is played in the general human lot by hereditary conditions in the largest sense' out of which comes her definition of tragedy, the conflict between will and destiny, as the terrible difficulty of adjusting 'our individual needs to the dire necessities of our lot'. She left off work on her poem in frustration in February 1865 and the next month began writing *Felix Holt*. But to the novel she brings one of the insights she had experienced while pondering *The Spanish Gypsy*: 'Looking at individual lots, I seemed to see in each the same story, wrought out with more or less of tragedy.' Tragedy is domesticated and generalised as the relationship between individuals and the conditions in which they find themselves, whether these are social, hereditary, or political. The more these are examined, however, the more difficult it becomes to differentiate between will and destiny, between one's needs and one's lot; for, as she commented on her poem, 'even in cases of just antagonism to the narrow view of hereditary claims, the whole background of the particular struggle is made up of our inherited nature'.[8] By the time of *Middlemarch* this complex relationship is expressed in terms of the 'social medium', that powerful determinant as omnipresent and as intangible as the air we breathe. In *Felix Holt*, the term 'conditions' carries this burden with the acknowledgement that everyone must be both a product of and defined against their conditions. If this is the case, what kind of world-view can achieve genuine insight and choice in the clotted social medium of 1832?

The opening of the novel stresses the multitudinous nature of these conditions, the prerequisite for anything, either mundane or apoca-lyptic, to take place. 'As to the weather of 1832', the narrator records at the end of the lengthy account of Treby, 'the Zadkiel[9] of that time had predicted that the electrical condition of the clouds in the political hemisphere would produce unusual perturbations in organic existence'; and then links this astrological prophecy to 'that mutual influence of dissimilar destinies which we shall see gradually unfolding itself'. The term is then used in the next sentence to refer to a substratum upon which specific events act and re-act. 'For if the mixed political conditions of Treby Magna had not been acted on by the passing of the Reform Bill, Mr Harold Transome would not have presented himself as a candidate for North Loamshire', and, after listing some of the unexpected events arising from this conjunction, concludes with a philosophical definition: 'conditions in this case essential to the "where", and the "what", without which, as the learned know, there can be no event whatever'. And the next sentence incorporates the eponymous hero into the all-encompassing scope of the term: 'For example, it was through these conditions that a young man named Felix Holt made a considerable difference in the life of

Harold Transome' (45–6). In other words, the term defines the given elements of the fiction in order to make, however arbitrarily, a beginning; and, by extension, character is conceived as a response to these conditions out of which it emerges and upon which it re-acts in the creation of a world-view. This reciprocal relationship in *Felix Holt* is defined in the politically charged terms of conformity and rebellion; and by this means the dialectic of the sacred rebel, epitomised in the martyrdom of Savonarola, is translated into an analysis of the condition of England in all its aspects in 1832.

At the beginning of the novel, the three characters of the central love triangle are shown in various forms of rebellion against the conditions which have formed them. As a result, they – like everyone else – are anomalies. Harold's response, for example, is to become a Radical parliamentary candidate, an apparently shocking rejection of his landed position which is difficult to interpret. Such people, says the Tory newspaper, 'were ready to pull one stone from under another in the national edifice', while the Liberals see it as a 'signal instance of self-liberation from the trammels of prejudice' (96). But the narrator quickly moves beyond the party labels to an account of Harold's upbringing, concluding that 'he had the energetic will and muscle, the self-confidence, the quick perception, and the narrow imagination which makes what is admiringly called the practical mind'. This is the key to understanding his political views for 'the man was no more than the boy writ large, with an extensive commentary' (97). With the help of the narrator, the reader is to be shown that a character's life comments on, interprets itself. This is a more reliable guide than the political commentators. Harold's character, then, is a text from which we can decipher the apparently anomalous relationship between the conditions of his life and his reaction to them.

The years had nourished an inclination to as much opposition as would enable him to assert his own independence and power without throwing himself into that tabooed condition which robs power of its triumph. And this inclination had helped his shrewdness in forming judgments which were at once innovating and moderate. He was addicted at once to rebellion and to conformity, and only an intimate personal knowledge could enable any one to predict where his conformity would begin. The limit was not defined by theory, but was drawn in an irregular zigzag by early disposition and association. (97)

The political slogans are dissolved into the psychology of rebellion and conformity which is itself dissolved into his initial disposition –

and that dissolves, in its turn, into the dark hints about his parentage which will gradually be revealed as his career unfolds. The crucial focus of the commentary is upon that 'irregular zigzag' between rebellion and conformity which it is not easy to interpret, as Romola found as she perused Savonarola's printed confession. Now, all character is envisaged as a difficult text with a commentary which both reveals and conceals its meaning, as the narrator acknowledges punningly with relaxed self-consciousness: 'A character is apt to look but indifferently, written out in this way. Reduced to a map our premises seem insignificant, but they make, nevertheless, a very pretty freehold to live and walk over' (98).

Harold's self-confidence springs from his ability to reconcile comfortably in all areas of life his tendencies to rebellion and conformity. In political terms this translates into a pragmatic reliance upon the machinery of election: 'A practical man must seek a good end by the only possible means; that is to say, if he is to get into Parliament he must not be too particular. It was not disgraceful to be neither a Quixote nor a theorist, aiming to correct the moral rules of the world' (162). But his ambition is held in check by his conformity, his fear of disgrace, and the code of a gentleman. And at the end of the novel, Esther comes to see what it is that underlies the apparently contradictory sides of his political views. The irregular zigzag conceals a solvent: 'the utmost enjoyment of his own advantage was the solvent that blended pride in his family and position, with the adhesion to changes that were to obliterate tradition and melt down enchased gold heirlooms into plating for the egg-spoons of "the people"' (344–5). As a practical man he sees the world as essentially passive, 'with a precocious clearness of perception as to the conditions on which he could hope for any advantages in life' (23). However, a series of events – defeat in the election, his disinheritance, the discovery of his real father, and his rejection by Esther – undermine both his aristocratic self-confidence and his British empiricism, forcing him into the various compromises of self-interest until the 'middle course' (292) which he always seeks becomes untenable. One purpose of this process is to redefine the true nature of pragmatism, both in politics and private life. It is expressed most clearly through the example of the quixotic Rufus Lyon: 'For what we call illusions are often, in truth, a wider vision of past and present realities – a willing movement of a man's soul with the larger sweep of the world's forces – a movement towards a more assured end than the chances of a single life' (161). It is, of course, Harold who is the man of illusions within his narrow horizon of self-interest, 'trusting in his own skill to shape the success of his own morrows, ignorant of what many yesterdays had determined for him beforehand' (161–2).

As a result of Jermyn's final revelation, Harold experiences the tragic relationship of will and destiny in the form of entail, inheritance, and progeny: 'for the first time the iron had entered into his soul, and he felt the hard pressure of our common lot, the yoke of that mighty resistless destiny laid upon us by the acts of other men as well as our own' (386). This is the negative version of the cultural and political inheritance which *Felix Holt* is so anxious to preserve. And it is only now that Harold begins to interpret the symbolic shorthand of his mother's life at Transome Court, the limbo to which her past has consigned her. 'He understood now, as he had never understood before, the neglected solitariness of his mother's life, the allusions and innuendoes which had come out during the election.' He responds by rebelling and conforming in a new, more honourable, way – 'with a proud insurrection against the hardship of an ignominy which was not of his own making' and a resolve that the 'character [of a gentleman] should be the more strongly asserted in his conduct' (383), now that he has lost his birthright. It is in this chastened, paradoxical, and more attractive form that he offers himself to Esther at the climax of the novel.

The testing of Harold, as of the other main characters, is carried out both in the present action of the novel and through the pasts of their parents, the two becoming inseparable as the plot unwinds. In each case it is the discovery in that past of an act of compromise with the world, an act of sacrilege against a system of values which the parent apparently lives by, which determines the life of the child. In each case the discovery is made in a different way and presented in a different mode. Harold's aristocratic obtuseness requires that the discovery be thrust upon him as Gothic melodrama ('I am your father') by the man he is seeking to destroy. This is the result of the way in which the earlier generation had responded to the conditions of *their* lives. Thirty-five years ago Mrs Transome and Jermyn 'had seen no reason why they should not indulge their passion and their vanity, and determine for themselves how their lives should be made delightful in spite of unalterable external conditions' (190). For Mrs Transome the nature of this act of rebellion is prepared in the lengthy and sombrely witty sketch of her upbringing and background in chapter one. Like

her son, she seems to combine rebellion and conformity in manageable proportions: 'She always thought that the dangerous French
writers were wicked, and that her reading of them was a sin; but many
sinful things were highly agreeable to her, and many things which she
did not doubt to be good and true were dull and meaningless . . . but
she believed all the while that truth and safety lay in due attendance
on prayers and sermons, in the admirable doctrines and ritual of the
Church of England, equally remote from Puritanism and Popery'
(27). Self-interest is again the solvent, and the narrator moves quickly
from the inadequacy of Mrs Transome's daring quotations and
correct opinions as 'a safe theoretic basis in circumstances of
temptation and difficulty', to the cares of her threadbare life which
has followed.

Between the daring youth and the anxieties of middle-age, there
has occurred the adultery with Jermyn and the birth of Harold: this is
the act of sacrilege to her unquestioning belief in blood, family, and
lineage, committed paradoxically for the purpose of producing a
healthy heir to the estate. And this contradiction in her life is still
unresolved when Esther goes to stay at Transome Court at the end of
the novel and has to listen to her talk of genealogies and heraldry, for
Mrs Transome 'still found a flavour in this sort of pride; none the less
because certain deeds of her own life had been in fatal inconsistency
with it'. 'She had no ultimate analysis of things that went beyond
blood and family', and yet it is these she has betrayed. Her
punishment, therefore, is to live 'in the midst of desecrated sanctities'
(320) in the hope that her apostasy will be justified by its results. In
Dantean terms, this is Mrs Transome's *contrapasso*, the appropriate
retribution for her sacrilege, which is endlessly repeated as she paces
the rooms at Transome Court, the frozen limbo in which the rebel-
conformist lives and which, in her case, can only be broken by the
return of a dutiful son and heir to redeem the estate.

This remarkable section of the novel dramatises Mrs Transome's
punishment as a perpetual re-enactment of the events surrounding
the birth of Harold thirty-five years ago, and the uncertainty and
anxiety associated with it. Beneath the cloak of sentimental romance
both lovers had their own self-interest in mind: she needed an heir to
supersede the imbecile Durfey, while Jermyn required a lever to
forward his legal career. The question is, will Harold prove malleable
to their plans? They have had to wait thirty-five years to find out, to
the moment of his return to his inheritance from abroad, the day on

which the novel opens. During this period Mrs Transome has waited at the decaying Court in a state of suspended animation; she has gambled and now must wait in the hope of becoming, in her sense of the term, the justified sinner. 'Such desires make life a hideous lottery where every day may turn up a blank' (22). Harold's return in the first chapter is presented as a re-living of the hopes and fears of his actual birth – the expectancy, the suspense, the ringing of the church bells, the arrival of an heir! Will he be able at last to play the role devised for him? 'Could it be that now . . . she was going to reap an assured joy? – to feel that the doubtful deeds of her life were justified by the result, since a kind Providence had sanctioned them?' (16). Harold arrives, she 'heard herself called "Mother!" and felt a light kiss on each cheek', but 'in the moment when their eyes met, the sense of strangeness came upon her like a terror' (17). The resemblance to the despised Jermyn has overlaid her own, and Harold's self-confident insensitivity indicates he has a will of his own. This crucial moment of Harold's rebirth into the lives of the adulterers is repeated in flashback as Mrs Transome ponders her situation later in the same chapter. 'The news came from Jersey that Durfey, the imbecile son, was dead. *Now* Harold was heir to the estate; now the wealth he had gained could release the land from its burthens; now he would think it worth while to return home.' From this promised fulfilment her memories take her back to Harold at the age of nineteen, then as a child of four, and finally to his birth. But again comes the sense of terror: 'An hour seemed to have changed everything for her.' This opening scene of the novel is Mrs Transome's apocalypse in which past, present, and future, are all revealed in their true colours. She now knows the full significance of Harold's birth and what it portends for the guilty lovers. 'The keenness of her anxiety in this matter had served as insight' (24) and it is aided by 'that quickness in weaving new futures which belongs to women whose actions have kept them in habitual fear of consequences' (21). She knows that the act of sacrilege will be revealed, that Harold will discover his father because he has inherited a combination of aristocratic pride and lawyer-like practicality from his parents, those qualities which make up his own blend of rebellion and conformity.

As soon as the moment of meeting and suspense is over, Mrs Transome is released from the lottery of life: now she knows what will happen and she begins to die. Like Lady Dedlock as the snows begin to melt in *Bleak House*, she is released from her frozen, aristocratic limbo. In the mirror she scrutinises her 'dried-up complexion, and the deep lines of bitter discontent about the mouth' and says to herself 'I am a hag' (22). And the ageing process, suspended by her hopes and the exercise of her will, begins again and accelerates through the novel. 'These fine clothes you put on me', she tells her maid, 'are only a smart shroud' (314). At last and belatedly, the 'habitual fear of consequences' has turned into a clear vision of consequences by means of which she is enabled to interpret the true meaning and significance of her life. This vision is also her punishment for, without hope any longer in her sacrilegious form of justification, she is forced to re-live the past in the present as its terrible consequences rapidly unfold. It is a form of typological fulfilment, what A. C. Charity calls in his study of Dante 'figural realism', in which characters' 'past life concerns them now chiefly as the process which disposed them to their present situation in death'.[10] Past and present events are juxtaposed in a bi-focal vision when Harold and Jermyn meet, for example, as adversaries for the first time: 'Mrs Transome was not observing the two men . . . she seemed to hear and see what they said and did with preternatural acuteness, and yet she was also seeing and hearing what had been said and done many years before, and feeling a dim terror about the future' (34). As the expectant 'nows' of the opening chapter turn into the pathetic 'ifs' of chapter eight – 'if all the past could be dissolved, and leave no solid trace of itself – mighty *ifs* that were all impossible' (99) – she is forced to live out a mimicry of the life she had hoped for.

Under the threat of Harold's discovery, Mrs Transome and Jermyn are forced remorselessly further and further back into the past to re-enact their adulterous liaison – the secret meetings, the innuendoes, the anxieties, the plotting – in full knowledge now of its consequences. The moribund relationship between aristocratic wife and family lawyer, between inherited wealth and the legal profession, is re-activated by fear. 'She was still young and ardent in her terrors; the passions of the past were living in her dread' (280), while even Jermyn's obtuseness is penetrated by the threat to his self-interest. But they still seek desperately to evade the full consequences of their past. In the two scenes (chapters nine and forty-two) in which they are alone, we see how their romantic affair has congealed into the mutual recrimination in which its true nature is revealed. At first, Mrs Transome cannot bear to discuss their situation with this man she now, in the scornful language of inheritance, despises: 'Moral vulgarity cleaved to him like an hereditary odour' (101). As a result, her bitterness is – in language echoing the silent tragedy of the introduction – 'suppressed because she could not endure that the degradation she inwardly felt should ever become visible or audible in acts or words of her own – should ever be reflected in any word or look of his' (101). Gradually, however, as the constraints tighten she is being forced to a full recognition that the 'unalterable external conditions' of her life thirty-five years ago, with which she dealt so cavalierly, are now enmeshing her in their 'fatal threads' (99). The conditions, apparently passive, have turned into the shirt of Nessus, poisoning her life so that, as she says later, 'every fibre in me seems to be a memory that makes a pang' (317).

As Mrs Transome is forced to redefine the nature of will and destiny in this way, her attempt to keep separate the formal parody of her life and its inner terror – the conformity and the rebellion – becomes increasingly untenable. The maid and confidante Denner, who represents the pagan, feudal world where her mistress's values originate, still manages the magical metamorphosis from private despair to public regality 'by throwing an Indian scarf over her shoulders, and so completing the contrast between the majestic lady in costume and the dishevelled Hecuba-like woman whom she had found half an hour before'. But the transition is no longer efficacious ('I am not at rest!'). Past and present, public and private, as they are forced together in judgment, require her to live out again in more and more vivid detail the past causes of the present consequences. The birth of Harold, at which Denner was present, has to be gone through again – but now with the wish that he will not be born. She 'grasped the little woman's hand hard, and held it so' and confesses her terrible recognition: 'if I could choose at this moment, I would choose that Harold should never have been born'. And the stoical Denner, for whom nothing has changed, replays her role at the birth: '"Nay, my dear" (Denner had only once before in her life said "my dear" to her mistress), "it was a happiness to you then"' (317). But Mrs Transome, in the full knowledge of her vision of consequences, has been granted a kind of second-sight through the veil of the future. Her punishment is that such a vision upon which choice is dependent, as the other half of the novel insists, is in her case belated.

The final, extraordinary re-enactment of the past occurs when Mrs Transome and Jermyn are forced together in desperate self-defence as Harold closes in on their secret. In parallel to their present position, their original romantic affair is sketched in with more and more detail through Mrs Transome's memories, as we move further back, from the birth of Harold to the adultery itself – 'and she had thought there was poetry in such passion beyond any to be found in everyday domesticity' (335). But Jermyn, too, feels himself a victim of the past now that the full implications of his rebellion are becoming clearer. With her terrible double vision, Mrs Transome listens to his self-exoneration as he repeats – he too has to re-enact what he now regrets – the very words she used to persuade him to save the Transome inheritance: 'A clever lawyer can do anything if he has the will; if it's impossible, he will make it possible' (336). This is how the justified sinners sought to combine conformity with rebellion as they manipulated the conditions of their lives. And now Jermyn, in his terror, suggests one more zigzag between rebellion and conformity by 'daring to urge the plea of right' (338) upon Mrs Transome. They should tell Harold his true parentage. To save his skin, he is prepared to let Mrs Transome lose her son. Now it is her turn to be revitalised by another memory – 'her whole frame thrilled with a passion that seemed almost to make her young again' (337) – as she recalls her previous sacrifices to save his marriage and career, another precise anticipation of their present situation. More and more, their true feelings are being articulated – his self-interest, obtuseness, and vulgarity, her pride, degradation, and scorn. But in their bitter alienation they are perversely dependent on each other: only Mrs Transom's disclosure to Harold can save Jermyn, only Jermyn's silence can help her retain her son. She ends the negotiations by delivering judgment on them both: 'But now you have asked me, I will never tell him! . . . If I sinned, my judgment went beforehand – that I should sin for a man like you' (338). Past and present, sin and judgment, are finally accepted as inseparable and simultaneous. Punishment is a continual re-enactment of the moment of sacrilege, a form of realised eschatology. Jermyn, however, sees things differently as he continues to weave between rebellion and conformity, seeking survival and refusing to acknowledge their contradictions. And the parable of the stolen pyx acts out the literal meaning of sacrilege. Jermyn becomes the temple robber who justifies his sin in the language of sacredness when he returns the stolen object in fear of justice: 'if in doing so he whispered to the Blessed Virgin that he was moved by considering the sacredness of all property, and the peculiar sacredness of the pyx, it is not to be believed that she would like him the better for it' (338). In the zigzag of self-interest, rebellion tries to turn itself into conformity, sacrilege into sacredness.

The crucial terms, it will be seen, in which the characters seek to find or create coherence in their lives in this part of the novel are defined in increasingly negative terms. The conditions of existence are transformed from a passive medium to a shirt of Nessus; the clever manipulation of conformity and rebellion results in the loss of the benefits of both; while the vision which might have predicted consequences becomes the fatalistic recognition of judgment. If the multitudinous conditions of life are so unpredictable that things become their opposites, the question is: how can one make sense of the world? To what does one conform and against what does one rebel? The response to this difficulty in George Eliot's later fiction can be seen in a double and complementary emphasis. On the one hand, there is the full recognition of the multiplicity of conditions in which cause and effect, will and destiny, are so hopelessly confused and entangled that any 'theory of life' is bound to prove misleading. But, on the other hand, as an escape from a fatalistic quietism, there is a new stress on the possibility of a vision of consequences, not belatedly as a recognition of judgment, but as the basis for 'a life of vision and of choice' (326). These two emphases are reciprocal and they culminate in the confrontation of the two disparate worlds of *Daniel Deronda*. In *Felix Holt* the darkly deterministic world of aristocratic inheritance, kinship, and progeny, is gradually transformed into a world of freedom and choice in the working-class milieu of the hero.

The narrator links Harold with the other male protagonist, Felix, by means of a disclaimer which claims a good deal: 'There could hardly have been a lot less like Harold Transome's than this of the quack doctor's son, except in the superficial facts that he called himself a Radical, that he was the only son of his mother, and that he had lately returned to his home with ideas and resolves not a little disturbing to that mother's mind' (46). The superficial facts are the basis for an elaborate comparison and contrast between the two characters, both of whom represent an interpretative model of society (and its political implications) to which they seek to appropriate the heroine. Like Harold, Felix is an obvious anomaly. He is an educated man who, refusing to climb the social ladder, has returned to the working-class origins rejected by his parents. His politics are based on this rejection and acceptance, another permutation of rebellion and conformity. 'I want', says Felix, 'to be a demagogue of a new sort; an honest one, if possible, who will tell the people they were blind and foolish, and neither flatter them nor fatten on them. I have my heritage – an order I belong to. I have the blood of a line of handicraftsmen in my veins' (224). This means that he rejects, in a characteristically Victorian way, the politics of class-warfare and the ballot as expressed by the trade-union leader at the election, in favour of the politics of responsibility, public morality, and a gradualism built firmly upon the past. The oddity of this form of working-class radicalism is acknowledged by George Eliot when the Tory voters misguidedly give it their blessing. The purpose of setting the aristocratic radical against the working-class conservative is to undermine simplistic political labels and focus the reader's attention on the real problem – conformity to or rebellion against the conditions in which one finds oneself and upon which all change and process take place. The 'irregular zigzag' of Harold's character which defined that relationship in a solvent of self-interest is very different from the brusque, self-conscious interaction of the same qualities in Felix. Unlike Harold, Felix provides his own commentary on the primary text of his character. 'You're thinking that you have a roughly-written page before you now', he says to the Reverend Rufus Lyon (54).

The roughness of his character, as opposed to the 'agreeable medium of Harold's personality', is an index of their essential difference. Whereas rebellion and conformity are carefully aligned by Harold the politician, with Felix we are meant to see them in the strongly dialectical relationship of the sacred rebel. He is, in the phrase from *Childe Harold*, antithetically mixed. Educated by his parents' money, he has rejected the role they planned for him; he has been 'converted' to his present views by six weeks of debauchery (55); and though of equable temper he can still lose self-control 'in a rage as ungovernable as that of boyhood'. His rage is the motor which drives the dialectic, though he attempts to avoid 'the conditions that might cause him exasperation' (243). The two men, and the two models of political action they represent, are epitomised in the motto to the chapter in which Felix first appears. The cautious citizen complains of the passionateness of youth 'That makes a vice of virtue by excess', and fatalistically accepts the fact that 'All things cool with time – / The sun itself, they say, till heat shall find / A general level, nowhere in excess'. But the more radical citizen questions this fatalism: "'Tis a poor climax, to my weaker thought, / That future middlingness' (53). For one, the dialectic is seen negatively as the dangerous reversal of opposites; for the other, the golden mean is seen equally negatively as an expression of the universal entropy eradicating all differences. The motto provides a succinct juxtaposition of the principles motivating the two characters and their world-views and, though the brief confrontation is unresolved, the dialogic form in which it is expressed – like the divided structure of the novel itself – implicitly supports the vital play of dialectical opposites.

One feature of the fully dialectical character is that he acts out openly the conflict of forces he embodies. So whereas the narrator carefully supplies the commentary which explains the primary text of Harold's life, Felix provides his own. Or, alternatively, he reports other peoples' interpretations which are again cast in a dialectical form: the phrenologist who diagnosed his 'large veneration' is contradicted by Felix's friend who considered him 'the most blasphemous iconoclast living'. '"That", says my phrenologist, "is because of his large Ideality, which prevents him from finding anything perfect enough to be venerated"' (60). Through semi-jocular definitions of this kind, George Eliot links the state of sacred rebellion – like that of the sacrilege of Transome Court earlier – to the condition of England and to the roots of character. In the aristocratic form of rebellion, the individuals contravene their system of values in pursuit of self-interest; in the working-class world, the rebellion – iconoclasm as distinct from sacrilege – is in the service of a higher truth. This invites misrepresentation, especially among the politicians, because the enactment of the dialectic within one person places that character outside the labels of the contesting parties. The paradoxes inherent in this kind of rebellion are dramatised through the relationship between Felix and his mentor, the dissenting minister Mr Lyon – a kind of Congregational Mordecai – who declares that 'Our great faith . . . is the faith of martyrs' (297).

It is Lyon who repeatedly checks Felix's bumptious self-confidence.[11] Though he recognises that Felix's apparent heresy is orthodoxy 'in the making' (105), he warns him against playing with paradox as an end in itself – 'the caustic . . . may happen to sear your own fingers and make them dead to the quality of things' – and points the dialectic towards its fulfilment: 'the right to rebellion is the right to seek a higher rule, and not to wander in mere lawlessness' (131). The realisation of that higher rule is expressed in suitably apocalyptic terms, not as a universal entropy or decadence – that ingredient is supplied by Transome Court – but as 'that crowning time of the millenial reign, when our daily prayer will be fulfilled, and one law will be written on all hearts, and be the very structure of all thought, and be the principle of all action' (131). Lyon forms the crucial bridge between biblical prophesy and typology and the secular use to which George Eliot applies them.[12] He is nicknamed 'Revelations' and the proportions of his body compared to those of 'a stone Hermes' (47). He may be 'absorbed in mastering all those painstaking interpretations of the Book of Daniel, which are by this time', says the narrator, 'well gone to the limbo of mistaken criticism' (326); but he is also aware, as he tells Felix, of a form of realised apocalyptic 'in what are called the waste minutes of our time, like those of expectation, [when] the soul may soar and range, as in some of our dreams which are brief as a broken rainbow in duration, yet seem to comprise a long history of terror or of joy' (207). Though the apocalyptic note is domesticated in Lyon's quaintness, he points in his own way beyond the conflict of interpretations to the time when events will confirm his beliefs 'in a sort of picture-writing that everybody could understand'. The narrator wistfully acknowledges the desirability of such a time but also the need for his own different kind of commentary: 'The enthusiasms of the world are not to be stimulated by a commentary in small and subtle characters which alone can tell the whole truth' (300). But it is Lyon's private life, as we shall see in a moment, which gives his statements authority.

When applied to the condition of England, Felix's world-view represents a very different interpretative key from that of Harold, the practical politician. The latter, seeking to reconcile rebellion and conformity through the self-interest of class, points only to that future middlingness of a world running down in compromise. Felix, on the other hand, is above the antagonisms of party politics with their focus on the suffrage and ballot-box, in his terms merely the machinery and engines of reform. His 'election sure' is closer to a religious vocation than an electoral majority. Genuine change will only come through education, culture, and the transformation of public opinion, 'the steam that is to work the engines' (250). At another level, Felix's views are *below* the concerns of party politics in that he seeks to address the actual conditions of the working classes. He is not concerned with the middle ground of political ways and means, the art of the possible, which Harold occupies. There, the vision of what might be and the actual conditions of life are continually accommodating each other because 'interests' rather than 'duties' are the criteria. Felix seeks to retain the tension, the dialectic between public morality and the social realities, the idea and the facts – it is an attempt to translate the hypothesis into political life. In addition, the relationship between the vision of a higher morality and the conditions of the poor must not be judged by any crude utilitarian calculus. As he tells Esther when she visits him in prison after his disastrous attempt to intervene in the election riot, 'Where great things can't happen, I care for very small things, such as will never be known beyond a few garrets and workshops' (364). In contrast to the man of politics who seeks to manipulate the system in which he becomes hopelessly entangled, this high-minded minimalism recognises the mysterious relationship between the single life and the movement of the world's forces.

The contrast between the two forms of radicalism is further developed in the two men's attitudes to the positions in which they find themselves at the beginning of their political careers. Unlike Harold, Felix accepts his situation in full knowledge: 'My course was a very simple one', he says to Esther. 'It was pointed out to me by conditions that I saw as clearly as I see the bars of this stile' (221). This is his kind of pragmatism. If he intends to stop his mother purveying Holt's injurious drugs then he must support her; and if he refuses a genteel profession then he must become a watchmaker. In his ignorance Harold, too, both conforms and rebels but in the mode of Gothic tragedy, while this is working-class farce in which Mrs Holt is developed at some length as another mother disappointed in her vision of a future containing grandchildren, a doctor son, a rich daughter-in-law, and outings in a gig. After betraying their working-class origins, the Holts have supported themselves on a mixture of bogus medicines and biblical justification, as Mrs Holt plaintively pleads: 'And my husband said, when he was a-dying – "Mary", he said, "the Elixir, and the Pills, and the Cure will support you, for they've a great name in all the country round, and you'll pray for a blessing on them" . . . for if it was wrong to take the medicines, couldn't the blessed Lord have stopped it?' (50). Out of this spurious compound of self-interest and religiosity Mrs Holt has constructed her own providential view of the world in which her justification is guaranteed: 'There's few women would have gone through with it; and its reasonable to think it'll be made up to me; for if there's promised and purchased blessings, I should think this trouble is purchasing 'em'. (52). There may even be a pun in the comparison between the two justified sinners: Holt's Cathartic Lozenges damage the 'blood' as much as Mrs Transome's adultery. And when Felix's arrest for murder appears to sabotage finally her ambitions, she too provides her own comic version of the end-time and her visions of consequences, 'regarding all her trouble about Felix in the light of a fulfilment of her own prophecies . . . worthy of a commentator on the Apocalypse' (297).

World-views are created and then collapse for, as the narrator comments, 'none of our theories are quite large enough for all the disclosures of time' (77). And the conditions out of which a character formulates a world-view are, as we saw most clearly in *The Mill on the Floss*, fragments of earlier world-views inherited from previous generations in a kind of infinite regress. This is why they don't simply constitute a passive medium, as Harold assumes, but a living reality consisting of elements from the past accepted or rejected, conformed to or rebelled against. In the last resort, the parents' values can be seen as a commentary, tragic or comic, upon the theories of the children out of which they are constituted. In Felix's case, his mother's spurious synthesis of religion and bogus drugs is a parody of his own dialectic of lofty purposes and particular measures to help the poor. The children provide in their turn a commentary upon their parents.

As the third major character, Esther, too, is an anomaly but of a different kind. Whereas the two men have fashioned out of their conformity and rebellion programmes of reform, Esther is mainly conscious of the incongruity between her refined tastes and the Dissenting milieu in which she lives, 'a sense of irreconcilableness between the objects of her taste and the conditions of her lot' (68). Fastidiously disaffected, 'surrounded with ignoble, uninteresting conditions, from which there was no issue' (68), she is, like Romola, inchoate but also potentially inclusive in her sympathies. One side of her nature touches the world of Transome Court: here she deploys 'a little code of her own about scents and colours, textures and behaviour, by which she secretly condemned or sanctioned all things and persons' (68). The other side, which rebels against her limited world and desires the higher life, links her to her stepfather and Felix. In what is by now a familiar ritual, the two male protagonists seek to appropriate her to their theories of life while she, the soul of England and passive catechumen, eventually learns to interrogate her dogmatic catechisers.

The incompatible elements of Esther's character are explained by her birth and upbringing, a past which contains again an act of sacrilegious compromise, a dislocation in her stepfather's system of values. Felix recognises Esther as an anomaly, a question mark against Lyon's public beliefs, when he asks himself: 'Now by what fine meshes of circumstances did that queer devout old man, with his awful creed, which makes this world a vestibule with double doors to hell, and a narrow stair on one side whereby the thinner sort may mount to heaven – by what subtle play of flesh and spirit did he come to have a daughter so little in his own likeness?' (66). If character is a text to be deciphered, then, as we have seen, the generations act as commentary on each other. And Felix's question is answered in the next chapter in one of those retrospects George Eliot characteristically employs to validate her clergyman on non-religious grounds. Here, the flashback is in the confessional mode of the Dissenting novel. Though a successful Congregational minister, Lyon had been aware of heterodox tendencies in his 'too restless intellect, ceaselessly urging questions concerning the mystery of that which was assuredly revealed' (71), in the same way as Mrs Transome's risqué questioning of established values was the fissure which was to undermine her social orthodoxy. Lyon subsequently fell in love with the forsaken French-woman, a Catholic with her child, and underwent 'a spiritual convulsion' (73). Here again, a character comes into existence as an act of sacrilege, a rebellion against a previously accepted set of beliefs. But, unlike Mrs Transome, Lyon 'was as one who raved, and knew that he raved. These mad wishes were irreconcilable with what he was, and must be, as a Christian minister; nay, penetrating his soul as tropic heat penetrates the frame, and changes for it all aspects and all flavours, they were irreconcilable with that conception of the world which made his faith.' This is a volcanic upheaval, the end of a world-view, an internalised apocalypse. Through this love for Annette, his previous doubts 'had now gathered blood and substance. The questioning spirit had become suddenly bold and blasphemous' (73).

Every world-view contains by its nature the criteria of justification and salvation in its own personal eschaton. What has been challenged by these events is Lyon's original Calvinistic belief in the limits of salvation so that his faith and his creed are – inevitably, as George Eliot's master-plot declares – at odds. He resigns his ministry which is only taken up again years later after the death of his wife. But, of course, his backsliding is very different from that of Mrs Transome, the self-justified sinner: 'Strange! that the passion for this women, which he felt to have drawn him aside from the right as much as if he had broken the most solemn vows . . . induced a more thorough renunciation than he had ever known in the time of his complete devotion to his ministerial career' (79–80). In George Eliot's terms, this is rebellion which is seeking a higher rule, a wider definition of salvation; but he, like Mrs Transome, is forced to re-live his past when the disclosures of the plot suggest that Esther's real father may still be alive. Lyon's response is again very different: 'if that wandering of his from the light had brought the punishment of a blind sacrilege as the issue of a conscious trangression, – he prayed that he might be able to accept all consequences of pain to himself' (139). Lyon is, in his own way, a sacred rebel and this is why he is a sympathetic guide and mentor to Felix upon whom his whole career is a commentary,[13] but he is a sacred rebel with a guilty conscience, still modifying covertly the strict doctrines of his church. And Esther's discovery of his past, an essential step in her education, explains her incongruous combination of qualities – the mother's genteel fastidiousness added to her stepfather's other-worldliness.

Harold and Felix appeal respectively to these two sides of Esther's character – the masterful gentleman who pays homage and the brusque craftsman who lectures and bullies. The contrast in their treatment of the heroine (and its political implications) is finely managed. Both men have returned to Treby with clearly defined plans, and for neither is marriage on the agenda. Through their views, George Eliot presents her most pungent definition of the woman question, that crucial indicator of the condition of England.[14] The world-views of neither of these contrasting radicals can accommodate an independent-minded woman. After his years in the Orient, Harold regards 'women as slight things, but he was fond of slight things in the intervals of business' (153). He has an heir from his previous slave-wife and he does not intend to re-marry, certainly not an opinionated English wife. 'Western women were not to his taste: they showed a transition from the feebly animal to the thinking being, which was simply troublesome. Harold preferred a slow-witted large-eyed woman, silent and affectionate, with a load of black hair weighing more heavily than her brains' (292). When Esther turns out to be the heiress of Transome Court, however, his mild initial interest quickly becomes more purposeful as the solvent of self-interest again reconciles competing demands and transforms him into a charming wooer. The implied commentary on this relationship is provided by his mother and Jermyn, the type of which this could become the antitype.

Felix, too, has no place for marriage in his radicalism. He sees it as the quickest way of compromising his Pauline apostolic mission: 'I'll never marry, though I should have to live on raw turnips to subdue my flesh. I'll never look back and say, "I had a fine purpose once – I meant to keep my hands clean, and my soul upright, and to look truth in the face; but pray excuse me, I have a wife and children . . ."' (66). The reasons are contrary but the dismissal is expressed in similar language. Felix shares the view that women are curious hybrids, that 'the utmost stretch of their ideas will not place them on a level with the intelligent fleas' (66). For him they are less than human, not because they seek to have ideas but because they replace them by good taste and codes of conduct: 'That's what makes women a curse; all life is stunted to suit their littleness' (109). In other words, both men disparage women because each sees in them what the other finds attractive – refined taste and opinions, of which Esther is an uneasy amalgam. And this is how the triangular relationship develops in the latter part of the novel. Harold seeks to win the heiress by means of his gentlemanly manners and tasteful homage, while being dimly aware of the opposing influence of Felix in the background, an influence he tends to discount because it is no part of his world. Similarly, Felix badgers and instructs Esther on the lofty role women might play if they could be liberated from the terrorism of good taste and manners. For the two men the triangle is a kind of shadow-boxing for neither understands or appreciates the attractions of his rival and so neither, consequently, understands Esther. The anomalies are trying to understand each other and their difficulties are those of interpretation at a time of crisis. Felix imagines he has observed her closely, 'But', the narrator warns, 'very close and diligent looking at living creatures, even through the best microscope, will leave room for new and contradictory discoveries' (197). Similarly, Harold is confident of Esther's feelings at the climax of the novel, 'But,' comes the warning again, 'we interpret signs of emotions as we interpret other signs – often quite erroneously, unless we have the right key to what they signify' (388). In the interpretative process both men come to revise their views as their original, dogmatic self-confidence is put to the test. The question for Esther is, which man's world-view offers a reprieve from Mrs Transome's terrible cry: 'God was cruel when he made women'(316).

Unlike the previous heroines, Esther is in a relatively detached and
privileged position. She is not suddenly appropriated or buffeted
between competing demands. She determines her own priorities in
the language of the novelist's master-plot: 'Her life was a heap of
fragments, and so were her thoughts: some great energy was needed to
bind them together' (152). Either Harold or Felix has to supply the
energy, the narrative assumes, and so she must scrutinise their systems
of value and what they imply. It is not easy for her to get them both in
focus simultaneously. The two men occupy her mind, challenging and
superseding each other as complementary images. She knows that
Felix would look different 'if I saw him by the side of a finished
gentleman' (106); and shortly afterwards this 'vaguer image of a
possible somebody who would admire her hands and feet' (152)
appears in the shape of Harold who quickly displaces 'the shaggy-
haired cravatless image of Felix Holt' (153). This is in turn dispersed
and replaced by Felix: 'now she had known Felix, her conception of
what a happy love must be had become like a dissolving view, in
which the once-clear images were gradually melting into new forms
and new colours' (197). Even when Felix is imprisoned and she goes to
live at Transome Court and begins to receive Harold's homage, the
other lover is 'present in her mind throughout: what he would say was
an imaginary commentary that she was constantly framing.' (306).
Each man comments implicitly on the other in words provided by
Esther, but she is not simply their mouthpiece: only she is in a position
to juxtapose and so assess their comments. Mrs Transome's double
vision was of the past and its fatal consequences; Esther's is of two
superimposed present realities and the dimly discerned future they
offer.

Esther is attracted and repelled by both men in turn, undergoing
with each 'a strange contradiction of impulses in her mind'. With
Felix she is repelled by his rudeness but seduced by his ideas: 'She
revolted against his assumption of superiority, yet she felt herself in a
new kind of subjection to him' (110). The language of rebellion and
conformity is now being extended into love relations and, prompted
by Felix's brusque confrontation, it is experienced in a strongly
dialectical mode in which the two sides of her character are forced into
open conflict. And as she comes to understand him more clearly, she
begins to imagine what life with a sacred rebel would be like – 'a sort of
difficult blessedness, such as one may imagine in beings who are
conscious of painfully growing into the possession of higher powers'

(197). But the more clearly she understands his role in life the more she realises he doesn't need her. His lofty view of the potential role of noble womanhood is expressed in typological rather than human terms: 'He was looking up at her quite calmly, very much as a reverential Protestant might look at a picture of the Virgin, with a devoutness suggested by the type rather than by the image' (223). As a result, she concludes that although 'he had seemed to bring at once a law, and the love that gave strength to obey the law', she can't love him because he is independent of her. What she really needs is 'a moral support under the negations of her life'. But she is not to be allowed to choose Felix from self-interest; that motive has to be purged from love as from politics. It would be a sacrilegious choice of the sacred rebel, a compromising of the 'first religious experience of her life' (227) which had come through him. This rejection of self-interest, of course, eventually makes her worthy of his love. It is the kind of dilemma that Janet Dempster and Gwendolen Harleth have to face with their own otherworldly mentors.

During Felix's period in prison, Esther learns of her inheritance and is given a preview of life at Transome Court where she is wooed by Harold in scenes which are carefully balanced against those with Felix, even down to the details of gesture and conversation. Harold's attitude, in precise contrast to Felix, is deeply coloured by his awareness of a dependence upon her which he means to reverse with 'the padded yoke' of marriage. He, too, is not in love 'but he was readily amorous', and through marriage he sees 'a mode of reconciling all difficulties' (322). The 'rehearsal of that demeanour amongst luxuries and dignities which had often been part of her day-dreams' (341) has a potent attraction for Esther, especially as 'the effort to find a clue of principle amid the labyrinthine confusions of right and possession', in other words the extraordinarily complicated legal inheritance, proves impossible. But Felix remains a countervailing tendency by means of which she begins to decode carefully the meaning of life at Transome Court, her imagined utopia. She begins to recognise that this utopia, like all others, 'was filled with delightful results, independent of processes' (304). Esther's 'intensest life was no longer in her dreams, where she made things to her own mind: she was moving in a world charged with forces' (306-7). Thanks to Felix, she begins to discern the nature of these processes and forces at work at Transome Court. Previously, her utopian dream had simply been a reaction 'from the presence of opposite conditions' in her life at

Malthouse Yard, but now that the dream is realised she 'found the balance of her attention reversed . . . she found herself arrested and painfully grasped by the means through which the ladyhood was to be obtained'. This is a dialectical as opposed to a utopian vision of the world, a vision in which 'a humiliating loss' must be 'the obverse of her own proud gain' (305). This new awareness, on Esther's part, is presented as an added faculty which links interpretation and vision in a way which is to become increasingly important. For example, when she makes an assumption a little later that Lyon would come to live with her at Transome Court, she experiences 'a vision, showing, as by a flash of lightning, the incongruity of that past which had created the sanctities and affections of her life with that future which was coming to her'. Thanks to 'this vision and its reversed interpretation which, five months ago she would have been incapable of seeing' (307), she begins to fit past, present, and future together.

As the moment of choice approaches, the alternatives become more and more equally balanced. In *The Mill on the Floss* and *Romola*, the heroines' hermeneutic vertigo culminated in a breakthrough into a mythic world where event and meaning were miraculously identical. The conflict of interpretation is handled with subdued melodrama in this novel. One reason is that Esther is kept passively in the wings observing both the legal and the political action until called upon to intervene in the lives of her two suitors and, in the meanwhile, she carefully observes and listens. This is not the grand educational detour Romola makes through European civilisation to prepare for her final act of textual interpretation, but it has its own kind of comprehensiveness. Not only has Esther experienced at first hand the contrasting world-views of Harold and Felix, the 'middling delights' of one and the 'difficult blessedness' of the other, but learnt of the trials of the previous generation in its attempt to reconcile conformity and rebellion, will and destiny. She has heard her stepfather's confession, listened to Mrs Holt's disappointed hopes, and is gradually beginning to decipher the mystery of Transome Court. Each contains a vision of possibilities, a commentary on her own position; and they range, like the opening coach ride, across the social spectrum of England, from the aristocracy and the legal profession through the world of Dissent to the working-class. Having absorbed the whole of the novel, as it were, the heroine is given the opportunity to choose. This is her final moment of suspended animation: 'Esther found it impossible to read in these days; her life was a book which she seemed herself to be constructing – trying to make character clear before her, and looking into the ways of destiny' (322). The other characters have provided and been provided with commentaries explaining and glossing their own and other people's primary texts; with the seals opening in this way, Esther has approached her own apocalypse. She is now in the process of writing her own text and her choice will conclude the novel.

Marriage to Harold would close the novel in a practical compromise, a disillusioned utopia already in existence. Everything, 'all outward conditions', seem to conspire 'to make this middling lot the best she could attain to' (358). Esther becomes increasingly passive as her destiny seems to be expressed through her inheritance of Transome Court and the complex plotting of the novel; in other words, the conventional ending to her utopian romance and so many condition-of-England novels. But this, she knows, represents a world running down in irreversible entropy, as she forsakes 'the high mountain air' and adjusts 'her wishes to a life of middling delights, overhung with the languorous haziness of motiveless ease, where poetry was only literature, and the fine ideas had to be taken down from the shelves of the library when her husband's back was turned' (357–8). She is intent on writing the text of her life, but from this perspective the alternative Felix offers seems impossibly demanding. The 'divided and oppressed' state of her heart is expressed as a contrast between the hard 'conditions' of her life and 'the easy invitations of circumstance' (360) which are leading her towards Harold and one kind of satisfactory closure. She is, however, acutely aware of the significance of her choice as she stands 'at the first and last parting of the ways'. The apocalyptic overtones increase as she acknowledges that the act of choice will bring into simultaneous existence a world and a self; only a correct choice, she knows, gives 'unity to life, and makes the memory a temple where all relics and all votive offerings, all worship and all grateful joy, are an unbroken history sanctified by one religion' (360). Such a choice would help to redeem in the future all the acts of sacrilege, iconoclasm, blasphemy, and desecration which underlie, in the novel's and England's past, the choice she has now to make. It will also precipitate Esther into the world as a character, not as 'a heap of fragments' but as a temple, with a future uncompromised by the past. But as she seeks 'the rest of final choice' (389), the question the novel asks implicitly and insistently is, how is choice possible in a world where the conditions of life determine the individual, where will and destiny are inextricably intertwined, a world where the apostolic suitor is sentenced for manslaughter and the aristocratic suitor turns out to be illegitimate? The answer is, by an act of faith and by a vision – the first publicly associates her with Felix, the second dissociates her from Harold and Transome Court. And both are expressed as acts of interpretation.

Her act of faith occurs at Felix's trial where, against strong circumstantial evidence, he attempts to explain himself to the bemused jury by claiming honest intentions in his violent behaviour during the election riot. He is, of course, neither a rebel nor a conformist. He reverences the law, he says, but holds 'it blasphemy to say that a man ought not to fight against authority'. The sacred rebel invokes his 'sacred feelings' which make 'a sacred duty' (370): the dialectic of conformity and rebellion cannot be frozen and this is the reason why he is supported by neither the Whigs or Tories. '[I]f he were a martyr', comments Lyon, 'neither side wanted to claim him' (300). The problem is that there are no standards or criteria by which to judge the sacred rebel and interpret his actions. This in turn disqualifies Felix from being able to 'calculate the effect of misunderstanding as to himself' which results in the fiasco of his intervention. Nature, we are told in terms reminiscent of Savonarola's fatal antithetical mixture, 'never makes men who are at once energetically sympathetic and minutely calculating' (268). Harold considers his rival irrational and in his defence concentrates pragmatically on the art of the possible, on 'adjusting fact, so as to raise it to the power of evidence' (311). But, characteristically, George Eliot introduces legal hermeneutics in order to transcend them. 'Man cannot', the narrator opines, 'be defined as an evidence-giving animal' (369). The crucial question is that of motives and these can only be validated by someone who shares them: Romola could interpret her sacred rebel because his spirit was dwelling in her, while in this trial Esther's 'woman's passion and her reverence for rarest goodness rushed together in an undivided current' (375). On this basis she delivers her public testimony: 'His nature is very noble; he is tender-hearted; he could never have had any intention that was not brave and good' (376). It is the most romantic and perfunctory of George Eliot's several trials in that it is Esther's 'inspired ignorance' which is meant to cut through the legal niceties and 'the stiffening crust of cautious experience' (375). Even though the verdict goes against him, she has, like the biblical Esther, made her 'confession of faith' (376) without a hint of the perjury of self-interest. Poetry has become, briefly, more than simply literature.

In her modest way she too has rebelled – against the dictates of good
taste. But both men are still misinterpreting her actions: Felix assumes
that she will eventually accept Harold, while the latter dismisses her
public confession as quixotic.

After the trial, a decision has to be made: Esther has publicly
defended Felix and also allowed Harold to woo her at Transome
Court. But no simple choice is possible as the hard ideals of the life of
one radical are counteracted by the beguiling circumstances of the
other. This is where vision is needed for, as the mottoes to chapters
forty-one and forty-nine insist, it is inseparable from genuine choice.
This is a new development in George Eliot's fiction. Maggie Tulliver
and Romola were suddenly precipitated from their impasse into a
new kind of reality; and even with Savonarola no vision was granted
and his prophecies were annulled. In *Felix Holt*, as the two worlds of
the novel are juxtaposed more and more closely in the heroine's mind,
there is a growing confidence that a vision of the future will be
forthcoming to facilitate her choice.[15] She creates her own rituals for
such an experience. To distance herself from 'the oppressive urgency'
of Transome Court she extinguishes the candles. 'And now . . . her
mind was in that state of highly-wrought activity, that large
discourse, in which we seem to stand aloof from our own life . . . "I
think I am getting that power Felix wished me to have: I shall soon see
strong visions"' (386). The influences of the two suitors are still
competing with each other as this remark of Felix's, recalled amidst
the luxuries of Transome Court, takes us back to an earlier
conversation: 'I want you to have such a vision of the future that you
may never lose your best self.' And Felix casually confided to her,
despite the evidence of his several misjudgments, that he himself was
'warned by visions': 'Those old stories of visions and dreams guiding
men have their truth: we are saved by making the future present to
ourselves' (224). In the complex conditions of life in post-Reform
England, a prophetic vision, however muted, is necessary for making
an informed choice. This, rather than Arnoldian culture, will
preserve the best self.

Her ritual is interrupted by Harold, agitated by the discovery of his
parentage, who has come to clarify honourably his changed position
in the world and to tell her about the public appeal he has organised
on behalf of Felix. Both actions make her choice even more difficult.
Alone again, she draws up the blinds – repeating that familiar
Victorian *topos* – and looks out into the moonlight: 'She wanted the

largeness of the world to help her thought' (389). She juxtaposes and rehearses her two courses of action, the two renunciations – a life of difficult blessedness or one of middling delights. The first offers an open-ended, dialectical conclusion to her life's story for, although she has no illusions about 'the dim life of the back street', the love of Felix would make such a life tolerable; but such a love is 'only a quivering hope, not a certainty' (390). The ideal must be embraced without any compromising self-interest as an act of faith which creates the reality it seeks. In contrast, the result of the second closure to her hopes, their apparent fulfilment, has become increasingly predictable during her stay at Transome Court. 'With a terrible prescience', she sees herself 'in a silken bondage that arrested all motive, and was nothing better than a well-cushioned despair' (390). But this double foreknowledge, hope or despair, is still not decisive as her thoughts oscillate, 'succeeding and returning in her mind like scenes through which she was living'.

The aristocratic world remains a mystery which has to be interpreted before she can choose – and the vision which enables her to do this is finally vouchsafed at midnight, when the ghost of Transome Court appears. It is Mrs Transome rejected by her son and now irredeemably trapped in a ghostly limbo, pacing up and down the corridor, unable to turn to Esther, despite her promptings to do so. 'She had never yet in her life asked for compassion – had never thrown herself in faith on an unproffered love' (392). This is again the *contrapasso* to which life has consigned her, repetitively 'pacing the corridor like an uneasy spirit without a goal' (393), as she was introduced to the reader in the first chapter. The woman who sought to control decisively her own life has spent the whole novel waiting. Now, having been rejected by her distraught son, she has died, 'age striking her with a sudden wand' (384), as her terrible vision of consequences at the opening of the novel is fulfilled. But simultaneously that fulfilment has 'come as a last vision to urge [Esther] towards the life where the draughts of joy sprang from the unchanging fountains of reverence and devout love' (393–4). She seeks to bring Mrs Transome back to life through reunion with her son, and then leaves Transome Court. Thanks to her lengthy education, Esther has been enabled to read the silent tragedy described in the introductory chapter – 'committed to no sound except that of low moans in the night, seen in no writing except that made on the face by the slow months of suppressed anguish and early morning tears' (84). She has correctly 'divined' the meaning of 'that image of restless misery' (596), the figure of Mrs Transome pacing the corridor, as a vision of consequences, a typological fulfilment of the life she must reject.

In conclusion, *Felix Holt* depicts a world in crisis on the verge of revolution. At the centre of the public events of the novel is the election riot which epitomises the inexplicable nature of this crisis as well as George Eliot's anxieties. 'As [Felix] was pressed along with the multitude into Treby Park, his very movement seemed to him only an image of the day's fatalities, in which the multitudinous small wickednesses of small selfish ends, really undirected towards any larger result, had issued in widely-shared mischief that might yet be hideous' (270). To interpret this crisis, the condition of England in 1832, it must be placed within a larger context. The reader is taken thirty years into the past and an equal distance into the future to the time of writing, in the attempt to achieve a glimpse of the apocalypse concealed within the crisis. Only in this way can any direction be discerned among the complex conditions of life out of which the self and society are constituted. In a variety of ways George Eliot offers, as we have seen, glimpses of the future to both generations of characters in the novel. These always occur at moments of crisis, of personal revolution. In the first generation, Mr Lyon's and Mrs Transome's sacrilegious reversals result in visions of consequence, either of damnation or salvation. 'Quick souls', says the narrator, 'have their intensest life in the first anticipatory sketch of what may or will be' (73). These reversals become the conditions out of which the second generation of characters is constituted, the pasts to which they have to respond in order to glimpse the future.

In all cases, whether of hope or despair, the moment of vision which makes choice possible arises from the collision of two world-views, one conformed to, one challenged or rebelled against. In political terms it represents the imminent collapse of a world, in personal terms the collapse of a world-view. This provides a moment of freedom as the character moves abruptly from the confines of one world – 'that conception of the world which made his faith' (73), as it is referred to with Mr Lyon – to an alternative, and in the process experiences 'a wider vision of past and present realities – a willing movement of a man's soul with the larger sweep of the world's forces – a movement towards a more assured end than the chances of a single life' (61). At this pivotal moment when part and whole interact, the limiting horizon of the character's world-view is breached in a form of secularised apocalypse which reveals the relationship of past, present, and future. The vision of the assured end may be the punishment of the justified sinner or the millenial expectations of the sacred rebel. At her moment of vision, the heroine is called out of the one into the other, out of the repetitive limbo of the infernal *contrapasso*, a decadent utopia, into the dialectical promise of the higher blessedness. It will be seen from this that the sense of crisis and the problems of interpretation reflect and explain each other; their only possible resolution in *Felix Holt* seems to be in the access to some kind of visionary experience. This is a development in George Eliot's hermeneutics which will be taken much further in *Daniel Deronda*, and in the light of which *Middlemarch* may be seen as a retrenchment.

CHAPTER 7

Middlemarch: empiricist fables

The sudden switch in chapter ten of *Middlemarch*, from Dorothea's career to Lydgate's, is the most unprepared and unsettling transition in George Eliot's oeuvre.[1] At that point, *Middlemarch* becomes a multiplot novel, different in kind from the other fictions, and as a result it foregrounds the question of interpretation in quite new ways. Each of the divided structures of her other novels, most strikingly *Silas Marner*, *Felix Holt*, and *Daniel Deronda*, implies and acts out a dialectic which comes to focus on a crucial conflict of interpretation, climax, and closure. However disparate the two halves of these novels, each half is read against the stable background of the other with which it is being brought into closer and closer relationship. The pressure in such double narratives focuses finally on the central interpretative crux, which is resolved either by an apocalyptic breakthrough into a new kind of reality or by a vision of consequences which makes choice meaningful. For instance, both Rufus Lyon, with his 'wider vision of past and present realities', and Mordecai, his Jewish counterpart in *Daniel Deronda* with his gift of second-sight, hint at some kind of transcendence at the borders of the real in the novels on either side of *Middlemarch*.

The persistent decentering of the narrative of *Middlemarch* denies such possibilities: 'the time was gone by', Dorothea Brooke acknowledges, 'for guiding visions and spiritual directors'.[2] In their absence, the reader experiences at first hand the life of the novel as a hypothesis continually collapsing under the weight of the new evidence which the different segments of the narrative bring to light. In her 'Notes on Form in Art', George Eliot had stressed the growth of knowledge achieved by that primordial form of interpretation, the hermeneutic circle, with its rhythm of expansion and contraction, of distinction and combination. *Middlemarch*, although it dramatises vividly this totalising search for unity and meaning – by narrator, characters, and readers – offers, as well, the opposite experience: the 'smaller and smaller unlikenesses' may not reveal 'a common likeness', just as 'the whole' into which they are to be combined may not enter into 'the fullest relation to other wholes'.[3] But both possibilities, positive and negative, are given such urgent and plausible representation in all aspects of this novel that literary critics have usually chosen a single emphasis in order to evade that uncomfortably fine balance between sameness and difference, credulity and scepticism, which seems to reflect ironically and step by step their own reading process.

An earlier generation of critics, prompted by the Prelude and Finale, sought to centre the novel in the career of Dorothea and her crucial discoveries about the human condition, climaxing in her dramatic confrontation with Rosamond. In such interpretations it is as if the shadowy presence of Dinah and Hetty and *their* climatic meeting in the prison in *Adam Bede* could be discerned within this more indeterminate structure. But, against such monocentric readings, increasingly sophisticated doubts have been raised, especially by J. Hillis Miller, in essays which provide a salutary stress on the negative, deconstructive side of the novel.[4] The emphasis here tends to fall on the commentary where the narrator generously adds his support to this kind of indeterminacy with such remarks as, 'Signs are small measurable things, but interpretations are illimitable' (24), or 'The text, whether of prophet or of poet, expands for whatever we can put into it, and even his bad grammar is sublime' (50). Now, the apparently totalising images – the web, the text, the pier-glass, the organism – all of which have been carefully articulated by a large body of scholarly writing are found to be trapped in their own metaphoric nature, a point the narrator also makes with the comment that 'we all of us, grave or light, get our thoughts entangled in metaphors, and act fatally on the strength of them' (84).

More recent studies of the novel have sensibly stressed the way in which both of these tendencies are, in any reading of *Middlemarch*, underpinned by the act of interpretation itself. Peter Garrett, for example, considers that 'the bond between reader and character [is] formed by their participation in a common process of interpretation', that the 'characters' responses to experience [can be seen] as varieties of interpretation', and that it 'is only a short step beyond this observation to say that *Middlemarch* is "about" interpretation'.[5] Similarly, D. A. Miller, in his perceptive discussion of the strangely ambiguous status of the novel, holds that '*Middlemarch* seems to be traditional and to be beyond its limit, to subvert and to reconfirm the value of its traditional status'; and this is because the 'text pluralizes the perspective from which traditional form is commonly perceived and delimited' so that the act of interpretation is again foregrounded.[6] This chapter shares the same emphasis as these recent studies, but its aim is to show even more sharply, if possible, how the act of interpretation itself is the dynamo which drives the narrative of this most interpreted of all Victorian novels; and that its different segments can best be understood as the fictionalisation of different hermeneutic modes. This will enable us, I believe, to appreciate better the reasons why this provincial 'home epic' achieves such an exemplary range and variety at the same time as it marks the limit of the traditional novel.

The high drama of George Eliot's master-plot is necessarily muted by the very structure of *Middlemarch*. That plot was driven, as we have seen, by the forming and testing of hypotheses in the search for a vision of larger and larger wholes incorporating more and more minutely discriminated parts. The extreme possibilities of such desire – total organic oneness or the collapse into 'miserable agglomerations of atoms' – are excluded from the middle ground which this novel occupies. But on its provincial borders the reader is allowed glimpses of the Pascalian abysses which lie in wait if the desire for meaning is pursued to excess and the veils of life unwisely lifted. If our senses were preternaturally heightened, if we could hear the grass growing, if the microscopes we apply to our neighbours' behaviour were increasingly powerful, where would interpretation end, how could meaning be stabilised? Well wadded with stupidity against such extreme possibilities, we turn, says the narrator, back to our humdrum lives. Such a turn is characteristic of nineteenth-century empiricism with its belief, derived from Hume, that knowledge is limited to phenomena and that, though relative, this knowledge of our sense impression is the closest we can get to the truth. The metaphysical speculations of ontology are to be discarded in favour of an epistemology which seeks to define the ever inaccessible physical world. But although this can lead, as J. M. Cameron has pointed out, to states of extreme anxiety, empiricism also rescues us from such speculation by not permitting us 'to reject those beliefs without which we should lose the appetite for life':

Empiricism is thus immensely strange and yet solidly commonsensical. It tells us that most of what we take to be susceptible of categorical statement should strictly be the subject of an indefinitely vast collection of hypotheticals; and yet that this need make no difference to how we talk and how we act. It is terrifying and it is consoling. With one hand it robs us of our familiar world; with the other it restores it to us.[7]

This 'empiricist fable' with all its anxieties and reassurances was, as we have seen, always part of George Eliot's thinking, though the nature of its deployment changed in the course of her career, as her reservations about the advance of grand theory increased. One expression of it occurred in 1874, shortly after the writing of *Middlemarch*, in her well-known reply to the Hon. Mrs Henry Frederick Ponsonby who had confessed to becoming indifferent to her fellow human beings after studying molecular physics. 'As to the necessary combinations through which life is manifested,' wrote the novelist, 'and which seem to present themselves to you as a hideous fatalism, which ought logically to petrify your volition – have they, *in fact*, any such influence on your ordinary course of action in the primary affairs of your existence as a human, social, domestic creature?' Mrs Ponsonby still takes a bath, George Eliot assumes, as she reminds her that 'the consideration of molecular physics is not the direct ground of human love and moral action . . . [which] have their peculiar history which makes an experience and knowledge over and above the swing of atoms'.[8] It is clear from this kind of advice that empiricism is not simply a theory of knowledge; it is also a state of mind, a certain ironic habit of thought and expression which is most readily recognisable in this novel.

In *Middlemarch*, the presence of this empiricist fable, thoroughly moralised and domesticated, can be felt at all levels of the narrative as both a compulsion to interpret the world, to create a coherent and comprehensive world view, and an acknowledgement of the dangers inherent in any such attempt. The narrator's comments on the compulsion can be balanced against his equally witty and wise comments on the dangers. But what drives the narrative is the desire for comprehensive meaning. Peter Brooks has recently drawn attention to the presence of some form of engine in every novel by Zola, suggesting that they 'represent the dynamics of the narrative, furnish the motor power by which the plot moves forward'. These engines are, he concludes, 'a *mise-en-abîme* of the novel's narrative motor, an explicit statement of the inclusion within the novel of the principle of its movement'.[9] In their different ways, the same can be said of Lydgate's and Casaubon's researches in *Middlemarch*. It is worth looking briefly at these as the interpretative motors of this novel as well as at their fate within the empiricist fable.

Lydgate's research demonstrates the genuinely hypothetical method in action, 'the exercise of disciplined power – combining and constructing with the clearest eye for probabilities and the fullest obedience to knowledge; and then, in yet more energetic alliance with impartial Nature, standing aloof to invent tests by which to try its own work'. In this way, the scientific imagination dissolves the familiar material world, goes beyond the evidence of the senses, and constitutes a new relation between itself and the object by revealing 'subtle actions inaccessible by any sort of lens, but tracked in that outer darkness through long pathways of necessary sequence by the inward light which is the last refinement of Energy, capable of bathing even the ethereal atoms in its ideally illuminated space' (161–2). Energy as the inward light of the mind illuminates the energy of the swing of the atoms, and in the process the Cartesian division of mind and matter, subject and object, is overcome. This is what the quest for the primitive tissue finally reveals, sameness without real difference.[10] It is not unlike Lewes's description of the relation between the organism and its medium which he wrote in 1874: 'Out of the general web of Existence certain threads may be detached and rewoven into a special group – the Subject – and this sentient group will in so far be different from the larger group – the Object; but whatever different arrangement the threads take on, they are not different threads.'[11] These are late nineteenth-century versions of the romantic sublime, scientific and philosophical translations of Wordsworth's 'spousal verse / Of this great consummation' between the mind and nature, which culminated in his vision on Snowdon.[12] From this sublime abyss, the empiricism of *Middlemarch* characteristically turns away with a mixture of pathos and irony to another and countervailing ideal construction on the next page of the novel: 'In Rosamond's romance it was not necessary to imagine much about the inward life of the hero, or of his serious business in the world' (163).

The second and equally specialised account of the activity of interpretation in *Middlemarch* is to be found in Casaubon's researches into myth. It has become customary to contrast the two men's intellectual activities, but from our point of view it is their similarities which are instructive. Both are searching for origins, the very stuff out of which life is constituted, and both are asking the wrong questions:

Casaubon's aim is to show 'that all the mythical systems or erratic mythical fragments in the world were corruptions of a tradition originally revealed' (23). Once this Archimedean point of origin has been established, then myth will be illuminated in the sublime glow of revelation. 'Having once mastered the true position and taken a firm footing there, the vast field of mythical constructions became intelligible, nay, luminous with the reflected light of correspondences' (23). The language of this interpretative enterprise is not unlike Lydgate's as he too seeks to overcome the dualism of mind and matter, 'to pierce the obscurity of those minute processes which prepare human misery and joy' in his 'ideally illuminated space' (162). The difference is that one man begins with the material world, the other with the mythical constructions of the mind. Both enterprises fail but whereas Lydgate glimpses the possible sublimity of the hermeneutic circle – described appropriately, in terms drawn from his own branch of science, as the systole and diastole of research – Casaubon's project turns out to be, equally appropriately, another spurious myth of origin. As Dorothea considers the task of labouring on her husband's notebooks and documents after his death, she conjures up a Gothic version of the negative sublime, a nightmarish continuation of the 'stupendous fragmentariness' of Rome: 'And now she pictured to herself the days, and months, and years which she must spend in sorting what might be called shattered mummies, and fragments of a tradition which was itself a mosaic wrought from crushed ruins' (469).

The empiricist fable takes us to the edge of the abyss in its search for reality, 'the very grain of things', and then turns back to other, quite different truths by which we live our daily lives. It is both chastening and reassuring. And it is the source of the irony which converts the careers of Lydgate and Casaubon into a sad commentary on the need to acknowledge other truths: despite the looming presence of Rosamond, Lydgate insists that the primitive tissue is still his 'fair unknown', while Casaubon neglects the sunshine in pursuit of his solar deities. But their research remains the most detailed expression of the interpretative quest for meaning, which is both unavoidable and dangerous. It is worth recalling the fate of those two other obsessively single-minded researchers, the Renaissance textual scholars Bardo and Baldassarre in *Romola*. They sought to recover the origin of classical antiquity in all its textual purity, but through their *hubris* only succeeded in releasing into Florence the agents – reborn pagan god and medieval saint – who rejected their begetters' scholarly quests in favour of the struggle for the soul of Florence. In all these cases, there is a suggestion of idolatry or sacrilege in the unilateral search for origins, the stable point outside the experiential flux, with a warning that the results are likely to be unpredictable or self-defeating. In *Middlemarch*, this drama is not presented explicitly as an allegory of European civilisation, but Lydgate and Casaubon in their provincial failure adumbrate the dangerous nature of the quest for the original life-stuff out of which existence is created. They too release into Middlemarch disruptive and destructive forces. And as the *mise-en-abîme* of the interpretative quest – one of science, one of religion – their researches provide a rich source of analogy and metaphor for the more down-to-earth activities of Middlemarch.

The reference to *Romola* also helps us to understand more clearly the reasons for setting *Middlemarch* at the time of First Reform Bill. This was for George Eliot, as we have seen with *Felix Holt*, a time of cultural crisis, of changing paradigms, a time when interpretation becomes a central issue.[13] If the earlier novel is a Renaissance epic, this is a Victorian 'home epic' in which all the established world-views are at risk as 'the boundaries of social intercourse' shift, 'begetting new consciousness of interdependence' (93). The kaleidoscopic coach ride of *Felix Holt* with its glimpses of different worlds has become a part of the structure of this novel. Everything is changing, even those who refuse to change are 'altering with the double change of self and beholder' (93–4). This points to the double hermeneutic which George Eliot now employs with great skill in representing the lives of even her relatively minor characters in the community. The narrator simultaneously represents and interprets. Mrs Cadwallader, for example, is a world-view, 'a well-bred scheme of the universe' based predeterminedly on blood, birth, and genealogy, which constitutes both her as a character and the world she inhabits. With appropriate irony, the mythical and religious language of *Romola* is displaced into these provincial theodicies which are beginning to feel themselves threatened: 'her feeling towards the vulgar rich was a sort of religious hatred: they had probably made all their money out of high retail prices, and . . . such people were no part of God's design in making the world' (59). And the world has to be made to conform to this view by Mrs Cadwallader's mind, 'active as phosphorous, biting everything that came near into the form that suited it' (60). Another minor character who displays this double hermeneutic even more elaborately is Caleb Garth with his creed of business. As a boy he was called to the worship of this secular and powerful many-headed divinity, 'that myriad-headed, myriad-handed labour', the sights of which 'had acted on him as poetry without the aid of the poets, had made a philosophy for him without the aid of philosophers, a religion without the aid of theology'. Though 'an orthodox Christian' it is, in reality, this 'sublime labour' which produces his 'sublime music', harmonising and controlling his interpretation of life: Caleb too is a scheme of the universe complete with a comprehensive classification of human activities, as well as 'virtual divinities' and his own 'prince of darkness'. His redeeming quality is that, unlike Mrs Cadwallader, 'he was ready to accept any number of systems, like any number of firmaments' (246–7), which places him alongside the narrator of this multi-plot novel.

With these minor characters, the double hermeneutic – the narrator interpreting the interpreters – is stabilised into relatively static world-views, secular religions evolved and modified to explain a time of crisis. But even here, George Eliot is cautious about any neat encapsulation of character: the act of interpretation, like the Heisenberg uncertainty principle, affects what it interprets. The 'double change of self and beholder' is not only a double, but also a reciprocal hermeneutic in which no one is neutral or omniscient, neither the narrator nor – as he is quick to point out – the readers with 'their own beautiful views' (59). The mystery of character is respected and maintained through anomaly or the discrepancy between belief and conduct: Mrs Cadwallader has married a poor clergyman while Caleb Garth is ignorant of profit-and-loss. An essential ingredient of the epic scope of *Middlemarch* is the representative nature of these various and subtly inconsistent theories of life. In contrast, the major characters are, by definition, those whose world-views are in the process of being formed, challenged, or dismantled. With these the dynamics of the interpretative quest are dramatised in much greater complexity, their narratives generated by a marked discrepancy between a hypothesis of reality and the world in which they find themselves. In *Romola*, such hypotheses were the founding myths of classical and Christian culture reborn into the confusing Florentine present. In *Middlemarch*, George Eliot achieves her home-epic scope by fictionalising in the lives of her protagonists some of the major myths articulating and controlling life in Victorian England, most of which are associated with vocation and marriage, and their interaction.

These myths, these theories of life, are subjected to the full stringency of a reciprocal hermeneutic at a time of cultural crisis. They are all, in fact, tested to the point of radical redefinition or destruction by each other and by the social medium of Middlemarch in which they seek to achieve their own coherence. The difference between success and failure is shown to be a fine one. And the crucial determining element is identified again and again as the social medium of provincial life, variously described as the 'embroiled medium' (283) or the 'dim and clogging medium' (484) through which the characters move and which determines the way they see and are seen. In the terms of Lewes' analogy, the social medium is 'the general web of existence' out of which 'certain threads' are detached and rewoven as the subject, and so distinguished from the remainder known as the object. This conveys the vivid sense in the novel of the medium as both palpable and infinitely subtle, or as the narrator describes one element in this medium, those 'prejudices [which], like odorous bodies, have a double existence both solid and subtle – solid as the pyramids, subtle as the twentieth echo of an echo' (318). And it is in this diffusive medium that the interpretations of both self and beholder have to be carried out, those sensitive hypotheses which partly determine the conclusions they seek. The question *Middlemarch* asks is, what survives of the inherited myths when they are translated and displaced into the embroiled provincial medium of English life at the time of the First Reform Bill? To answer this question, it is necessary to disentangle a few of the major myths of vocation from a multiplot novel whose purpose is to juxtapose, interweave, and problematise.

Dorothea Brooke's career is cast in the form of a saint's life.[14] She is compared variously to St Theresa (85), St Barbara (86), St Clara (211), St Catherine (523) and the Virgin Mary (758). She takes over, as it were, from Romola at the point of that character's canonisation, a point flamboyantly recapitulated by Naumann in the Vatican Museum when he catches a glimpse of this provincial 'perfect young Madonna' and describes her as an expression of 'antique form animated by Christian sentiment – a sort of Christian Antigone – sensuous force controlled by spiritual passion' (185). This ironic reprise of *Romola* alerts us to the kind of experiment this novel is carrying out. Can the life of a saint with its hagiographic sequence of renunciation, testing, and martyrdom, provide a hermeneutic for the heroine's career in the decentered world of Middlemarch?[15] That the descent from lofty ambitions to mundane realities will be sudden, is sharply outlined in the Prelude to the novel which provides the model not only for Dorothea's career but for all the protagonists. We quickly discover that even St Theresa's initial search for 'some illimitable satisfaction' proved belated: the 'martyrdom' she sought as a child was denied her by 'domestic reality . . . in the shape of uncles', so she had to satisfy her epic ambitions 'in the reform of a religious order'. For the 'later-born Theresas', the discrepancy between their 'spiritual grandeur' and 'the meanness of opportunity' is even more acute and their lives end in negatives, the 'goodness' they seek 'unattained', 'foundress[es] of nothing' with their lives not 'centering in some long-recognizable deed'. And the reason offered is that they 'were helped by no coherent social faith and order which could perform the function of knowledge for the ardently willing soul'; or, as the narrator says in the Finale, 'the medium in which their ardent deeds took shape is for ever gone' (825). In the absence of this shared world-view, they try, nevertheless, 'to shape their thought and deed in noble agreement'; just as we try, with equal difficulty, to interpret their lives, for 'to common eyes their struggles seemed mere inconsistency and formlessness' (3). Can the model of the secularised life of a saint provide any guidance to this double hermeneutical problem?

It is important to recognise that the key turning-point for Dorothea is the Roman honeymoon: before this, she is still seeking in the tradition of her saintly predecessors her own form of 'illimitable satisfaction', while after her renunciation she accepts the fully secularised sainthood of a decentered universe. The form of satisfaction her intense 'religious disposition' (28) initially aspires to is theologically imprecise; it is 'that spiritual religion, that submergence of self in communion with Divine perfection' (24) to be expressed in 'some lofty conception of the world' (8) which will regulate her day-to-day conduct. But as we have seen, the medium of faith in which such a religious need can be met has disappeared and so Dorothea has to turn to the medium of knowledge and Mr Casaubon; 'since the time was gone for guiding visions and spiritual directors, since prayer heightened yearning but not instruction, what lamp was there but knowledge? Surely learned men kept the only oil; and who more learned than Mr Casaubon?' (85). He, the clergyman scholar, is appropriated willy-nilly by this insatiable need for 'a binding theory':

'she was looking forward to higher initiation in ideas, as she was looking forward to marriage, and blending her dim conceptions of both' (84). The language of religious vocation is displaced onto this dream of comprehensive knowledge so that when the scholar, upon whom 'the radiance of her transfigured girlhood' has happened to fall, proposes marriage – 'as good as going to a nunnery' (58), says Mrs Cadwallader – Dorothea becomes 'a neophyte about to enter on a higher grade of initiation' (44). She is 'on her way to the New Jerusalem' via the pamphlets annotated in Mr Casaubon's own hand (37).

During the betrothal, the religious language becomes increasingly hermeneutical as Dorothea earnestly justifies her faith in Casaubon by explaining away the gaps in her expectations. Her need for a binding theory demands no less. 'She filled up all blanks with unmanifested perfections, interpreting him as she interpreted the works of Providence, and accounting for seeming discords by her own deafness to the higher harmonies' (73). Or alternatively, his conversation is perused as a sacred text. 'Dorothea's faith supplied all that Mr Casaubon's words seemed to leave unsaid: what believer sees a disturbing omission or infelicity? The text, whether of prophet or of poet, expands for whatever we can put into it, and even his bad grammar is sublime' (50). The discords and omissions can, of course, point in other directions, as Dorothea discovers finally in Rome which is both their honeymoon destination and the anti-climax of her pilgrimage towards that 'illimitable satisfaction' of complete knowledge. Here, the gaps and discords point not beyond themselves to the higher harmonies but find definitive expression in the fragments of European culture and civilisation. Instead of penetrating to the holy of holies, she finds that the temple is in ruins. This is the moment of radical decentering in her saintly quest: brought by her guide and mentor to the 'Imperial and Papal city', the holy place of culture, she finds only 'stupendous fragmentariness' and 'broken revelations' (187–8).

All the materials are present in Rome, 'the city of visible history', as they were in Renaissance Florence, for a comprehensive vision of classical and Christian civilisation. But what was presented in *Romola* as a series of collections of heterogeneous objects, here becomes a compound image of negative sublimity. The sight of '[r]uins and basilicas, palaces and colossi, set in the midst of a sordid present', culminates in 'the huge bronze canopy' of St Peter's with 'the excited intention in the attitudes and garments of the prophets and evangelists in the mosaics above'. It is not that history and culture are dead and reified. Rather, they are too active and violent in their unintelligibility: the 'eager Titanic life gazing and struggling on walls and ceilings', 'the vast wreck of ambitious ideals, sensuous and spiritual', all these 'first jarred her as with an electric shock, and then urged themselves on her with that ache belonging to a glut of confused ideas which check the flow of emotion'. The 'gigantic broken revelations' for which Dorothea had been longing in her pilgrimage of knowledge are suddenly 'thrust abruptly' on her meagre notions. The 'city of visible history' turns into 'the oppressive masquerade of ages, in which her own life too seemed to become a masque with enigmatical costumes'. Her insatiable need for meaning is checked and turned violently back on her like a violation; and as she becomes helpless, '[f]orms both pale and glowing took possession of her young senses and fixed themselves in her memory' (187–8) for the rest of her life.

This kind of vertigo is different from the oscillations experienced by, say, Maggie Tulliver at the climax of *The Mill on the Floss* or Romola undecided between her 'clashing deities'. There, the precise balancing of conflicting interpretations made the choice of action impossible; here, there is simply no correlation between Dorothea's provincial hypothesis and the European reality it seeks to understand but which overwhelms it. This is the definitive representation in the fiction of the 'miserable agglomeration of atoms', that deconstruction of the self and the world which George Eliot's master-plot demands. But this need not necessarily be the response which Rome elicits, the narrator assures us; high culture can become a living reality. 'To those who have looked at Rome with the quickening power of a knowledge which breathes a growing soul into all historic shapes, and traces out the suppressed transitions which unite all contrasts, Rome may still be the spiritual centre and interpreter of the world' (188). The Eternal City can be reclaimed and recentered by this kind of imaginative knowledge, a secular version of the Holy Spirit, as the language of the quotation suggests. Like Lydgate's inward light of energy which illuminates the ethereal atoms, so knowledge of this kind breathes a living soul into dead shapes and reveals their unity. But this form of recovery and renewal is denied not only to Dorothea but also to her spiritual mentor, Casaubon. He had described his own hermeneutic mode earlier in the novel: 'My mind is something like the ghost of an ancient, wandering about the world and trying mentally to construct it as it used to be, in spite of ruin and confusing changes' (17). He brings nothing to the task but his learning and a fixed premise, so that no dialogue between the present and the past takes place; 'such capacity of thought and feeling as had ever been stimulated in him by the general life of mankind had long shrunk to a sort of dried preparation, a lifeless embalmment of knowledge' (191). This form of knowledge – the exact opposite of Dorothea's engulfment – takes on the imagery of Gothic horror, affecting Dorothea with 'a sort of mental shiver' as 'the large vistas and wide fresh air which she had dreamed of finding in her husband's mind were replaced by anterooms and winding passages which seemed to lead nowhither' (190–1).

The New Jerusalem Dorothea hoped to find in the glories of Rome turns into various kinds of labyrinths, imprisonments, dead-ends, constraints, and confusions. The complex imagery leads in several directions – towards, for example, the Cretan labyrinth with Casaubon as the Minotaur and Dorothea as Ariadne. Or, closer to the life of a saint, it suggests that the heroine's spiritual mentor has led her down into a Gothic dungeon, 'a virtual tomb, where there was the apparatus of a ghastly labour producing what would never see the light' (348). Ladislaw embellishes this with the thought 'of beautiful lips kissing holy skulls and other emptinesses ecclesiastically enshrined' (355).[16] But whether it leads into solar or classical mythology, the source of this imagery seems to lie precisely in Casaubon's hermeneutic: in the fact that he deploys his theory of myth rigidly as a key. As such, it is not part of a living dialogue or relationship with the world which is itself therefore moribund. This is why the fragments of dead evidence – 'shattered mummies' – are not tested but simply offered sacrificially 'as foison for a theory which was already withered in the birth like an elfin child' (469). George Eliot's horror is uniquely aroused by the thought of an *a priori* theory refusing, rigidly and remorselessly, to test itself against the world it seeks to explain. We have seen how she turned against Comte when theory, separating itself from practice, became doctrine 'liable to putrefy when kept in close chambers'.[17] Here, in one complex, parallel sentence, we are told that Casaubon's theory 'was not likely to bruise itself unawares against discoveries ... it floated among flexible conjectures ... it was a method of interpretation which was not tested by the necessity of forming anything which had sharper collisions than an elaborate

notion of Gog and Magog . . . it was as free from interruption as a plan
for threading the stars together' (469-70). No bruising, no collision,
no interaction, no interruption. This is a denial of the experimental
method, of life itself, and as a result there is no possibility of turning
back – until death intervenes in this gloomiest version of the empiricist
fable – to the solidly commonsensical world of everyday, because all
Casaubon's hopes and ambitions are tied to the proof of his theory. It
is this that has led Dorothea away from the revelations and into the
catacombs of the Eternal City.

There is a character who represents a startling contrast in his
response to Rome. Just as Bardo and Baldassarre, in their fanaticism,
bring into existence the amanuenses who both complement and reject
them, so Casaubon conjures up, as it were, his second-cousin,
Ladislaw, simultaneously dependent and rebellious. He, like Dorothea, is an embodiment of the myths that Casaubon is so
painstakingly studying, 'an incarnation of the spring' (462) with a
smile like 'a gush of inward light' touched by Ariel (199). But beneath
the obvious contrasts of spring and winter, youth and age, and so on,
the basis of their opposition is essentially hermeneutic. Instead of a
Casaubon with his 'small taper of learned theory exploring the tossed
ruins of the world', Ladislaw places himself in 'an attitude of
receptivity towards all sublime chances' (82). He rejects Aristotle's
precepts about the application of means to ends, as well as any desire
to search for origins: 'he said he should prefer not to know the sources
of the Nile, and that there should be some unknown regions preserved
as hunting-grounds for the poetic imagination' (80). When he
reappears in Rome his negative capability reveals its more creative
side, though his depiction remains uneasily sprightly, as if George
Eliot is self-consciously experimenting with a new kind of character.
His rootlessness and classlessness enable him to respond to the
fragmentariness of the city without inhibition: 'he confessed that
Rome had given him quite a new sense of history as a whole: the
fragments stimulated his imagination and made him constructive'
(206).

Ladislaw is, in effect, a kind of bricoleur who Lydgate describes
later in the novel as 'rather miscellaneous and *bric-a-brac*' (428), and it
is this which enables him to respond with enjoyment to the *bric-a-brac*
and 'the very miscellaneousness of Rome' (206). And when Mr
Brooke, that wise quintessence of miscellaneousness, claims him as
alter ego (499), we realise that Ladislaw represents a significant

response to a decentered world – open-minded, receptive, *ad hoc*, ungrounded, 'a creature who entered into every one's feelings, and could take the pressure of their thought instead of urging his own with iron resistance' (487). And yet, because of this, because he is his own creation, he presents the most serious challenge to the assumptions of Middlemarch as a community and to the other protagonists individually. 'There are characters which are continually creating collisions and nodes for themselves in dramas which nobody is prepared to act with them' (186). He is the anomaly which tests all the accepted Middlemarch paradigms. If Casaubon's career is the relentless and deadly imposition of a theory, Ladislaw embodies the creative hypothesis flexibly and reciprocally initiating its engagement with the world. His closest predecessor is the painter Piero di Cosimo in *Romola* who responded to the heterogeneousness of Florence in a similar way, rejecting a comprehensive and fixed vision in favour of a creative and constantly changing mythic reconstruction.[18] This, unbeknown to Casaubon, is the true nature of myth, as George Eliot's own dense network of allusions shows. As we saw with Piero, the significant feature is metamorphosis; and this is dramatised in Ladislaw's temperament, 'his point of view shifted as easily as his mood' (378), as well as his appearance: 'Surely, his very features changed their form; his jaw looked sometimes large and sometimes small; and the little ripple in his nose was a preparation for metamorphosis' (203). He is not so much a world-view as a receptive state of mind, and 'the universe had not yet beckoned' (82).

We can now see that Dorothea's path to her vocation is through an understanding of these two men and their complementary relationship, a scenario flippantly evoked in Naumann's reference to Schiller's play, *Der Neffe als Onkel* (186).[19] Dorothea desires a binding theory but also the creative freedom that Ladislaw offers; she has to marry both men to achieve her own synthesis as each man alerts her through their mutual misrepresentations to the true nature of the other. It is, for example, the contrast between Ladislaw's sunny metamorphoses and Casaubon's rayless gloom that prompts in Dorothea, while still in Rome, 'the first stirring of a pitying tenderness fed by the realities of [Casaubon's] lot and not by her own dreams' (203). Then, in her own version of the empiricist fable, she turns from the illusions of grand theory and their final demolition in the Roman honeymoon to the solid ground of the otherness of people. She is now able 'to conceive with that distinctness which is no longer reflection

but feeling – an idea wrought back to the directness of sense, like the
solidity of objects – that [her husband] had an equivalent centre of
self, whence the lights and shadows must always fall with a certain
difference' (205). In a decentered world the empiricist turns back to
the solidity of objects or the centres of self of other people,
impenetrable but there. This is an acknowledgement that the inside
view and the outside view, subjective and objective, understanding
and explanation, can never coincide – but that it is upon this lack of
correspondence, this difference, that the solidity of the world rests
rather than upon any unitary key or primitive tissue. In a world
lacking 'a coherent social faith and order' in which belief has to be
recovered through painful interpretation, this is George Eliot's
rephrasing of Jesus's second commandment (Matthew 22.39).

It should be added that such an account of Dorothea's career is
inevitably partial. In this most hermeneutic of fictions it all depends,
as D. A. Miller has demonstrated, on who is telling the story or
carrying out the interpretation – the narrator, the community, or the
protagonists.[20] From the community's point of view, for example,
Saint Dorothea appears both bizarre and quixotic, and in her
widowhood is urged by its spokeswoman, Mrs Cadwallader, not to be
'always playing the tragedy queen and taking things sublimely': 'You
will see visions. We have all got to exert ourselves a little to keep sane,
and call things by the same names as other people call them by' (525).
This is the kind of radical deconstruction the novel performs at all
levels; Ladislaw's cosmopolitan negative capability, for example, is
persistently ridiculed as a sign of his 'cursed alien blood, Jew,
Corsican, or Gypsy' (707). And as the saint's life is cut down to
provincial size, the novel persistently asks if there is anything left of
those high ideals which has any relevance to Middlemarch. Can that
particular model of a life withstand the various suspicions of
provincial society which at the same time – by their very variety –
create the complexity of character which no single perspective can
bring into focus? Similarly with Mr Casaubon, the narrator protests
against 'any absolute conclusion' on his character: 'If to Dorothea Mr
Casaubon had been the mere occasion which had set alight the fine
inflammable material of her youthful illusions, does it follow that he
was fairly represented in the minds of those less impassioned
personages who have hitherto delivered their judgments concerning
him?' (82). If Dorothea is a saint, then he could be seen as her spiritual
director, 'a living Boussuet', 'a modern Augustine' (24), himself

briefly canonised in Rome as St Thomas Aquinas (209). But he is also a pedant who sees everything in bibliographical terms, whose memory is a *vide supra* (26), whose life has no awkward backward pages (43), and whose ambition is to leave a copy – not of himself – but of his mythological key (272). And when the community delves further, again in the person of Mrs Cadwallader, he is reduced to a parchment code, and finally when she metaphorically and character-istically tests his blood under a magnifying glass it is found to be made up of 'semicolons and parentheses' (69). He is rescued to some extent by the narrator's diagnostic turn – 'Mr Casaubon, too, was the centre of his own world' (83) – but in *Middlemarch* no character can escape being embroiled in, misrepresented, and undermined by the unfriendly social medium of which they are a product.

One way to describe this social medium is as a complex network of hypotheses which seek both to explain and also to control the individual characters, and to which they inevitably contribute. Interpretation is an inescapable fact of life. So a character like Dorothea is not only seeking a coherent world-view, she is also combating, appropriating, being influenced by other world-views which impinge upon hers. Under their influence, as we have seen, her demands for a binding theory have given way to a foundational act of faith – the acceptance of the equivalent otherness of her husband. This is the beginning of a different kind of sainthood. That state has changed from a theory to be imposed to a hypothesis engaging itself with the world: 'She was no longer struggling against the perception of facts, but adjusting herself to their clearest perception' (356). Despite Casaubon's rigidity and cruelty, 'the noble habit of [her] soul reasserts itself' as she undergoes the testing of her new vision: 'the resolved submission did come' (418). And these spiritual exercises culminate at the time of her husband's death in the submission to his further paranoid demands. 'Neither law nor the world's opinion compelled her to this – only her husband's nature and her own compassion, only the ideal and not the real yoke of marriage' (472). But these tests are only a preparation for her ultimate trial and martyrdom, the compromising of Ladislaw – on one level simply the confirmation of Middlemarch gossip which she has been trying to ignore, on another the supreme test of her faith. This is where the life of the saint, that mythic hypothesis with its language of torture, sacrifice, and martyrdom, engages most intimately with the Jane Austen-like gentilities of provincial life.

Just before the discovery scene, Dorothea has had evidence of the power of faith. By expressing her confidence in Lydgate against her friends' careful advice, she has enabled him to believe once more in his own integrity through speaking to someone, as he says, 'where belief has gone beforehand' (752). Her faith in his character prompts him to accept her hypothesis of his conduct rather than the suspicious alternative of Middlemarch gossip, and by doing so makes it a reality. This is George Eliot's redefinition of saintliness: a complete absence of 'subtle constructions and suspicions of hidden wrong', combined with 'that simplicity of hers, holding up an ideal for others in her believing conception of them, [which] was one of the greatest powers of her womanhood' (761). Such constructions and suspicions, however, seem inescapable later in the same chapter when she comes unexpectedly upon Ladislaw and Rosamond. There follows her dark night of the soul when she weeps 'after her lost belief' in Ladislaw, with its hopes and joys: 'In that hour she repeated what the merciful eyes of solitude have looked on for ages in the spiritual struggles of man.' The pain is expressed as the conflict between 'two images – two living forms that tore her heart in two', like a mother seeing her child divided by the sword, one 'bleeding half' embraced, the other 'carried away by the lying woman that has never known the mother's pang'. This is the beginning of the violent metaphors which articulate the climax of Dorothea's saintly career. The two images are those of Ladislaw, first, as 'the bright creature', the mythic 'spirit of morning', and second, as a 'detected illusion – no, a living man' who has betrayed her belief, the belief which had again 'gone beforehand' as with Lydgate but is now seen to be unfounded (775). There seems no possibility of synthesising the two images – one based on her trusting hypothesis, the other on the evidence of her senses – so as to rescue Ladislaw's integrity from the confirmed suspicions of the interpretative community. Even he now anticipates 'a future where he himself was sliding into the pleasureless yielding to the small solicitations of circumstance' (772).

The agony of the dark night of the soul is traditionally the discovery of God through his absence; by analogy Dorothea now recognises her love for Ladislaw – 'she discovered her passion to herself in the unshrinking utterance of despair' (775). Love and suffering – both contained in the word 'passion' – have to be brought together in this way for both to be given meaning, so that Dorothea may awaken later in the twilight 'to a new condition', freed from her terrible conflict, 'looking into the eyes of sorrow' and accepting her grief. The foundational act of faith in the equivalent centres of self of others survives the test and finds expression in the 'deliberate' act of decentering: she now begins 'to live through that yesterday morning deliberately again, forcing herself to dwell on every detail and its possible meaning. Was she alone in that scene? Was it her event only?' (776). The questions bring together the self-transcendence of the saint and the hypothesis of the experimental method, and they prepare her for her crucifixion. 'What should I do – how should I act now, this very day, if I could clutch my own pain, and compel it to silence, and think of those three?' (777). And to strengthen her in this resolve she is granted in the dawn her beatific vision. This combines the awareness of anonymous individuals – a man, a woman, a baby, a shepherd – with that of 'the largeness of the world'. In its Wordsworthian bareness it is the opposite of the negative sublimity of Roman fragmentariness. It is an organic vision of part and whole in unity, and 'she was a part of that involuntary, palpitating life' (777); or it can be seen as the realisation of the hermeneutic circle – the radical otherness of individual centres of self now complemented and completed by holistic oneness, the 'alternating processes of distinction and combination'. This vision may seem hopelessly remote from its negative, provincial version – individual egoisms in a context of communal prejudice – but that is where the vision has now to be empirically tested. As Dorothea sets off again on her mission to Rosamond, the saintly sequence of virgin and bride is completed in that of *mater dolorosa* (777).

To compare the scene that follows with the climactic prison scene in *Adam Bede*, underlines both the persistence of George Eliot's concerns and the distance she has travelled from her first novel. There are striking similarities in the contrast between Dinah and Hetty and that between Dorothea and Rosamond; in both climactic scenes the spiritual madonnas come to help the worldly magdalenes. What is different is the way in which the earlier contrast is now thoroughly enmeshed in the details of provincial life, that social medium which both realises and obfuscates the moral dilemmas. This, of course, is the nature of that final and rigorous testing of the saintly model: the attempt to help Rosamond is beset with provincial misunderstandings, as each imagines the other to be the preferred woman so that neither is in a position to reveal the truth. Dorothea, like Dinah, brings her beatific vision to this meeting; but whereas Dinah recounted her typological prayer in the form of the narrative of Jesus's dereliction, crucifixion, and resurrection, to which Hetty finally responded, Dorothea, lacking such a coherent faith, can only bring her own experience of marriage with Casaubon, followed by the shock of her disillusionment with Ladislaw, to bear on Rosamond's situation. This has been her secularised *imitatio Christi* which is now to be completed in the rescue of three other people. Love and suffering again become indistinguishable as Dorothea re-enacts the 'death' of the loss of Ladislaw for her rival's sake: 'The waves of her own sorrow, from out of which she was struggling to save another, rushed over Dorothea with conquering force.' Then, as in *Adam Bede*, the two women cling to each other, and Rosamond finally, like Hetty, confesses the truth. This is Dorothea's miracle. She has briefly transformed Rosamond into performing a 'generous effort', 'not counting that the effort was a reflex of her own energy' (786–7). Her own sacrificial act has elicited its reflection, its echo – *imitatio* of *imitatio* – in a precise form: she was the only person capable of rescuing Lydgate from the misinterpretations of Middlemarch; Rosamond responds by doing the same for Ladislaw. Both acts of self-abnegation arise from suffering and rejection. The miracle of Dorothea's redemption is that the two bleeding halves of the dismembered Ladislaw are re-united as Rosamond hands her half back; or, less melodramatically, that Dorothea's ideal image and the social medium of Middlemarch in which she discovered him are forcibly reconciled. No longer will they think of each other, in Ladislaw's terms, 'as in a world apart, where the sunshine fell on tall white lilies, where no evil lurked, and no other soul entered' (793). Dorothea, in any case, only discovered her love when he was compromised by another woman, and now she ends her saintly career promising to 'learn what everything costs' (801), while he is rescued from the 'motiveless levity' (772) which even the most creative flexibility can turn into.

As Dorothea's career has become more and more enmeshed in the prejudices and ambiguities of provincial life, its saintliness has been increasingly jeopardised by the hermeneutics of suspicion – the initial hypothesis finally modified out of all recognition. Its epitaph in the Finale represents a fine balancing of alternative perspectives. One 'tradition' in Middlemarch persists in seeing her pilgrimage simply as a marriage to 'a sickly clergyman, old enough to be her father', followed promptly by marriage to his cousin, 'young enough to have been his son' (824). This perspective will never coincide with that of sacred biography. The narrator, too, has to acknowledge that this particular saint's tomb is 'unvisited' and that 'her full nature . . . spent itself in channels which had no great name on the earth'; but then he turns this dispersal dialectically into the very means of redeeming the social medium: 'the effect of her being on those around her was incalculably diffusive' (825). The extreme difficulty of this balancing act is finally demonstrated in George Eliot's revision of the penultimate paragraph of the novel (824), the unique occasion of her responding to critical disapproval. Her revision acknowledges that she had overbalanced in exonerating Dorothea from blame at the expense of Middlemarch. The saint is also a Quixote. A possible formulation of this final ambivalence is suggested by a concealed allusion in the novel which has been uncovered by Gillian Beer: 'the boy in the legend' (215) Dorothea is compared to by Ladislaw in Rome, turns out to be Anskar, a ninth-century missionary, whose life-long expectation of martyrdom appeared to have been disappointed until he is reassured by a death-bed revelation. His martyrdom, this tells him, was not to be a martyr.[21] In the time of the absence of coherent faith, this paradox accommodates – as it did for Savonarola at the beginning of that collapse – both the hermeneutic of innocence and the hermeneutic of suspicion.

With Bulstrode's career we have a different hermeneutic model. The language and concepts remain religious, but the model of sainthood is exchanged for that of election, justification, and predestination. The banker is a 'justified sinner', the origins of his beliefs a Calvinistic dissenting church (601), and his ethos that of 'sacred accountableness' (124). He is a classic version of the Puritan type defined by Max Weber as the coalescence of the Protestant ethic and the spirit of capitalism: the 'duty to attain certainty of one's own election and justification in the daily struggle of life' must come from intense worldly activity in one's calling and the assurances of salvation this provides.[22] Victorian fiction, acknowledging the influence of this ethic, is full of hypocritical Evangelical Christians but none is treated with the subtlety with which George Eliot scrutinises the spiritual-worldly paradoxes at the heart of Calvinism and upon which Bulstrode's career is based. It is presented as a series of hermeneutic dilemmas.

The theory, the absolute duty even, by which the Calvinist lives his life is, according to Weber, 'to consider [him]self chosen, and to combat all doubts of insufficient faith, hence of imperfect grace'.[23] This is the opposite of a working hypothesis and yet, because God's purposes remain impenetrable, salvation is never secure. There always remains the anxious gap between the details of one's life and the assurance of salvation. The need to scrutinise and interpret these details is a form of hermeneutic responsibility of which Bulstrode's inner life consists. As his influence in Middlemarch increases, he devotes considerable effort to its justification, in both senses of the word: 'It was a principle with Mr Bulstrode to gain as much power as possible, that he might use it for the glory of God.' Since he is not 'a coarse hypocrite' (606), not even an antinomian, this means that self-interest and the divine purposes require constant and careful alignment and re-alignment. 'He went through a great deal of inward argument in order to adjust his motives, and make clear to himself what God's glory required' (153). As with Dorothea, it is the sincerity and validity of this hermeneutic which is to be tested in the novel, and the motto to chapter thirteen which introduces Bulstrode warns of the difficulties. 'How class your man? – as better than the most, / Or, seeming better, worse beneath that cloak? / As saint or knave, pilgrim or hypocrite?' As well classify your books by their covers as by using such typological labels, is the reply. But Middlemarch has no such inhibitions. It is quite clear in its own mind that this interloper is a 'Pharisee' as well as an Evangelical (121), that he 'must be first chop in heaven' (128), that his Protestant ethic is 'a sort of worldly-spiritual cliqueism' (172), and that since he did not enjoy life as they did, 'worreting himself about everything', the motives of this 'saintly Kill-joy' (717) are profoundly suspect: 'he must have a sort of vampire's feast in the sense of mastery' (153). They are all true to some extent, and yet none exclusively so. They are, once again, the stereotypes which are to be tested in the narrative of the home epic.

Bulstrode's assurances, however, seem amply justified by his successful career, crowned halfway through the novel by the acquisition of Stone Court which 'he interpreted . . . as a cheering dispensation' and with regard to which the narrator characteristically warns the reader against the reflex of suspicion: 'it was as genuinely his mode of explaining events as any theory of yours may be, if you happen to disagree with him' (510–11). The banker has at this stage achieved a fine balance between his theory of life and his circum-

stances, between his spiritual election and its worldly assurances, or in
more theological terms that he is a justified sinner, *simul justus et
peccator*. 'He was doctrinally convinced that there was a total absence
of merit in himself; but that doctrinal conviction may be held . . . with
intense satisfaction when the depth of our sinning is but a measure for
the depth of forgiveness, and a clenching proof that we are peculiar
instruments of the divine intention' (511–12). This belief has been
called by theologians a 'legal fiction', according to which 'God
reckons sinners to be what in reality they are not – righteous', by
reason of their faith which is a form of incipient righteousness.[24] But
Bulstrode, we are about to discover, is a justified sinner in a rather
different sense. He has achieved his present position of influence, his
evidence of salvation, through chicanery; in other words, he has
himself justified his sins in the same way as those two sinners in *Felix
Holt*, Mrs Transom and Jermyn, sought to justify their past actions –
by results. The legal fiction of orthodox Calvinism is, however, still in
place as Mr Bulstrode pauses outside Stone Court one summer
evening to enjoy in 'good spiritual frame' (511) the successful
completion of his plans and the signs of divine approval. It is at exactly
such a moment in the classic fictional study of Calvinistic spirituality,
The Private Memoirs and Confessions of a Justified Sinner, that the Sinner,
feeling an 'exaltation of spirit [which] lifted [him], as it were, far
above the earth, and the sinful creatures crawling on its surface', is
confronted by his daemon, his 'second self', who leads him in his pride
to destruction.[25]

With the re-appearance of Raffles from Bulstrode's hidden past, the
concurrence of divine and human purposes – the proof of instrumentality – is revealed as a 'legal fiction' in another sense. In order to
prove the theory of his election Bulstrode had tampered not only with
his conscience over the Dunkirks' shady pawnbroker business, but
also with the evidence of the disappearance of their daughter through
which he has come into his present fortune. As the agent of the
banker's past 'equivocation', Raffles challenges the symmetrical
edifice of Bulstrode's life. 'Five minutes before . . . sin seemed to be a
question of doctrine and inward penitence, humiliation an exercise of
the closet, the bearing of his deeds a private vision adjusted solely by
spiritual relations and conceptions of the divine purposes.' In the
empiricist fable, however, all such comprehensive theories have
sooner or later to return to everyday human realities. 'But even while
we are talking and meditating about the earth's orbit and the solar

system', comments the narrator, 'what we feel and adjust our movement to is the stable earth and the changing day' (515). The reappearance of Raffles threatens the stability of his position in Middlemarch. 'And now, as if by some hideous magic, this loud red figure had risen before him in unmanageable solidity – an incorporate past which had not entered his imagination of chastisements' (513). Raffles not only embodies past chicanery, the actual means by which the sinner has been justified in a worldly sense; this 'thick-set Adonis of bar-rooms and back-parlours' (405) is also the second self who complements, completes, and parodies the banker – in his grotesque appearance, his moral cynicism, his flamboyant indiscretion, his sleazy lack of respectability, and his bogus religious language.[26] As with Casaubon and Ladislaw, the exclusive world-view of the one implies and calls the other into existence; this is the inexplicable 'hideous magic' by which the excluded, the repressed, returns to challenge, undermine, and claim its rights. And this can only be done through the assertion of a different interpretation of events. In George Eliot's play on the word 'equivocation', Raffles is the alternative and equal voice which gloatingly reduces Bulstrode's spiritual wrestlings to crude self-interest: 'Still in the Dissenting line, eh? Still godly? Or taken to the Church as more genteel?' (518).

In this most extreme version of interpretative conflict in the novel, the question of which version will triumph becomes a matter of public acceptance or disgrace, and finally of life or death. In the course of the struggle the language of Calvinism is displaced on to matters of self-interest and self-survival in the here and now. It is not the divine judgment that Bulstrode fears but that of Middlemarch and his wife. This is George Eliot's own hermeneutic of religious suspicion in action, pursuing Bulstrode's motives into the intimate privacy of his prayers. The banker's doctrine of instrumentality, for example, is now represented as a very unCalvinistic bargain with God: '"I am sinful and nought – a vessel to be consecrated by use – but use me!" had been the mould into which he had constrained his immense need of being something important and predominating' (607). To be used by a God who rewards and punishes, justifies Bulstrode's own use of others as instruments of his purposes; and it is against this that Raffles, the instrument, now rebels by asserting his own instrumentality in the language he has been taught: 'you see, I was sent to you, Nick – perhaps for a blessing to both of us'. The only weapon he has is his own version of events which Bulstrode has tried to suppress; and he must threaten to make this public, as a means of blackmailing himself back into existence as an independent agent.[27] When Bulstrode asks him, 'What is your calling?'; he replies, 'I want an independence' (516–17). And like Bulstrode, this wished-for independence depends on *his* version of the past narrative which he conceals (as a blackmailer must) but then relays in various garbled forms in Middlemarch.

In his long retrospects, Bulstrode is now forced to re-live his past, re-examine the evidence of his election, and try to explain this act of 'hideous magic' in terms he understands. 'The spirit of evil might have sent [Raffles] to threaten Mr Bulstrode's subversion as an instrument of good; but the threat must have been permitted, and was a chastisement of a new kind' (515). Which is it? As the sinner approaches judgment, he – like the guilty lovers of *Felix Holt* – is required to experience again the narrative of his life: 'intense memory forces a man to own his blameworthy past' (601). His punishment begins with this detailed exegesis which he is now forced to carry out on his own life: on the one hand, he uses the language of instrumentality, external leading, and providence; on the other, the language of adjustment, shrinking, equivocation. Can they be assimilated? In a wonderfully complex image, the past is shown interfering with his present life 'as obstinately as when we look through the window from a lighted room, the objects we turn our backs on are still before us, instead of the grass and the trees'. Like Wordsworth in *The Prelude*, leaning over the edge of his boat and looking into the depths of the lake through the reflections of the clouds and mountains, unable to 'part / The shadow from the substance',[28] Bulstrode sees his past and present there 'in one view' but ana-morphically distinct: 'though each might be dwelt on in turn, the rest still kept their hold in the consciousness' (601). The theory of his life and the evidence cannot be brought into accord. He is forced finally to acknowledge 'the bare fact' of his chicanery in the form of 'the rigid outline with which acts present themselves to onlookers', but 'the fact was broken into little sequences, each justified as it came by reason-ings which seemed to prove it righteous' (604). He accepts the facts and then re-interprets them. In language which recalls Dorothea's own dark night of the soul ('Was it her event only?'), Bulstrode to rather different effect 'would have adopted Cromwell's words – "Do you call these bare events? The Lord pity you!"' (604–5). His whole life has been an interpretation of these events to justify his need for power: 'He was simply a man whose desires had been stronger than his theoretical beliefs, and who had gradually explained the gratification of his desires into satisfactory agreement with those beliefs' (606). This should no longer surprise us, nor is it 'peculiar to evangelical belief', adds the narrator as he is forced back again – in this novel which questions all the generalisations of grand theory – onto his own theoretical statement. It is another rephrasing of Jesus's second commandment in the form of an attack upon the first: 'There is no general doctrine which is not capable of eating out our morality if unchecked by the deep-seated habit of direct fellow-feeling with individual fellow-men' (606). Like the Cretan paradox, it is a general statement which denies general statements, one suitable for a decentered universe.

Yet even Bulstrode is now forced to acknowledge that the acts he has reconciled himself to are being used to darken 'the divine glory'. 'If this were to be the ruling of Providence, he was cast out from the temple as one who had brought unclean offerings' (607). In desperation he begins to change the terms in which he has articulated his life's story: 'The divine tribunal had changed its aspect for him; self-prostration was no longer enough, and he must bring restitution in his hand.' Justification by faith in a remote Calvinistic God is replaced by the propitiation of, and negotiation with, a god of sacrifices, for 'the religion of personal fear remains nearly at the level of the savage' (607). But Ladislaw refuses the proffered restitution and, at the same time, forces upon Bulstrode, 'with the air of a judge' (611), the full acknowledgement of his past equivocations, the details of which have already been provided by Raffles. It is, characteristically, Ladislaw who glimpses the true relations between the two men who are working together to checkmate each other: 'It seemed like the fluctuations of a dream – as if the action begun by that loud bloated stranger were being carried on by this pale-eyed sickly-looking piece of respectability . . . as repulsive to him as their remembered contrast' (608). It is a form of metamorphosis. After Ladislaw's rejection, the struggle between the briber and the blackmailer enters its final phase, each in turn threatening and cajoling, each in turn seeing the other as the devil's agent. Bulstrode is still trying to keep intact the narrative of his life while realising that Raffles in his delirium tremens and in fear of his own judgment seeks to exonerate himself – just as the banker had tried and failed to do – by relating 'his minute terror-stricken narrative' (686) to anyone who will listen.

When Raffles falls ill, however, and Bulstrode insists on looking after him in his final illness, the banker is offered a last opportunity to recover the sincerity of his original belief in God's providence. This is the point where the model of the justified sinner – and the true meaning of justification – engages most intimately with the circumstances which test and threaten its validity. 'He knew that he ought to say, "Thy will be done"; and he said it often. But the intense desire remained that the will of God might be the death of that hated man' (685). With Raffles getting weaker and weaker, this is the finely balanced climax to Bulstrode's career of spiritual struggle. He, too, with 'the air of an animated corpse returned to movement without warmth', is between life and death as he seeks to reconcile his prayers with 'the images of the events he desired'. 'Should Providence in this case award death, there was no sin in contemplating death as the desirable issue – if he kept his hands from hastening it – if he scrupulously did what was prescribed' (692). The crucial test lies in whether this hypothesis is allowed to interpret the events now unfolding – 'And Bulstrode set himself to keep his intention separate from his desire' (693) – or whether it turns into a theory which demands proof by further equivocations, by further tampering with the evidence. In such a situation, can the hypothesis and the events be kept separate? 'A man vows, and yet will not cast away the means of breaking his vow' (695). The narrator even pursues Bulstrode into his prayers to scrutinise the purity of his motives: 'Does any one suppose that private prayer is necessarily candid – necessarily goes to the root of action? Private prayer is inaudible speech, and speech is representative: who can represent himself just as he is, even in his own reflections?' (698). Representation and interpretation, in both their private and public forms, are inseparable.

The equivocation occurs, almost inevitably as these questions suggest, but its decisiveness is obscured in the dim regions into which the narrative now moves. As George Eliot comments in one of her own mottoes, it is no use 'putting a dead mechanism of "ifs" and "therefores" for the living myriad of hidden suckers whereby the belief and the conduct are wrought into mutual sustainment' (508). Bulstrode is able, first, to exploit the complexities and ambiguities of medical ethics; and this is where his career interacts most decisively with that of Lydgate to whom he has taken the precaution of making a sizeable loan. Lydgate has given clear instructions as to how to deal with this case of alcoholic poisoning according to the latest ideas; and it is these which Bulstrode disobeys by allowing the continued dosage of opium and brandy, a practice quite in conformity, however, with traditional Middlemarch thinking. Bulstrode's equivocation, further-more, appears less decisive because it is another of his sins of omission: he failed to provide the information that the Dunkirks' daughter was not dead; he now fails to give the instructions to his housekeeper, his latest instrument, to stop administering the opium and brandy. In his deviousness, Bulstrode simply 'had accepted what seemed to have been offered' (706). Perhaps God might have predestined this in any case? 'And who could say that the death of Raffles had been hastened?' (700), asks the banker as he prepares to pick up the threads of his career once more, his life waxing vampire-like as Raffle's wanes, his version of events apparently secure.

In his dying moments Raffles felt himself 'sinking down through the earth' (698) in judgment, and Bulstrode, too, has not escaped his tribunal, since the 'haunting ghost of his former life' has not been laid with 'the corpse of Raffles' (706). It survives hale and hearty in the medium of Middlemarch gossip. When the briber and blackmailer no longer justify each other's existence, both are lost. The Calvinistic language of justification is essentially juridical (the legal fiction), but we have seen how that changed for Bulstrode under the pressure of events to a different kind of justice through propitiation. When that was rejected, he was left to his own devices, and Providence ('Yes, Providence', adds the narrator) seems to have allowed him to escape (706). But punishment has been handed over to the community. In the social medium of Middlemarch the 'vague conviction of indeterminable guilt' (709) is quickly transformed by the hermeneu-tic of suspicion: 'Everybody liked better to conjecture how the thing was, than simply to know it; for conjecture soon became more confident than knowledge, and had a more liberal allowance for the incompatible' (709). His summary conviction by the community in this way offers a striking contrast to the forensic debate in The Rainbow in *Silas Marner*. Mrs Dollop, the landlady of The Tankard, also believes like the landlord of the earlier novel that 'It's well known there's always two sides, if no more' (711), but this simply enables her to make the blackest of definitive interpretations: 'When a man's been 'ticed to a lone house, and there's them can pay for hospitals and nurses for half the country-side chooses to be sitters-up night and day, and nobody to come near but a doctor as is known to stick at nothing . . .' (712). In this milieu a loan must be a bribe. So that when Bulstrode appears at the meeting of the hospital board to resume his position in the town, he finds himself unexpectedly before his tribunal, accused of 'acts which, owing to circumstances, the law cannot visit' (715). Divine judgment has been replaced by public disgrace based on conjecture.

The nature of his disgrace is so agonising because the individual is constructed out of the same social medium, the community, by which he is condemned. 'Who can know how much of his most inward life is made up of the thoughts he believes other men to have about him, until that fabric of opinion is threatened with ruin?' (677). In this form of the double, reciprocal hermeneutic, suspicion destroys just as faith, as we have seen, redeems. Bulstrode now 'must quail before the glance of those towards whom he had habitually assumed the attitude of a reprover', or translated into his own language, 'that God had disowned him before men' (715–16). This is his moment of despair, abandonment, and dereliction: 'all this rushed through him like the agony of terror which fails to kill, and leaves the ears still open to the returning wave of execration' (716). But a second and worse trial awaits Bulstrode. From the first appearance of Raffles we have known that 'the loss of high consideration from his wife . . . would be as the beginning of death to him' (600). He waits as the news of his disgrace percolates to her through the vicious interpretative medium of Middlemarch gossip and innuendo; and then he has to appear before this ingenuous yet most intimidating of judges. She has, however, already forgiven him in George Eliot's own version of imputed righteousness: 'with one leap of her heart she was at his side in mournful but unreproaching fellowship with shame and isolation' (739). But the sinner, in this the most moving scene in the novel, awaits judgment in ignorance, 'perishing slowly in unpitied misery' with nowhere to turn: 'And if he turned to God there seemed to be no answer but the pressure of retribution.' When she comes in he dare not raise his eyes until she speaks ('Look up, Nicholas') and he discovers his judge transformed not – in their religious tradition – into a saint but into 'an early Methodist'. And she does not ask for an explanation: 'His confession was silent, and her promise of faithfulness was silent' (741). In this way, Bulstrode becomes once again the justified sinner, and the legal fiction of Calvinism – righteous and sinner at the same time – is restored, but this time through his wife's compassionate agency. And as to which version of events was true – with the accompanying gossip, accusations, and public disgrace – all this is placed in abeyance. 'She could not say, "How much is only

slander and false suspicion?" and he did not say, "I am innocent"'
(741). The constraints of the human are retained in this act of natural
supernaturalism.

As with Dorothea, the rest of Bulstrode's life is projected as a kind of
radically redefined martyrdom. The motto which introduces the
banker's preparation for exile – the trial and judgment of Faithful in
The Pilgrim's Progress – is a Puritan counterpoint to his own ambiguous
situation. 'The pitiable lot is that of the man who could not call
himself a martyr even though he were to persuade himself that the
men who stoned him were but ugly passions incarnate.' George Eliot
won't allow her fictions to be allegorised in this way and, as a result,
the presence of his wife remains, despite her compassion, 'a tribunal
before which he shrank from confession and desired advocacy', a more
intimidating judge than the 'Omniscience whom he prayed to' (811).
He is a martyr who is not able to witness, for these are the continuing
martyrdoms of the home epic. In varying ways, they are caused by the
inevitable gap between the binding theory and circumstances,
between belief and conduct, between the hypothesis and the facts, or
in Bulstrode's case, 'for not being the man he professed to be' (602).
And since, as the narrator of *Felix Holt* tells us, 'None of our theories
are quite large enough for all the disclosures of time', martyrdom in
this redefined sense is the experience of being alive. This is how the
controlling models, the types of saint or justified sinner, are absorbed
into the social medium of provincial life.

Lydgate's provincial martyrdom is the most painful of the frequent
tragedies which 'have not yet wrought [themselves] into the coarse
emotion of mankind' (189). This is because his career originates in a
moment of 'intellectual passion', an epiphany in which 'the world was
made new to him' (141), and contains, as we have seen, glimpses of
possible sublimity through his scientific research which seem far more
realisable than, say, those of Dorothea. But, in terms of the empiricist
fable, this puts him more at risk when 'the gradual action of ordinary
causes'[29] which begins to impinge on his life is ignored, and then it is
simply a matter of time before he becomes 'shapen after the average
and fit to be packed by the gross' (142).

In one sense, Lydgate represents a new type coming into
prominence in the 1820s with the growth and increasing specialisa-

tion of the professions. He aims to combine his various roles – family doctor, medical scientist, and provincial citizen – in order ultimately to make a link in the chain of discovery. As Alan Mintz writes, 'The very possibility of a doctor's being an expert – that is to say, the possibility of a connection between his professional activity and the actual curing of people – first became thinkable at this time'.[30] And Lydgate maps out his future career like a research proposal. His scientific and professional work 'would illuminate each other: the careful observation and inference which was his daily work, the use of the lens to further his judgment in special cases, would further his thought as an instrument of larger inquiry'. Middlemarch is to fit into these plans as the suitable location which 'could hold no rivalry' (144) with this projected inquiry. In another sense, however, Lydgate is – like the saint and the justified sinner – a recognisably traditional type, the scientific discoverer. This is an ambivalent role. In his own private typology he identifies himself with the sixteenth-century anatomist, Vesalius, in the tradition of 'the great originators', the 'Shining Ones', as he builds upon the work of Bichat and strives 'towards final companionship with the immortals' (144). But there is another image of the scientist in competition with that of the heroic reformer and discoverer. Surfacing from the depths of Middlemarch prejudice and primitivism is the mistrust of scientific knowledge of any kind, 'the world-old association of cleverness with the evil principle being still potent in the minds even of lady-patients who had the strictest ideas of frilling and sentiment' (176). The 'pride of intellect' (290), as Mrs Bulstrode describes it at one social level, is quickly translated at another into Mrs Dollop's conviction that Lydgate's main aim in the New Hospital is to acquire, by whatever means, dead bodies for his experiments. And when to this are added growing rumours of his 'power of resuscitating persons as good as dead' (434), his research into 'the homogeneous origin of all the tissues' (447) becomes increasingly Frankenstein-like.

The question the plot initially frames is, which of these two models or stereotypes interprets his career most adequately? Which provides the more plausible interpretation of that 'cluster of signs for his neighbours' false suppositions' (139)? In the home epic the answer must, of course, be neither. But, as with the other protagonists, such typologies enter the social medium and prove decisive when the climactic crisis of interpretation occurs. The danger signal in all cases is the wide gap which opens up between the conflicting interpretative models, a gap which Lydgate cheerfully acknowledges to Rosamond as he discourses on his hero Vesalius: 'They called him a liar and a poisonous monster. But the facts of the human frame were on his side, and so he got the better of them.' In his enthusiasm he fails to register Rosamond's disapproving reaction ('I do *not* think it is a nice profession, dear') nor the end of his hero's career ('He died rather miserably') which she elicits from him (450). The gap is exacerbated by the division between his intellectual activity and the rest of his life, the one rigorously scrutinised, the other led by habit and convention with 'that *naïveté* which belonged to preoccupation with favourite ideas' (340). It is a more subtle, psychological version of the kind of arrangement Dr Frankenstein makes as he is about to begin his sacrilegious quest for the secret of life: 'I wished, as it were, to procrastinate all that related to my feelings of affection until the great object, which swallowed up every habit of my nature, should be completed.' If this is the price, then the notorious doctor acknowledges in retrospect – and in line with the empiricist fable – 'that study is certainly unlawful, that is to say, not befitting the human mind'.[31]

The representation of Lydgate's career provides George Eliot with the opportunity to exploit the fictional possibilities of two other hermeneutic disciplines – diagnostic medicine and anatomical research. She employs them with the searching irony of her own double hermeneutic: as Lydgate practises these disciplines they are practised upon him by the narrator and the community. This dramatises the true nature of the *hubris* of his life in Middlemarch: he thinks that he, uniquely, is the observer, the experimenter, the interpreter who, despite everything, 'may work for a special end with others whose motives and general course are equivocal, if he is quite sure of his personal independence' (458). His martyrdom is to discover otherwise, as the different elements in his life, far from supporting, checkmate each other. Each of his initiatives – the New Hospital and its chaplaincy, the non-dispensing of drugs, his advanced practices – becomes enmeshed in the 'petty medium of Middlemarch' (182) and so progressively misinterpreted. A wonderfully subtle contrast is provided by Farebrother, that true denizen of the home epic, who manages to accommodate his various activities – pastoral duties, scientific hobby, and family responsibilities – to the provincial world in a low-key, dispirited, occasionally heroic way.

It was clear as early as *Scenes of Clerical Life* that George Eliot was fascinated by the role of the family doctor in the community. He serves as a focus for the hermeneutics of everyday life, a professional deliverer of opinions on whom everyone has an opinion. First of all, there are the practitioners themselves with their outdated medical theories: 'For the heroic times of copious bleeding and blistering had not yet departed, still less the times of thorough-going theory, when disease was called by some bad name, and treated accordingly without shilly-shally.' But the patients upon whom they practise their theories respond by diagnosing the diagnosticians, with everyone swearing by his own doctor: 'each lady who saw medical truth in Wrench and "the strengthening system" regarding Toller and "the lowering system" as medical perdition'. The evidence for their cleverness 'was of a higher intuitive order' (139), as the citizens decide who to follow. When in a more serious crisis the physicans have to be called in, the choice is easier as each man becomes a metaphor for his mode of treatment. Dr Minchin is 'soft-handed, pale-complexioned', while Dr Sprague is 'superfluously tall' and noisy: 'In short, he had weight, and might be expected to grapple with a disease and throw it; while Dr Minchin might be better able to detect it lurking and to circumvent it.' The complex situation of patients interpreting doctors who interpret patients becomes a kind of caricature of the double hermeneutic. And it is into this traditional symbiotic relationship, 'the mysterious privilege of medical reputation' (177) as the narrator calls it, that Lydgate briskly and ingenuously intrudes, as a new type of family doctor with the latest modern methods. Then they all, doctors and patients alike, bring their interpretative skills to bear upon him. Keen to see how this interloper 'might be wrought into their purposes', they misunderstand both his successes and his limitations, as Lydgate gradually comes to realise: 'it was as useless to fight against the interpretations of ignorance as to whip the fog' (440–1). There is a remorselessness in the complacency with which Middlemarch 'counted on swallowing Lydgate and assimilating him very comfortably' (152).

The narrator, too, switches into the medical mode in interpreting the 'cluster of signs' by which Lydgate is known. To begin with, prognosis points out 'all the niceties of inward balance' upon which his future depends and 'which makes many a man's career a fine subject for betting'. For character like disease 'is a process and an unfolding' which requires careful observation, as Borthrop Trumbull's symptoms demonstrate when subjected to Lydgate's 'expectant theory'. Then from the general diagnosis of both faults and virtues the narrator passes, like a discreet physician, to 'the particular faults from which these delicate generalities are distilled [which] have distinguishable physiognomies, diction, accents, and grimaces'. This requires an examination of 'the minutiae of mental make in which one of us differs from another', and leads to that definitive diagnosis which combines succinctly the language of character analysis with that of the medical practitioner: 'Lydgate's spots of commonness lay in the complexion of his prejudices' (147). The whole of chapter fifteen is a deservedly famous piece of extensive character analysis, and it vividly demonstrates the extraordinary facility with which the novelist adopts in her narrative commentary the hermeneutic language and perspective of the character under discussion. Interpretation and representation again become one in this refinement of the double hermeneutic. Just as the narrator scrutinises Bulstrode's life for the true evidences of salvation, so he diagnoses Lydgate's spots of commonness as the doctor begins his own career of medical practitioner.

Lydgate's other activity, his scientific research, is used in a similarly ironic manner to reveal the *naïveté* of his relationship with women. 'Plain women he regarded as he did the other severe facts of life, to be faced with philosophy and investigated by science. But Rosamond Vincy seemed to have the true melodic charm' (92).[32] Then he puts aside his science and becomes himself the bewildered object to be experimented on. In the earlier episode with the actress, for example, he 'left his frogs and rabbits to some repose under their trying and mysterious dispensation of unexplained shocks', while he himself is subjected to 'some galvanic experiments' (148) at the hands of Laure. He is saved from 'hardening effects' (151) by his good nature but he has learned very little. And the experimental language is continued into his relationship with Rosamond as he persists in 'bringing a much more testing vision of details and relations into [his] pathological study than he had ever thought it necessary to apply to the complexities of love and marriage' (161). Unwittingly subjected to the 'shaping activity' of Rosamond's idea of marriage while his own 'lay blind and unconcerned as a jelly-fish which gets melted without knowing it', he returns home to his own experiments in maceration and other scientific reveries: 'the primitive tissue was still his fair unknown' (266). Much later in the novel, after their marriage, the double experimenting continues with Lydgate preoccupied with 'the construction of a new controlling experiment' (643-4), but he is forced soon after to accept the results of Rosamond's research: 'Nevertheless she had mastered him' (656).

Rosamond is able to turn the experimental tables in this way because her world-view is coherent and her life undivided. She embodies 'that combination of correct sentiments, music, dancing, drawing, elegant note-writing, private album for extracted verse, and perfect blond loveliness, which made the irresistible woman for the doomed man of that date' (262). She never questions this model on which her life is constructed – it is the pier-glass analogy which ironically confirms that 'Rosamond had a Providence of her own' (258) – and, crucially, it is accepted by the community from which it draws its strength. As with the other protagonists, George Eliot subjects this mode of interpreting the world to hermeneutic scrutiny in various ways, but especially in the way Rosamond deploys and realises her own idea of what is called her 'social romance' (114). It is an idea which requires intense observation of social niceties and assumes, in competition with the novelist, its own form of narrative: 'Rosamond had registered every look and word, and estimated them as the opening incidents of a preconceived romance – incidents which gather value from the foreseen development and climax' (163). In one sense she is the most persistent idealist in the novel, as she insists on shaping, interpreting, subduing everything to this romantic idea.

More specifically, her power consists in not allowing the double hermeneutic of interpreting and being interpreted, of self and beholder, to escape from her control. Her 'eyes of heavenly blue', for example, are 'deep enough to hold the most exquisite meanings an ingenious beholder could put into them, and deep enough to hide the meanings of the owner if these should happen to be less exquisite' (109). This is the power of the stereotype she embodies. There is no gap, no discrepancy possible between what she projects and the recognised image. 'She was by nature an actress of parts that entered into her *physique*: she even acted her own character, and so well, that she did not know it to be precisely her own' (114). And to stress the formidable nature of such characters in which there is no slippage, as it were, between role and identity, George Eliot feels it necessary to introduce the episode of Laure. That actress utilises her role in the melodrama in which she is supposed to stab her lover in error, actually to murder her husband. The appalled Lydgate finally begins to grasp what has happened ('And you planned to murder him?'), but her reply closes the gap between intention and role: 'I did not plan; it came to me in the play – *I meant to do it* (151). This could well have been Rosamond's comment when her rare 'moment of naturalness' becomes the 'crystallizing feather-touch' (294) which successfully completes the first part of her preconceived romance with Lydgate. 'What she liked to do was to her the right thing' (570). Both women spontaneously act their roles to achieve their desired ends. The roles, of course, have been established and tested by others, but each time they are assumed they are subtly adapted and modified, as Rosamond's piano-playing from which 'a hidden soul seemed to be flowing forth' demonstrates: 'and so indeed it was, since souls live on in perpetual echoes, and to all fine expression there goes somewhere an originating activity, if it be only that of an interpreter' (158). As J. Hillis Miller points out, interpretation is recognised paradoxically as a foundational activity.[33] But this is an *imitatio* of a different kind from Dorothea's.

Lydgate is vulnerable to these stereotypes, not only because of his emotional callowness, but also by reason of his intellectual acuity from which, as we have seen, it is inseparable. Unlike Farebrother he is not interested in the traditional taxonomies of natural history but in origins, the homogeneous origin of the tissue, the morphology beneath appearances, so that when his emotional commonness mistakes Rosamond for something special, his science is ready to hand to justify his perception. 'After all, he thought, one need not be surprised to find the rare conjunctions of nature under circumstances apparently unfavourable: come where they may, they always depend on conditions that are not obvious' (158). It takes them both some time to realise their mutual misinterpretation, that powerful shaping activity of which human, especially marital, relationships are shown to consist. Lydgate eventually links together his two actresses 'in a sudden speculation about this new form of feminine impassibility revealing itself in the sylph-like frame which he had once interpreted as the sign of a ready intelligent sensitiveness'. 'Would *she* kill me because I wearied her?' he asks (578). Form and function are finally discriminated, as the motto to the next chapter confirms in its juxtaposition of the soul and its 'fleshy self': 'And see! beside her cherub-face there floats / A pale-lipped form aerial whispering / Its promptings in that little shell her ear' (585). By then Lydgate's scientific work has been sabotaged. But Rosamond is thoroughly disappointed, too, in that the 'group of airy conditions' with which she had fallen in love and had tried to turn into her aristocratic dreams have proved insubstantial. If she is the 'anencephalous monster' that Lydgate acquires from Farebrother, then he displays 'a morbid vampire's taste' in his obsession with his scientific research. She begins to extend her ideas of romance to include the making of 'captives from the throne of marriage with a husband as crown-prince by your side' (429); but the 'thin romance' (743) with Ladislaw collapses at the climax of the novel when all the romantic conventions are shattered. Her chevalier turns viciously on her so that she almost loses 'the sense of her identity'; and with 'her little world in ruins' (769), she is further bewildered to find the preferred woman coming to plead heroically on behalf of her (Rosamond's) disgraced husband.

It is with the death of Raffles that the three strands of Lydgate's life finally compromise and checkmate each other. Was Raffles murdered? Did Lydgate's advanced treatment make possible Bulstrode's equivocation? Lydgate's open, experimental mind is aware of the complexity of the situation and so reacts against any simple conspiracy theory: 'What we call the "just possible" is sometimes true', he acknowledges to himself, 'and the thing we find easier to believe is grossly false' (728). But this scientific open-mindedness prevents Lydgate himself acting decisively so that there remains an 'uneasy corner of [his] consciousness while he was reviewing the facts and resisting all reproach' (729). Had he allowed his indebtedness to Bulstrode to influence his interpretation of the symptoms? Suddenly, scientific niceties about the nature of the experimental hypothesis take on a very different significance.[34] Had he colluded in murder? This is where George Eliot locates, characteristically, her crisis of interpretation. Both of the obvious explanations – bribed accomplice or victimised healer – are shown to be inadequate the more they have become enmeshed in the details of provincial life. Lydgate, however, knows he has slipped from his own earlier high standards when 'he had denounced the perversion of pathological doubt into moral doubt' under the conviction that 'the very breath of science is a contest with mistake, and must keep the conscience alive' (729). This is the nature of his indeterminate crime and, though it is beyond a court of law, it is punished, as with Bulstrode's, by the community. Self-exculpation is self-defeating, as Lydgate's knows. 'The circumstances would always be stronger than his assertion' (728) because 'it is always possible for those who like it to interpret them into a crime', says Farebrother cautiously: 'there is no proof in favour of the man outside his own consciousness and assertion' (724).

This is the unresolvable interpretative crux of Lydgate's career in the town. To what extent was he influenced by Bulstrode's loan? *Middlemarch* gossip is in no doubt, and even his friend Farebrother, 'with a keen perception of human weakness', can understand his falling from his own high standards (719). But George Eliot creates these ambiguous situations in order to show that the final analysis really depends on one's premises – and these are breathed in like air from the social medium in which we live. On this occasion, Dorothea initiates a countervailing interpretation by offering to her friends the proof of 'a man's character beforehand'. But Farebrother ('smiling gently at her ardour') counters with his statement that 'character is not cut in marble . . . It is something living and changing, and may become diseased as our bodies do'. Picking up the medical metaphor, Dorothea leaps over the question of guilt or innocence in her reply: 'Then it may be rescued and healed' (724–5). It all depends on one's hypothesis, the act of faith (or suspicion) which – and this is where *Middlemarch* points ahead to *Daniel Deronda* – brings into existence what it believes to be true. This is the necessary response to that interpretation of the evidence which imputes guilt which cannot be refuted, 'the public belief', as Lydgate describes it, 'that [a man] has committed a crime in some undefined way, because he had the motive for doing it' (753). It is left to Dorothea to initiate this alternative interpretation based on different premises which will also create what it hypothesises. With Lydgate himself at the point of uncertainty between the two hypotheses, Dorothea decisively tips the balance by providing him with, in terms of his own scientific research, an 'illuminated space' in which confused things can be seen clearly. 'The presence of a noble nature . . . changes the lights for us: we begin to see things again in their larger, quieter masses, and to believe that we too can be seen and judged in the wholeness of our character' (751–2). The various fissures and divisions in Lydgate's character are briefly overcome at this point when he simply describes to Dorothea what happened: it is George Eliot's secularised version of the moment when we shall see as we are seen. Lydgate undergoes no miraculous cure but the healing begins as he makes his confession – the confession denied to Bulstrode – narrating his version of events without equivocation, and 'recovering his old self in the consciousness that he was with one who believed in it' (752). Within this illuminated space, as in the account of his research, the hypothesis and the reality it explains become inseparable as each creates the other; or, in religious terms, Dorothea imputes righteousness to Lydgate and so imparts it. His future martyrdom spent between London and a Continental bathing-place

– 'he always regarded himself as a failure' (821) – is made more bearable.

George Eliot's main aim in *Middlemarch* can now be seen to be to bring some of the major myths or models of life, active at the beginning of the Victorian period, into alignment with the actual conditions of nineteenth-century society. Repeatedly, the protagonists set out with a belief in some kind of unquestioned, providential scheme as the basis for their world-views and subsequent vocations. An extreme and comic version of this is Fred Vincy's belief in that powerful Victorian myth of 'great expectations': 'What can the fitness of things mean, if not their fitness to a man's expectations? Failing this, absurdity and atheism gape behind him' (132). All are brought to recognise – 'under the varying experiments of Time' (3) – that such schemes cannot be grounded or sustained in the decentered world represented by this multi-plot novel. The empiricist fable requires that the benign designs of Providence and the apparently comprehensive theories based upon them, are subjected to the unpredictable forces of Destiny who 'stands by sarcastic with our *dramatis personae* folded in her hand' (93). Here are two narratives in conflict, as it were, of which *Middlemarch* consists: the imaginary one projected in the career of the modern saint, the justified sinner, or the scientific explorer, and that enforced by 'the stealthy convergence of human lots', by the community's suspicion, and by the conditions of provincial life. Each side in the conflict seeks to impose its own interpretation upon the careers of the protagonists in a variety of complex ways. Do you call these bare events? implies the novel with incredulity, when at the climax of each narrative strand a crisis occurs so full of ambiguities, indeterminacies, and misunderstandings that it becomes inevitably an interpretative crux. This is the space in which a trial of competing, adversarial interpretations takes place, each seeking to establish its claim on the truth – what a person is – according to its own premises. In the earlier fiction, this was the moment when verisimilitude gave way to mythic re-enactment. But, in *Middlemarch*, George Eliot remains true to her empiricist fable in which there is no 'grand life here – now – in England' (28): a temporary salvation is allowed through the generous hypothesis which briefly redeems, stabilises, and makes tolerable the gap between a character's world-view and the facts of life of which provincial martyrdom consists.

CHAPTER 8

Daniel Deronda: coercive types

The radically new mode in which *Daniel Deronda* is written abandons the technique of depicting character as an embodied world-view, that painfully negotiated equilibrium between the self and the world through which both are constituted. In the unstable world of *Middlemarch*, which is 'altering with the double change of self and beholder', that negotiation becomes more and more difficult: from one point of view the characters are simply clusters of signs for their neighbours' misinterpretations, and yet they know that their own inner life is made up of what they imagine those neighbours think about them. Each of the empiricist fables of which *Middlemarch* is made up underlines the same point, as it deconstructs and harshly redefines the providentially based world-views with which the characters embark on their careers. At the crises of their lives they become, once again, simply clusters of signs subject to conflicting interpretations in a suspicious community.

Daniel Deronda starts from this assumption and explores its implications more radically. If the representation of the self and its interpretation form no stable relationship, what are the implications for culture and characters? George Eliot's answer is to explore the psychic roots of character anterior to the formation of a coherent view of the world, and at the same time to uncover the psychic roots of religion anterior to the formation of creeds and rituals. In what one critic has called this 'modern reflective epic',[1] each entails the other in answer to the question, where does genuine coherence originate in a fragmented and materialistic culture? The answer is articulated in the conflict between two typologies, biblical and social, those two powerful interpretative modes. Instead of the negotiated world-view as the norm of character, we have two radically contrasting versions of the type. And the conflict of interpretations which results is given increased urgency by the fact that the novelist foregoes the stabilising

273

irony of historical hindsight of her previous novels in order to locate this final fiction in contemporary England.[2] Destiny no longer stands by sarcastic with our *dramatis personae* in its hands, as it did in *Middlemarch*; now 'destiny in the shape of Mephistopheles play[s] at chess with man for his soul'[3] in the present. In this high-risk game, one kind of typology imposes the dead hand of the past, the other offers spiritual liberation in the future.

The clearest indication of this new emphasis is to be found in the mysterious opaqueness of character, a point George Eliot is keen to stress through the mottoes of her own composition early in the novel. (The persistent use of her own mottoes to challenge our fictional expectations is a significantly new departure.) In the chapter in which Grandcourt first appears, for example, the motto reads: 'The beginning of an acquaintance whether with persons or things is to get a definite outline for our ignorance' (97). The opening paragraph then describes him in terms of what he is not – the reversal of Gwendolen's expectations – until he virtually disappears from view. 'It was not possible for a human aspect to be freer from grimace or solicitous wrigglings; also it was perhaps not possible for a breathing man wide awake to look less animated.' But it would be a mistake, adds the narrator, to see him as the 'correct Englishman', for that implies a tension between a rigid bearing and an inner suppressed vivacity; Grandcourt is as featureless and characterless as he appears. Even his complexion can only be described as the subtraction of something that was added in the first place – 'a faded fairness resembling that of an actress when bare of the artificial white and red'. The switch of gender distances us even further, and then shortly afterwards the narrator abandons the effort: 'Attempts at description are stupid: who can all at once describe a human being? . . . We recognise the alphabet; we are not sure of the language' (97–8). This should not be seen as a promise that the novel will fulfil as, for instance, it is fulfilled in *Middlemarch* when we turn from 'outside estimates of a man' to 'the report of [Casaubon's] own consciousness'. Fourteen chapters later the narrator returns to the frustrated interpretation of this cluster of cryptic signs, in a chapter headed by another of George Eliot's mottoes which begins: 'How trace the why and wherefore in a mind reduced to the barrenness of a fastidious egoism, in which all direct desires are dulled, and have dwindled from motives into the vacillating expectation of motives: a mind made up of moods, where a fitful impulse springs here and there conspicuously rank amid the general weediness?' (258). As entropy takes hold, the tracking of character from desires to motives to moods to impulses becomes an endless and obscure regression.

The other male protagonist, Deronda, is described in a similarly abstract way. The chapter in which he is formally presented begins with a motto acknowledging the impossibility of the narrator's task. 'Men, like planets, have both a visible and an invisible history. The astronomer threads the darkness with strict deduction, accounting so for every visible arc in the wanderer's orbit; and the narrator of human actions, if he did his work with the same completeness, would have to thread the hidden pathways of feeling and thought which lead up to every moment of action' (149). Grandcourt is defined by negations, Deronda by the invisible arcs not available for examination. And the incident which follows in the Gothic cloisters at the Abbey – 'the moment [which] had been burnt into his life as its chief epoch' (149) – is not, like Lydgate's, a moment of vocation, but the discovery that he doesn't know who he is, that his life is a hypothesis. The hidden orbits of the planets which explain their visible history remain hypothetical, however strict the deduction, and in a novel full of astronomical imagery provide a fittingly vertiginous sense of the mysteries of character. For Deronda is, like Grandcourt, without motive, drifting in his skiff on the Thames, wondering what the world holds for him. The golden youth, the English milord – these are the outlines for our ignorance which the novel provides, raising the questions: Is there such a thing as a character without qualities? Is it possible to engage with the world simply as a hypothesis?

In the previous fiction, as we have seen, characters oscillated wildly or deliquesced into other people's views of them at moments of intense crisis. In the abstract mode of *Daniel Deronda*, this becomes the norm as most of the mediations of character description and analysis are discarded for the purpose of focusing on the theme announced by the motto to the novel: 'Let thy chief terror be of thine own soul.' Not that the fate of the heroine's soul is a new concern, but the terror which accompanies it is, as well as the terms in which it is formulated. In order to carry out this most fundamental exploration of the moral self, George Eliot utilises on a grand scale the fictional structure she first employed in 'Janet's Repentance', where the two male protagonists and the worlds they represent pivot upon and effect the heroine's salvation or damnation. The shadowy nature of the male protagonists pushes the novel towards the psychomachia where the heroine plays at dice for her soul. To understand the nature of her gamble, it will be best to examine the psychic forces which form her character and then to trace the influence of Deronda and Grandcourt upon her which culminates in the drowning episode off Genoa.

The two men are essentially passive – Grandcourt inert, Deronda unrealised – for reasons we shall examine later, while Gwendolen is given an irreducible, unstable vitality. This vitality, this elemental life-stuff, is the prize for which the forces of the novel compete. In order to suggest its pristine, unformed quality, George Eliot again presents the young woman stepping into life, but the previous heroines seem positively weighed down with definable qualities at the beginning of their narratives compared to Gwendolen. Her spark is so vital because it can't be categorised, nor has it reached any kind of accommodation with the world. Contradiction and paradox are the only means of representing this 'princess in exile':

and those who feared her were also fond of her; the fear and the fondness being perhaps both heightened by what may be called the iridescence of her character – the play of various, nay, contrary tendencies. For Macbeth's rhetoric about the impossibility of being many opposite things in the same moment, referred to the clumsy necessities of action and not to the subtler possibilities of feeling. We cannot speak a loyal word and be meanly silent, we cannot kill and not kill in the same moment; but a moment is room wide enough for the loyal and mean desire, for the outlash of a murderous thought and the sharp backward stroke of repentence. (36)

In other words, she is uninterpretable both to herself and to others; character as a cluster of signs becomes the constantly changing colours of iridescence.

Though their workings are unpredictable, the 'contrary tendencies' of Gwendolen's character are extreme expressions of the opposed moral dimensions of George Eliot's fictional world. There is, first, the self and the innate belief in the self, that 'inborn energy of egoistic desire' (36) which intimidates and fascinates. Its power is that it seems self-sustaining so that even when results are random and unpredictable, as in roulette, Gwendolen always assumes she will win. To the onlookers there is something both charming and sinister in a self-confidence not in relation to a world which would never be 'equal to the demands of her fine organism' (72). This quality is defined in

George Eliot's motto to the chapter in which the heroine seeks to rescue the family fortunes by becoming, with Klesmer's assistance, a professional singer. 'The most obstinate beliefs that mortals entertain about themselves are such as they have no evidence for beyond a constant, spontaneous pulsing of their self-satisfaction – as it were a hidden seed of madness, a confidence that they can move the world without precise notion of standing-place or lever' (232). It is a disturbing statement. At its deepest level, the rhythm of the self originates in these mysterious, quasar-like pulsations, out of relation to the world in which it finds itself – mad.

The other dimension – one is encouraged by the novel to use spatial terms – is the terror of self-destruction, the submergence of the self, expressed as a form of agoraphobia. This is 'that liability of hers to fits of spiritual dread' and it is again depicted in a primitive and abstract mode: 'Solitude in any wide scene impressed her with an undefined feeling of immeasurable existence aloof from her, in the midst of which she was helplessly incapable of asserting herself' (57). The self is an exile in an astronomical vastness – the motto to this particular chapter is from Fontenelle's *Pluralité des Mondes* – from which it retreats in terror. Gwendolen's dread surfaces when 'her horizon [which] was that of the genteel romance' safely circumscribed 'by the ordinary wirework of social forms' (47), is suddenly breached by a glimpse of the immeasurable. Such a moment, the first of several which articulate her career in the novel, occurs during the Hermione tableau. This scene dramatises the violent conflict between the two dimensions of Gwendolen's character: before the mysterious painting is revealed she is about to achieve another social triumph as the awakened Hermione, while immediately afterwards she breaks down in terror. 'She wondered at herself in these occasional experiences, which seemed like a brief remembered madness, an unexplained exception from her normal life' (56). It is 'remembered', but it is also proleptic of the brief scene, a different kind of tableau, towards which her life must move before the answer to Deronda's opening question – 'Was the good or evil genius dominant in those beams?' – can be answered. The painting of 'the dead face and the fleeing figure' (54) ambiguously combines an extreme expression of the will (murder) with the terror of the unknown (flight).

The self is everything, the self is nothing. One is reminded of that early letter ('the fate of poor mortals') which contains the most succinct version of George Eliot's master-plot. After describing that continuous process of breakdown and renewal, the letter switches in the next paragraph to a more extreme state of mind which offers no hope of resolution. 'I feel a sort of madness growing upon me – just the opposite of the delirium which makes people fancy that their bodies are filling the room. It seems to me as if I were shrinking into that mathematical abstraction, a point – so entirely am I destitute of contact that I am unconscious of length or breadth.'[4] This description explores deeper levels of alienation, and it is upon this Pascalian sense of disproportion that Gwendolen's character is based. On each side is a form of madness, of extreme unrelatedness. These are the irreducible elements of morality and religion which have to be brought into the dialectical relationship Feuerbach compares to the 'perpetual systole and diastole' of life: 'In the religious systole man propels his own nature from himself, he throws himself outward; in the religious diastole he receives the rejected nature into his heart again.'[5] Each state is grounded in the other, but if they are unrelated they oscillate randomly; and it is because Gwendolen has no way of relating them – she finds religion tiresome – that George Eliot is enabled to present them in their pristine, extreme forms as a superstition 'which attached itself both to her confidence and her terror' (257). This is Browning's 'dangerous edge of things' where the self cannot be categorised, at risk at each moment because character has not crystallised or congealed into a world-view: 'one step aside, / They're classed and done with'.[6] This is the virginal iridescence, the 'potent charm' of a character which fascinates the male protagonists.

What became the unresolvable conflicts of interpretation at the climaxes of the previous heroines' careers is now taken as the starting-point for Gwendolen's character. And just as they awaited, longed for, and sometimes (as in *Felix Holt*) achieved a vision of consequences to guide them, so she is granted hers early in the novel but is unable to interpret it. This is the 'unmapped country' (257) *Daniel Deronda* explores. The significance of the painted panel remains uncertain until the end of the novel when Gwendolen links it to the drowning of Grandcourt, but it is clearly a glimpse of the self's possibilities beyond temporal and moral constraints, a prevision granted to the superstitious, primitive self. It is also a power granted to the spiritually sophisticated, as we see in this comment on Mordecai:

'Second-sight' is a flag over disputed ground. But it is matter of knowledge that there are persons whose yearnings, conceptions – nay, travelled conclusions – continually take the form of images which have a foreshadowing power: the deed they would do starts up before them in complete shape, making a coercive type; the event they hunger for or dread rises into vision with a seed-like growth, feeding itself fast on unnumbered impressions. (439)

In its creative form such a faculty is defined in terms of biblical and Cabbalistic typology[7] which Mordecai expounds to Deronda, but the key terms – image, foreshadowing, type, vision – refer equally to Gwendolen's fits of spiritual dread and to the event which is to fulfil as antitype her fearful vision. In either case, the seed of the future is to be found in the present. But why should the heroine share this faculty with the seer? One possible answer is provided by the *Shemah*, the Hebrew confession of the divine unity, which Mordecai describes as 'a binding theory to the human race': 'Now, in complete unity a part possesses the whole as the whole possesses every part: and in this way human life is tending toward the image of the Supreme Unity.' It is the most explicitly spiritual version of organic unity in the novels, or the most formalised account of the hermeneutical circle which has here achieved completion, for through participation in such a unity 'in a brief day the soul of man may know in fuller volume the good which has been and is, nay, is to come, than all he could possess in a whole life where he had to follow the creeping paths of the senses' (683). In its own primitive, superstitious way, Gwendolen's character is also 'quiveringly poised' between the whole which, in her case, threatens annihilation and the part which wilfully asserts its independence – and at certain shattering and key moments of her career the two dimensions of the moral life touch briefly before springing apart again. In the Hermione episode, the anticipated exultation of the self is immediately, almost simultaneously, invaded by the terrifying image of the unknown which it unwittingly conjures up; and then Gwendolen's past, present, and future coalesce in a vision. Neither Mordecai nor Gwendolen is negotiating with the world in any conventional sense; both his 'binding theory' and her fearful vision are hermeneutics of a different kind, suitable for the prophet and the princess, both in exile.

If the novel moves towards the vision of divine unity, it starts in the gambling casino at Leubronn where chance is the only power and confidence in one's luck the only motive. The scene is an infernal parody of divine unity, in which all Europe is represented and reduced to its lowest common denominator, gambling for money. 'Here certainly was a striking admission of human equality' (4). The players are separate but united, and the unity is that of self-interest with its 'uniform negativeness of expression which had the effect of a mask – as if they had all eaten of some root that for the time compelled the brains of each to the same narrow monotony of action' (5). Though Gwendolen is gambling, she does not yet share this stupor of self, and that is why Deronda asks his questions about her. But she is at risk, having just fled from Grandcourt's very desirable proposal of marriage in fear and uncertainty. Her 'favourite key to life – doing as she liked – seemed to fail her, and she could not foresee what at any given moment she might like to do' (121). Her state of mind finds expression in roulette, where the self is pitted against a random universe, and not only does she come to believe in her luck but others are beginning to do so too: 'she had visions of being followed by a *cortège* who would worship her as a goddess of luck and watch her play as a directing augury' (6). All the other gamblers have their systems, those parodies of second-sight, while Gwendolen imagines herself Fortuna controlling the turn of the wheel, determining the future, until Deronda appears and in another of her sudden reversals she begins to lose. His scrutiny from 'a region outside and above her' (6) is the beginning of the long process by which the rampant self will be brought into relationship with its vertiginous, annihilating agoraphobia.

Madness, superstition, chance – these are the controlling elements of the world in which the moral embryo emerges to seek its identity. Gwendolen's iridescence is the expression of the vital uncertainty of this search, and it is this unpredictability which challenges Grand-court and Deronda. In *Felix Holt*, both Felix and Harold ignored and condescended to Esther until they decided they needed her to fulfil their political and social aims; in this novel the motivation is more mysterious. The two men are united, as we have seen, by their impenetrable passivity: Grandcourt appears to be in the final lingering atrophy of the will, Deronda is unable to be born into the world. Gwendolen's appearance on the aristocratic scene prompts them both into a realisation and fulfilment of the qualities they mysteriously embody.

Grandcourt is the culmination and epitome of the aristocratically decadent world of *Daniel Deronda*, validated by his lengthy genealogy in the same chapter in which Deronda discovers that he doesn't know who he is. The Gothic cloister in which the latter is being tutored is overlooked by the gallery in which portraits by Lely, Kneller, Reynolds, Romney, and Lawrence trace the descent of the Mallinger line to Sir Hugo and his brother who had married Miss Grandcourt, 'thus making a junction between two equally old families . . . uniting their highest advantages in the prospects of that Henleigh Mallinger Grandcourt' (150–1). Despite his detailed provenance, he is a mysterious figure defined, as we have seen, by negatives. The 'outline for our ignorance' that he presents seems to be that of the typical bored aristocrat of the Dickensian James Harthouse kind, wilful, predatory, and inconsistent. But he is an aristocrat who has left off doing aristocratic things; as with his appearance he can only be described in terms of qualities added and then subtracted. Despite a murky past he remains, according to Mr Gascoigne, a good marriage prospect, for 'whatever Grandcourt had done, he had not ruined himself' (83). He has no marked characteristics because he appears not to be in relation to the world. He has done everything and has now left off doing it. In his attempt to explain the cold and formal opacity of this man without qualities, Deronda cites his native culture: 'the English fondness for reserve will account for much negation; and Grandcourt's manners with an extra veil of reserve over them might be expected to present the extreme type of the national taste' (386). But he is a type in the most abstract sense with all particular features, claims, motives, and desires negated, and this is, of course, why Gwendolen in her refusal to be coerced by the world finds him 'not ridiculous' (98) and draws her fatal conclusion: 'the less he had of particular tastes or desires, the more freedom his wife was likely to have in following hers' (122). As a type, he *is* his formal, perfect manners, always responding with that apparent absence of demand which is the only trap into which Gwendolen in her 'fierceness of maidenhood' (63) could have fallen. So that in the superb proposal scene, when he offers himself by his absence ('Do you command me to go?') and Gwendolen accepts him with a 'no', she experiences her only affection for him: 'She had a momentary phantasmal love for this man who chose his words so well, and who was a mere incarnation of delicate homage' (279). In one sense, she is correct, for not only does he embody the wealth and luxury she desires, but also there is no character there with whom to relate – except phantasmally with a type.

In his case, the type implies aristocracy, empire, power, and

wealth, though these too must be distanced. 'Grandcourt's importance as a subject of this realm was of the grandly passive kind which
consists in the inheritance of land.' Even 'his most careful biographer'
need know nothing about the contemporary political situation,
'trade-unions, household suffrage, or even the last commercial panic'
(543). But his true passivity is that of the will which is atrophying as it
feeds upon itself. In genealogical terms, he is the end of the line,
epitomising and fulfilling all that has gone before – the end, it should
be stressed, of descent through the male line to which, as Gillian Beer
has pointed out, 'the dwindling energy of England is related
directly'.[8] In the novel he does virtually nothing, he hardly speaks.
When he admits to the 'confounded strain' of gambling, Sir Hugo
suggests 'somebody should invent a wheel to do amusements for you,
my dear fellow, as the Tartars get their praying done' (145). This
'inert specimen of personal distinction' (396), this 'remnant of a
human being' (376), in Deronda's words, is slowly running down as,
in a 'gratification of mere will' (135), it asserts itself by denying its own
satisfactions as they are about to be realised. His only contact with the
world is maintained indirectly through his go-between and *alter ego*,
the brilliantly conceived Lush who embodies the sleaziness and
grubbiness rigorously excluded from his master's life of good form.
This is Grandcourt's most enduring relationship but it dramatises
even further the mysteriousness of his motives: 'to know Grandcourt
was to doubt what he would do in any particular case' (261). The will
in its terminal state is entirely unpredictable. Grandcourt, for
example, hesitated to approach Gwendolen again after the family
bankruptcy either because he feared rejection or because he was
certain of acceptance; 'Lush could only toss up his chin in despair of a
theory' (266). But the two men are essential to each other and, in the
wooing of Gwendolen, Lush performs the useful function of deflecting
her antipathies from his master to himself. The cold formality of the
one is the most desirable alternative to the oily obsequiousness of the
other. And even when Lush imagines he is plotting against his master
by arranging the meeting with Mrs Glasher he is – in his entire
ignorance of motives – strengthening Grandcourt's hand.

How close do we ever come to a knowledge of Grandcourt's
motives? It seems that, before Gwendolen's appearance, his bloated
will is simply running down entropically into a 'diseased numbness', a
final inertia 'sublimely independent of definite motive' (135).
Interpretation and representation have become unrelated. No one,

neither the narrator nor the characters, can fathom his character which is simply represented through the negations of an abstract type. With the arrival of Gwendolen, however, his inert will is aroused to a final conquest for she seems to represent a wilfulness and unpredictableness equal to his own. The oscillations of her nature provide a continual titillation to his will and sadism: 'He meant to be master of a woman who would have liked to master him' (294). Even when his concentration lapses and the will desists out of self-gratification, Gwendolen's unexpected flight arouses him again; and the titillation is mutual for his slowness to respond challenges her ambitions. The furthest we penetrate into Grandcourt's motives, however, is in the mysterious scene at Diplow when he is alone, 'sitting meditatively on a sofa and abstaining from literature – political, comic, cynical, or romantic'. Time passes unnoticed – 'from a state of the inward world, something like premature age, where the need for action lapses into a mere image of what has been, is, and may or might be; where impulse is born and dies in a phantasmal world, pausing in rejection even of a shadowy fulfilment' (292). There is still nothing here to be interpreted. This is another kind of mysticism, the mysticism of the will, which turns everything into finer and finer negations, transcends temporal constraints and is cut off in its completeness from the world which it despises. And yet, on this occasion, the apparent passivity conceals a profound inner disturbance: 'Grandcourt's thoughts this evening were like the circlets one sees in a dark pool continually dying out and continually started again by some impulse from below the surface. The deeper central impulse came from the image of Gwendolen' (293). Momentarily, the will's rejection of even 'a shadowy fulfilment' is countermanded by an image which demands its fulfilment in the mysterious economy of Grandcourt's psyche. This is a new kind of double hermeneutic: the narrator can only delineate that psyche by an extended image, and what the psyche broods upon is, in its turn, an image of Gwendolen who is herself constituted from those mysterious images in 'the dark seed-growths of consciousness' (271). It is a *mise-en-abîme* of interpretation of a kind which opens up in all directions in *Daniel Deronda* and which its typologies seek to stabilise.

George Eliot is depicting a character who is both unpredictable and obsessive, living in a world where the only reality is the power of its will. Lush knows that 'there was no telling what might turn up in the slowly-churning chances of his mind' (142) for it is like a roulette-wheel. And yet even he is disturbed by his master's perverse reaction to Gwendolen's unpredictability, for 'in his freak about this girl he struck Lush rather newly as something like a man who was *fey* – led on by an ominous fatality' (291). His fate is crystallised in the image of Gwendolen deep in his consciousness. Her iridescence, the primitive life-stuff she represents, must be controlled, but even after the marriage she remains unknown to him – as she does to Deronda – because each man only glimpses part of her nature. The uninterpretable dangers of her undulations and oscillations are expressed through the imagery of the serpent, the demonic, the 'Nereid in sea-green robes' (7) at Leubronn; and just as lawyer Dempster failed to control the serpentine metamorphoses of Janet (under the influence of Tryan) so Grandcourt is drawn into the depths which Gwendolen's image disturbs.

That Grandcourt's pursuit of Gwendolen marks the final stage of his life is chillingly suggested by his hurried visit to Gadsmere to tell his mistress of his forthcoming marriage and claim back the family jewels. Mrs Glasher, though 'a standing banquet for his delight in dominating', represents the remants of his last human relationship. This is now to be severed and she knows there is no appeal: she 'shrank from crying in a dead ear and clinging to dead knees, only to see the immovable face and feel the rigid limbs' (318). But to his surprise and annoyance, she refuses to hand over the jewels, insisting that she herself will give them to Gwendolen, even though her resistance is suicidal both for herself and her children. 'I will not bear to have it denied me.' As we penetrate further into the pathology and dialectics of the will, even Grandcourt is bewildered: he 'had a baffling sense that he had to deal with something like madness; he could only govern by giving way' (323). Mrs Glasher is forced to submit but must be allowed her revenge. 'There is no quailing . . . which has not an ugly obverse: the withheld sting was gathering venom' (313). The delivery of the jewels with the hidden note achieves both her aims; it is simultaneously sadistic and masochistic. She discharges her venom through the letter which acknowledges her own rejection: 'The man you have married has a withered heart. His best young love was mine . . . It is dead; but I am the grave in which your chance of happiness is buried as well as mine' (330). As she hands over the cadaver of her lover to Gwendolen, she exacts her revenge through the poisoned gems which symbolise that dead love – 'and the poison had entered into this poor young creature'. To Grandcourt, his bride's hysterical screaming as he comes into her boudoir is another sign of perverse, uncontrollable, female madness: but the poison has been handed on and will have to be discharged. And the poison is the truth Mrs Glasher has just discovered: Grandcourt is dead and the mysterious painting at Offendene comes closer to its fulfilment. He is incapable of further human relationships, for even the novelty Gwendolen represents cannot elicit feeling from the corpse he has now been declared to be. She has simply roused him from the penultimate atrophy of the will to a final convulsive effort, leading the doomed man – now fully the type, the phantasm, the corpse – on to his ultimate and paradoxical assertion which is self-annihilation. As for Gwendolen, the triumph of the marriage is immediately invaded by the mistress's curse as one extreme again triggers off the other: 'Hers was one of the natures in which exultation inevitably carries an infusion of dread ready to curdle and declare itself' (329).

Whereas Grandcourt is cryptic, silent, and opaque but equipped with an impeccable pedigree, Deronda is constantly speculating at considerable length about his unknown origins. The former can only be delineated in ambiguous images while the latter is an insecure exercise in recurrent self-interpretation. Deprived of origins he makes 'conjectures about his own history', trembling at what might be 'a fiction of his own' (152). Just as any sense of Grandcourt's individuality disappears in the fixity of the type (which simply masks and expresses the will), so Deronda's uncertainty turns his life into a hypothesis, the visible arcs accounting for the invisible arcs of his trajectory: 'there came back certain facts which had an obstinate reality, – almost like the fragments of a bridge, telling you unmistakably how the arches lay' (153). But the hypothesis can be challenged by new facts to which he has to remain receptive; he embodies a state of suspense, open, uncommitted, undefined. Outwardly, he shares some of the qualities of his opposite, Grand-court: both men appear inert, directionless, and suffering from *ennui*, but Deronda's passivity arises from an excess of sympathy. His lack of a genealogy, his 'sense of an entailed disadvantage' takes 'the form of fellowship and makes the imagination tender' (160).

If Grandcourt appears at the penultimate stage of the self-negation of the will, Deronda is seeking to be born into the world without the originatory facts upon which to base a world-view. Sir Hugo's materialistic complacency, reflecting brilliantly the ethos in which Deronda is an exile, throws into relief the hero's mysterious inchoateness. He doesn't mind him 'doffing some of our national prejudices': 'But, for God's sake, keep an English cut, and don't become indifferent to bad tobacco! And – my dear boy – it is good to be unselfish and generous; but don't carry that too far' (168). Just as Grandcourt's character becomes deliquescent and oozy with 'the want of regulated channels for the soul to move in' (141), so Deronda's wide sympathies and 'meditative yearning after wide knowledge' prevent him engaging 'in the fight for prize acquirements in narrow tracks' (162). So, like his rival, he holds back when fulfilment is near: 'how could a fellow push his way properly when he objected to swop for his own advantage . . . when he was within an inch of victory?' (162). Grandcourt has left off such vulgarity, Deronda has never taken it on. Thanks to his privileged position, the latter can remain in 'a state of social neutrality', his 'reflective hesitation' becoming paradoxically the motivating force of his life: 'He longed now to have the sort of apprenticeship to life which would not shape him too definitely, and rob him of that choice that might come from a free growth' (164). As he acknowledges later, it is his fear of 'turning himself into a sort of diagram instead of a growth' (486), a fear of premature foreclosure, which prevents commitment and action. The two men provide a fascinating comparison and contrast which is itself an investigation into the representation and interpretation of character. Each man crystallises one fictional mode: Grandcourt is all external representation, a cluster of signs and images, of genealogy and conventions, which others fail to interpret; while Deronda is all self-interpretation and self-interrogation with no social signifiers to call his own.

The most extreme expression of Deronda's cultivated negative capability occurs in the episode in which he rescues Mirah and which signals the beginning of the end of his neutrality. He is sculling on the Thames, drifting with the tide and 'questioning whether it were worth while to take part in the battle of the world' (169), in a scene which corresponds to Grandcourt abstaining from polite literature. Here, it is Deronda's sympathy not his will that is meditating upon itself, but he too summons up the image of a woman, that of Mirah, by singing Rossini's plaintive arrangement of Dante's '*Nessun maggior dolore*'. He sees 'a figure which might have been an impersonation of the misery he was unconsciously giving voice to', as his words enter 'her inner world' (171) and they each briefly signify each other's feelings. This glimpse of Mirah, however, simply deepens his sense of universal sorrow and confirms him in the reasons 'why he should not draw strongly at any thread in the hopelessly-entangled scheme of things' (172). Unseen in his boat, he drifts away with the tide, watching the sunset fade on the river, seeking to merge himself with the objects he was looking at in the visionary landscape, and wondering 'how far it might be possible habitually to shift his centre till his own personality would be no less outside him than the landscape' (173). If Grandcourt's abstentions represent the pathology of the will, this is the pathology of sympathy and, like the former, it negates character because it denies relationship. But, at this moment of self-nullification, a movement on the bank opposite, 'the moving figure' (173), returns him to himself and the world in an act of rescue. In the remote depths of character there is registered once again an image with some of the same ingredients – a woman, fleeing and forsaken, water and drowning – as in Gwendolen's painted panel and Grandcourt's dark pool of meditation. Here, the forsaken girl with 'her eyes fixed on the river with a look of immovable, statue-like despair' (171), becomes Deronda's fate. The self-consuming will, the self-dissipating sympathy, or in Gwendolen's case the violent oscillation of the two, are determined in their courses by mysterious images which the self both calls up and is determined by.

It is Mirah who is to lead Deronda eventually to the discovery of his Jewish origins, but it is a tortuous and paradoxical quest. He cannot simply choose to be a Jew; and, when he finds he is one, the commitment to his people need not necessarily follow. It is an extreme version of the relationship between will and destiny out of which character is created but which is here disrupted. How does one discover and become what one is? Gradually, Deronda's search for the origins of his enigmatic self – the 'apparent indefiniteness of his sentiments', the 'reflective analysis which tends to neutralise sympathy', his inability to form 'a strong partisanship' (335–6) – is linked more and more closely to his growing interest in Judaism. His self-questioning is a form of the hermeneutic circle, not its rhythmic workings or its visionary completion, but its paradoxical initiation. Any understanding of a text or the world demands an initial and inadequate projection of its meaning on the basis of partial experience. This is what, in the ignorance of his origins, Deronda is incapable of making: 'what he most longed for was either some external event, or some inward light, that would urge him into a definite line of action, and compress his wandering energy' (336). It is the classic Victorian liberal dilemma. 'Man must begin with an Idea of the world', wrote Matthew Arnold, 'in order not to be prevailed over by the world's multitudinousness.'[9] Deronda waits for some insight or impingement. 'But how and whence was the needed event to come? – the influence that would justify partiality, and making himself what he longed to be yet was unable to make himself – an organic part of social life, instead of roaming in it like a yearning disembodied spirit?' (336). The partiality of that initial commitment is denied him because of his 'innate balance' which makes him simultaneously sympathetic and inactive, democratic and conservative, speculative and traditional. Deronda describes his lack in a self-deprecating conundrum (for even his desperate search for selfhood must not be overstated): 'To pound the objects of sentiment into small dust, yet keep sentiment alive and active, was something like the famous recipe for making a cannon – to first take a round hole and then enclose it with iron; whatever you do keeping fast hold of your round hole' (337). Which has priority, the round hole or the iron? Deronda is an absence seeking to be present, and his inner life is a protracted meditation on this dilemma.

   His second crucial experience occurs in the Judengasse in Frankfurt where he finds himself partly because of Mirah, and partly because of his vague interest in 'the faint beginnings of faiths and institutions, and their obscure lingering decay' (337). In the synagogue he gives 'himself up to that strongest effect of chanted liturgies which is independent of detailed verbal meaning – like the effect of an Allegri's *Miserere* or a Palestrina's *Magnificat*'. In other words, this is religion without doctrine or belief. 'The most powerful movement of feeling with a liturgy is the prayer which seeks for nothing special, but is a yearning to escape from the limitations of our own weakness and an invocation of all Good to enter and abide with us' (339). This sounds like the hole without the cannon, but Deronda is receptive because the liturgy has, like himself, no 'fixed local habitation' (336), 'a national faith, which had penetrated the thinking of half the world, and moulded the splendid forms of that world's religion, was finding a remote, obscure echo' (339). It is acceptable because it has been assimilated and superseded; it is not identified with one place; and it is declining but still echoing obscurely through the world. Time has purged it of its excrescences and left religion's essential common denominator – a sense of 'passionate regret' (339). Judaism is presented in this way to appeal to a character without qualities who sings Rossini arias to himself on the Thames. And this is how Deronda describes his long awaited religious experience: 'He wondered at the strength of his own feeling; it seemed beyond the occasion – what one might imagine to be a divine influx in the darkness, before there was any vision to interpret' (339). This is the pre-hermeneutic moment to which Deronda's state of suspension, his negative capability, his habitual self-emptying or *kenosis*, enables him to respond. This is the primal religious experience, the divine influx, the spirit breathing upon the waters, not only before interpretation gets to work but even before there is a vision to interpret. (One of the central aims of Cabbalistic mysticism to which this experience leads him was to restore to Judaism the idea of *creatio ex nihilo* in the form of myth.)[10] This moment of influx links up to those inexplicable pulsations, impulses, ripples in the darkness, all of which are used to define the mysterious and primitive forces of character in the novel, and all of which either precede or – in the case of Grandcourt – postdate the act of interpretation. Deronda is able to respond because he has the correct form of pre-understanding, that of a man whose life is the open hypothesis which hasn't yet crystallised into a theory or a character.

His task is now to carry this experience of 'the divine influx' into the mundane world of Victorian London and submit it to 'the pressure of that hard unaccommodating Actual, which has never consulted our taste and is entirely unselect'. He becomes squeamish at the thought of Jewish ideals becoming 'warmly incarnate' (351), as he searches for Mirah's missing family and the meaning of his own experience. The impingements of the Actual repeatedly disturb the hypotheses which he is formulating and reformulating at this stage of his career and through which George Eliot is questioning our deterministic view of circumstances and character. Do we make circumstances or circumstances us? Again, how is Deronda to become what he is? 'Might there not come a disclosure which would hold the missing determination of his course? What did he really know about his origin?' (437). But no such disclosure of his past comes, nor is he any more than Grandcourt granted a glimpse of the future, for 'Deronda's nature was not one of those quiveringly-poised natures that lend themselves to second-sight' (438). Instead – and this is his third crucial experience – he becomes the focus of someone else's second-sight, the figure in whom Mordecai's prophetic vision crystallises. The result is that Deronda's disparate experiences – his education among the Gentiles, his wide uncommitted sympathies, his deliverance of Mirah, his response to the divine influx – all become unified and meaningful under this formative influence. Mordecai's vision is a hypothesis which helps to interpret Deronda into existence. It is a radical development and enlargement of the act of faith through which Dorothea enabled Lydgate to recover his selfhood; and it is combined with the mentor-pupil relationship, explored in *Adam Bede* and *Romola*, in which each person defines and fulfils the hopes of the other. The relationship is, of coure, sharply contrasted with any simply deterministic, circumstantial, or genealogical view of character we find in the Gentile half of the novel. In this sense, *Daniel Deronda* challenges the assumptions and conventions of a great deal of Victorian realistic fiction.

Deronda has then become, in his turn, an image. For Mordecai's yearnings, conceptions, and conclusions find their initial expression in 'images which have a foreshadowing power', as we have seen. To fulfil his prophetic role Mordecai must find the 'executive self', the agent who will mediate and interpret his message to the world: 'and hence it was that his imagination had constructed another man who would be something more ample than the second soul bestowed according to the notions of the Cabbalists, to help out the insufficient first' (441). More substantial than the ghostly Golem,[11] this self will complement and complete the prophet's life. To shape and define this initially phantasmal figure Mordecai searches for strong images in both men and paintings 'which might feed his hopefulness with grave and noble types of the human form' (440). If society is envisaged as a whispering gallery in *Middlemarch*, in this novel it becomes a picture-gallery of types, both threatening and promising.[12] Mordecai imagines this other self in a visionary landscape, first 'darkened by the excess of light in the aerial background', then turning towards him as it advances 'a face became discernible . . . hardly individual but typical [in] form and colour', until finally 'the visionary form became a companion and auditor' (442), both in his waking imagination and his dreams. Deronda had dispersed himself empathetically into the visionary landscape of the evening river; Mordecai and Mirah call him from it into the world. With his life coming to an end, Mordecai's vision demands that fulfilment must be at hand: 'The deliverer's footstep must be near – the deliverer who was to rescue Mordecai's spiritual travail from oblivion, and give it an abiding place in the best heritage of his people' (443).

It will be clear that in depicting this relationship in terms of image and type, George Eliot is establishing a contrast with the Gentile half of the novel. There, everything was subordinated to the idea of the type – embodied supremely in Grandcourt – as the social stereotype, expressive of convention, genealogy, and power. Here, in the Jewish half, the idea of the type is deployed in a creative, flexible, and spiritual form, based on biblical typology. The contrast between these two typologies, two ways of interpreting the world, epitomises the difference between the two halves of the novel. *Daniel Deronda* is the culmination of George Eliot's fictional use of biblical typology, that pervasive and powerful mode of Victorian thought with which she was familiar from her early evangelical years and from her work in the Higher Criticism. She began her redefinitions of typology, as we have seen, as early as *Scenes of Clerical Life*. The Victorians adapted in a variety of ways the orthodox form of this hermeneutic in which an event or person in the Old Testament, the type, is fulfilled by a later event or person (usually Christ) in the New Testament, the antitype. As George P. Landow has written, it appealed to the Victorians' powerful sense of history: 'typology promises a means of linking two conceptions of the real within a coherent intellectual framework' – on the one hand, there is 'the essential historicity' of the type and antitype, on the other, there is 'typology's implicit theory of progressive revelation [which] encourages meliorist theories of historical development'.[13] There is a fruitful tension also, between the free will of the individual as historical type and his or her function in the divine plan. In her adaptation and internalisation of typology (which incorporates ideas of metempsychosis from the Cabbala as well as ideas of nemesis from Dante), George Eliot exploits this tension in order to counter the deterministic, class-bound thinking of the Gentile world. In *Daniel Deronda*, it is not one character or event foreshadowing another by which it is fulfilled – except in a negative, genealogical sense; it is rather one character imagining and choosing an executive self who reciprocally recognises and accepts the source of his or her selfhood.

It is worth looking at the way in which the two men realise each other in this form of spiritual genealogy. The images in Mordecai's mind have a 'foreshadowing power' which takes the form of a 'coercive type'. When he meets Deronda he recognises 'a face and frame which seemed to him to realise the long-conceived type' (447) and, despite evidence to the contrary, he persists in his belief because 'the long-contemplated figure had come as an emotional sequence of Mordecai's firmest theoretic convictions; it had been wrought from the imagery of his most passionate life'. It could be a novelist bringing what Deronda thought of as the 'fiction' of his life into sharper and sharper reality. Now the figure becomes more individualised in a process compared to the reverse effects of memory: 'Deronda had that sort of resemblance to the preconceived type which a finely individual bust or portrait has to the more generalised copy left in our minds after a long interval' (447). He is next imagined in the visionary landscape which signals the crucial transitional moment, the death of the type and the birth of the antitype, 'painted on that golden sky which was the doubly blessed symbol of advancing day and of approaching rest' (447). The fulfilment occurs two chapters later when Deronda, rowing on the Thames out of the sunset, catches sight of Mordecai's face looking over Blackfriars Bridge, 'an illuminated type of bodily emaciation and spiritual eagerness' (459), who in turn recognises his antitype, 'the nearing figure [which] lifted up its face towards him – the face of his visions – and then immediately, with white uplifted hand, beckoned again and again' (459). From the initial image the type is now fully transformed into the prophetic vision and its fulfilment with, as E. S. Shaffer writes, 'the appearance of the Son of Man in the clouds'.[14] Or in the terms of Mordecai's poem in which the cherubim, the ark of the of the covenant, and the law are all buried in Mount Nebo (from which the Promised Land is to be glimpsed), the 'clay of the founder' has been shattered from around 'the golden image' (445).

Deronda remains in an ambivalent position throughout these events, balancing his receptivity with a sceptical commentary, a characteristically Gentile hermeneutic of suspicion. 'What, after all, had really happened?' (474). His lengthy meditations on this question are George Eliot's most theoretical discussions in her fiction on the relationship between selfhood and events, anticipating the musings of Theophrastus Such who also begins by deconstructing the self ('Looking Inward') and ends by acknowledging the central role of Judaism ('The Modern Hep! Hep! Hep!'). Deronda is trying to interpret himself into existence by choosing between two hypotheses. On the one hand, there is the apparently solid Gentile world where his life was based on 'a pure supposition, namely, that Sir Hugo was his father'. This has accustomed him to a life lived in the expectancy of some revelation. 'To be in a state of suspense which was also one of emotive activity and scruple, was a familiar attitude of his conscience' (476). But the kind of revelation he has been granted would, he knows, be interpreted very sceptically in this world, as he imagines Sir Hugo's comments: 'A consumptive Jew, possessed by a fanaticism which obstacles and hastening death intensified, had fixed on Deronda as the antitype of some visionary image, the offspring of wedded hope and despair' (474). Typology constructs but it also – as Strauss showed – deconstructs. The type is fulfilled in the antitype which in turn has been foreshadowed in the type; like double mirrors each reflects the other. But as for the ground on which this is based, that, writes the Gentile debunker Hans Meyrick, is 'the world-supporting elephant' or rather it could be called a 'mystery' – 'a sort of gas which is likely to be continually supplied by the decomposition of the elephants' (598). Under the influence of this scepticism, which is part of his Gentile inheritance, Deronda desperately seeks sound empirical reasons, 'plainly discernible links' (478), for Mordecai's influence upon him.

The other hypothesis for Deronda's future comes from Mordecai, his spiritual as opposed to his worldly mentor. This is based on a Cabbalistic vision of unity and growth:

> 'The world grows, and its frame is knit together by the growing soul; dim, dim at first, then clearer and more clear, the consciousness discerns remote stirrings. As thoughts move within us darkly, and shake us before they are fully discerned – so events – so beings: they are knit with us in the growth of the world. You have risen within me like a thought not fully spelled: my soul is shaken before the words are all there. The rest will come – it will come.' (468)

The whole and the parts, the world and the soul, thoughts and events, work together – without priority – into clearer and clearer relationship and definition. It is, like the *Shemah*, another description of the hermeneutic circle, a mystical version of the act of interpretation itself, through which everything achieves meaning and significance. Out of that divine influx in the darkness 'before there is a vision to interpret', which Deronda glimpsed in Frankfurt, grows this unitary cosmic vision of which he is a part, 'a thought not fully spelled'. Within this unity the relation of type and antitype is a form of spiritual parenthood and childbirth, superseding the genetic and patriarchal descent whose absence has made this possible, as Deronda is formed like a hypothesis: 'the sense of spiritual perpetuation in another resembles that maternal transference of self' (462). What is being brought into being is Deronda's spiritual, as opposed to his dubious Gentile, genealogy and this is defined in terms of Cabbalistic metempsychosis: 'souls are born again and again in new bodies till they are perfected and purified, and a soul liberated from a worn-out body may join the fellow-soul that needs it' (501). In a later version, the hypothesis becomes a prayer which we utter just as we fulfil other people's prayers (537).

These, then, are the two paradigms, the secular and the spiritual, out of which the possible hypotheses of his life emerge. And Deronda is the only character who can mediate between them in his long meditations. To the question mark over Mordecai's visionary excitability and his readiness to 'read outward facts as fulfilment' (477), for example, Deronda responds with his own sceptical scrutiny of the scientific paradigm, that alternative net for containing and interpreting the universe. 'Men may dream in demonstrations, and cut out an illusory world in the shape of axioms, definitions, and propositions, with a final exclusion of fact signed Q.E.D.' (478). It certainly seems that the typology being used by Mordecai to link past, present, and future, runs counter to the empirical assumptions of causality, but in this, her most ambitious novel, George Eliot is not prepared to divorce the interpretative modes of religion and science, the research of Casaubon and Lydgate. To acknowledge their common basis has been, in one sense, the foundation of her fictional experiments from the beginning. Here, in confirmation, Mordecai's 'exultation' as he discovers his antitype, we are told, 'was not widely different from that of the experimenter, bending over the first stirrings of change that correspond to what in the fervour of concentrated prevision his thought has foreshadowed' (460). As Northrop Frye has recently explained, the causal thinker can only understand phenomena by thinking of them as effects for which he must find the causes. 'These causes are the antitypes of their effects, that is, revelations of the real meaning of the existence of the effects . . . An exposition founded on causality, however, is likely for the sake of greater clarity to reverse this movement again, and proceed forward from cause to effect. Hence causality and typology are rhetorically similar in form, and typology might in fact be thought of as an analogy of causality.'[15] As Hans Meyrick might have said, it depends on whether you are talking of 'the effects of present causes' or 'the present causes of past effects' (597).

Each paradigm, however, deconstructs the other. Mathematics becomes 'a dreamland where nothing is but what is not' (478), while typology becomes a form of wish-fulfilment. Yet, as we have seen, this helps to bring them closer together. The question Deronda finally asks is, can their positive elements be combined, can Mordecai's visionary excitement co-exist with a clear awareness of cause-and-effect consequences? Is it possible to transcend the conflict upon which Savonarola was martyred? Deronda's tentative answer is George Eliot's most all-embracing synthesis of religious typology and scientific hypothesis:

perhaps [Mordecai's] might be one of those natures where a wise estimate of consequences is fused in the fires of that passionate belief which determines the consequences it believes in. The inspirations of the world have come in that way too: even strictly-measuring science could hardly have got on without that forecasting ardour which feels the agitations of discovery beforehand, and has faith in its preconception that surmounts many failures of experiment. And in relation to human motives and actions, passionate belief has a fuller efficacy. Here enthusiasm may have the validity of proof, and, happening in one soul, give the type of what will one day be general. (477)

The hypothesis creates the reality it predicts, the type foreshadows the antitype through which it is fulfilled. Both reverse the logic of cause and effect, and it is upon this reverse logic that the Jewish reality is constructed (and all that this implies for the realistic novel). Deronda turns out eventually to have been born a Jew – a birthright quickly denied him – but the fact has been pre-empted by the claims of Mordecai's spiritual parenthood and Deronda's response, the present causes of past effects and a far surer sign of his Jewish inheritance than the precise details of his circumcision which pre-occupy some of the irredeemably 'realistic' readers of *Daniel Deronda*. As Deronda seeks to reconcile his two genealogies – the Gentile and the Cabbalistic – we see the Jew who is also the 'accomplished Egyptian' preparing himself as a new kind of deliverer to the modern world. An earlier Victorian version of this synthesis occurs in *In Memoriam*, in the merging of the typology of evolutionary science with that of Christian faith in Hallam, that 'noble type', 'To which the whole creation moves'.[16]

The social and political implications of the deliverance he will offer are spelled out by Mordecai at the Hand and Banner, when he rebuts the arguments of both the rational and the strictly orthodox Jews with his own form of mystical rationalism, which perceives 'more and more of the hidden bonds that bind and consecrate change as a dependent growth' (490). This is true development. And it is based on the constant return of Judaism, that most hermeneutical of all religions, to its founding records and covenant: 'The native spirit of our tradition', says Mordecai, 'was not to stand still, but to use records as a seed, and draw out the compressed virtues of law and prophecy; and while the Gentile . . . was reading the letter of our law as a dark inscription . . . our Masters were still enlarging and illuminating with fresh-fed interpretation' (493–4). Development as inevitable progress is rejected in favour of an organic process linked to continual interpretation and re-interpretation. If this lapses, then the vision is lost and that is why 'the organic centre' of Judaism (494) needs to be revived so that the world can rediscover a sense of divine unity. This process of rediscovery, interpretation, and growth is expressed by Mordecai in a complex image: 'What is needed is the leaven – what is needed is the seed of fire. The heritage of Israel is beating in the pulses of millions; it lives in their veins as a power without understanding . . . it is the inborn half of memory, moving as in a dream among writings on the walls, which it sees dimly but cannot divide into speech. Let the torch of visible community be lit!' (497). The soul of Israel is the 'seed among the tombs' (484), the 'seed of fire' which creates both new growth and the light by which the dark inscriptions of the past can be deciphered and recovered.[17] It is a process of genesis and revelation, the bringing together of activities which must not be separated. The ambitiousness of *Daniel Deronda* is to suggest that the seed of fire might even be brought to illuminate the lives of the Gentile aristocrats at the Abbey. In their Ruskinian discussion (ch. 35) of restoration and improvement, the landowners discuss the pros and cons of renovating their stately homes, while Deronda respectfully removes his hat in the old chapel which has been turned into a stable.

Each phase of Gwendolen's career culminates, as we have seen, in a scene of violent contradiction. The Hermione theatricals, the gambling at Leubronn, her wedding-day, each dramatises in the form of a tableau a public triumph which turns abruptly into a private nightmare. Each moment of 'exultation' carries its 'infusion of dread'. It is as if the disrupted dialectic of life – the self is everything, the self is nothing – which Gwendolen embodies in its most primitive form is briefly re-activated and the self becomes horrifyingly aware of what it is capable of in the absence of any redemptive vision. This is the dark side of Mordecai's prophetic second-sight which also acknowledges the 'remote strivings' of consciousness, 'As thoughts move within us darkly, and shake us before they are fully discerned' (468). In Gwendolen's case, the series of frozen tableaux points ahead to its end term, the drowning off Genoa, the antitype and fulfilment of the mysterious panel at Offendene. The question all these scenes pose, but the last one supremely, is that asked by Deronda in the first paragraph of the novel: 'was the good or the evil genius dominant in those beams?'. Which guiding spirit will triumph in Gwendolen's psycho-machia? This is the struggle for the soul of England that Deronda and Grandcourt are engaged in at the centre of *Daniel Deronda*, and the answer is to be found in the typologies the two men embody, express, and use to influence and control the heroine. Gwendolen's early career, on the other hand, is a wilful and paradoxical attempt to reject all typologies and predictions. 'Clairvoyantes are often wrong', she tells Rex Gascoigne, 'they foresee what is likely. I am not fond of what is likely; it is always dull. I do what is unlikely' (61). But her future is already in the past, on the painted panel at Offendene; it is a question of which man interprets it correctly by bringing into existence what it foreshadows.

The implications of this central triangular relationship spread far beyond the rivalries of a genteel misalliance. Grandcourt, as the type of decadent aristocracy, sits at the centre of the web of imperial power through which Britain controls the world, 'fitted as possessors of the most truth and the most tonnage', as George Eliot wrote later in *Impressions of Theophrastus Such*, 'to carry our purer religion over the world and convert mankind to our way of thinking'.[18] As the final version of this type which represents the withered simulacrum of a culture, Grandcourt is the focus for the novelist's devastating anatomy of British assumptions, values, and class-system. Deronda's empire which he is belatedly discovering for much of the novel is, in contrast, that of the spiritual realm, defined eclectically through Judaic and Cabbalistic lore. The motivating force here is not 'Buy cheap, sell dear', but the transmission of a spiritual and unifying vision to the world. The radical irony of *Daniel Deronda* consists of the way in which these two visions mirror, parody, and deconstruct each other at all levels of the novel. The aristocratic obsession with lineage, inheritance, and property in one half of the novel, for example, is translated into the transmigration of souls, spiritual rebirth, and sacred texts in the other. The relationship is established through an elaborate system of punning between the material and the spiritual, what Feuerbach called a 'deuteroscopy' of theology and pathology.[19] It is an enormously expanded version of the device employed in that pastiche of the temperance tract, 'Janet's Repentance', by means of the pun upon 'spirit'. Occasionally, the two realms come into collision: Klesmer – a cultural version of Deronda's messianism – appears out of the east and wins the prize of Catherine Arrowpoint from her aristocratic suitors; or, in reverse, the mysterious and predatory count – a shadowy version of Grandcourt – enters the Jewish world to acquire singers and actresses for his own sinister pleasures. But for the most part, the worlds are kept separate and the reader becomes hyper-sensitive to the way each acts as both figure and ground to the other. It is another form of second-sight, a subtle anamorphism, and it persists to the very end of the novel, with Sir Hugo still imposing his own sentimental ending to the story now that 'the unsuitable husband [had] made his exit in such excellent time' (710).

The worlds intersect most challengingly in the double appropriation of Gwendolen's character. As far as Grandcourt is concerned, that image which disturbed his meditative inertia has to be defined, controlled, and subdued into the type of his wife, the 'delicate vessel' chosen to bear his son and heir. 'He had not repented of his marriage; it had really brought more of aim into his life, new objects to exert his will upon; and he had not repented of his choice. His taste was fastidious, and Gwendolen satisfied it' (543). But it is only by constant surveillance that he can 'monitor' her behaviour, check the slightest divergence from the type, and so satisfy the aestheticism of the will. The crucial skill in this enterprise is to know how to see and be seen: 'If Grandcourt cared to keep any one under his power he saw them out of the corner of his long narrow eyes, and if they went behind him, he had a constructive process by which he knew what they were doing there' (384). As Gwendolen begins to understand the implications of her marriage, the terrible price to be paid for her gamble, she develops a superstitious dread of his 'power of suspicious divination' (565) into her motives. And as she does so, she congeals into the type of consort that satisfies him: 'she might as well have tried to defy the texture of her nerves and the palpitation of her heart . . . She sat in her splendid attire, like a white image of helplessness, and he seemed to gratify himself with looking at her' (417–8). His appropriation is so powerful because she partly shares his interpretation of her role and the world, and so the double hermeneutic becomes a terrifying instrument of implicit control. 'No chemical process shows a more wonderful activity than the transforming influence of the thoughts we imagine to be going on in another' (394), as the exchange of glances with which the novel opened has shown.

The specific reason for Grandcourt's power over Gwendolen is that he knows she entered marriage in the full knowledge of Mrs Glasher's existence. This is the hidden interpretative key to her behaviour which he deploys tacitly to suppress any incipient rebellion and retain his 'empire of fear' (395). He would, we are told, have made an excellent colonial governor (552). Gwendolen quickly comes to feel as helpless under his mastery as under the will of 'a crab or a boa-constrictor which goes on pinching or crushing without alarm at thunder' (394). But, whatever her impression, Grandcourt's power is dialectical: it depends on her response. The point is made casually several times about the supercilious, *savoir-vivre* attitude of the aristocratic world in the novel. Grandcourt might 'not care a languid curse for any one's admiration; but this state of not-caring, just as much as desire, required its related object – namely, a world of admiring or envying spectators' (544). Similarly, Grandcourt's control of Gwendolen can only be validated by a resistance she dare not express but which he needs to be conscious of; this is the challenge which titillates his sadism and which has roused him from his deathly torpor, this 'contentment that his wife should be in a temper which would dispose her to fly out if she dared' (544). He plays upon the two sides of her nature, her wilfulness and her fear, with subtle expertise, rousing and suppressing her pride, goading and silencing her rebellion, using both his secret knowledge and the understated codes of good breeding. 'Oblige me in future by not showing whims like a mad woman in a play' (417). Grandcourt is exacerbating so as to control that iridescence of her contradictory character which challenged him in the first place, and which must now be frozen into the desired type. As with Janet Dempster's less refined torture, this incited war in the members is a necessary part of Gwendolen's salvation: 'In fact, she was undergoing a sort of discipline for the refractory which, as little as possible like conversion, bends half the self with a terrible strain, and exasperates the unwillingness of the other half' (553).

Since power is dialectical, Grandcourt, too, is gambling when he contorts Gwendolen to his will. As the demands of his sadism grow, 'led on by an ominous fatality', she has to be roused and tempted to ever more daring acts of rebellion which she must not be allowed to express. Grandcourt raises the stakes by letting her know that he was aware of her meeting with his mistress and mother of his putative son and heir, in order to aggravate her jealousy 'and yet smite it with a more absolute dumbness' (555). But his divination fails to extend to the other, countervailing force in her character that is slowly being elicited and developed under Deronda's tutelage. Here Grandcourt in the amorality of his power is both innocent and vulnerable. 'He had correctly divined one half of Gwendolen's dread – all that related to her personal pride, and her perception that his will must conquer hers; but the remorseful half, even if he had known of her broken promise, was as much out of his imagination as the other side of the moon' (554). We glimpsed such a moment of obtuseness in his relations with Mrs Glasher when he experienced, ominously, a sense of powerlessness in the face of her wilful submission in a desperation which he called madness. Gwendolen too is being pushed towards a similarly extreme contradiction in which submission and rebellion are indistinguishable (398), her iridescence congealed into the perfect type of his wife. This is the unknown territory into which Grand-court's gamble is leading him. Like Browning's duke, he is baffled by the wife he has purchased; and the reason is embodied in her relationship with that fop Deronda who is as much 'an unexplored continent' (384) to Grandcourt as Grandcourt is to Deronda.

In this world of watching and being watched, a genteel world in which nothing momentous appears to happen, Deronda too has Gwendolen under close surveillance, but with a stillness which denotes receptivity. He also is her 'monitor' (417), and gradually becomes her mentor and confessor, as he seeks to counteract 'the hardening effects' of Grandcourt's humiliating galvanic experiments (394). He too becomes part of the fabric of her nerves, but in his case she wants him to know everything about her without the need for telling him (400), so that he will become 'a part of her conscience' (386), and finally her 'priest' (401). This is where the significant action of this epic of empire increasingly comes to focus: who occupies Gwendolen's mind?[20] Deronda also comes to realise that her betrayal of Mrs Glasher could be 'a key by which to interpret her more clearly' (404), but instead of exploiting this as a form of blackmail and control he seizes upon her self-reproach as a possible means of salvation. It is still a deployment of one part of the self against the other, but instead of freezing rebellion against submission in a perpetual torment, Deronda – as he explains in the library at the Abbey which is 'as warmly odorous as a private chapel in which the censers had been swinging' (419) – uses it as a means of controlling her future actions, a form of spiritual exercise in which the monitor will become fully internalised. The dread of performing some terrible action which Grandcourt has played on must now be countered by the fear of increasing her bitter remorse. 'Take your fear as a safeguard. It is like quickness of hearing. It may make consequences passionately present to you. Try to take hold of your sensibility, and use it as if it were a faculty, like vision' (422). Deronda's spiritual therapy is based on his growing acceptance of Mordecai's typological thinking, but here in the Gentile world he is applying it in a preventative way. The image of the painting, the type of what Gwendolen most desires and dreads, must be used as a vision of the consequences to be avoided; the antitype when it occurs will then be an image of the dread and not a fulfilment of the temptation.

As the novel moves towards the enactment of the horrifying picture, the conflict between the two interpretations of her character, now thoroughly internalised, becomes extreme. She is convinced she will be finally forced by Grandcourt into an irrevocable crime: 'When my blood is fired I can do daring things – take any leap; but that makes me frightened at myself' (422). But the picture is ambiguous. Will the leap be away from the crime or away from her criminal desires? Gwendolen can imagine no form of deliverance as she seeks Deronda's help more and more desperately. 'What release, but death? Not her own death . . . It seemed more possible that Grandcourt should die: – and yet not likely. The power of tyranny in him seemed a power of living in the presence of any wish that he should die' (563–4). This is the nature of his power in all its abstractness: he lives *because* she wishes him to die. Her desire for vengeance gives him not only life but the power to kill her, a reflex of her criminal desire: 'The thought of his dying would not subsist: it turned as with a dream-change into the terror that she should die with his throttling fingers on her neck avenging that thought' (564). She persists in her attempts to see Deronda, but Grandcourt's patience has run out. He announces his decision to take Gwendolen yachting in the Mediterranean; *le jeu ne va plus* and the roulette wheel is now spinning. Which man's interpretation of her contradictory character will prevail? Each has powers of divination into one side of her nature as they seek to counter the 'infection' (565) of the other, yet the larger irony of George Eliot's *Divine Comedy* is that the two men – torturer and confessor – are working together to spark the heroine's spirit into life.

The three protagonists proceed to Genoa to fulfil their destinies. Grandcourt relishes a yachting expedition through the Mediterranean because of 'its dreamy do-nothing absolutism, unmolested by social demands', a kind of anticipatory death-in-life. He can now focus entirely on the subjection of his wife: 'he wanted to feel more securely that she was his to do as as he liked with, and to make her feel it also' (622). Here, at the culmination of her brilliant career, Gwendolen's triumph and terror again come terrifyingly together in a tableau which symbolises the two dimensions of her character. On the one hand, there is the elegant yacht on which she and Grandcourt appear to act out to perfection their marital and aristocratic roles; on the other, beyond the wirework of social forms, there is the vast macrocosm of the sea and the sky. But there has been a crucial change in her reaction: now it is the world of social forms, contracting further under Grandcourt's control, which terrifies and the larger landscape which brings hope. 'Inarticulate prayers, no more definite than a cry, often swept out from her into the vast silence, unbroken except by her husband's breathing or the plash of the waves or the creaking of the masts' (628). As he uses his own refined versions of the thumbscrew and the rack (634), the torturer is forcing her to turn outwards to the moon and the stars, 'with less of awed loneliness than was habitual to her – nay, with a vague impression that in this mighty frame of things there might be some preparation of rescue for her' (629). She dreams of Deronda and he materialises on the steps of their hotel, raises his hat, and passes on.

Each monitor is offering her his own psychic model, his own interpretative key. In *Felix Holt*, the male protagonists became 'commentaries' on the heroine's fate, while here each man becomes a 'medium' through which Gwendolen perceives the world: 'The beings closest to us, whether in love or hate, are often virtually our interpreters of the world, and some feather-headed gentleman or lady . . . may be acting as a melancholy theory of life in the minds of those who live with them – like a piece of yellow and wavy glass that distorts form and makes colour an affliction.' In George Eliot's final novel, human relationships are in this way defined in more and more explicitly hermeneutic terms. The two men are 'mediums' also in psychic terms, clairvoyants predicting a future they are seeking to

realise. The distorting window Grandcourt provides turns Gwendolen's life into 'a promenade through a pantheon of ugly idols' (626),
and her only corrective is to try to perceive the world from the point of
view of her 'terrible-browed angel': 'she had learned to see all her acts
through the impression they would make on Deronda: whatever relief
might come to her, she could not sever it from the judgment of her that
would be created in his mind' (627). As the climax is anticipated in
clearer and clearer detail, the question is what kind of deliverance is
possible? Or, more specifically, through which medium will the crisis
be interpreted? Deronda offers remorse before commission, the
safeguard of a vision of consequences, which is beginning to prompt
her 'inarticulate prayers'. As her religious sense flickers into being in
this way, Grandcourt cultivates in her 'a constructive vindictiveness,
an imaginary annihilation of the detested object, something like the
hidden rites of vengeance with which the persecuted have made a
dark vent for their rage, and soothed their suffering into dumbness'
(627). The religious vision of consequences and the sacrilegious vision
of revenge come to be balanced in her mind in a precise, antithetical
equilibrium. The deed will be committed in a dream, but its effects
will be real – 'instead of darkness, daylight; instead of satisfied hatred,
the dismay of guilt; instead of freedom, the palsy of a new terror – a
white dead face from which she was for ever trying to flee and for ever
held back' (627).

'Passion is of the nature of seed' (626), comments the narrator, and
these are the primitive seeds of selfhood which find expression in the
images which the male protagonists are seeking to elicit and shape
according to their very different typologies, that of the will and that of
the spirit. And at this point of perfect equilibrium in the heroine's
psychomachia, Grandcourt and Deronda become fully internalised:
'In Gwendolen's consciousness Temptation and Dread met and
stared like two pale phantoms, each seeing itself in the other – each
obstructed by its own image; and all the while her fuller self beheld the
apparitions and sobbed for deliverance from them' (628). It is an
extraordinary image of opposition and reciprocation between the
'two pale phantoms' which validate each other in a Manichean
nightmare. But deliverance of some kind becomes inevitable when
Grandcourt decides to turn the screw tighter. From her gilded cage in
London, to the yacht in the Mediterranean, now the prison gets even
smaller as husband and wife go out in a sailing-boat in which his
control will be absolute. In proof of this, he hands over the tiller to

Gwendolen in his final dangerous titillation of the will: 'As she sat guiding the tiller under her husband's eyes, doing just what he told her, the strife within her seemed like her own effort to escape from herself' (635). She holds the tiller, he gives commands; the parody of marital union epitomises their aristocratic life as they sail into the bay of Genoa in this culminating but cryptic scene. The climax is determined in one sentence: 'Yet suddenly Gwendolen let her hands fall, and said in a scarcely audible tone, "God help me!"' It is the moment of appeal ('That selfsame moment I could pray') to which the echoes of *The Ancient Mariner* have been pointing and to which both men have conducted her, the moment when the 'fuller self' turns beyond the conflict of temptation and dread, and – to Grandcourt's bafflement – accepts its helplessness. 'I shall like nothing better than this' (635). The self abandons itself. But with Gwendolen's prayer Grandcourt's power has come to an end, the curse is lifted, and, as we discover in the next chapter, he dies.

Meanwhile, in Genoa, Deronda is about to be born into the world (or, according to the motto to chapter 50 from Browning's *Paracelsus*, reborn at 'His true time's advent'). It is to be a difficult birth. As he waits word from his mysterious mother, his life of suspended animation reaches a crescendo of sympathetic inactivity. He too takes a boat in the bay, but instead of the world contracting under the will, his meditations expand to include the whole novel. He thinks of Mordecai and Mirah, of the Spanish Jews in exile, of his ancestry, and of Gwendolen, while in the background occurs the struggle for Italian independence. But he looks out on an uncreated world, 'on the double, faintly pierced darkness of the sea and the heavens', where action is impossible 'because the point of view that life would make for him was in that agitating moment of uncertainty which is close upon decision' (580). When the uncertainty is finally resolved, the dialectics of the novel insist that it is the opposite of what is expected. If Grandcourt's moment of supreme triumph is simultaneously the moment of his annihilation, so Deronda's birth is a painful death of rejection. Like one of Dickens's will-less heroes, Arthur Clennam say, he discovers the secret of his original wounding: his mother did not want him to be born and declared him dead. To escape from her father's patriarchal Judaism and its coercive typology – the rigid 'pattern' by which 'a woman's heart . . . must be pressed small, like Chinese feet' (588) – she agreed to marry to achieve her independence. She pretends to be what she is not in order to become,

ironically, an actress. It is another version of the will desperately
seeking its freedom at all costs, even through submission; and out of
this conflict Deronda was born, as she sought a career on the stage
'with no more ties, but such as I could free myself from' (591). The
success and freedom she achieves, however, as the great Alcharisi – 'I
was living a myriad lives in one' (584) – has become a parody of a true
relation between the individual and her kind. In the search for
selfhood, everything she does has become a form of acting: 'experience
immediately passed into drama, and she acted her own emotions'
(586). But now, in her fatal illness, there rises into memory from
beneath the regal Gentile trappings, 'the poor, solitary, forsaken
remains of self' (593), which have forced her to tell Deronda he is a
Jew in an act of exculpation.

The harrowing confession of the dying Princess is the most extreme
version in the novel of the self, always the female self, seeking salvation
on its own terms in a world of fixed types. In the process, the women
are all demonised: Gwendolen becomes Lamia, Lydia Glasher was
the Medusa, and now the Princess appears as Melusina in these
carefully staged scenes. Her confession is a re-statement of the
dilemma debated at the Hand and Banner: should the Jews preserve
themselves by separating or assimilating? Mordecai sought to
mediate there, just as Deronda does here as his mother pleads with
him to mediate between her two lives: 'You will come between me and
the dead' (618–9). Now he begins to shape his future more explicitly
and the way in which he does this, as he listens to his mother, is to
experience with sudden intensity the growing up which has been
denied him. Even before the meeting 'he felt some revival of his
boyhood' (582); when she appears he blushes and trembles nervously
when she declares her motherhood, becoming 'breathless' when she
announces, 'I did not want a child' (584). He is witnessing,
participating in, 'the strange mental conflict under which it seemed
that he had been brought into the world' (587) – then rejected and
handed over to the Gentiles. He has now to bring himself back to life
by recovering his lost inheritance, and he does this by angrily rejecting
his mother's self-justifying interpretation of his life. Each of the
decisions by which she tried to determine his birthright is now
challenged and revised by Deronda on his own behalf, as he finally
and forcibly commits himself to a series of choices. 'He could not have
imagined beforehand how he would come to say that which he had
never hitherto admitted' (585). As he challenges his mother's

account, he is bringing to birth his true self – already planted by
Mordecai, his spiritual parent – by choosing to become what he is.
'But that stronger Something has determined that I shall be all the
more the grandson whom also you willed to annihilate' (618). Against
her will but through her rebellion, she has given birth to the Deliverer
who seeks to reconcile the Judaic tradition she despises with the
Gentile world to which she handed him over in a new world vision,
separation with communication. The crucial, reconciling act is
Deronda's re-interpretation of her confession through which will and
destiny become one, as he brings himself into existence. It is a skill he is
to need at the impending climax of the novel when Grandcourt, in
contrast, is about to leave off doing everything.

Still overwrought after the second interview with his mother,
Deronda is pitched into the climax of the novel, the drowning of
Grandcourt and Gwendolen's confession. In her characteristic way
George Eliot does not depict the drowning directly. Deronda listens
unobtrusively to various kinds of inconclusive evidence, preparing
himself for his most difficult interpretative task. The ambiguity as to
what actually happened – 'Few details came to light' (641) – finally
shifts the centre of significance to Gwendolen's consciousness. This is
the novelist's culminating dramatisation of the crisis of interpretation,
and once again the word crisis is inseparable from its cognate,
judgment, though never in such startlingly Dantesque terms.
Gwendolen emerges from the sea, 'pale as one of the sheeted dead,
shivering, with wet hair streaming . . . as if she had waked up in a
world where some judgment was impending' (638–9). Deronda must
now listen to her distraught confession. As in the scenes with his
mother, his responses and reactions are crucial to the unfolding of the
confession and its results for this, as we have seen repeatedly, is the
most intimate and intense form of reciprocal interpretation. In both
cases, Deronda applies a hermeneutic of suspicion: having rejected his
mother's self-justifying confession in order to re-interpret himself into
his messianic role, he now rejects Gwendolen's self-condemnation so
that she can be redeemed. The crucial question remains: which
typology has been fulfilled? She must be persuaded to replace
Grandcourt's interpretative code with Deronda's.

Substantially what we get in the confession is an account of the drowning from a Gwendolen categorically convinced of her own guilt. She has murdered Grandcourt: 'His face will not be seen above the water again . . . Not by any one else – only by me – a dead face – I shall never get away from it' (642). In his final act of the will, his self-annihilation, Grandcourt has apparently triumphed over his victim who is damned to an eternity of his control, trapped in the frozen tableau of the painting, the fulfilled antitype of her guilty desires. Deronda is appalled by the responsibility he has to assume. The Deliverer of the Jews has suddenly to become the personal deliverer of Gwendolen: 'He was not a priest. He dreaded the weight of this woman's soul flung upon his own with imploring dependence' (642). The confessor is repeatedly shattered by what he hears and yet he knows that she must be allowed to tell her story if there is to be any hope of redemption: 'And all the while he felt as if he were putting his name to a blank paper which might be filled up terribly' (643). This is an extension of the birth-pangs he experienced with his mother, but now the messianic role is being tested and validated through the suffering individual. He hands himself over to her (imputed) better self in an act of faith and love – 'He must let her mind follow its own need' (645) – just as Grandcourt had gambled on her evil will in the bay of Genoa, supremely confident in the sustaining power of her desire for vengeance.

In her confession of guilt, Gwendolen acknowledges that the only countervailing influence had been Deronda: 'And if I had told you, and knew it was in your mind, it would have less power over me' (645). This is what she is now belatedly achieving. As she circles back to the actual drowning, the 'two creatures' (643) within her, temptation and dread, become more and more finely balanced and interdependent, as we have seen. Implicit in such unresolvable conflicts, as early as *Scenes of Clerical Life*, has been the Pauline war in the members of Romans chapter 7 ('for the good that I would I do not: but the evil which I would not, that I do') with its desperate appeal: 'who shall deliver me from the body of this death?' But all she had been able to do was repeat Deronda's words about remorse, and then the temptation returned and the oscillation continued. As with Janet Dempster, Maggie Tulliver, Romola, and now Gwendolen, this represents the removal of any ground in which the self can come to rest as it spins out of control with no possibility of closure. As she re-lives this moment of despair in her confession, Gwendolen repeats one of the few details recorded by the narrator previously: 'I remember then letting go the tiller and saying "God help me!" But then I was forced to take it up again and go on'. The evil thoughts return and Grandcourt drowns and she is damned: 'I only knew that I saw my wish outside me' (648). The motto to this chapter from *The Ancient Mariner* underlines the irrevocable guilt ('The pang, the curse with which they died, / Had never passed away . . .') but also implies the appeal, the prayer, she is finally – thanks to her two monitors – forced to make beyond the endless dialectic of the self. This is what delivers her from Grandcourt's control. It is, once again, the influx in the darkness before there is a vision of any kind to interpret. Deronda has now to elicit its meaning.

Gwendolen narrates and interprets these climactic events as an expression of the alternating forces within the self. First, the drowning is related according to one law of the members in which she sees herself as the guilty agent, succumbing to temptation ('and I held my hand, and my heart said "Die!" – and he sank'). Then, there follows the reaction of dread: 'and I felt "It is done – I am wicked, I am lost!" . . . I was leaping away from myself. I would have saved him then. I was leaping from my crime, and there it was – close to me as I fell – there was the dead face – dead, dead. It can never be altered' (748). What the account represents is the inability of the narrative sequence to depict the contradictory fluctuations of Gwendolen's emotions and the manner in which they have determined her actions. The question of her precise responsibility, which way she jumps, is never answered. As we saw earlier, Macbeth's rhetoric 'referred to the clumsy necessities of action and not to the subtler possibilities of feeling'. In a moment there *is* room 'for the outlash of a murderous thought and the sharp backward stroke of repentance'. Just as Maggie Tulliver runs away with Stephen Guest and does not, so Gwendolen in a much more ambiguous scene both murders Grandcourt and tries to save him. Since the ambiguity is never cleared up, it is true to say that both typologies are fulfilled.

Now, for the second time, Deronda applies the hermeneutics of suspicion to a confession, in order to disentangle the events from Gwendolen's interpretation of them. But since all event is interpretation, or as the narrator has commented earlier, 'all meanings, we know, depend on the key of interpretation' (51), this is impossible, especially when there are no other witnesses. He has therefore to interpret her interpretation as evidence against her own testimony: 'for Gwendolen's confession, for the very reason that her conscience made her dwell on the determining power of her evil thoughts, convinced him the more that there had been throughout a counterbalancing struggle of her better will' (648). Definitive judgment is impossible and quickly becomes almost incidental: 'But her remorse was the precious sign of a recoverable nature.' The culminating image is, as with St Paul, the crucifixion which promises deliverance from the war in the members. 'Deronda could not offer one word to diminish that sacred aversion to her worse self – that thorn-pressure which must come with the crowning of the sorrowful Better, suffering because of the Worse' (649). The judgment which Gwendolen accepts and which begins the process of redemption remains, of course, hypothetical; and this is thrown into relief by the fact that the only coherent account of the climactic events is in the form of Gwendolen's own confession, the crucial narrative kernel, which incriminates her. Although 'fitful' and 'wandering' (643), it is a narrative of cause and effect, guilty desires leading to criminal action. It is the typology of the will. In any narrative such an explanation is bound to be powerful. Deronda, however, elicits her cause-and-effect account so that it will invalidate itself by its over-determined coherence. Instead of causes he concentrates on effects: her remorse and conviction of guilt is the ground for not accepting the narrative. She is innocent because she insists she is guilty. The hermeneutic of suspicion prepares the way for the hermeneutic of restoration. In the terms of Hans Meyrick's paradoxes, 'antithesis is the sole clue to events' which can best be understood as 'present causes of past effects' (597). In this logic, the drowning of Grandcourt fulfils as antitype the painted panel but as a warning which offers choice.

In her fine discussion of these climactic scenes, E. S. Shaffer points out that the Pascalian wager on the existence of God is here powerfully redefined for the nineteenth century in terms of 'the central myth of our civilization', the freedom of the will: 'the premises are atheistic; the assumption of moral responsibility is a myth; belief in the myth is an unmitigated good ... Moreover, the power of the myth is affirmed, in that although Gwendolen's certainty of guilt is a compulsion for her, for Deronda it is evident that she has made a moral choice. Both are possible because she has been struggling in moral terms.'[21] This myth is the ultimate hypothesis, the belief which, as in the case of Mordecai's vision, 'determines the consequences it believes in'. In *Daniel Deronda*, George Eliot does not resolve the impasse of interpretation by switching into the symbolic mode. Here, the affirmation of the self's grounding in the freedom of choice is a much more gradual and painful process: Gwendolen has to be brought to accept freely Deronda's interpretation of the drowning as her own. The difficulty is that she 'identified [Deronda] with the struggling regenerative process in her which had begun with his action' (717); and yet to assert her freedom (and his) he must sever their relationship. The steps by which this relationship is redefined and the myth articulated are in the same Christian trinitarian terms (with Cabbalistic additions) as George Eliot used in the relationships of Dinah and Hetty, Savonarola and Romola. To emphasise its centrality, the process is gone through twice, once in Genoa and again in London. Each is a recapitulation of the whole novel.

In Genoa, Deronda appears to Gwendolen first as the judge to whom she confesses her sins, then he becomes the Christ who shares her guilt and her crucifixion ('that sacred aversion to her worst self'), and finally he leaves her while declaring his continuing presence: 'It could never be my impulse to forsake you' (652). In London, where Gwendolen is living 'through and through again the terrible history of her temptations' (740), the process has to be repeated and brought to a conclusion. The proceeding from God the Father, to God the Son, to God the Holy Spirit, has to be gone through as a form of moral psychotherapy. Again, the first stage is based upon Gwendolen's need for the judgment of that 'severe angel' Deronda (716), which had begun in Leubronn: 'It is hard to say', comments the narrator, 'how much we could forgive ourselves if we were secure from judgment by an other whose opinion is the breathing-medium of all our joy . . . In this way our brother may be in the stead of God to us, and his opinion which has pierced even to the joints and marrow, may be our virtue in the making' (709). She accepts his judgment, confident of a future 'where she would be continually assimilating herself to some type that he would hold before her' (740), not realising that this has to be fully internalised as her psychotherapy comes to an end. Then he tells her with trepidation of his forthcoming marriage – to one who has taken her place in *his* soul 'as a beloved type' (692) – and his messianic destiny. She responds with her cry of dereliction ('I am forsaken') which echoes through these chapters as a counterpoint to the deliverance the messiah is offering, and she experiences again the drowning scene. Then in their joint agony they enact a crucifixion. 'Deronda's anguish was intolerable. He could not help himself. He seized her outstretched hands and held them together and kneeled at her feet. She was the victim of his happiness.' In this 'crowning of the sorrowful Better, suffering because of the Worse' (649), they each play both crucifixion roles, forgiving and justifying each other. This is the second gamble, the 'risk' (718), Deronda has had to take to bring Gwendolen's free spirit into being; and his words as he leaves echo Christ's to the disciples: 'I shall be more with you than I used to be' (750). He will now 'live in' her as Mordecai – that transmitter of 'the Ruach-ha-kodesh, the breath of divine thought' (466) – is beginning to live in Deronda (504).

How has Gwendolen's moral selfhood been achieved? In the biblical terms which George Eliot adapts, the answer is – by conviction of sin and remorse, by confession and judgment, by redemptive love and the empowering of the spirit. In the more specific terms of the novel's structure, the answer is by one coercive type, Deronda, complementing and completing what the other, Grandcourt, had begun. The latter offered her through marriage the opportunity for betrayal, the curse of Mrs Glasher, on which her life contracted to the drowning, the fulfilment of her evil wishes. Deronda has redeemed her from this fulfilment but he can only complete the process by betraying her in turn. The shock of his imminent departure returns us to the beginning of the novel, to the heroine's bewildering alternations of agoraphobia and claustrophobia, to the vastness of the world and the minuteness of the self, each seeking for domination. Grandcourt's galvanic experiments played upon her will, rousing it through suppression. Now, on Deronda's news, Gwendolen 'felt herself reduced to a mere speck' as 'the larger destinies of mankind' (747) invade her life: 'she was for the first time feeling the pressure of a vast mysterious movement, for the first time being dislodged from her supremacy in her own world, and getting a sense that her horizon was but a dipping onward of an existence with which her own was revolving' (748). In one sense, what Deronda has released into her life is a glimpse of the other half of the novel, where the spiritual forces which are to rescue the Gentiles are operative, but to the very end the language echoes, while it reverses, that of Grandcourt. 'But here had come a shock which went deeper than personal jealousy – something spiritual and vaguely tremendous that thrust her away, and yet quelled all anger into self-humiliation' (748). This is the moment – the result of their joint experiments – when the primitive psychic forces, the systole and diastole of the self and world, achieve relationship and give birth to the moral being.

For this to be achieved, both the male protagonists have to betray Gwendolen on behalf of the women they, in their very different ways, understand and love. (Gwendolen meets and interviews both Mrs Glasher and Mirah and belatedly recognises this.) They betray her because they can't understand her; her character remains opaque to the end because it encompasses them both. Each man gambles in applying his typology – that of the will, that of the spirit – to this iridescent creature, and both typologies are fulfilled in the drowning scene, the ambiguous antitype. In that fulfilment both men achieve, in contrasting ways, their own apotheosis: the will finds its own self-annihilation, sympathy turns into messianic deliverance, and the two phantoms in her soul are transcended. Then they disappear. The two mentors, the two clairvoyants, are proved both right and wrong, for Gwendolen finally begins to tell her own story which incorporates both of their typologies. What we are left with at the end of George Eliot's epic of empire is the heroine's first religious experience, a glimpse of the true relationship between the self within its own horizon and a plurality of other horizons, the most sophisticated expression of which is Mordecai's vision of the divine unity. From the pulsations of the self, the influxes in the darkness, the mysterious seed-like images, has emerged this embryonic moral being, the self and the world stabilising at last into a world-view which is Gwendolen's own.

Conclusion

Lord Acton praised George Eliot for knowing uniquely how to think or feel as people do who live 'in the grasp' of various systems of thought and belief.[1] It will be clear that one of the aims of this study has been to show that much of the narrative energy of George Eliot's fiction comes from the dismantling of these same theories of life which seek, as they must, to escape their own provisional nature. Whether they are expressed as religious truths, theodicies, family codes of practice, founding historical myths, political programmes, models of vocation, or class ideologies – all are subjected to the hermeneutic of suspicion which reveals their inner contradictions. Representation and interpretation proceed simultaneously. The fictional experiments which elicit these disconfirmations are various, but an essential feature of any comprehensive world-view in George Eliot's fiction is the inevitability of its self-deconstruction. One form, in particular, of the novelist's double hermeneutic epitomises this irony: that in which a character is subjected to his or her own interpretative language and concepts. Whether the narrator is diagnosing the doctors, experimenting on the scientists, or carrying out exegesis on the clergymen, the depth of the irony is proportional to their claims to comprehensiveness.

Individuals, families, societies, are all subjected to the same rigorous scrutiny. In the earlier novels, the relatively stable communities are disturbed by the arrival of aliens, hybrids, or anomalies who challenge the *status quo*. At first ostracised or marginalised, these characters eventually elicit and act out the contradictions within the community which comes in this way to an understanding of its own incarnate history. Then the community is able once more to stabilise its view of the world. In this process, the protagonists – Amos Barton, Hetty Sorrel, Maggie Tulliver – become the scapegoats who not only articulate but exorcise the community's contradictions. The culmination of this tendency occurs in *Romola*, where the sacred rebellion of Savonarola which leads to his betrayal, trial, and execution is cast in the form of an *imitatio Christi*. The acting out of the antagonism of valid claims, the essential conflict of interpretations, is a sacred and sacrificial task in which no one is victor. It is a martyrdom which witnesses to no settled truths but to the onward movement of the dialectic, as world-views cohere and then fragment.

What does this hermeneutic of suspicion finally uncover? The careers of the heroines which act out most explicitly the sequence of the master-plot provide the clearest answer. The temporary coherences they achieve may be the 'adjournments' from Maggie's various crises or the staging-posts of European civilisation Romola passes through, but they all eventually reach the impasse, the oscillation, or vertigo in which meaning and verisimilitude end. In other words, their long detours in which every possible resolution or world-view has been dismantled brings them to an end which is also a beginning. At this point, the hermeneutic of suspicion turns into the hermeneutic of restoration. They break through briefly into another fictional reality, a story unclogged by commentary and interpretation, where they re-create and redefine through their actions the foundational myths from which they and their communities originated in the first place. In one sense, they discover the place where they have been situated all the time.

With the disappearance of the traditional communities after *Silas Marner*, the detours of the master-plot become longer and more tortuous. 'This the fate of poor mortals . . . the state of prostration – the self-abnegation through which the soul must go, and to which perhaps it must again and again return'.[2] There is no way in which the process can be short-circuited; as 'The Lifted Veil' warns, premature knowledge is poison, while probability is the only honey. And the longer the detour and the more fragmented the world in which it takes place, the more symbolic is the final discovery. Romola eventually and briefly achieves a reality where event and meaning are identical, but this recovery of 'a second naiveté' can only be attained through interpretation and its painful disclosures.[3] These pre-hermeneutic moments – like Maggie in the flood, or Daniel Deronda in the synagogue – are the rediscovery of the primal experience before the long martyrdom of life began. It was there all the time – childhood is within us still, and Judaism is beating unrecognised in the pulses of millions – but only the conflicts of interpretation will reveal it.

These fictional detours which the novels and the protagonists represent are, of course, expressions of the hermeneutic circle; like the reading of a text, experience in the world involves a projection of its meaning on the basis of partial understanding. The further we read the more we regress, as that understanding is extended and deepened. As in typology, type and antitype fulfil each other both proleptically and retrospectively though, in George Eliot's fiction, fulfilment can never be more than a continual approximation. But even though the hermeneutic circle never stops turning, there are in the final novels moments of rest, pauses, illuminations, when glimpses of the whole are offered. These epiphanies are not an escape from the circle but momentary crystallisations in which the true relationship of part and whole in the dynamics of interpretation is revealed. Just as Wordsworth looks out from the summit of Snowdon to discover the 'perfect image of a mighty mind' reflected and embodied in nature,[4] so Dorothea's vision of the true social medium in the dawn – people are other and also one – and Deronda's discovery of the *Shemah* are recognitions of the image of a whole of which they are simultaneously a part.

To what extent one considers this a hermeneutic of restoration, depends on where one enters the circle of interpretation. One perceptive Victorian critic, having recognised that George Eliot's religion of humanity 'was essentially incompatible with system, or even with maxim', concluded ironically: 'It is no small victory to show that the godless humanitarianism of Strauss and Feuerbach can be made to appear the living centre of all popular religions.'[5] For this writer, the novels represent not an act of restoration but the triumph of suspicion and substitution. And yet he ends his discussion by praising the novelist's ethics in these terms: 'her books may be read not only with pleasure and profit, but – unless the reader is possessed by squint suspicion – without a conception of the hidden meaning which lies under their plot, their dialogue, and their characters'.[6] In the hermeneutic circle, as in the hypothetical method, suspicion and restoration are difficult to separate. Lord Acton's description, quoted in the Introduction, can now be seen to place the novelist precisely at a particular historical moment in the nineteenth-century crisis of interpretation and belief: 'The sleepless sense that a new code of duty and motive needed to be restored in the midst of the void left by lost sanctions and banished hopes never ceased to stimulate her faculties and to oppress her spirits.'[7] This captures both the heroism and the pathos of George Eliot's career as a writer.

NOTES

INTRODUCTION

1 *The Mill on the Floss*, ed. Gordon S. Haight (Oxford: Clarendon Press, 1980), pp. 452–4.
2 *The George Eliot Letters*, ed. Gordon S. Haight, 9 vols (New Haven: Yale University Press, 1954–78), VI, p. 216.
3 *Felix Holt*, ed. Fred C. Thomson (Oxford: Clarendon Press, 1980), p. 77.
4 *George Eliot Letters*, I, p. 264.
5 Lord Acton in his review of J. W. Cross's *George Eliot's Life* in *The Nineteenth Century*, 17 (1885), 471.
6 See, especially, E. S. Shaffer, '*Kubla Khan' and the Fall of Jerusalem: the Mythological School in Biblical Criticism and Secular Literature 1770–1880* (Cambridge University Press, 1975); Gillian Beer, *Darwin's Plots: Evolutionary Narrative in Darwin, George Eliot and Nineteenth-Century Fiction* (London: Routledge and Kegan Paul, 1983). Other recent studies which emphasise the influence of hermeneutics on Victorian literature include: George P. Landow, *Victorian Types, Victorian Shadows: Biblical Typology in Victorian Literature, Art, and Thought* (London: Routledge and Kegan Paul, 1980); Linda H. Peterson, *Victorian Autobiography: the Tradition of Self-Interpretation* (New Haven: Yale University Press, 1987).
7 See, for example, Hans-Georg Gadamer, *Truth and Method* (London: Sheed and Ward, 1975); or, for a more accessible account, Richard E. Palmer, *Hermeneutics: Interpretation Theory in Schleiermacher, Dilthey, Heidegger, and Gadamer* (Evanston: Northwestern University Press, 1969).
8 For a convenient survey of these, see Hans-Georg Gadamer, *Reason in the Age of Science* (Cambridge, Mass.: M.I.T. Press, 1981), pp. 88–112.
9 J. Hillis Miller, *The Form of Victorian Fiction* (Notre Dame: University of Notre Dame Press, 1968), p. 64.
10 *The Mill on the Floss*, pp. 437–8.
11 *Middlemarch*, ed. David Carroll (Oxford: Clarendon Press, 1986), p. 139.
12 *Middlemarch*, p. 58.
13 *Letters of Lord Acton to Mary, Daughter of the Right Hon. W. E. Gladstone*, ed. Herbert Paul (London, 1904), pp. 60–1.
14 *Middlemarch*, p. 59.

15 Thomas Carlyle, 'Biography' (1832), in *Essays of Thomas Carlyle* (London: J. M. Dent, n.d.), II, p. 65.
16 *Middlemarch*, p. 83.
17 *Middlemarch*, p. 146.
18 *Middlemarch*, p. 59.
19 *Daniel Deronda*, ed. Graham Handley (Oxford: Clarendon Press, 1984), p. 322.
20 *Daniel Deronda*, p. 149.
21 *The Complete Prose Works of Matthew Arnold*, ed. R. H. Super, 11 vols (Ann Arbor: University of Michigan Press, 1960–77), III, p. 109.
22 *Middlemarch*, pp. 187–8.
23 'A Word for the Germans', reprinted in *Essays of George Eliot*, ed. Thomas Pinney (London: Routledge and Kegan Paul, 1963), pp. 386–90. See Rosemary Ashton, *The German Idea: Four English Writers and the Reception of German Thought 1800–1860* (Cambridge University Press, 1980).
24 The first four reviews are reprinted in *Essays of George Eliot*. The two reviews of Stahr appeared as 'The Art of the Ancients', *Leader*, 17 March 1855, 257–8; and 'The Art and Artists of Greece', *Saturday Review*, 31 May 1856, 109–10.
25 *Essays of George Eliot*, pp. 29–30.
26 Ibid., pp. 148, 153.
27 See George Levine's important article, 'George Eliot's Hypothesis of Reality', *Nineteenth-Century Fiction* 35 (1980), 1–28.
28 *Essays of George Eliot*, p. 31.
29 See Palmer, *Hermeneutics*, pp. 87–8.
30 *Essays of George Eliot*, pp. 33–4, 45.
31 Ibid., p. 41.
32 Ibid., pp. 255–60
33 Paul Ricoeur, *Freud and Philosophy* (New Haven: Yale University Press, 1970), p. 35.
34 Ludwig Feuerbach, *The Essence of Christianity*, trans. George Eliot (New York: Harper, 1957), pp. 13–14.
35 Ibid., p. 80.
36 *George Eliot Letters*, II, p. 403.
37 *Essays of George Eliot*, pp. 30–1.
38 Ibid., p. 413.
39 Diana Postlethwaite, *Making It Whole: a Victorian Circle and the Shape of Their World* (Columbus: Ohio State University Press, 1986). I am indebted to this study in what follows.
40 See Raymond Aron, *Main Currents in Sociological Thought*, trans. Richard Howard and Helen Weaver, 2 vols. (New York: Basic Books, 1965–7), I, p. 80.
41 Quoted in Postlethwaite, p. 212.
42 *George Eliot Letters*, II, p. 341.
43 Ibid., III, p. 227.

44 Ibid., i, p. 162.
45 *Essays of George Eliot*, p. 28.
46 Ibid., pp. 287, 290.
47 Ibid., pp. 271–2.
48 *George Eliot Letters*, ii, p. 439.
49 Ibid., ii, p. 40. Quoted in Postlethwaite, p. 182.
50 Thomas Pinney, 'More Leaves from George Eliot's Notebook', *Huntington Library Quarterly*, 29 (1965–6), 353–76. In addition to this Huntington notebook there is also a Princeton notebook, recently published: see K. K. Collins, 'Questions of Method: Some Unpublished Late Essays', *Nineteenth-Century Fiction* 35 (1980), 385–405.
51 'Questions of Method', pp. 387–9.
52 Ibid., pp. 363–5.
53 Ibid., p. 390.
54 'More Leaves', pp. 371–3.
55 Quoted by Pinney, 'More Leaves', p. 361.
56 'More Leaves', pp. 374–5.
57 Quoted by Collins in 'Questions of Method', p. 400.
58 Michael York Mason, '*Middlemarch* and Science: Problems of Life and Mind', *Review of English Studies*, 22 (1971), 151–69. This important article describes the scientific debate and its relevance to the novel.
59 K. K. Collins, 'G. H. Lewes Revised: George Eliot and the Moral Sense', *Victorian Studies*, 21 (1978), 467, 477–8.
60 *George Eliot Letters*, iii, pp. 382–3.
61 Ibid., iii, pp. 339–40
62 Ibid., v, pp. 323–5.
63 Ibid., iv, pp. 256.
64 Ibid., iii, pp. 170–1.
65 Ibid., viii, pp. 383–4
66 Ibid., iii, pp. 365–7
67 Ibid., iii, pp. 427–8.
68 Edward Said, *Beginnings: Intention and Method* (New York: Basic Books, 1975), p. 263. The whole of chapter 4 is relevant to my discussion.
69 *George Eliot Letters*, vi, pp. 216–17.
70 G. H. Lewes, *The Principles of Success in Literature*, ed. Fred N. Scott (Boston: Allyn and Bacon, 1894), pp. 25–6.
71 Ibid., pp. 26–7.
72 Ibid., p. 31.
73 *George Eliot Letters*, iv, p. 300.
74 *Essays of George Eliot*, p. 15.
75 Ibid., pp. 17–18.
76 Ibid., p. 433.
77 *George Eliot Letters*, i, p. 264.
78 *Impressions of Theophrastus Such*, Cabinet edition (Edinburgh and London: Blackwood, 1880), p. 12.

79 Ibid., pp. 17–18.
80 Ibid., pp. 195–7.
81 Ibid., pp. 268, 292.
82 *Silas Marner, The Lifted Veil, Brother Jacob*, Cabinet edition (Edinburgh and London: Blackwood, 1878), p. 278. All subsequent page-references will be included in the text.
83 For an illuminating discussion of Balzac's story from this point of view, see Peter Brooks, *Reading for the Plot: Design and Intention in Narrative* (Oxford: Clarendon Press, 1984), pp. 48–61.
84 Anthony Giddens, *New Rules of Sociological Method: A Positive Critique of Interpretative Sociologies* (London: Hutchinson, 1976), p. 162.

1 *SCENES OF CLERICAL LIFE*

1 *Scenes of Clerical Life*, ed. Thomas A. Noble (Oxford: Clarendon Press, 1985), pp. 7–8. All subsequent page-references are included in the text.
2 See, e.g., Ludwig Feuerbach, *The Essence of Christianity*, trans. George Eliot (New York: Harper, 1957), pp. 91–2.
3 *The George Eliot Letters*, ed. Gordon S. Haight, 9 vols. (New Haven: Yale University Press, 1954–78), IV, p. 300.
4 Wordsworth, 'Simon Lee', 67–8.
5 Peter Brooks, *The Melodramatic Imagination: Balzac, Henry James, Melodrama, and the Mode of Excess* (New Haven: Yale University Press, 1976), pp. 13, 2.
6 Referred to in Peter Brooks, *Reading for the Plot: Design and Intention in Narrative* (Oxford: Clarendon Press, 1984), p. 232.
7 In *George Eliot's Early Novels: The Limits of Realism* (Berkeley: University of California Press, 1968) U. C. Knoepflmacher discusses the counter-pointing of these two characters in similar terms (p. 78).
8 For a more detailed discussion of Dempster's career, see David Carroll, ' "Janet's Repentance" and the Myth of the Organic', *Nineteenth-Century Fiction* 35 (1980), 341–4.
9 Walter Benjamin, 'The Storyteller', in *Illuminations*, trans. Harry Zohn (London: Fontana, 1973), pp. 100–1.
10 See D. A. Miller, *Narrative and Its Discontents: Problems of Closure in the Traditional Novel* (Princeton: Princeton University Press, 1981), p. 120.

2 *ADAM BEDE*

1 See *The Oxford Companion to Art*, ed. Harold Osborne (Oxford University Press, 1970), pp. 43–4.
2 George Eliot, *Adam Bede*, Cabinet edition, 2 vols. (Edinburgh and London: Blackwood, 1878), I, pp. 265–6. All subsequent page-references will be incorporated in the text.
3 Raymond Williams discusses the tensions integral to pastoral in

The Country and the City (London: Chatto and Windus, 1973). See especially pp. 23–47, and on *Adam Bede*, pp. 202–20.

4 See, e.g., Erwin Panofsky, 'Et in Arcadia Ego', *Pastoral and Romance*, ed. Eleanor Terry Lincoln (Englewood Cliffs: Prentice Hall, 1969), pp. 25–46.

5 *George Eliot: the Critical Heritage*, ed. David Carroll (London: Routledge and Kegan Paul, 1971), p. 75. A perceptive summary of the debate can be found in Kenny Marotta, '*Adam Bede* as Pastoral', *Genre*, 9 (1976), 59–72. 'Although one kind of critic sees Eliot's pastoralism as decoration and the other sees it as allegory, both find it inconsistent with Eliot's pretensions to realism, and both see it as a form of self-deception' (p. 61).

6 *George Eliot: the Critical Heritage*, p. 74.

7 'Theodicy', *A New Dictionary of Christian Theology*, ed. Alan Richardson and John Bowden (London: SCM Press, 1983), pp. 564–6.

8 *The George Eliot Letters*, ed. Gordon S. Haight, 9 vols. (New Haven: Yale University Press, 1954–78), II, p. 503: 'the scene in the prison being of course the climax towards which I worked'.

9 Ludwig Feuerbach, *The Essence of Christianity*, trans. George Eliot (New York: Harper, 1957), p. 80.

10 See W. J. Harvey, 'The Treatment of Time in *Adam Bede*', in *A Century of George Eliot Criticism*, ed. Gordon S. Haight (London: Methuen, 1965), pp. 298–306.

11 Byron, *Childe Harold*, Canto III, st. 36.

12 See Peter V. Marinelli, *Pastoral* (London: Methuen, 1971), pp. 25–6.

13 U. C. Knoepflmacher compares the two novels in *George Eliot's Early Novels: The Limits of Realism* (Berkeley: University of California Press, 1968), pp. 123–5.

14 Sir Walter Scott, *The Heart of Midlothian*, ed. Claire Lamont (Oxford University Press, 1982), pp. 232–3.

15 E. S. Shaffer comments on the complexity of historical transmission in *Adam Bede* in '*Kubla Khan*' and the Fall of Jerusalem* (Cambridge University Press, 1975), which 'turns on the very intermittence of omniscience' (p. 245).

3 THE MILL ON THE FLOSS

1 *The Mill on the Floss*, ed. Gordon S. Haight (Oxford: Clarendon Press, 1980), p. 237. All subsequent page-references will be included in the text.

2 See Gillian Beer, *Arguing with the Past* (London: Routledge, 1989), pp. 124–6.

3 *The Prelude* (1850), I, 460.

4 On the plurality of Maggie's world, see John Kucich, 'George Eliot and Objects: Meaning as Matter in *The Mill on the Floss*', *Dickens Studies Annual*, 12 (1983), 319–40.

5 The curious Bob Jakin is their only link for long sections of the novel. He is

the gipsy-like alien on the periphery of St Ogg's society, 'amphibious', 'diabolical', but guardian angel to both Tom and Maggie.

6 As well as the *Imitation* Maggie uses a range of other texts to define her own future: *The Pilgrim's Progress*, Scott's *The History of the Devil* and *The Pirate, Corinne*, etc. See Margaret Homans, 'Eliot, Wordsworth, and the Scenes of the Sisters' Instruction', *Critical Inquiry*, 8 (1981), 223–41, on Maggie's discovery of the 'inexorable laws of feminine plotting' (p. 227).

7 *Essays of George Eliot*, ed. Thomas Pinney (London: Routledge and Kegan Paul, 1963), p. 265. See Gerhard Joseph, 'The *Antigone* as Cultural Touchstone: Matthew Arnold, Hegel, George Eliot, Virginia Woolf, and Margaret Drabble', *PMLA*, 96 (1981), 22–35.

8 For an extreme emphasis on this aspect of Maggie's character, see Nina Auerbach, 'The Power of Hunger: Demonism and Maggie Tulliver', *Romantic Imprisonment* (New York: Columbia University Press, 1985), pp. 230–49.

9 See, e.g., *George Eliot: the Critical Heritage*, ed. David Carroll (London: Routledge and Kegan Paul, 1971), pp. 15–16, 109–66.

10 Peter Brooks, *The Melodramatic Imagination: Balzac, Henry James, Melodrama, and the Mode of Excess* (New Haven: Yale University Press, 1976), p. 5.

11 See Felicia Bonaparte's comments on the myth of St Ogg's, in *The Triptych and the Cross: the Central Myths of George Eliot's Poetic Imagination* (New York University Press, 1979), pp. 151–2.

12 Nina Auerbach, *Romantic Imprisonment*, p. 243.

13 Northrop Frye, *The Great Code: The Bible and Literature* (London: Routledge and Kegan Paul, 1982), refers to Kierkegaard's *Repetition* with its 'psychological contrast between a past-directed causality and a future-directed typology' (p. 82).

4 *SILAS MARNER*

1 Walter Benjamin, 'The Storyteller', in *Illuminations*, trans. Harry Zohn (London: Fontana, 1973), pp. 87–90.

2 Ibid., p. 99.

3 *The George Eliot Letters*, ed. Gordon S. Haight, 9 vols. (New Haven: Yale University Press, 1954–78), III, p. 382.

4 *Silas Marner, The Lifted Veil, Brother Jacob*, Cabinet edition (Edinburgh and London: Blackwood, 1878), p. 181. All subsequent page-references will be included in the text.

5 Reprinted in *George Eliot: The Critical Heritage*, ed. David Carroll (London: Routledge and Kegan Paul, 1971), pp. 175–8.

6 Ibid., p. 171.

7 Ibid., pp. 186–8.

8 See especially, Harold Fisch's article, 'Biblical Realism in *Silas Marner*', in *Identity and Ethos: A Festschrift for Sol Liptzin*, ed. Mark H. Gelber (New

York: Peter Lang, 1986), pp. 343–60, with its emphasis on the covenantal pattern of the novel.

9 *George Eliot: The Critical Heritage*, p. 182.

10 See Sally Shuttleworth, 'Fairy Tale or Science? Physiological Psychology in *Silas Marner*', in *Languages of Nature: Critical Essays on Science and Literature*, ed. L. J. Jordanova (London: Free Association Books, 1986), pp. 244–88. In this important essay the author relates this question to Victorian ideas of physiological psychology which, she maintains, both challenge and affirm conceptions of organic unity and continuity.

11 For a discussion of the narrative of solitary confinement, see Frank Kermode, *The Sense of an Ending* (London: Oxford University Press, 1966), ch. 6.

12 Titus Burckhardt shows in *Sacred Art* (London: Perennial Books, 1967), how the creation of the universe was frequently represented through the activity of weaving (p. 59).

13 Gillian Beer refers to Midas in *George Eliot* (Brighton: Harvester, 1986), p. 126.

14 See Brian Swann, '*Silas Marner* and the New Mythus', *Criticism*, 18 (1976), 117–18.

15 Job 7, 6. See *George Eliot: The Critical Heritage*, p. 185.

16 Gillian Beer, *Darwin's Plots* (London: Routledge and Kegan Paul, 1983), p. 113.

17 'Signs of the Times' (1829) in *Essays of Thomas Carlyle* (London: J. M. Dent, n.d.), I, p. 226.

18 *George Eliot: The Critical Heritage*, p. 176.

19 Genesis 8. 22: 'While the earth remaineth, seedtime and harvest, and cold and heat, and summer and winter, and day and night shall not cease.'

20 See David Carroll, '*Silas Marner*: Reversing the Oracles of Religion', in *Literary Monographs* (Madison: University of Wisconsin Press, 1967), I, pp. 165–200.

21 *Silas Marner*, ed. Q. D. Leavis (Harmondsworth: Penguin Books, 1967), pp. 259–60.

22 Isaiah 62. 4: 'Thou shalt no more be termed Forsaken; neither shall thy land be any more termed Desolate: but thou shalt be called Hephzibah, and thy land Beulah: for the Lord delighteth in thee, and thy land shall be married.'

23 See Swann, '*Silas Marner* and the New Mythus', pp. 106, 110–11.

24 Matthew 12. 43–4: 'When the unclean spirit is gone out of a man, he walketh through dry places, seeking rest, and finding none. Then he saith, I will return into my house from whence I came out; and when he is come, he findeth it empty, swept, and garnished.'

25 Measure and chance, respectively.

26 There are interesting parallels between the gold, the child, and the gap of sixteen years in *Silas Marner* and the same elements in *The Winter's Tale*. See Carroll, 'Reversing the Oracles', p. 313.

27 See Carroll, 'Reversing the Oracles', pp. 190–3.
28 Jerome J. McGann, *The Beauty of Inflections* (Oxford: Clarendon Press, 1985), p. 150.
29 Ibid., p. 154.

5 *ROMOLA*

1 *Middlemarch*, ed. David Carroll (Oxford: Clarendon Press, 1986), pp. 187–8.
2 Robert Browning, *The Ring and the Book* (1869), I, 719–23.
3 John Ruskin, 'The Nature of Gothic', *The Stones of Venice*, II, ch. 6, section 8.
4 *Romola*, Cabinet edition, 2 vols (Edinburgh and London: Blackwood, 1878), I, p. 2. All subsequent page-references will be included in the text.
5 The episode seems to have been suggested by Dante's meeting with Cacciaguida, *Paradiso* xiv–xviii.
6 Felicia Bonaparte, *The Triptych and the Cross: the Central Myths of George Eliot's Poetic Imagination* (New York University Press, 1979), p. 27. I am indebted to this study of *Romola* which substantiated for the first time the extraordinary scope of the novel.
7 W. B. Yeats, 'The Scholars', 2, 11–12.
8 See Margaret Homans' important discussion of textuality in *Romola*, in *Bearing the Word: Language and Female Experience in Nineteenth-Century Women's Writing* (Chicago University Press, 1986), pp. 189–221.
9 Matthew Arnold, *Culture and Anarchy*, The Complete Prose Works of Matthew Arnold, ed. R. H. Super (Ann Arbor: University of Michigan Press), Vol. v (1965), p. 185.
10 Pater, *The Renaissance: Studies in Art and Poetry* (London: Macmillan, 1893), pp. 231–2. On Arnold's and Pater's Hellenism, see David J. DeLaura, *Hebrew and Hellene in Victorian England: Newman, Arnold, and Pater* (Austin: University of Texas Press, 1969), pp. 171–81, 202–22.
11 Homans, *Bearing the Word*, pp. 208–12.
12 Bonaparte, *The Triptych and the Cross*, p. 118.
13 George Eliot explained to Alexander Main in 1871 that the name Romola was 'the Italian equivalent of Romulus' (*The George Eliot Letters*, ed. Gordon S. Haight, 9 vols (New Haven: Yale University Press, 1954–78) v, p. 174), the mythical founder of Rome. See Bonaparte, pp. 19–20.
14 On the significance of Piero di Cosimo, see William J. Sullivan, 'Piero di Cosimo and the Higher Primitivism in *Romola*', *Nineteenth-Century Fiction*, 26 (1972), 390–405; Hugh Witemeyer, *George Eliot and the Visual Arts* (New Haven: Yale University Press, 1979), pp. 56–60.
15 Robert Browning, 'Fra Lippo Lippi', 387.
16 See Hayden White, *Tropics of Discourse: Essays in Cultural Criticism* (Baltimore: The Johns Hopkins University Press, 1978), pp. 71–4; Stephen Bann, *The Clothing of Clio: A Study of the Representation of History in*

Nineteenth-Century Britain and France (Cambridge University Press, 1984), pp. 42–53.

17 George Levine, '*Romola* as Fable', in *Critical Essays on George Eliot*, ed. Barbara Hardy (London: Routledge and Kegan Paul, 1970), p. 84.

18 Neil Hertz discusses Baldassarre's 'thoroughly imperialistic' mastery of language, in 'Recognizing Casaubon', *Glyph*, 6 (1979), 33–5.

19 *The Mill on the Floss*, ed. Gordon S. Haight (Oxford: Clarendon Press, 1980), p. 437.

20 *George Eliot Letters*, IV, p. 104.

21 The Dantean idea of the perfectly appropriate 'retribution' is discussed by A. C. Charity in *Events and their Afterlife: the Dialectics of Christian Typology in the Bible and Dante* (Cambridge University Press, 1966), pp. 189–98.

22 Bonaparte, *The Triptych and the Cross*, p. 227.

23 Ibid., pp. 235–9; and Homans, *Bearing the Word*, pp. 205–8, on Romola as 'the Madonna bearing the Word'.

24 See Gennaro A. Santangelo, 'Villari's *Life and Times of Savonarola*: A Source for George Eliot's *Romola*', *Anglia*, 90 (1972), 118–31.

25 Pasquale Villari, *Life and Times of Savonarola*, 2 vols, trans. Linda Villari (London, 1888), II, p. 418.

26 Ibid., I, p. 312.

27 Ibid., I, p. 322.

28 Charles C. Hennell, *An Inquiry Concerning the Origin of Christianity*, 2nd edn (London: 1841), pp. 449, 423.

29 E. S. Shaffer, '*Kubla Khan*' *and the Fall of Jerusalem* (Cambridge University Press, 1975), p. 220.

30 See Marjorie Reeves and Warwick Gould, *Joachim of Fiore and the Myth of the Eternal Evangel in the Nineteenth Century* (Oxford: Clarendon Press, 1987), pp. 115–31.

31 John Henry Newman, *The Dream of Gerontius*, section 5. In Newman's hymn, 'Praise to the Holiest in the height' (1868), derived from this section of the poem, the 'double agony' refers to the secret agony of Gethsemane and the public crucifixion.

32 For a discussion of the martyr as witness which has considerable relevance to George Eliot's treatment of Savonarola, see Paul Ricoeur, 'The Hermeneutics of Testimony', in *Essays on Biblical Interpretation*, ed. Lewis S. Mudge (London: SPCK, 1981), pp. 119–54.

33 For a discussion of the Victorian view of myth as the embodiment of irreducible contradictions, see Steven Connor, 'Myth and Meta-Myth in Max Müller and Walter Pater', in *The Sun is God: Painting, Literature and Mythology in the Nineteenth Century*, ed. J. B. Bullen (Oxford: Clarendon Press, 1989), pp. 199–222.

6 FELIX HOLT

1 *Felix Holt*, ed. Fred C. Thomson (Oxford: Clarendon Press, 1980), p. 76. All subsequent page-references will be included in the text.

2 Frank Kermode's comments on apocalypse in *Middlemarch* in *Continuities* (London: Routledge and Kegan Paul, 1968), pp. 136–51, are equally relevant to *Felix Holt*. George Eliot's own fears about the condition of England are expressed more explicitly in 'Address to Working Men, By Felix Holt' (1868), reprinted in *Essays of George Eliot*, ed. Thomas Pinney (London: Routledge and Kegan Paul, 1963), pp. 415–30.

3 The allusions to Dante and their typological significance are of increasing importance in *Felix Holt*. See *Felix Holt*, ed. Peter Coveney (Harmondsworth: Penguin, 1972), pp. 9–10, 36, 645, 647.

4 The discussion by Raymond Williams in *Culture and Society 1780–1950* (Harmondsworth: Penguin, 1961), pp. 112–19, remains the most perceptively succinct account of George Eliot's tentativeness in addressing these problems in *Felix Holt*.

5 Robin Sheets, '*Felix Holt*: Language, the Bible, and the Problematic of Meaning', *Nineteenth-Century Fiction*, 37 (1982), 146–69, provides a comprehensive account of the ambiguities of meaning at all levels of the novel. 'For George Eliot, discourse – in speech or in writing – has become fraught with difficulty . . . Words provoke controversy because they yield a variety of meanings, and the community cannot agree upon strategies of interpretation' (p. 148).

6 In *The Industrial Reformation of English Fiction: Social Discourse and Narrative Form 1832–1867* (University of Chicago Press, 1985), Catherine Gallagher effectively places *Felix Holt* within this fictional sub-genre.

7 *OED.*, I. 4.

8 J. W. Cross, *George Eliot's Life as Related in her Letters and Journals* (London: Blackwood, 1885), III, pp. 43–4.

9 In rabbinical writings, Zadkiel was the angel of the planet Jupiter – and the pseudonym of the author of *Herald of Astrology* (1831).

10 A. C. Charity, *Events and their Afterlife: the Dialectics of Christian Typology in the Bible and Dante* (Cambridge University Press, 1966), p. 184.

11 In seeking to relate the problems of literary and political representation, Catherine Gallagher in her innovative reading sees Felix's self-contradiction as an index of George Eliot's unresolvable problems (aesthetic and political) rather than an expression of the dialectic of his character (*The Industrial Reformation*, pp. 237–43).

12 For George Eliot's interest in apocalyptic narrative, see Mary Wilson Carpenter, *George Eliot and the Landscape of Time: Narrative Form and Protestant Apocalyptic History* (Chapel Hill: University of North Carolina Press, 1986), pp. 3–30. The subsequent use of the numerological implications of apocalypse as an interpretative key to the novels is less convincing.

13 The two men are linked through Pauline analogies: Lyon is compared to St Paul at Ephesus (p. 71), while Felix quotes 1 Corinthians 9. 16, 'necessity is laid upon me' (p. 222).

14 See Bonnie Zimmerman, '*Felix Holt* and the True Power of Womanhood', *English Literary History*, 46 (1979), 432–51.

15 An earlier mention of Byron's poem, 'The Dream' (p. 61), has, despite Felix's sarcasm, anticipated Esther's own vision of the future: 'I would recall a vision which I dream'd / Perchance in sleep – for in itself a thought, / A slumbering thought, is capable of years, / And curdles a long life into one hour' (23–6).

7 *MIDDLEMARCH*

1 For a detailed account of the transition, see Jerome Beaty, '*Middlemarch*' *from Notebook to Novel: A Study of George Eliot's Creative Method* (Urbana: University of Illinois Press, 1960), pp. 3–42.

2 *Middlemarch*, ed. David Carroll (Oxford: Clarendon Press, 1986), p. 85. All subsequent page-references will be included in the text.

3 *Essays of George Eliot*, ed. Thomas Pinney (London: Routledge and Kegan Paul, 1963), p. 433.

4 J. Hillis Miller, 'Narrative and History', *English Literary History*, 41 (1974), 455–73; 'Optic and Semiotic in *Middlemarch*', in *The Worlds of Victorian Fiction*, ed. Jerome H. Buckley (Cambridge, Mass: Harvard University Press, 1975), pp. 125–45.

5 Peter K. Garrett, *The Victorian Multi-plot Novel: Studies in Dialogical Form* (New Haven: Yale University Press, 1980), pp. 150–1.

6 D. A. Miller, *Narrative and Its Discontents: Problems of Closure in the Traditional Novel* (Princeton University Press, 1981), pp. 108–9.

7 J. M. Cameron, 'Newman and the Empiricist Tradition', in *The Rediscovery of Newman*, ed. J. Coulson and A. M. Allchin (London: Sheed and Ward, 1967), p. 77.

8 *The George Eliot Letters*, ed. Gordon S. Haight, 9 vols. (New Haven: Yale University Press, 1954–78), VI, pp. 98–9.

9 Peter Brooks, *Reading for the Plot: Design and Intention in Narrative* (Oxford: Clarendon Press, 1984), p. 45.

10 In one of her *Middlemarch* notebooks the novelist transcribed a lengthy description by the French chemist, F. V. Raspail, of the '*substance membraneuse*': 'il reste une substance blanche comme l'albumine coagulée, mais bien moins élastique, que les alcalis ou les acides concentrés désorganisent ou dépouillent, mais ne dissolvent jamais entièrement.' *(George Eliot's Quarry for 'Middlemarch'*, ed. A. T. Kitchel (Los Angeles, 1950), p. 31.)

11 G. H. Lewes, *The Problems of Life and Mind, First Series: The Foundation of a Creed*, 2 vols. (London: Trübner, 1874), I, p. 189. Quoted by Sally

Shuttleworth, 'The Language of Science and Psychology in George Eliot's *Daniel Deronda*', in *Victorian Science and Victorian Values: Literary Perspectives*, ed. James Paradis and Thomas Postlewait (New Brunswick: Rutgers University Press, 1981), p. 298.

12 William Wordsworth, 'Prospectus' to *The Recluse*, 57–8.

13 Carlyle's essay, 'Signs of the Times' (1829), provides a vivid account of these changing paradigms at the period of the novel.

14 See Gillian Beer on the saint's life in George Eliot, in 'Myth and the single consciousness: *Middlemarch* and *The Lifted Veil*', in *This Particular Web: Essays on 'Middlemarch'*, ed. Ian Adam (University of Toronto Press, 1975), pp. 106–10; *Darwin's Plots* (London: Routledge and Kegan Paul, 1983), pp. 176–9; *George Eliot* (Brighton: Harvester, 1986), pp. 122–4.

15 See Thomas J. Heffernan, *Sacred Biography: Saints and Their Biographers in the Middle Ages* (Oxford University Press, 1988), p. 265.

16 It leads in many directions as Clerk Maxwell's ingenious, tongue-in-cheek solar mythological reading of the novel in 1873 shows. It is quoted by Gillian Beer in 'Victorian Solar Physics and Solar Myth', *The Sun is God: Painting, Literature and Mythology in the Nineteenth Century*, ed. J. B. Bullen (Oxford: Clarendon Press, 1989), pp. 173–4.

17 See Introduction, p. 21.

18 See Beer, *Darwin's Plots*, pp. 113–14, who quotes Cassirer: 'The mythic consciousness does not see human personality as something fixed and unchanging, but conceives every *phase* of a man's life as a new personality, a new self' (*Language and Myth*, trans. S. K. Langer (New York: Harper, 1946), p. 51).

19 'The Nephew as Uncle', a comedy by Schiller (1803) in which the hero disguises himself as his uncle to win the woman he loves.

20 D. A. Miller, *Narrative and Its Discontents*: 'In *Middlemarch* the different ways of perceiving and delimiting the story all conspire to identify what is, in terms of its main actions, *the same story*. Yet if they are narratologically identical, they remain to the end hermeneutically distinct' (p. 109).

21 Beer, 'Myth and the single consciousness', pp. 105–6.

22 Max Weber, *The Protestant Ethic and the Spirit of Capitalism*, trans. Talcott Parsons (New York: Scribner, 1958), p. 111.

23 Ibid., p. 111.

24 *A New Dictionary of Christian Theology*, ed. Alan Richardson and John Bowden (London: SCM Press, 1983), p. 315.

25 James Hogg, *The Private Memoirs and Confessions of a Justified Sinner*, ed. John Carey (London: Oxford University Press, 1969), pp. 116–17.

26 See David Carroll, '*Middlemarch* and the Externality of Fact', in *This Particular Web*, pp. 79–84, for a more extended treatment of this relationship.

27 See Alexander Welsh, *George Eliot and Blackmail* (Cambridge, Mass: Harvard University Press, 1985), especially pp. 243–55.

28 William Wordsworth, *The Prelude* (1850), IV, 263–4.
29 *George Eliot Letters*, V, p. 168.
30 Alan Mintz, *George Eliot and the Novel of Vocation* (Cambridge, Mass: Harvard University Press, 1978), p. 76.
31 Mary Shelley, *Frankenstein; or, The Modern Prometheus*, ed. M. K. Joseph (Oxford University Press, 1969), pp. 55–6.
32 Mintz refers to this as an example of Lydgate's 'fatal taxonomic carelessness' (p. 95).
33 J. Hillis Miller, 'Narrative and History', p. 468.
34 The best account of this scientific dispute between John Stuart Mill and William Whewell and its relevance to the novel is Michael York Mason, '*Middlemarch* and Science: Problems of Life and Mind', *Review of English Studies*, 22 (1971), 151–69.

8 DANIEL DERONDA

1 E. S. Shaffer, '*Kubla Khan' and the Fall of Jerusalem: the Mythological School in Biblical Criticism and Secular Literature 1770–1880* (Cambridge University Press, 1975), p. 253. The final chapter of this study examines in compelling detail George Eliot's 'own contribution to the long discussion as to the origins of Christianity and the course of the early life of Jesus' (p. 269) in *Daniel Deronda*.
2 Since *Daniel Deronda* was published many critics have tried to define its essential difference from *Middlemarch*. R. E. Francillon, for example, wrote a perceptive review on its first appearance, declaring 'it is practically a first book by a new author' (*George Eliot: the Critical Heritage*, ed. David Carroll (London: Routledge and Kegan Paul, 1971) p. 396). Two recent articles address the same question in a manner relevant to my discussion: Peter Dale, 'Symbolic Representation and the Means of Revolution in *Daniel Deronda*', *The Victorian Newsletter*, 59 (1981), 25–30; Lyn Pykett, 'Typology and the End(s) of History in *Daniel Deronda*', *Literature and History*, 9 (1983), 62–73.
3 *Daniel Deronda*, ed. Graham Handley (Oxford: Clarendon Press, 1984), p. 424. All subsequent page-references will be included in the text.
4 *The George Eliot Letters*, ed. Gordon S. Haight, 9 vols. (New Haven: Yale University Press, 1954–78), I. p. 264.
5 Ludwig Feuerbach, *The Essence of Christianity*, (New York: Harper, 1957), p. 31.
6 'Bishop Blougram's Apology', 395, 400–1.
7 See Gershom G. Scholem, *On the Kabbalah and Its Symbolism*, trans. Ralph Manheim (New York: Schocken Books, 1965), especially ch. 3, 'Kabbalah and Myth', pp. 87–117.
8 See Gillian Beer, *Darwin's Plots* (London: Routledge and Kegan Paul, 1983), p. 200. The whole of the following chapter, 'Descent and Sexual Selection: Women in Narrative' (pp. 210–35) is also relevant.

9 *The Letters of Matthew Arnold to Arthur Hugh Clough*, ed. H. F. Lowry (Oxford: Clarendon Press, 1932), p. 97. See Robert Preyer, 'Beyond the Liberal Imagination: Vision and Unreality in *Daniel Deronda*', *Victorian Studies*, 4 (1960), 33–54; and Alexander Welsh, *George Eliot and Blackmail* (Cambridge, Mass: Harvard University Press, 1985), p. 302.

10 Scholem, *On the Kabbalah and Its Symbolism*, p. 101–3.

11 Ibid., p. 158–204, for the idea of the Cabbalistic Golem.

12 For the relationship between painting and typology in *Daniel Deronda*, see Hugh Witemeyer, *George Eliot and the Visual Arts* (New Haven: Yale University Press, 1979), pp. 92–104.

13 George P. Landow, *Victorian Types, Victorian Shadows* (London: Routledge and Kegan Paul, 1980), p. 54.

14 Shaffer, '*Kubla Khan*', p. 255.

15 Northrop Frye, *The Great Code: The Bible and Literature* (Routledge and Kegan Paul, 1982), p. 81.

16 Tennyson, *In Memoriam*, Epilogue, 138, 144.

17 The 'seeds of fire', according to the Cabbalists, were the sparks of Adam's soul scattered in exile at the Fall when they became diffused in matter. 'In the course of its exile Israel must go everywhere, to every corner of the world, for everywhere a spark of the *Shekhinah* [divine presence] is waiting to be found, gathered, and restored by a religious act' (Scholem, *On the Kabbalah and Its Symbolism*, pp. 115–16).

18 *Impressions of Theophratus Such*, Cabinet edition (Edinburgh and London: Blackwood, 1880), p. 270.

19 *The Essence of Christianity*, pp. 87–8; Shaffer, '*Kubla Khan*', p. 253.

20 Welsh, *George Eliot and Blackmail*, pp. 289–93.

21 Shaffer, '*Kubla Khan*', p. 282.

CONCLUSION

1 See Introduction, p. 6.

2 *The George Eliot Letters*, ed. Gordon S. Haight, 9 vols (New Haven: Yale University Press 1954–78), I, p. 264.

3 For the 'second naiveté' and the detour of interpretation, see Paul Ricoeur, *The Symbolism of Evil* (New York: Harper and Row, 1967), p. 351.

4 William Wordsworth, *The Prelude* (1805), XIII, 69.

5 Richard Simpson in the *Home and Foreign Review* (1863), reprinted in *George Eliot: the Critical Heritage*, ed. David Carroll (London: Routledge and Kegan Paul, 1971), p. 225.

6 Ibid., p. 250.

7 See Introduction, p. 3.

Index

331